The
Reformation of
American
Quakerism,
1748-1783

The Reformation of American Quakerism,

1748-1783

JACK D. MARIETTA

University of Pennsylvania Press
PHILADELPHIA

Library of Congress Cataloging in Publication Data

Marietta, Jack D.
    The reformation of American Quakerism, 1748–1783.

    Bibliography: p.
    Includes index.
    1. Society of Friends—United States—History—18th
century. 2. Society of Friends—Doctrines. 3. United
States—Church history—Colonial period, ca. 1600–1775.
I. Title.
BX7636.M37 1984   289.6'73   83–23502
ISBN 0–8122–7922–0

Printed in the United States of America

For *my mother*
and the memory of *my father*

Contents

Figures and Tables

All figures are three-year moving averages, 1682–1776.

Preface

Atransformation occurred in the Society of Friends in America
between 1748 and the end of the American Revolution that
radically altered the course of Quaker history. It began and
found its fullest expression among Pennsylvania Friends but eventually spread to all corners of the Society. It was the sum of many
particular changes, some of them rare or unique in religious history
and of unmistakable consequence to American history generally.
Taken together, these changes represented an attempt by the Society
of Friends to become a more distinctive and "purified" religious
community and amounted to the withdrawal of American Friends
from the mainstream of American society and government. This
book is a history of that transformation, particularly as it occurred
in Pennsylvania and the adjoining colonies and states of New Jersey,
Delaware, and Maryland.

The original Quaker settlers of Pennsylvania emerged from the
recesses of society in the British Isles to occupy a place of renown in
history. Even though they failed to achieve many of the lofty objectives of William Penn's Holy Experiment in Pennsylvania, they created
an illustrious record. They exercised power on behalf of some of the
most lauded ideals in Western history: religious and civil liberty,
progressive law codes and equal justice, openness and diversity, and
political autonomy, among others. Here, if anywhere in the American colonies, was the prototypical liberal American society. Of Pennsylvania, Voltaire wrote, "William Penn might glory in having brought
down upon the earth the so much boasted golden age, which in all
probability never existed but in Pennsylvania." Nevertheless, in the

middle of the eighteenth century, the children and grandchildren of these Quaker founders elected a distinctly different course for themselves, away from many hallmarks of Quakerism in the New World and from that Experiment that was envied by people of that age on all levels of society. This book describes the causes of the change, its extent and variety, and discusses what was new and possible in the reformed Quakerism that emerged. It is an account of withdrawal and reform and of the substitution of a different vision from the one that inspired the Holy Experiment.

The evil attacked most vehemently by those who would purify Quakerism in the mid-eighteenth century was the attempt by some Friends to divide human behavior into autonomous spheres and to separate the church and religion from all other forms of behavior. Traditionally, Friends believed, more strongly than most other Christians, that life could not be meaningfully separated into various aspects or spheres, with the church allotted the spiritual one, the government the political one, an "invisible hand" the economic one, and so on. If the religious impulse really exists in a person, it infuses all. All behavior is interconnected and religion is sovereign.

In the interest of simplicity and in keeping with a convention of historical writing, I have nevertheless divided the account of the Quaker reformation into its social and its political aspects. The division necessarily distorts the unity of Quaker reformers' vision and activities, but with sufficient cross-references between the two aspects, the distortion can be minimized. The social aspect is discussed first, in chapters 1 through 5; the political aspect in chapters 6 through 11. While the most dramatic way in which the Society of Friends changed was by withdrawing from the government of Pennsylvania, equally important and much less conspicuous was their undertaking to transform the Society of Friends by strengthening the members' commitment to a host of Quaker mores such as endogamy, "guarded" childrearing, sexual continence, honesty, simplicity, humility, and asceticism, among others. By the stern determination of Quaker reformers, the members either adhered to these mores or else were expelled from the Society, whatever the cost to its membership rolls. In the terms that Ernst Troeltsch made famous in his work *The Social Teachings of the Christian Churches*, Friends were transforming the Society from a Church into a sect. (To avoid confusion, I have capitalized the word *Church* when I mean Troeltsch's term; I have used the word sect only in the sense that Troeltsch intended.) The transformation meant that Friends increasingly regarded the world—

its civil government, social institutions, and some of its religious denominations—as alien and hostile. At the same time, they directed much more of their attention and energy inward toward their own community. The Society quit accepting and retaining members upon a largely formal and perfunctory procedure and began to test their worthiness before admitting them. More important, members were retained only as long as they demonstrated their commitment to Quaker beliefs and practices. Membership was no longer secure once it was granted, and expulsion became common. This transformation, in a church of this size and consequence, was unique.

The treatment here of political change differs from that of social changes. I discuss the social changes in a topical and analytical manner; the political aspect appears in a narrative of Quaker experiences from 1748 through 1783. And while most of the quantitative information in the first five chapters is new to Quaker historiography, the political history of Pennsylvania Friends has been told many times. One reason for retelling it is that the story of Friends' withdrawal from government has never before been accurately depicted in any book in English. Historians have failed to understand the tension that existed between government service and Quaker ethics because they did not know Quaker ethics, especially pacifism. Additionally, the complexity of the Friends' situation and the magnitude of their dilemma in the 1750s has been missing from previous accounts. Whereas the reformers could accomplish their agenda of social reform largely by the force of their own wills and by hard labor, they could not so easily accomplish political reform. There was neither the clear agenda nor the freedom from interference that existed in social reform. Obstinate Quaker opponents and intractable events limited the reformers' choices and created difficulties they had not foreseen. The actions of imperial policy-makers at Whitehall, the proprietary Penn family, hostile politicians in Philadelphia, discontented settlers in the province, and aggrieved Indians complicated plans and frustrated the reformers' concern for their Christian ethics, their best historical traditions, and their obligations to others. Through a maze of unwelcome events and conflicting counsel, the reformers were obliged to plot a course that respected Quaker pacifism and yet acknowledged a Quaker tradition of leadership. Only in these circumstances did Friends come to appreciate the precariousness of their service in two worlds and the vulnerability of their rule in Pennsylvania.

To this era of reformation also belongs the growth of Quaker philanthropy and, most conspicuously, the birth of Quaker abolition. Friends made an everlasting name for themselves by being the first people to abolish slavery among themselves and to champion abolition everywhere. This epochal development gained for the Society of Friends as much renown as did the Holy Experiment. Quaker antislavery and other benevolences have been accepted as having been in keeping with the original Quaker doctrines of religious equality and peace and therefore as having occurred naturally in the course of Quaker history. This assumption does not take into account, however, the eighteenth-century transformation in American Quakerism which altered the course of the Society and separated the abolitionists from the Quaker founders of Pennsylvania not only by time but also by spirit. One purpose of this book is to locate innovations, philanthropy, and abolition, especially, in the proper context of reformed Quakerism and thereby to better explain the causes of abolition, including the time and place of their appearance. I take up the origins of Quaker philanthropy also because my account of those origins differs markedly from that of Sydney James, the current authority on the subject.

I will be pleased if this account of the Society of Friends helps to refurbish the respect for the importance of religious sectarianism in American history. In my opinion, sectarianism has not been treated adequately or judged fairly by some eminent historians and others; the value to society of there having been Americans who chose to be different from the majority needs to be better explained. As Protestant evangelicalism grew in America after the Great Awakening of the mid-eighteenth century, the churches or sects that did not put a premium on proselytization, and which often fell behind in relative size or numbers, were commonly regarded as declining or failing. This assumption indicates a quantative bias and error: What counted most was what could be most easily counted. The more elusive functions of the churches such as their providing counsel or pastoral aid and various forms of benevolence were belittled.

Historians have insinuated that sectarianism was selfish, sterile, and un-American. In Edmund S. Morgan's works on the Puritan family, John Winthrop, and the Half-Way Covenant, he praises the Puritans for not moving toward sectarianism at important junctures in their history. To have done so, he judges, would have meant forfeiting a redeeming mission to the world for a tribalistic concern for one's brethren. The Quakers suffer by inference in Morgan's works, but in

Daniel Boorstin's they suffer directly. Boorstin offers colonial Quakers as a model of error because they spurned the pragmatic genius of American politics. They retreated behind "ghetto walls," devoting themselves to sectarian dogmas "unfit for building a new society in a new world." For Boorstin, dogma is the bane of American politics and ought to be rejected in favor of the formless consensus that has fostered American greatness.

Sydney V. James, in his *A People Among Peoples,* disagrees with Boorstin while simultaneously recounting the benefits of joining American society.[1] James does not find Quakers deliberately retreating behind ghetto walls. Rather, he says, Quakers respected American society and in the late eighteenth century wished to acquit themselves with the mass of Americans. They attempted to do so through their philanthropy to native Americans, blacks, and others. (Boorstin portrays native Americans as villains and gives Quaker abolition barely a nod.) Quakers' heightened sectarianism, says James, helped to prepare them for a greater role in American life. Their benevolence and their reinforced or reformed mores are therefore evidence of their participation in the American consensus or their desire to belong to it through service to shared American values.

Boorstin, in his short acknowledgment of Quaker philanthropy, says it was the measure of what Quakers no longer gave to politics—the presumption being they could equally well have given in both respects. James says that the Quakers stayed in the mainstream of American society (although not in government) *and* gave their benevolences. I find that the Quakers could not have simultaneously contributed to both philanthropy and politics, as Boorstin implies they could have. I find, furthermore, that the Quakers did not stay in the mainstream of American society and advocate abolition, as James says they did. Especially in the Quakers' advocacy of abolition, their criticism of American society required that they stand off from it and out of government in order to see its faults. They, as much as nineteenth-century abolitionists, did not wholly belong to American society. Their philanthropy was the product of separation and not of joining, of sympathizing with people who got little sympathy from other Americans.

The topic of the Quaker reformation is not itself novel. Frederick B. Tolles, in the conclusion of his classic work *Meeting House and Counting House,* limned the story.[2] This work expands that suggestion to a history of late eighteenth-century Quakers. It draws on a

great mass of evidence barely touched before, which is the disciplinary records of the Society of Friends. Here are some ten thousand
cases in which Quakers violated the regulations of the Society between
1682 and 1776. This evidence provides a historical record without
equal among American churches and supplies us with an uncommon
insight into what the Society wished and required its members to be
or do. The chronological continuity reveals changes in what the Society required, and the picture drawn from all the evidence assists us
in understanding the characters, events, and changes in this history
of reform.

   I have not included quite all the Quakers who lived in Pennsylvania. I have used Quaker meetings as my units of study, and at all
organizational levels some Quaker meetings straddled provincial
boundaries. I have omitted meetings that lay predominantly outside
Pennsylvania. In 1760, Pennsylvania comprised the largest part of
Philadelphia Yearly Meeting; the province contained four quarterly
meetings, and nineteen subordinate monthly meetings. These nineteen comprehended the Quakers represented in my statistics.

   In yet another sense I have slighted political boundaries. Quakerism was an Atlantic community, just as Frederick Tolles emphasized. No part of it can be explained without reference to others. No
adequate history of Quakerism in Pennsylvania can omit John Woolman, Samuel Fothergill, Elizabeth Wilkinson, Warner Mifflin, and a
score of other Friends who did not live in Pennsylvania. I have not
omitted them either. For these reasons and also because the reformation in Pennsylvania spread to the other corners of Quakerism in
America, I have chosen to use the adjective American in the title of
this book.

   Among the persons who assisted me in this work are two friends
now deceased: Frederick Tolles and Dorothy Harris. The task of
examining the mass of Quaker meeting records at Friends Historical
Library would have been discouraging had it not been for their kind
help over the course of many months. I am immensely indebted
to Haverford College and Edwin B. Bronner for awarding me the
T. Wistar Brown Fellowship in Quaker history. It permitted a year
of uninterrupted study under the best conditions. Also, part of the
computing for this study was done at Haverford and I thank the
College for that aid. Barbara Curtis, archivist of the Quaker Collection at Haverford, unsparingly lent her assistance during my year

there and on other visits. In recent years, at Friends Historical Library, J. William Frost and Jane Rittenhouse Smiley have extended the same assistance I received from Frederick Tolles and Dorothy Harris. I also thank Jerry Frost for being such a patient listener. At the Historical Society of Pennsylvania, Peter Parker and his staff in the Manuscripts Department have assisted me year in and year out.

Alice Allen, for years the librarian of the former Friends Records Department, deserves special mention, not only for her knowledge of Quaker records, but also for her unfailing hospitality. She is also the custodian of a Quaker oral history, as those who have been privileged to know her have been delighted to learn.

To Herman Bateman, Rudolph Bell, Robert Gough, Joseph Illick, Thomas Wendel, and copy editor Debby Stuart who read and improved the manuscript, I am indebted. The mistakes and the infelicities are, of course, mine; but without their eyes and ears, I would have more to apologize for. Rudy Bell patiently shared with me his extensive knowledge of statistics and computer programming and eased my initiation into these mysteries. Paul Seaver and William Clebsch of Stanford University directed my earliest research into Quakerism. The benefits of their guidance appear in this work as well. Marilyn Bradian and Nikki Matz typed the manuscript and Gwyn Roske prepared the illustrations. Jan McCoy solved programming difficulties and Joseph Fineman coded much of the data. The American Philosophical Society assisted in the expense of travel to Philadelphia. The University of Arizona generously assisted in the expense of keypunching, computing, and publication. Part of chapters 3, 7, and 12 have appeared in different form in the *Pennsylvania Magazine of History and Biography, Quaker History,* and *Church History,* respectively.

In the years that I have spent working on this history, I have come to know well some of the persons named above. Their friendship has been abundant repayment for the labor invested. To my wife, Katherine, whom I tried to convince that all our trips to Philadelphia were vacations, I am dearly thankful. It has taken a long time, and she has always been patient.

The Social Reformation

1

The Context of Reform: Quaker Discipline

How a Quaker was expected to conduct his or her life was prescribed by the discipline of the Society of Friends. This body of rules for Quaker behavior originated in the late seventeenth century and was amended in the following decades. The rules sprang from the sectarian self-consciousness of English Friends and the persecution they suffered after the restoration of King Charles II. To effectively deny and disprove their oppressors' slander of them, Friends had to display some reasonably uniform conduct based upon their religious professions. Eccentrics in their midst jeopardized them all. For example, when Friends were accused of dishonesty or sedition, they could not attest to their honesty or lawful behavior or promise it for the future with a sacred oath. Their faith and the Scriptures taught them to "swear not at all." Instead, they insisted that their word—an affirmation—was sufficient. But if some Friends were dishonest and subversive, the simple word of any given Friend could not be trusted. When magistrates pressed them to swear oaths, Friends could not object that their word was sufficient. The skepticism of the magistrate and the persecution of Friends was warranted. Because of this danger to all Friends, it became the Society's duty to make honesty a fact; to cull from their ranks the dishonest and untrustworthy. Furthermore, they must see that the world learned of their zeal for honesty and for every other manifestation of the religious "Truth" they professed. They must publicize their explusion of irregular members—in their words, disown them before the world.

In this chapter, we examine the rules or articles of discipline as well as the Society's record of whom and what behavior it disciplined in Pennsylvania. It is a commonplace among students of crime and law enforcement that legal and other codes represent sometimes more and at other times less than the behavior that a society desires or requires. By examining not just the code, but also what Quakers enforced upon their brethren, we get a considerable degree closer to the actual desires of the Society of Friends and the actual lives of Friends. And while the code of the Society usually remained unchanged, the requirements of the Society changed in an unmistakable manner.

An examination of discipline reveals the historic importance of correct conduct to Friends—by, among other things, their use of evidence to prove a member's deviance, their anxiety that deviants be publicized, their willingness to diminish their membership and create tensions within families and meetings, all to uphold their standards of ethics. With a sense of their concern for their corporate record or character, we may better understand their extraordinary refusal to assimilate the "world's ways" or to pragmatically go along with the prevailing social and political customs of their day. Finally, this is the tradition and environment that produced reformers zealous to restore or refine the "primitive purity" of the Society in the eighteenth century.

The Practice of Discipline

Quaker discipline governed a Friend's life from birth to death: The Society registered his birth, oversaw his religious and secular education, approved his choice of spouse, and buried him "decently, orderly, and publickly."[1] To assure that the Society could effectively oversee the lives of its members, the Quaker discipline required that Friends live within the physical confines of a monthly meeting. Since the meeting encompassed at least one township—more in rural areas—Friends had more room to disperse than was permitted early New England Congregationalists. Yet the disciplinarians were untroubled by the distances separating Friends. They showed in fact that within their monthly meetings they could very effectively inspect the lives of the members. But a Friend did have to live within the confines of a meeting; living beyond them exposed him to possible disownment. Temporary escape from Quaker oversight was curtailed too. Prolonged travel and migration required the approval of the meeting and a certificate of removal and membership, which testifed to one's good standing in the Society. That certificate had to be presented to the Quaker meeting at one's destination, and without any undue, questionable delay.[2]

Between the important and vital junctures in most Friends' lives, the Society might exercise its oversight in scores of ways that are not fully revealed in the disciplinary code. An examination of the behavior for which monthly meetings disciplined members gives a truer picture of the scope of Quaker oversight (see table 1).

Whatever the error a Friend committed, the disciplining of members took much the same procedural course. Every Friend belonged to a congregation called a meeting for worship. Typically, two or three congregations of Friends comprised a monthly meeting. In Pennsylvania, from four to eight of the monthly meetings comprised a quarterly meeting. The three quarterly meetings in Pennsylvania—Bucks, Chester, and Philadelphia—contained most of the membership of the Philadelphia Yearly Meeting, the highest organizational unit.[3] It was in the monthly meetings that most of the business, including the disciplining of members, occurred. The higher meetings heard appeals and determined policy. Each monthly meeting appointed two members as overseers and gave them the special responsibility of looking after the behavior of the other members, although notice of a Friend's transgression might come to the monthly meeting by any channel—overseer, Friend, or non-Friend.

When a delinquent Friend was reported to a monthly meeting, the meeting appointed several Friends to visit the delinquent to inform him of the allegation against him and to ascertain his disposition. In most cases it appears that the meeting was already certain of the guilt of the accused before visitors were appointed, and their primary task was usually to learn whether the delinquent was disposed to admit and condemn his breach of discipline or would refuse to condemn it and be disowned. To condemn his breach, he had to prepare a written statement for the meeting confessing his

Table 1
Varieties of Quaker Delinquency
(N = 12,998)

Offense	Number	Percentage of Total	Percentage Disowned
Marriage delinquency	4925	37.4	45.8
Sectarian delinquency			
Drunkenness	1034	7.8	60.9
Military activity	504	3.8	71.0
Inattendance	497	3.8	70.8
Disciplinary[1]	408	3.2	77.1
Loose conduct	359	2.7	54.3
Profanity	231	1.8	68.9
Attending irregular marriage	217	1.6	27.4
Quarreling	214	1.6	41.1
Entertainments	178	1.4	39.9
Neglecting family responsibilities	142	1.1	49.6
Use of law[2]	129	1.0	31.7
Gambling	107	0.8	48.1
Disapproved company	81	0.6	75.0
Business ethics	64	0.5	70.3
Schism	54	0.4	28.8
"Gospel Order"[3]	38	0.3	56.8
Oaths	35	0.3	60.0
Voluntary withdrawal	35	0.3	94.3
Courting and fraternizing	23	0.2	54.5
Public activity[4]	22	0.2	50.0
Lying	21	0.2	76.2
Disobeying parents	21	0.2	81.0
Dispensing liquor	21	0.2	23.8
Theology	15	0.1	20.0
Dress and speech	11	0.1	68.8
Printing	7	0.0	71.4
Sabbath breaking	5	0.0	60.0
Miscellaneous	42	0.4	31.7

Table 1 (*continued*)
Varieties of Quaker Delinquency
(N = 12,998)

Offense	Number	Percentage of Total	Percentage Disowned
Sexual delinquency			
Fornication with fiance(e)	1311	9.9	39.6
Fornication	727	5.5	70.6
Incest	174	1.3	75.7
Adultery	46	0.3	87.0
Delinquency with victims			
Debt	613	4.6	51.4
Assault	391	3.0	41.3
Slander	124	0.9	35.2
Slaveholding	123	0.9	22.0
Fraud	118	0.9	58.1
Theft	61	0.5	60.0
Violating laws	17	0.1	17.6
Destroying property	11	0.0	36.4
Fleeing master	9	0.0	76.2
Counterfeiting	7	0.0	57.1
Smuggling	6	0.0	50.0

[1]Disciplinary violations were occasions when the offender showed contempt for the Society's authority over his conduct.
[2]This violation is the prosecution at law of one Friend by another, without having exhausted the arbitration procedure of the Society.
[3]"Gospel Order" was Quaker arbitration. Violators ignored it in various ways. One of them was to seek redress at law and this error is separately tabulated here.
[4]Prohibited public activity was the holding of public offices that entailed activity that violated Quaker ethics.

guilt and attesting to his contrition. He had to attend the monthly meeting with this paper, have it checked for its adequacy, and later attend his own meeting for worship when the paper was read to his brethren. If he chose disownment, the monthly meeting prepared a statement of his transgressions and a declaration of its disunity with him. A copy was given to him for his inspection. If he did not object, the statement would be published among Friends. The procedures were strictly observed. In one of the very few cases in which a higher meeting reversed the decision of a monthly meeting, Bucks Quarterly Meeting reinstated C. B. because Falls Monthly Meeting did not show him a copy of his disownment before it published it.[4]

The procedure for readmission to the Society alone might dissuade the sensitive man or woman from attempting it, for it exposed him and his error to the community. S. P. told Newgarden Monthly Meeting that she would condemn her fornication in writing, but she would not appear at the meeting in person to condemn her act. The appearance was mandatory; she was disowned.[5] Friends demanded a personal appearance so that they might judge the sincerity of the delinquent who had to prove his contrition and his reformation to the meeting.[6] For the normally sober Friend who committed an angry or passionate act, proof of good character and of regret were sufficient for prompt pardon. For the chronic drunkard, contrariwise, proof of reformation might require years.[7] The surest way to fail the test was to treat the test flippantly. T. V. committed the minor offense of attending a prohibited wedding. If he had acknowledged that he had made a mistake, he would have been pardoned. Instead, he suggested to Uwchlan Monthly Meeting that his was a minor violation and that they ought to ignore it. He was disowned.[8] Friends expected humility in an offender who petitioned for pardon, an awareness that he indeed was a petitioner. When J. K. committed fornication his offense was "much aggrivated by his presuming to preach to others when he was very faulty himself." For his show of pride, Bradford Monthly Meeting disowned him despite his readiness to fulfill its other demands.[9] In hundreds of cases the task of assessing the sincerity of the petitioner was more difficult: Did the gestures of the delinquent demonstrate humility? Was his confession declamatory or evasive? How well had he attended meetings for worship?[10]

When the misdeed involved a victim, the meeting had a more substantial means of testing the sincerity of the confessor. He had to satisfy the just demands of the victim and compensate the victim for damages. In 1754, Goshen Monthly Meeting disowned T. P. for alleged fornication with a girl in Virginia. Fourteen years later, T. P. condemned his misdeed. Before the meeting would reinstate T. P., it demanded that he produce a letter from the victim in which she acknowledged that he had satisfied her demand for restitution. When he produced such a letter from her two years later, Goshen reinstated him.[11]

If the Friend did not appeal, the meeting published his disownment; if he had condemned his misdeed, the meeting published his condemnation. Publication of the papers was as important to the meetings as was the treatment of their authors. Friends were anxious that persons inside and outside the Society recognize the evildoer and the personal nature of his guilt. To acquit the Society, Friends publicized the revelations about the evildoer. The Yearly Meeting ordered that the "condemnation be published . . . in such a manner that it may reach as far and become as publick as the offense hath been."[12] The concern over the need to publicize a misdeed sometimes influenced a meeting's decision about an evildoer. Z. G. had committed fornication. Wrightstown Monthly Meeting recorded that "he thought he was not in a proper condition to satisfy Friends but that if they would wait sometime with him he was in hopes he would be enabled to do something . . . but . . . we believe the reputation of the society will suffer through delay of publishing our disunity with such practices."[13]

To publish the papers, Friends would read the disownment or condemnation in the meeting for worship to which the delinquent belonged. Thereafter, the procedure varied. It commonly involved posting the paper on the door of the meetinghouse or in the public marketplace.[14] If a specific group of people had observed the offense, a Friend read the paper to them. If the offense occurred in a particular location, the paper was posted there. Exeter Monthly Meeting read S. W.'s condemnation at the tavern where he became drunk. When R. M. got drunk at S. H.'s house, Newgarden Monthly Meeting ordered R. M.'s paper be read there, and that R. M. be present when it was read.[15]

For extraordinary offenses or delinquents, the papers were given extraordinary circulation. In 1706, Edward Shippen married his third wife in a manner contrary to the discipline of the Society. Shippen was one of the wealthiest merchants of provincial Pennsylvania. He had been mayor of Philadelphia, speaker of the Pennsylvania House of Representatives, president of the Provincial Council, a justice of the Supreme Court, and acting governor of the province. He condemned his irregular marriage and heeded the customary procedure of standing in meeting for worship when his paper was read to the assembled Friends. However, Shippen's renown extended beyond Philadelphia Friends. To clear the Society of the reproach he had brought upon it, Philadelphia Monthly Meeting sent copies of his paper of condemnation to New England, Long Island, New Jersey, Maryland, Barbados, London, and Antigua.[16]

When Friends were satisfied that the papers were adequately published and that "Truth" was free from reproach, the disciplinary procedure ended. If it had ended in disownment, the disowned person, after a period of time long enough to permit him to understand his guilt and show genuine contrition, could petition the meeting for reinstatement. The normal period of disunion for those who were reinstated was a year or longer; some returned fifteen to twenty years after disownment.[17] Nevertheless, within any category of offense, one finds disowned Friends who were later readmitted. Disownment was never final; there was no kind of behavior or belief which Friends in Pennsylvania never forgave.

Friends did not claim that admission to the Society indicated salvation or a state of grace. They were singularly quiet about the inner state of members. Quite consistently, then, they did not claim that disownment signified a fall from grace or damnation. Through disownment, Friends really showed more concern over the reputation of the Society or its religious testimonies than they did for the delinquent member.[18] As they indicated in scores of cases, they were especially concerned "that Truth not suffer" from the confusing effects of deviant behavior. Friends comprised a self-conscious religious community with a perfectionist bent, and that became increasingly evident in the reformation of the Society.

The Varieties of Delinquency: Sexual Misconduct

For this study, the varieties of Quaker delinquency have been grouped into four categories, which appear in table 1: marriage, a category by itself because of its size; sectarian misbehavior, which is behavior that offended mostly Quaker sensibilities; sexual misconduct; and delinquency involving victims. Marriage deserves extended discussion and will appear later in the context of the Quaker family. We take up sexual misconduct first, because although it is the third largest category, the category is almost entirely fornication, and

fornication was, next to marriage, the largest single concern of
Quaker discipline.

Monthly meetings had no systematic means of detecting fornication. Friends observed acquaintanceships and courtships, listened
to rumors, requested explanations of conduct that aroused suspicion,
and warned suspects. Many of these practices appeared in Philadelphia Monthly Meeting's dealings with W. F. who "for a long series of
years occasioned much grief and trouble to our religious society arising from the various reports of his vicious and scandalous behavior
towards women." But, the meeting complained, "as such secret
works are often difficult to prove, nothing more could be done for a
long time." The meeting was reduced to admonishing him to prevent
the rumors and to apply to God "for power over temptation."[19]

Some offenders quickly undid themselves. Two of these were
going about boasting of frequent fornication with a young woman.
She utterly denied the fact. Richland Monthly Meeting never questioned the honesty of the young men and disowned them. The curiosity of Friends was aroused by some men and women who were
found living together. Several of these women even bore children.
When their respective monthly meetings asked to see evidence of
their marriage, they all refused to produce their marriage certificates.
Friends concluded that the suspects were not married and disowned
them all. Four persons forged or altered the dates of their marriage
certificates so that nine or more months appeared to have elapsed
since their marriages. Appearing to believe that Chester Monthly
Meeting would find his explanation reasonable, a man there told the
meeting that he was feigning marriage to escape a tax on bachelors.
It disowned him. In rare cases, the evidence was much less circumstantial. One man was found in bed with a woman of "debauched"
character; another was caught "with a woman of ill fame in the
woods."[20]

Paternity was the most common form of evidence. For the single
or widowed woman who bore the child, there was no evasion once
her pregnant condition had been perceived by other Friends. With
very few procedural complications, she was charged and usually
disowned.

More than simple pregnancy was necessary to prove newlywed
Friends guilty of fornication. These Friends comprised the largest
group of fornicators—1311 as compared with 727 unmarried. The
monthly meetings had to ascertain that the child was born signifi-

cantly less than nine months after marriage and therefore had to know the time elapsed between marriage and birth. When the couples were married by Friends, the monthly meeting had little trouble determining the dates and time. If Friends did not have the dates, the meetings requested the information from the couple they suspected. Self-incrimination was no defense and refusal to divulge the dates was a disownable offense. W. B. was disciplined by Middletown Monthly Meeting not for fornication but for refusal to "give them any satisfactory account of the time of his marriage, or the space of time between that and the birth of the child." C. B. showed contempt for the discipline of the Society by his refusal to cooperate, but in his case his meeting did not proceed against him for his contempt but rather waited him out. Six months later, when a child was born, the meeting straightaway disowned him. B. S. and his wife were repeatedly questioned because she appeared pregnant. They "always denied their indecency with an uncommon . . . assurance she alleging indispositions of another kind for her appearance . . . of being pregnant." She continued "inflexibly obstinate" until she delivered a child. Then the meeting wrote: "whereas such an obstinate, evasive, and deceitful deportment must be attended with pernicious consequences, as well as adding sin to sin and that repeatedly," even while "they knew themselves guilty of such heinousness," they are "forthwith disowned."[21]

Because some babies were delivered prematurely, fornication could not explain every untimely birth. To determine the circumstances of a birth, the meeting might question the midwife or other witnesses. The suspected couple, protesting their innocence, might bring such witnesses in their defense. J. R. did so when he and others witnessed an accident to his wife that provoked a miscarriage.[22]

These foregoing couples were guilty of compounding the sin of fornication with the additional error of marrying within the Society of Friends while aware that they were guilty of fornication. Obedient couples would have confessed fornication when they petitioned for marriage, whether or not the fiancees knew themselves pregnant and foresaw their embarrassment and exposure. Very few volunteered such information. If fornication did not produce pregnancy, we can suspect that Friends rarely learned of the sinful condition of the betrothed. If it did produce pregnancy, the couple often proceeded to sully Quaker marriage anyway, rather than reveal the condition that only they detected. Months later, their sin was exposed and they were charged with "imposing their marriage upon Friends." This show of moral obtuseness added to the burden of their guilt. Of a woman in these circumstances, Philadelphia Monthly Meeting said "that after so much hypocrisy and falsehood for which there does not at present appear any reason to believe she is truly penitent, the usual course of dealing is neither necessary nor expedient." She was immediately disowned.[23]

The near certainty of being disowned for this double delinquency should have prevented any thoughtful couple from having the Society solemnize their marriage. To explain the fact that many couples nevertheless did impose upon the Society, one may surmise that at the time of their Quaker marriage neither partner knew that the fiancee was pregnant. Many births occurred seven months after marriage. In the two months before the marriages, the fiancees might not have detected the pregnancy, or might not have been sure and dared to marry anyway.

Most of the 1311 Friends who committed fornication with a fiance(e) or subsequent spouse, did not marry under the care of Friends. The dilemma of one of these couples illustrates the situation of most of them. The young man was not a Friend but was petitioning Abington Monthly Meeting for admission. He intended to become a member, then become engaged and marry a young woman of the meeting. While Abington Friends were spending months observing his conduct and examining his qualifications for membership, they learned that he had married the young Friend outside of Quaker auspices. Several months later she bore a child.[24] The couple had changed their plans for an orderly marriage upon learning of her pregnancy. At least 70 percent of the Friends found guilty of fornication were also discovered when they married outside the Society and too soon became parents.

The Society more readily forgave fornication when committed by affianceed or later-married persons than fornication unaccompanied by marriage or the promise of it—even though the marriage was not solemnized in Quaker meeting. The Society disowned 39.6 percent of the affianceed fornicators, but 70.6 percent of the single members guilty of fornication. And whereas fornication by single members was the tenth most severely treated variety of delinquency (measured in terms of percentage of offenders disowned), fornication by affianceed members ranked thirty-third.[25]

Several possible reasons for the difference in treatment come to mind. Friends might have wished to add to their numbers the children of the union and even convert a non-Quaker spouse. But other facts discount this possibility: the Society of Friends was not a proselytizing church and after the beginning of reformation in the 1750s, the Society discouraged rather than eased the admission of children and spouses of errant Friends and undependable unions. Another possibility is suggested by the practice current in society at large in the eighteenth-century America. There "any public prosecution associated with an impending or currently existing marriage reduced the significance and punishment of the act of fornication."[26] The reason for the leniency was to save the public treasury the expense of maintaining a bastard child. The act of fornication itself bothered the public authorities less than the economic consequence of bastardy. This trend toward leniency in the eighteenth century appeared in Pennsylvania as well as in the rest of America, and in places where Friends held most of the public offices.[27] Friends looked after their own members' needs regardless of public assistance, and every child conceived out of wedlock by a married couple was an expense that the Society did not have to bear. Single mothers and fatherless children would likely prove to be a burden, and so the Society may have wished to discourage such situations by severer treatment. Finally, fornication among affianced persons probably appeared less promiscuous than fornication among people who had no commitment to each other and therefore was more easily forgiven.

The treatment of bachelor males and the proof of their paternity was more varied and interesting than the treatment of other groups. The Society felt easy about disowning some, such as T. P., who was discovered "applying to physicians to prevent if possible his wicked actions to come to light" and whose conduct the Meeting called an "abomination." The most ingenious of all the bachelors tried to get the woman with whom he had committed fornication to marry another man, secretly and quickly, but he was caught. Several men fled with their pregnant accomplices.[28] They, however, did not have the Society's reaction in mind, because leaving the jurisdiction of a monthly meeting without its approval was reason enough to get one disowned. They likely fled to escape public prosecution for paternity or marriage to the mother. Men Friends who did not flee but tried quietly instead to compensate the mother were in deep jeopardy whenever the Society learned of such compensation. It took the payment as sufficient evidence to warrant disownment. It discovered men Friends who paid sums of money from £5 to £160 for support of a child, for the woman's "lying in," or for release from responsibility and public prosecution.[29]

In most cases there was no circumstantial evidence. In some cases the monthly meetings reported that no evidence could be produced by either accuser or accused to prove or disprove the charge. Nevertheless, the meetings judged the accused guilty.[30] For the meetings, the accusation itself was sufficient cause for prosecution and, if the defendant did not disprove the accusation to the satisfaction of Friends, for disownment. The burden of the proof was clearly upon the defendant. When accused, W. B. demanded "Friends to make proof: wherefore . . . [two Friends] are appointed to acquaint him that the Meeting looks upon it [as] his business to clear himself." If the accused could not disprove the charge or refused to do so, he would probably be disowned.[31]

The statements disowning these accused Friends have a tone of equivocation that suggests uncertainty about guilt. One Friend was "somewhat guilty of the matter he is charged with or otherwise hath acted indescreet." Another "has not cleared up the matter in his own favor . . . [and] by several circumstances which appears in his conduct and management of the said affair, there is great room to suspect his being too far concerned in the said charge, and that he is not so clear thereof as he alleges, and would have the world to think he is." Abington Monthly Meeting announced:

We are of the mind that the said [J. P.] . . . hath not at all times so prudently avoided the said [M.'s] . . . company as he ought to have done, considering the diverse temptations respecting her, which he himself acknowledges he hath at times met with and on the whole, it doth not appear to us, that anything the said [J.] hath urged in favor of his case, is sufficient to clear him from remaining under the imputation of being guilty of unchaste familiarity with her.[32]

The Society employed a less exacting standard of proof when disciplining men for fornication or paternity than women. The effect of its zeal in disciplining men shows up not only in the preceding cases but also in the totals for 1682–1776 of men and women disciplined for fornication: 344 men (48.7 percent of 707 total) and 363 women (51.3 percent). Also, the figures for fornication with a

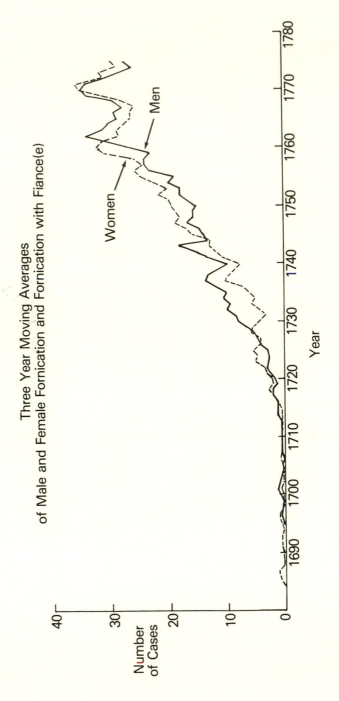

Three Year Moving Averages
of Male and Female Fornication and Fornication with Fiance(e)

Number
of Cases

Year

Figure 1.

fiance(e) balance—656 men and 655 women. Were Friends to have adopted a standard for men as positive as pregnancy was for women, the number of women would certainly have far outnumbered men; however, that was not the case. This balance contrasts with statistics on discipline from the Congregational churches of colonial Massachusetts. There the number of women disciplined for fornication significantly exceeded the number of men.[33] In both Massachusetts and Pennsylvania, fornication was a civil crime as well as a religious one, and fornicators were liable to be prosecuted within both jurisdictions. The Massachusetts churchmen may have been content when the state alone punished the male fornicator—church and state were far more intimate in Massachusetts than in Pennsylvania. But, Friends were not content with whatever the state did in Pennsylvania; they prosecuted fornicators regardless and for their own sectarian purposes.

The Society of Friends disciplined male fornicators upon scant evidence mostly because of their self-consciousness as a religious community. Although they did wish to see justice done to hapless, unwed mothers or their children, justice, deterrence, and retribution were not the motives commonly expressed in the records. Rather, Friends wished to clear the Society of Friends of the "scandal" that might attach itself to the church. That was nothing new; the discipline originated in the seventeenth century in a large part to distinguish regular Friends from deviants and imposters and from slanderous stories.[34] And so it was, for example, that Abington Monthly Meeting accused B. G. of paternity without any complaint from the pregnant young woman. He remained silent. The young woman still refused to accuse B. G. The meeting said "she would rather take the blame to herself, than say who the father was." This case had no plaintiff, no grievance, and no proof. Yet B. G. and the young woman were disowned. In another case, a woman accused J. E. of paternity. J. E.'s father came to the meeting on the day J. E. was to be publicly disowned and said, "They need not do it: for I am the wretched man that have done the thing and I believe my son to be clear." Exeter Monthly Meeting disowned the father "for the heavy reproach which he . . . hath brought upon the Truth and Friends." Yet the investigation continued. Four months later the meeting disowned the son;

as there is a probability that he is not clear of unchaste familiarity with the said woman and as a heavy reproach hath [been] brought upon our holy profession by the said charge, we think it most for the honour of Truth to testify against him . . . until his innocence (if innocent) appears to the satisfaction of Friends; or until he (if guilty) manifests that Godly sorrow for his transgressions.[35]

J. B. was disowned as the *reputed* father of a bastard child; J. K. disowned "in order to clear the truth and the society from such scandal (which otherwise it might be charged with)."[36]

After satisfying any demands for redress, the delinquent, male or female, had to condemn the act of fornication. If the monthly meeting accepted the written condemnation, it published the paper, possibly severely embarrassing a timid Friend. The monthly meeting had placed such a Friend in a dilemma. If he earnestly desired to be pardoned he could decry his sin. He would have impressed the meeting, embarrassed himself, and been pardoned. If he chose to retain his composure, he could equivocate and avoid all pejoratives in describing his sin. He would appear composed, insincere, and unworthy of pardon. H. H. condemned her "carnal knowledge of him that is now my husband before marriage, a crime very odious and heinious in the sight of God and scandalous to his Church and people." She convinced the meeting; others could not muster the equanimity to do so. Many disowned Friends who ignored the Society when they were accused probably feared making the public confession more than they feared disownment.[37]

A very few instances of sexual delinquency involved incest and adultery. One hundred seventy-four cases of incest comprised 1.3 percent of all sexual offenses; 46 cases of adultery comprised 0.4 percent. To a non-Quaker, incest was a less notable matter than the statistic may indicate, because Friends defined incest very broadly. To secular society's typical discouragement of unions with persons as close as or closer than first cousins, Friends added second cousins. And further, in 1753 the Society prohibited marriages of affinity parallel to the forbidden degrees of consanguinity. A Friend could not marry the sibling of a dead spouse, or spouse of a dead sibling, for example. These broad strictures raised one of the warmest protests ever, yet Philadelphia Yearly Meeting did not retreat from them, nor were violators casually dismissed.[38] Almost 76 percent of them were disowned, making incest the fifth most severely treated violation.

There was no controversy whatever about adultery. Without recriminations, the Society treated this error the most seriously of all, disowning 87 percent of all offenders.[39] Whereas the number of males accused of incest moderately exceeded the number of females (98 to 76), the number of accused male adulterers doubled the number of female offenders (30 to 16). Meetings occasionally insisted that Friends quit, avoid, or decry situations that threatened adultery. A Bucks County couple once slept a male lodger, a Friend, in the same bed with themselves "which probably did excite lust in him to lie with her," because "he used indeavours to tempt . . . her . . . by salutations, wantonness, and unseemly discourses." It happened a second time, which "hardened him [the lodger] with expectation that he should succeed with her."[40] The husband, now feeling aggrieved, demanded and got a payment of money from the offending lodger and thought the case was closed. But the Society did not, for those involved had to decry such suspect intimacy and remove any scandal or blame that might redound to the Society of Friends. Error was corporate and the grievance not merely personal.

As for other sexual misconduct, there was no record of rape, and except for one case of beastiality, no eccentric sexual episodes.

Sectarian Delinquency

The category of sectarian delinquency (excluding marriage) includes two subcategories of behavior. There is behavior that only Friends considered wrong, such as inattendance at worship, "loose" behavior, and keeping bad company. There is also such behavior as drunkenness, gambling, profanity, and sabbath-breaking, which was prohibited by both Friends and the laws of Pennsylvania. These are classified here with the sectarian errors, however, because the law enforcement officials of Pennsylvania increasingly ignored them, while Friends paid increasingly more attention to them.[41]

Drunkenness was the most common error in the sectarian category and the one that worried Friends most. It comprised 7.8 percent of all delinquency and 22.9 percent of the sectarian category. Drunkenness distressed Friends especially because, as Abington Monthly Meeting recorded, it "is an inlet to many other evils." Of the Friends accused of drunkenness, 50.1 percent had violated church discipline in some other way that was often "scandalous." A Friend was so drunk that he was found lying dangerously in the public highway; a woman was "seen with a young man acting such things as are a shame for a woman to be found doing." A man wagered on the amount he could drink, and so was "unexpectedly induced . . . to drink to excess which occasioned his death."[42]

Friends guilty of drunkenness were sometimes very conspicuous. J. M., a minster from Chester Monthly Meeting, repeatedly became drunk. Upon his third such offense he went "riding about the country craving for [liquor] and taking it after a clandestine manner and when intoxicated thereby presumptuously pretended to preach." The clerk of Concord Monthly Meeting was persistently drunk. Mordecai Yarnall, Jr., the eighteen-year-old son of a senior Quaker minister, was drunk almost every day in 1763, and some Friends once had to carry him off the street to Pennsylvania Hospital.[43]

Of the evils most often appearing in conjunction with drunkenness, inattendance ranked first (17.4 percent of the time), then swearing (12.4 percent), "loose" behavior (8.3 percent), prohibited marriage (7.8 percent), assault (7.2 percent), and delinquent indebtedness (6.8 percent). The minutes occasionally show a syndrome of behavior which added one of these upon another—keeping bad company, drinking to excess (often in that bad company), contracting debts, neglecting one's livelihood, and perhaps neglecting the care of one's family. If the drunken Friend added any other misbehavior to his drunkenness, he could not expect the tolerance the Society showed any typical offender or even any merely drunken offender. The Society disowned 69.8 percent of all who drank to excess and otherwise erred, while it disowned 52.0 percent of merely drunken delinquents.

On the other hand, Friends often showed extraordinary patience with drunkards who showed a willingness to reform. A good example was D. E. of Philadelphia, who had stopped attending meetings, neglected his business and family, and was often drunk. Some Friends visited him officially in January 1760, and learned that he wanted to improve. In April, the meeting told him "to putt out his children" into other Quaker homes because he had not reformed. In the following six months he almost convinced Friends that he had reformed and was stable again, but in December he relapsed and would have been disowned had he not begged for forbearance. In June 1762, he condemned his condition, and the Meeting accepted his condemnation on trial of his conduct. By the end of the year he had completely relapsed. In January 1763, when he was again almost disowned, he acknowledged the justice of the charges against him

and again resolved to reform. Seven months later he was living a
sober life and had recovered his business. Since he continued sober
and industrious in the next year, the meeting watched him less
intently.[44]

The number of Friends who recovered from chronic drunkenness,
however, was too few to satisfy their concerned brethren, and the
Society believed that ever more effort and changes were needed to
remedy this intractable problem.

Inattendance at meetings for worship was the second most
common sectarian offense and was treated seriously by Friends; they
disowned 70.8 percent of the offenders. The severity of treatment,
however, needs qualifying, lest anyone deduce that the Society
required all Friends to consistently attend worship. Inattendance was
infrequently the sole charge against any offender; not quite one in
five of all persons charged with inattendance committed only that
offense. The other four were most commonly guilty, in addition, of
drunkenness (28.4 percent of them), prohibited marriages (19.3
percent), "loose" behavior (10.1 percent), indebtedness (9.3 percent),
and keeping bad company (5.0 percent). One may surmise that in
some of these cases, the offenders stayed away from religious meetings because of another offense, such as marrying a non-Friend, keeping the company of non-Friends or irreligious people, or avoiding
Quaker creditors (or the Quaker advocates of non-Quaker creditors
since any delinquent debt was a violation of discipline). Inattenders
who had not compounded the error had a 49.5 percent chance of
being disowned, while other offenders had a 78.1 chance of disownment. Monthly meetings required delinquents, rather than reliable
Friends, to attend religious meetings regularly in order to test their
contrition for their errors.

Showing contempt for the disciplinary authority of the Society
was a very effective way to get disowned, and 313 such proud
persons, or 77.1 percent of all such offenders, were disowned. Whatever a Friend was charged with or required by the Society to perform,
if he or she did not finally attend monthly meeting, explain or excuse
himself, acknowledge the error, or beg pardon, he would finally be
disowned. The Society had to insist on its authority to command
the attention and compliance of members, or else see the whole
institution of discipline crumble.

Finally, there was a significant amount of sectarian misbehavior
which might be described as deviance from a humble and cautious

style of conduct. In the disciplinary records it appears as the correction of "loose" conduct (or "vain," "airy," "unseemly," or "unbecoming" conduct), of keeping bad company, and of courting and fraternizing with the opposite sex in an unseemly way.[45] Although the expression comes from Roman Catholicism, Friends had a similar sense of the "near occasions of sin," which ought to be avoided to forestall unequivocal sins. And so, when Quaker records were specific enough about "loose" and other such behavior, one finds cases of strong speech without slander, anger without assault or threats without violence, flirtations without fornication, and liasons without adultery. In one case, a male Friend had to explain his behavior to Newgarden Monthly Meeting, which had taken him to task because of his "lighting of [dismounting] his horse, and using the freedom of asking her [a newlywed Friend] how she liked marriage." Abington Monthly Meeting accused J. P. of keeping bad company and he denied he had accompanied the people in question. But the Meeting produced two witnesses who said they had hailed him as he sat with these other people in a tavern. According to the witnesses, when he had heard himself called, he had hidden his face with his handkerchief. When the witneses had hailed him again, he had replied that he was not the person they sought and he had left. Later, he returned wearing a different coat for disguise. Abington eventually disowned J. P. because "Truth and the Society may suffer reproach." Radnor Monthly Meeting told J. E. to stop seeing J. C., a married woman, so frequently, but he told Radnor that he would see her as often as the "necessity" occurred. Radnor disowned him three months later, because the necessity was occurring whenever J. C.'s husband was away.[46] In sum, the Society of Friends had not just a code of behavior, but a style as well, and one could be disowned just for ignoring the style.

There is a conspicuous absence from the sectarian category of any significant number of offenses against the use of "plain" speech, specifically the use of "thee" and "thou," and the wearing of uniformly dull-colored and unornamented "plain" dress. Because these are possibly the most famous hallmarks of Quakerism, one might expect to find the Society strict about requiring them of the members, but the records show otherwise. There are only eleven explicit references to plain speech and dress (0.1 percent of all offenses). Perhaps behind the vague accusations of "looseness" and its variants lie more cases of speech and dress, but the nature of these will remain moot. The fact that there were so few cases of explicit censure of speech and dress may indicate that Friends either kept to their plain speech and dress, or that they did not and were content not to. Frederick B. Tolles's work on the wealthy Quaker merchants of Philadelphia leads one to discount the first explanation. Wealthy Friends did indulge their inclination for extraordinary dress and furnishings.[47] And too, Quaker letters and journals indicate that more Friends discarded the thee and thou than disciplinary records would lead us to believe. Despite the considerable Quaker reputation for plainness, the Friends of colonial Pennsylvania do not seem to have been especially concerned to maintain these badges of Quakerism.

Delinquency Involving Victims

Delinquency involving victims was the least of the Society's problems with its members. The category comprised only 11.2 percent of all delinquency. Other than slaveholding, none of the components of the category raised much apprehension among stalwart Friends and disciplinarians. Delinquent indebtedness comprised the largest part of the category (42.6 percent). Friends had a reputation for economic acumen among their admirers and detractors alike, and a reputation for honesty at least among the former.[48] A good part of the reputation can be attributed to the discipline of the Society. Rash enterprises and insupportable borrowing and contracts were discouraged and Friends who did not do their utmost to repay debts and fulfill contracts were disowned. The tendency of the discipline was to leave the prudent, solvent, and honest in the Society.

Indebtedness was not delinquency in itself, and the monthly meetings had to examine each case to see whether the debtor was neglectful, malicious, or otherwise blameworthy. Often, they found that the debt was associated with other reprehensible conduct. Indebtedness occurred together with other errors 49.8 percent of the time, almost as often as drunkenness did. Drunkenness was often the other error (9.0 percent of the cases) and presumably a contributor. Inattendance followed it in frequency (7.5 percent), then neglecting one's business or vocation (4.9 percent), "loose" behavior (4.6 percent), fraud (4.1 percent), prohibited marriage (4.1 percent), and neglecting the care of one's family (3.8 percent). Much more common than any of these and almost all of them together was the additional offense of fleeing from one's monthly meeting. It occurred in 27.2 percent of the cases of indebtedness. It was taken as positive proof of malice that the debtor was clearly fleeing his creditors, and because it showed contempt for Quaker disciplinary authority, the offender was almost invariably disowned. Yet the evil of delinquent indebtedness did not depend upon the means by which the debt was incurred or repayment delayed. Lack of business acumen, misjudgment, and bad luck—not blameworthy in themselves—also caused some Friends' undoing and disownment.[49]

Disownment was not the rule in cases of debt, which was the twenty-third most severely treated delinquency. When the Society pardoned delinquent debtors, however, the Society required more than a confession; debts still had to be repaid, as Sadsbury Monthly Meeting made clear to a woman whom it required to give up her chattels, place her children in the homes of other Friends, and condemn her indebtedness.[50]

Cases of delinquent indebtedness did not consistently show up at expected times and places. Although the number of cases rose to their highest point in the depression following the French and Indian War, they did not increase during the depression of the 1720s. Indebtedness was only slightly more common in the city of Philadelphia than in rural Pennsylvania. Of all the cases of delinquency throughout the Quaker community under study, 4.6 percent were for indebtedness, whereas of all cases of delinquency in Philadelphia, 5.8 percent were for indebtedness. Yet in Radnor and Gwynedd Monthly Meetings—the Welsh Tract—debt comprised 12.1 and 8.1 percent of all delinquency, respectively.[51]

Violence was no problem among Friends either. Assault and battery was only 3.0 percent of all offenses and most of the cases involved little physical harm to anyone. Nor did monthly meetings deal especially harshly with assault; they disowned 41.3 percent of the offenders, which makes assault rank thirtieth in severity of treatment. The only identifiable group of victims of these assaults were servants; fourteen Friends were disciplined for physically abusing servants. At least one was a black man, whose Quaker master refused to condemn his attack upon the man, because, he said, he did not find striking a Negro a blameworthy act.[52] The absence of women as victims of assault and as perpetrators too provides a contrast with Pennsylvania society generally. Records of the crimi-

Three Year Moving Average of Indebtedness

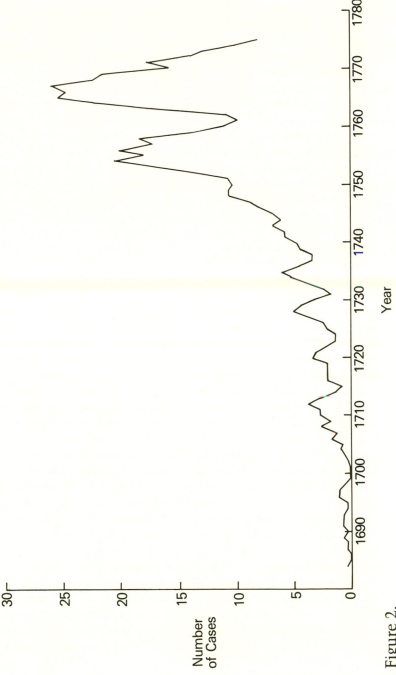

Figure 2.

nal courts of Pennsylvania show that women were the victims of assault by men, and that to a lesser degree, women also committed assault.[53]

Violence was not common in urban areas, nor was it confined to the frontier. Philadelphia Monthly Meeting had, in proportion to all its delinquency, one of the two lowest rates of assault in Pennsylvania (1.6 percent). Warrington Monthly Meeting, on the western edge of Quaker settlement in Pennsylvania and near the frontier, had the third highest rate. The two meetings with the highest rates were rural (but not frontier) ones in central and southwestern Chester County, Goshen (6.3 percent) and Newgarden (5.3 percent). Of all cases of deliquency in all meetings, on the average, 2.9 percent of the cases were for assault.

Regional Differences

In addition to the regional variations we have already noted in the numbers and treatment of cases of debt, violence, and fornication, several other differences existed. The most striking is the severity of several monthly meetings in Chester and Lancaster counties (see table 2). The fact that Uwchlan disowned 63.3 percent more offenders than it pardoned makes it appear draconic even in comparisons within the Society of Friends, but Uwchlan was the only meeting created after the reformation brought severer discipline to the Society. The most severe monthly meetings—the five that exceeded the average for Chester Quarter—covered a nearly contiguous region stretching from Concord Township on the Delaware border east of Brandywine Creek, northeast to Downingtown, and west to Lancaster. Most of this area lies in southern Chester County and was settled by Irish Quaker immigrants. Their common ethnic identity helps to explain the stern use of discipline there. These Friends were accustomed to severe discipline in Ireland: Irish meetings in the 1700s were disowning two out of three offenders (and after 1755, 22 out of 23). Moreover, from this area of Chester County came important innovations of the Quaker reformation, especially regarding pacifism and abolition, as we will later see.[54] Unquestionably, some of the seeds of the Quaker reformation were transported from Ireland.

As for characteristic kinds of delinquency, Philadelphia Monthly Meeting showed the most definition. Delinquent slaveholders were

Table 2
Severity of Discipline in Monthly Meetings

Monthly Meeting	Offenders	Percentage Disowned Minus Percentage Pardoned
Uwchlan (C)[1]	134	63.3
Sadsbury (C)	293	32.0
Bradford (C)	313	25.8
Newgarden (C)	559	25.5
Concord (C)	700	25.0
(Chester Quarter)	(3,883)	(22.6)
Goshen (C)	704	21.9
Philadelphia (P)	1,683	21.2
Warrington (C)	395	17.0
Abington (P)	889	14.5
Chester (C)	785	13.5
Exeter (P)	176	9.7
Darby (P)	257	9.3
(Philadelphia Quarter)	(4,199)	(8.7)
Buckingham (B)	568	7.3
Falls (B)	584	−8.5
(Bucks Quarter)	(1,972)	(−10.5)
Gwynedd (P)	653	−12.3
Middletown (B)	510	−17.3
Radnor (P)	454	−22.9
Richland (P)	87	−32.5
Wrightstown (B)	292	−33.8

[1]C, P, and B indicate, respectively, Chester, Philadelphia, and Bucks Quarterly Meetings.

typically Philadelphians. Somewhat less exclusively, Philadelphians were volunteers for military service, although privateers came only from the city. Once the reformation was under way, Philadelphia almost alone disciplined members who neglected their businesses, and also members who kept company with people the meeting disapproved of. Chester Quarter distinctively reprimanded shows of contempt for its disciplinary authority and procedure.

Gender Differences and the Nature of the Society

There were a number of differences between men and women delinquents and their offenses. Among the delinquents, there were almost twice as many men as women (1.8 to 1) whereas women outnumbered men in the Society—by 14.1 percent in Philadelphia in 1760, for example. Almost three times as many men as women committed multiple offenses. When those who committed the multiple offenses of fornication and prohibited marriage are subtracted, the ratio is twenty men to one woman. The broadest generalization about women's offenses is that prohibited marriages and fornication (including fornication with fiance) comprise 82.7 percent of all offenses. By contrast, one must sum the twelve most common varieties of male delinquency before a cumulative 82.7 percent is reached. Other than prohibited marriage, the most common offense, and sexual delinquency, women did comparatively little wrong. The most effective descriptor for men offenders was, not surprisingly, military activity, followed by drunkenness, debt, and assault.

The statistics on disownment and pardon show very little evidence of unequal treatment of male and female offenders. Overall, the Society disowned 1.8 percent more of its women offenders than its men. Were the inequity removed to show women disowned at the same rate as men, 61 fewer women out of 3,377 offenders would have been disowned. The greatest statistical bias against women offenders appears, in descending order, in the five categories of theft, gambling, slander, "loose" behavior, and fornication. If the bias were removed herein, 43 of the 61 (or 70 percent) of the disownments differentiating the sexes would disappear.[55]

The reason for the similar treatment of both men and women offenders is that in the Society of Friends, the women had their own monthly meetings for discipline. If men Friends were biased against women, they conceded their best opportunity to exercise that bias by assigning to the women the oversight and regulation of women—which is itself a testimony to the men's lack of bias. Some historians have questioned whether the women were assigned anything more than busy work while the determination of disciplinary cases and especially disownments remained with the men. The record among Pennsylvania Friends shows otherwise.

In most monthly meetings, the records of women disciplined are in the men's minutes, permitting the inference that the sanctions of Quakerism—or power—rested with the men. But in Bucks Quarterly Meeting (Buckingham, Falls, Middletown, and Wrightstown Monthly Meetings) the minutes of the men's monthly meetings reveal little or no attention to women's disciplinary business. That

business is found in the women's monthly meetings. This exceptional practice never raised a comment or criticism from other Pennsylvania Friends. They were not silent because it escaped their attention. Quaker ministers, Yearly Meeting committees, and other
official Quakers crossed and recrossed the province (and all the colonies) leaving no meeting at any level uninspected. When Yearly
Meeting authorities found something amiss in the practice of discipline they might even threaten to dissolve an incorrigible monthly
meeting. Bucks Quarter was never mentioned or criticized for its
women's practices because Friends in Philadelphia Yearly Meeting
found nothing exceptionable about it. And that attitude in turn
implies that throughout the Yearly Meeting the power to judge
women's behavior resided in the women's meetings. The fact that
women's disciplinary business appeared in the men's minutes repre-
sents a formality rather than the practical exercise of power there.

The authority of Quaker women over their sisters in profession
is consistent with Friends' equal treatment of women in other
respects. From the inception of the Society, women were admitted
to the ministry and eventually they appeared at every level of the
Society's government. Equal treatment flowed naturally from
Quaker theology. George Fox and others applied Quakerism's central
tenet of spiritual rebirth to women as well as men. Consequently,
Judeo-Christian disabilities upon women, supported by Scripture,
were annulled by revelations tendered to all by the Inner Light.[56]

We would be mistaken to attribute to Quaker women equality in
the economic and professional world, civil government, and private
households. As J. William Frost writes, in the colonial period, "no
Quaker writer transferred the spiritual equality of women into other
spheres."[57] Frost corrects anyone who might mistake Quaker sexual
equality with the goals of modern feminists. But at the same time,
he slights the freedom and the possibilities which religious equality
legitimized for Quaker women. In any church which limited the
purview of religion to the spiritual realm, equality was likewise
limited. But as an examination of table 1 will confirm, Quakerism
did not so limit the play of religion upon everyday life. Within the
broad range of behavior which came under the church's scrutiny,
women exercised a legitimate voice and oversight. And that voice
was not confined to the behavior of women only. Subsequently in
this book, we will learn of Quaker women advising the clerk of
Yearly Meeting, its highest office, in the proper nature of his voca-

tion, haranguing a South Carolinian on his degeneracy, advising Pennsylvania legislators on public policy, inciting rebellion within families to promote pacifism, and opposing the American Revolution, all in the name of Quaker discipline and religious testimonies—for peace, abolition, and humility. The discipline of the Society opened the way for women to express themselves in social, economic, and political spheres where women were, in seventeenth- and eighteenth-century ideology, allegedly dull and certainly disabled. By the nineteenth century, the way was even broader. By Mary Maples Dunn's count, 40 percent of female abolitionists were Quakers, 19 percent of feminists born before 1830, and 15 percent of suffragists born before 1830.[58] The record of women in Quakerism since Fox's day, their equality in the regulation of Quaker life, and the extension of their activity in late colonial America, makes their appearance as protestors in the nineteenth century no surprise.

As mentioned in the Preface, one of the errors that the reformers attempted to correct was the separation of life into distinct spheres and the exclusion of the church from some of them, such as politics and business. In America, such separation of activities occurred in Protestant churches. It has been labeled the "feminization" of American religion and it means that the churches, populated more by women than men, but run by men, avoided politics and business and focused their attention upon education, families and domesticity, and philanthropy. Men exclusively ran the worlds of politics and business and promoted there such values as aggressiveness, strength, and power—"masculine" virtues. Churches taught such "feminine" values as love and gentleness, empathy, and meekness. The exclusion of women and the churches from the domain of men helped to avoid the danger of conflict and disharmony. Thus, "when a society as a whole suffers from a serious conflict of its goals," concludes Mary Maples Dunn, "it can *use* gender differences to resolve the conflict." It assigns one set of goals to men, another to women, depreciates the women's, and thus leaves men free to ignore them and pursue male goals.[59]

The history of Quakerism runs counter to this separation of spheres. Values of love, humility, empathy, and philanthropy were not feminized in Quakerism. They were values fit for men and women alike. And the tendency to exclude women from the men's world did not grow with time, but rather decreased, and so religious values did not become identified solely with women. The grounds for this unity of values was maintained in part because of the Quaker patriarchs' doctrine regarding women, the continued admission of women to the regulation of church life through discipline, and above all the broadening way afforded women by the reformation of Quakerism. Before 1750, the Society was in fact in some danger of becoming a male-dominated institution, cut off from areas of life other than the spiritual. But the reformers, both men and women, had scotched that tendency by the end of the century.

The most obvious difference within Quaker discipline, however, does not appear in comparisons among meetings or regions, or between genders, but in a comparison of all meetings and genders before the reformation of the 1750s with those after the reformation.

2

The Beginnings of Reform,
1748-1755

John Churchman and Sectarian Reform

The Quaker reformation was not the work of any one person and no actor in it was irreplaceable. Yet it is possible to specify the first person to have expressed a hope to reform the Society and to have begun working at it. That was John Churchman of Chester County. Churchman was a lifelong resident of Nottingham Township in that county, a farmer, and a deputy surveyor of the province. Although he was not of Irish stock, he lived among the Irish Quaker immigrants to Pennsylvania, who settled in southern Chester County. These were sturdy and stern Friends and their attitudes may well have influenced Churchman.

Churchman became an active Friend early in life. At the age of nineteen he became concerned for the "good order of the church" and began conscientiously to attend the meetings for business and discipline—both in his own monthly meeting and in others. At the age of twenty-six he reluctantly became an elder. The Friends who had promoted him did not question his qualifications, but he did, and they had to overcome his diffidence. To their dismay, he shortly turned his scrupulosity upon them.[1]

At one particular quarterly meeting of ministers and elders, Churchman interrupted their routine of hackneyed responses to questions about the vitality of the ministry. When the elders said "that the ministry was well received," Churchman, not satisfied by their thoughtless replies, pointed out that the ministry was well "approved of," but could be "better received." That is, he said, the people approved of the ministry because they believed that what they heard was right, but if they were to receive it well they must put it into practice. If the auditors had done that, the "Society would appear more beautiful than at present." Before the next quarterly meeting in 1734 Churchman was replaced. The Friend had judged Churchman well who had once told him, "I preceive thou art born for a warrior."[2]

In the winter of 1748, Churchman suffered a fit of despondency. In his low condition, he said, the call came to him to "gather thyself from all the cumbers of the world, and be thou weaned from the popularity, love, and friendship thereof." Shortly, some friends promoted him for justice of the peace, contending that he would provide a superb model for other magistrates and improve the public service. But Churchman knew that however indefinite his call, God had not intended him to pursue such temporal business as that. His summons became clear to Churchman in 1749 when he understood that he must visit the British Isles and Holland in the service of "Truth."[3]

Quaker ministers typically described themselves, their messages, and the Society most adequately when they were traveling in the ministry; the more extraordinary their journeys were, the more informative the records they left. Churchman's four-year stay in the British Isles and Holland produced an exceptional account of the Society and its ministry, useful for studying British Friends as well as American ministers and the strength of Anglo-American ties. No eighteenth-century Quaker minister other than John Woolman recorded more insights about his auditors than did Churchman; not even Woolman outdid Churchman's attention to homiletics.

Churchman went to England in the spring of 1750 accompanied by his brother-in-law, William Brown, and John Pemberton, the youngest son of Israel Pemberton. The three ministers, occasionally joined by another Pennsylvanian, Daniel Stanton, spent the next four years engaged in the same task. That task was initially unclear. Shortly after debarking in London, Churchman felt an impulse to preach to non-Friends, but then, he recorded, he felt cautious and heard an instruction: "Go not into the way of the Gentiles, and into any city of the Samaritans enter ye not; but go rather to the lost sheep of the house of Israel." John Pemberton supported him: many other ministers "choose to proclaim the Gospel to others and endeavor to gather unto the Church, when behold the corruption which is in the Church is cause of humbling." The mission of Churchman and his colleagues was not to evangelize or to preach to throngs of unchurched Englishmen and others; the task that begged for attention was the cleansing of their own church. "The greatest enemies of the Truth were the professors of it who did not observe the instructions of the grace of God," and they had to be made to understand their faults and their danger to the church.[4]

Churchman sat silent through most of the meetings in London—"sealed up." Some Friends did not take his silence kindly and censured him as "singular and narrow." So it is, Churchman reflected, with "those who [love] to hear words eloquently delivered, and to have the itching ear pleased," who have been "fed with words and hungered for them more than for the instruction of the pure word of life . . . that they might not only hear it but be found doers thereof." Unusual though it may seem in a denomination well known for holding silent meetings, Friends of that day were not accustomed to sitting through a meeting without hearing preaching, especially not when joined by a minister who had come three thousand miles presumably to tell them something. Still Churchman sat mute through the London meetings and a score elsewhere. In his words, "Nehemiah quietly viewed the state of Israel by night."[5]

Churchman intentionally compounded his odd behavior. At Chippenham Monthly Meeting in Wiltshire he attempted to persuade the members to put the discipline into practice "for religion was at a low ebb in that country." But they did not even understand what he was talking about and so he quit trying to explain. When at the end of the meeting his listeners insisted he stay for dinner, claiming they "would think it very strange if I went away," he replied to his hostess that he was not free to eat or drink in her house. When she asked why, he answered enigmatically, "Inquire of the Truth in your own heart for the cause," and then left. Churchman had encountered people in America who had told him they were unaccustomed to being passed by, and "would not take it kind if I did not [join them]." The fault with all of them, Churchman believed, was that "their religion lay much in thinking that good Friends were familiar with them and thought well of them." Churchman had refused almost all the invitations he had received in London. He believed that there is great need to be exceedingly careful, when the Lord is pleased to reach unto and convict disorderly walkers by instrumental means, that we do not lessen the weight of Divine reproof, by being familiar with such, as if all was well; for they are apt to be fond of the instrument through whom they have been reached, and if by their fondling, they gain the esteem of such a Friend, it seems to heal them before their wounds are searched to the bottom; so that I rather chose . . . to live as privately as I well could.[6]

Shortly before leaving England, Churchman wrote an epistle to the "living remnant" among the Wiltshire Friends and warned them to stay clear of Friends "who have a smooth and fawning behavior, and flattering tongues, and do seek the love and friendship of such as are Friends of truth, for their own honour and credit . . . of such beware, for their friendship is poison, and . . . benumbing, even to insensitivity."[7]

Churchman understood his own weaknesses too, especially his susceptibility to "fondling"; by going from house to house among London Friends he suspected he would likely contradict his message of "self-denial and temperance in eating and drinking . . . [and] a steady inward attention to the teachings of the Spirit of grace." Sharing the more innocent hearthside pleasures of Quaker homes would disincline him from cautioning these Friends about unrighteous behavior. Best stay away.[8]

The "corruption" that offended Churchman and his colleagues included, among other things, extravagance, payment of tithes, drunkenness, exogamous marriages, and deism. Whole monthly meetings, they found, protested that any Friend ought to be free to pay tithes without being censured or criticized. Mostly, however, the American group criticized English Friends for their pride, vanity, and high-mindedness and the accompanying spiritual dullness, stupidity, and callousness. The walls of the church lay in "ruinous heaps" because of "dead lifeless members." They could not or would not understand their own deficiencies. They had lived their lives without ever becoming convinced, as their parents and grandparents had, of their lowness, insufficiency, and meanness; had never despaired for the sake of their souls, or even felt uneasy about their condition. They believed that to have entered the Society by birthright was to have gained for their spirits all the succor that their forebears had through the most fear-filled diffidence. They were "unsavoury salt." Unless they were willing to let their wounds be laid open to be cleansed, "their professed soundness would prove rottenness." If, Churchman believed, he would lead these men and women to understand how profound was their controversy with the Lord and how willfully they had fought "the Lamb," maybe then they would be open and receptive to suggestions that they change their profitless lives and correct their grievously delinquent ways. But it was difficult, almost impossible to make some see.[9]

In many places, persons at the head of the Society's affairs were of no help, or worse. They acted according to the "wisdom and carnal apprehension of man"; they transacted "the weighty affairs of the church in as light and easy a manner as men commonly buy and sell in a market"; they brought "death over a meeting [rather] than life." In such monthly meetings "earthly mindedness prevails, or love of the world and its friendship; there is a secret giving way to, and a gradual reconciliation with its sordid practices."[10]

When Churchman chose to speak he told peccant Friends pretty much what he recorded about them in his journal. And he and his colleagues warned the blameworthy leaders that "the days would come, when such as these should be laid aside, or taken away, and those raised up who would depend on the Lord for wisdom and counsel and live uprightly." The Lord "will shake his rod [over followers as well as leaders], and sweep the wicked with a besom of destruction. . . . it was in the Lord's power to cut the thread of their lives, and appoint them their portion agreeable to their doings."[11]

Churchman was rather an oddity in the Society of Friends and if he succeeded in his mission he would make the Society an oddity in eighteenth-century Protestantism. Unlike John Wesley, who had been riding up and down England for a decade reaching thousands outside the Anglican churches, and unlike George Whitefield, Gilbert Tennant, and Jonathan Edwards, who were proselytizing the 90 percent unchurched Americans, Churchman had no message for non-Quakers and felt no need to evangelize. His journey was no part of the pietist revival in England and no extension of the Great Awakening in America. At times Churchman refused to preach even to Friends. The prospect of being heard by crowds of Friends appealed to him little more than being heard by crowds of "Gentile" listeners.

He did not cultivate "enthusiasm" or "strangely warmed" hearts among his listeners. He did not equate his eloquence with the motion of the Holy Spirit in others, nor an enthusiastic response to the preacher with religious conversion and commitment. Listeners who were lifted off on clouds of words, he returned to earth with the advice that they "receive" the message well: "If ye love me keep my commandments," Jesus taught; anything less "would not do the work."[12] Churchman had an insight into the psychology of revivalism; too often listeners, emotionally moved by a sermon, become satisfied that being moved emotionally, they have atoned for their misbehavior and unbelief. But, in Churchman's homely language, that "would not do the work."

At first glance, Churchman appears to have been resisting pietism and to have done so deliberately; yet, it was not so. He never mentioned the revivals or the revivalists; nor for that matter any denomination but Friends. But he was thoroughly a Quaker. He hardly took a decisive step without first assuring himself that the inward spirit had employed him in its business. Ten years he delayed going to the British Isles out of a suspicion that he might act prematurely and by his own mere whim. Voices, visions, and dreams were his instructors; once he had heard or seen them he did not deliberate upon them or explain the instructions pragmatically. He was a pietist too because he encouraged an autonomous spiritual life among other Friends, especially other ministers like the novice John Pemberton. Rather than depend upon him, Churchman, men and women must hear "the instruction of the pure word of life" within themselves. Indeed, Churchman's expectations of the spiritual life—like the expectations of many Quaker ministers—appear too great. Insipid meetings for worship, and even those for business, disheartened him. When he himself was "dried up" and nothing stirred within him, he could not easily dismiss it from mind and hope for a better tomorrow; he kept dwelling upon his deficiency as though it were his error. Among such Quakers no religious business, it seemed, could be done routinely or indifferently.

Wherever Churchman went he redoubled—revived, in some places—attention to discipline, right conduct, education, and nurture of children; which made him more the pastor and teacher than most of his peers, Quaker and non-Quaker. Churchman's oddity was not his qualified opposition to pietism, but his appreciation of those aspects of Christian life that suffered when pietism became merely enthusiasm—that is, discipline, education, and nurture. He understood the hazards for ministers who, infatuated by their own preaching, became subservient to their flocks and were stripped of their faculties as teachers and prophets. Because Churchman felt that the faults of the Society were great he became predominantly the prophet, trying to stop the inroads of the age, or the world, upon his church.

Souls had to be cured, but equally, discipline enforced upon peccant Friends and the church put in good order. Everywhere the small group of Americans and their English collaborators preached discipline. Like George Fox's, the reformers' genius lay in bureaucracy as well as in ministry. Together they devised some reforms of church government which they expected to improve discipline: first, a national meeting of ministers and elders to meet immediately before the London Yearly Meeting convocation—a duplication of the practice in Philadelphia Yearly Meeting; and second, a yearly meeting for women. Both of these bodies would perfect the hierarchy of meetings that the reformers had been building; more and more monthly meetings were adding meetings of ministers and elders and meetings for women to benefit the cause of stricter discipline. It is impossible to prove that all or even most ministers were enthusiastic about reform; but on the other hand, almost every Friend on record as having been enthusiastic about reform was a minister. Also, male and female reformers asserted for some thirty years that women's oversight of women's conduct in their own meetings promoted reformation.

Although the reformers would willingly speak to a handful of Friends at a remote meeting, they had no intention of waiting for the leaven to work. If perverse or dull meetings of Friends refused to change their behavior, then the reformers anticipated making them change. Yearly meeting, quarterly meetings, and new meetings to be created would bring the reformers' authority to bear. Autonomy never characterized the organization of Friends, and the reformers were last among their contemporaries to permit more liberty.

At the 1753 London Yearly Meeting, the proposals for the two new meetings failed. The "generality" favored them, but London Friends, "stiff and self willed," resisted. For the sake of harmony, the reformers dropped the proposals for a session. The following year, when illness and business "providentially" kept three principal opponents from the meeting, the reformers got their meeting for ministers and elders. Agreement to the women's meeting had to wait until 1783.[13]

Although Churchman, Brown, and Pemberton rarely complained of their personal treatment, they were being "buffeted" and "slighted" by the opposition, treated as meddlers in other people's concerns, and discouraged from attending some meetings for discipline. More than anyone else it was the Londoners who oppressed the Americans, as they likewise oppressed the English supporters of reformation. John Pemberton reported from the Yearly Meeting of 1753 that the Londoners frequently gave William Brown "heavy blows." Then and later they accused the reformers of trying to introduce innovations into the Society with their new meetings. They asked that such proposals be laid aside for fear they would cause a separation—a request that may have sounded like a threat. All the while the Londoners "think themselves so whole, happy and well they need not a reformation," one English reformer, Mary Weston, complained.[14]

Once the Meeting for Ministers and Elders passed Yearly Meeting, it was still not secure. Its first clerk, a leading Friend, resigned in a theatrical manner, complaining that he did not understand the purpose of the meeting. If there were more subtlety than dismay in his protest, he failed, because a reform-minded Friend replaced him. Then the conservatives tried to keep women ministers out of the Meeting, but failed. While the reformers gained ground, the Londoners became increasingly perverse. In 1755, London Quarterly Meeting refused to answer some of the queries that Yearly Meeting had directed to all meetings. London presumed to tell Yearly Meeting that the queries were not intended for them! Time did not help Londoners to digest the unpalatable changes, for in 1757, they still refused to answer queries and further defied Yearly Meeting by refusing to visit families and to erect women's meetings for discipline at the local level.[15]

Two months after the gratifying Yearly Meeting of 1754, Churchman left the British Isles. He had spent four years abroad, traveled over nine thousand miles by land, and visited some one thousand meetings or more, as well as countless families. He had averaged five meetings a week for four years. His companions, Brown and Pemberton, did almost as much. If great changes were to appear in English Quakerism, their work would be the cause.[16]

Samuel Fothergill and the American Awakening

When Churchman returned home, Samuel Fothergill came with him. The friendship between Churchman and Fothergill was the

most notable of several that had arisen between the American visitors and English Friends, including Daniel and Mary Weston, John
Griffith, Hannah Harris, Thomas Gawthorp, Jonah Thompson, and
Elizabeth Wilkinson. All shared with the American Friends the same
apprehensions about the low state of the Society. All were ministers
and had either traveled to America or would do so in the next twenty
years. A small community of reformist ministers was gathering,
single-minded in purpose and taut with energy.

Fothergill's journey to America in 1754–56 was the most important by an English minister since that of George Fox in 1671–73.
Unlike Churchman, who often preferred silence to preaching, Fothergill spoke to throngs of people at some places, and spoke more
eloquently than any other Quaker minister of the eighteenth century. In letters, diaries, journals, and even poetry, Friends remembered how significantly Fothergill had affected them and their
communities. Israel Pemberton, Jr., accompanied Fothergill on his
journey through the Southern colonies and wrote to his wife that
Samuel "hath this day exceeded anything I have heard . . . [he spoke]
with Such Elegance of Language attended with so great [a] demonstration of Power, past anything I am capable of repeating or describing." Another Friend recorded that "Such, indeed, was the force of
divine evidence which attended him, that Friends' minds were seized
with awful dread, and had to say to each other, after meeting,—Is
this the last warning that we are to receive? it seems so like that of
Jeremiah to the Jews, just before the destruction of Jerusalem."
Young men like George Churchman, son of John, and Benjamin
Ferris were encouraged by Fothergill to devote their energies to the
church. Churchman eventually became clerk of Philadelphia Yearly
Meeting.[17]

Fothergill's popularity might have disclosed little more than his
talent at filling people who hungered merely after words. But he did
not aim to please anyone at the expense of right conduct; he judged
American Friends at least as severely as Churchman had judged the
English: "the Church . . . sits in the dust"; "the crooked footsteps of
the old professors . . . and the lethargy of the more morally clean,
seem to threaten the utter extirpation of the profession from various
parts of the province [of Pennsylvania]."[18] Fothergill pronounced his
now famous excoriation of Pennsylvania Quakers:

Their fathers came into the country in its infancy, and bought large tracts of
land for a trifle; their sons found large estates come into their possession,

and a profession of religion which was partly national, which descended like the patrimony from their fathers, and cost as little. They settled in ease and affluence, and whilst they made the barren wilderness as a fruitful field, suffered the plantation of God to be as a field uncultivated, and a desert. Thus, decay of discipline and other weakening things prevailed, to the eclipsing of Zion's beauty; . . . A people who had thus beat their swords into plowshares, and the bent of their spirits to this world, could not instruct their offspring in those statutes they had themselves forgotten. As every like begets its like, a generation was likely to succeed, formed upon other maxims, if the everlasting Father had not mercifully extended a visitation, to supply the deficiency of their natural parents.[19]

"Before Zion shines in her ancient glory, judgment must begin at the house of God," Fothergill insisted. And he traveled at least seven thousand miles in America from Massachusetts to South Carolina, instructing Friends, reprimanding them, correcting "the weak & almost ruined state of our discipline." In Pennsylvania and Philadelphia Yearly Meeting he visited every monthly and quarterly meeting, for business and discipline, in addition to meetings for worship and families. "I have been led into very close and laborious work amongst them . . . in the discharge of my duty[,] . . . the hardest labor that I ever yet met with in public or private." Older Friends especially troubled Fothergill; "many of the elders are dead, and some, though alive in the body, are dead to God." "As it is hard to lift up a hand against grey hairs, my progress has been more difficult and afflicting than I can express."[20]

Fothergill did not bear these burdens alone. "That truly great and good man, John Churchman," occasionally accompanied him, as did Israel Pemberton, Jr., William Brown, John Pemberton, William Logan, and John Smith. Two English ministers, Mary Peisley and Catherine Payton, came to America before Fothergill, stayed longer, traveled at least as much, and promoted the same reformation as he did—but sometimes more pugnaciously. In New England, they sat silently through one meeting after another, which "drew upon us great reproach, lies and slander." In Charleston, South Carolina, however, Peisley did not hesitate to tell their Quaker host, who had married a non-Quaker, that she "was much ashamed to walk the streets with one under our name who deviated so much from our principles as he did." She pronounced Charleston "a city of refuge for the disjointed members of our Society."[21]

By 1755 at the latest, a group of the most vigorous Friends, mostly ministers, were cooperating to bring about a reformation. The movement had begun with two concerned Friends traveling in the ministry who had soon been joined in their effort by scores of Friends and lent support by hundreds more at Yearly Meeting. The ministers crossed and recrossed the land, bringing to meetings their message of concern over the decline of Quakerism. Mary Peisley recorded that by December 1755 she had attended six meetings a week while in Philadelphia and visited 160 families—more than 35 percent of the Friends in the city. Probably every Friend in the city knew she was there, understood why she had come, and what she expected of them. Fothergill spoke to far more Friends than Peisley and with greater effect. An effort to bring about reform that had begun with only a few people was to affect the whole Anglo-American Quaker community.

Lay Leadership

Among the inspired leaders of reformation in the Society of Friends were not only ministers but also laymen. One of the most notable laymen was Israel Pemberton, Jr., who, after 1750, filled the preeminent office in American Quakerism of clerk of Philadelphia Yearly Meeting. Pemberton was a reformer and a very pugnacious one— which distinguished him from all his predecessors.[22] His appointment to the highest office from which he subsequently helped to direct Quakerism into a new course was made inadvertently by unreformed Friends and before his conversion to the ideals of reform. Few Friends expected what they subsequently got in Israel Pemberton.

In the 1740s, Pemberton did not appear to be the potential leader of a root-and-branch change in the Society. It was not that Pemberton had neglected the Society or led an irreligious life before 1750; rather, he seemed to be obsessed with politics—one of two candidates certain to become Speaker of the Assembly, the preeminent political post among Pennsylvanians. He had gained the reputation of being the most aggressive young member of the new Quaker party. Like most members of the party, Pemberton subscribed to its credo that their opposition (the Penn family, the governors, and some jealous non-Quaker Pennsylvanians) was attempting to eliminate civil and religious liberties in the province. Indeed, Pemberton seemed by his behavior to have helped to spread that suspicion.

In 1739, Pemberton slandered Lieutenant-Governor George Thomas, who was pushing the Quaker legislators to create a provincial militia. Pemberton was quoted as having said that he knew it was Thomas's "Design or Endeavor to overturn the Constitution and reduce this to a King's Government, and that they would prove it on him." When Pemberton later learned that his audacious comments had reached the governor, he supposedly added that he was glad, because the sychophants that Thomas had surrounded himself with would never tell him the truth. Thomas sought to prosecute Pemberton, but relented.[23]

Later, William Allen, leader of the opposition Proprietary party, did sue Pemberton for slander. Pemberton responded by stirring up a rebellion against the authority of the Philadelphia city corporation, which was controlled by Allen and a clique from the Proprietary party.[24] The Penns and their friends called Pemberton worthless, rude, the worst of "a set of the meanest wretches" and "dirty Politicians," and "the most turbulent creature that has appeared in the Province." After 1750–51 and his only service in the Assembly, they did not change that opinion. From his private station, they complained, he "prys into and has a [still] greater share in the conduct of all matters [of public business]." "With a high Spirit & no discretion [he] pushes himself into every thing."[25]

It was Pemberton's clear capacity for Whig outrage and his genius for mischief that led Pennsylvanians to expect that upon John Kinsey's retirement, Pemberton would obtain the Speaker's chair. That Pemberton might at the same juncture become clerk of Yearly Meeting would have struck no one as odd or inconsistent. The two offices, and yet others, were often united in one man. Kinsey was assemblyman (1731–50), Speaker of the House of Representatives (1739–50), attorney-general (1739–41), chief justice (1743–50), acting trustee of the Loan Office (1739–50), and head of the Quaker party. Kinsey was only the most recent of a series of politician-clerks: Griffith Owen, Caleb Pusey, and Isaac Norris, Sr.[26] These men could be said to have followed William Penn's advice that Friends ought to cultivate the two plantations of government and church. In precept as well as practice, the leadership of Friends was not incompatible with leadership in provincial politics, and most likely having one helped in obtaining the other. For Pemberton, his aggressive Whiggery could only improve his chances of becoming clerk of Yearly Meeting, not diminish them.

To the surprise of many and the relief of the Proprietary party, Pemberton did not become Speaker. Isaac Norris II did.[27] Upon Kinsey's death in 1750, his two preeminent offices were divided, ending the combination of the previous sixty-eight years. The new arrangement left Norris free of any official responsibility for the spiritual health of the Society of Friends, and Pemberton free of distractions from his religious responsibilities.

Soon after Pemberton became clerk of Yearly Meeting, reformer Friends caught his ear. Mary Weston, an English minister then traveling in America, warned him not to become infatuated with the glory and applause of any political office or activity. "Thou are qualified I grant to be serviceable both in church and state, but oh let the lesser always give place to the greater." The church was in a shambles, she told him, and he must rebuild the waste places. "The Lord has anoynted and appointed thee a ruler in Israel," William Brown told him. "I desire thee will rule with diligence and I believe thou will be made as eyes for many. . . . But if those who are placed as watchmen on the walls do not give a . . . sound the City will suffer. . . . The work will lay heavy on thee, and I believe the Lord intends to prosper it in thy hands." Increasingly, between 1750 and 1755, Pemberton adopted such counsel.[28] Pemberton's detractors missed the shift in his interests and vocation, especially because they could put a political construction upon his philanthropy in the 1750s.

While Pemberton's commitments shifted, his character did not. His friends, relatives, and religious brethren as well as his opponents noted and suffered from his volatile temper and sanctimoniousness. And being as extreme in his religious commitments as he had been in his political ones, he was not likely to err inconspicuously. At the Easton Indian conference in 1758, he publicly accused his cousin William Logan of lying about a minor matter, which brought Logan almost to the point of assaulting him. At Philadelphia Yearly Meeting, Pemberton embarrassed some Friends by his "preaching, Crying, & Great Concern that *Truth does not Suffer.*" "Abandon foolish pity," reformer John Churchman had counseled him, but sometimes he merely abandoned all pity.[29]

Quaker reformers were able to forgive Pemberton his shortcomings in light of the very great energy, personal fortune (the largest estate in Pennsylvania), eminent station, and name he brought to the service of the reformation. He had had one career already among merchants and politicians and now he began a second in the church. In the second career, he freely shared both his time and the advantages of his first career with Friends like John Churchman, John Woolman, Anthony Benezet, and other reformers. He lent to these ascetic and severe men the gravity of his station and the respectability of his person, so that those in the Society most in need of reforming might not casually dismiss them as mere eccentrics or visionaries. In light of the church's needs, of the inroads of politics on Quaker ethics and the Quaker mission, and of Pemberton's resources, the change in leadership was important and fortunate.

3

Social Reforms: Personal Behavior and Families, 1755–1783

It is easy to specify when the reformers began to have an effect upon Quaker life in Pennsylvania. It was on the heels of the Yearly Meeting of September 1755. Changes unmistakably appeared in the administration of discipline throughout the province and with dramatic speed. The evidence of the change lies in the statistics on discipline. To appreciate the magnitude of the change, it is necessary first to compare the record of the post-1755 period with that of earlier decades.

The Disciplinary Record

Pennsylvania's colonial past may be conveniently divided into periods of approximately thirty years each. The first period, 1682–1715, shows very little delinquency; only 3.7 percent of all the offenses recorded in the period 1682–1776 were recorded then.[1] At the beginning of the period—1682 through 1685—there were few Quaker immigrants to commit errors and a very low rate of delinquency is to be expected. Yet, by 1715 the immigration of Friends to Pennsylvania was nearly complete while the delinquency rate had little more than doubled.[2] Nor was it that Quaker misconduct was recorded elsewhere; for example, in the public court records. The court records show few offenses by Quakers and non-Quakers, and in some periods they show fewer total offenses than do the Quaker records. Moreover, the Quakers in the public record are a minority who are in the Quaker record too.[3]

In the first period, the errors Friends committed were overwhelmingly sectarian, and even when prohibited, irregular marriages are excluded from the record. Quarreling, "loose" conduct, and drunkenness were common sectarian errors of the period, but the distinguishing features of the period's delinquency were schismatical activity (due to the Kethian separation of 1692) and theological deviations.

Within two or three years of 1715, the number of cases of delinquency began to grow in a clear and unequivocal manner. By 1745, the number of cases for the year was eight times greater than for any year before 1716, and the total for the period 1716–45 was 4.4 times greater than for the previous period. Before the increase may be attributed to a change in the behavior of Friends or the scrutiny exercised by monthly meetings, we must examine Quaker population to determine whether its growth accounts for the increase in delinquency.

There are only two Quaker meeting censuses for Pennsylvania and they serve as our points of departure in estimating population. In 1688, Chester Monthly Meeting reported that it had 72 adult, male members. In 1760, a census of Philadelphia Monthly Meeting produced a total of 2,250 members.[4] The figures in Barry J. Levy's demographic work on Chester Friends suggest that Chester Monthly Meeting had between 538 and 561 members in 1688.[5] As for Philadelphia Friends in 1688 or thereabout, we are warranted in estimating that Philadelphia Monthly Meeting was twice the size of Chester or greater. That would result in a Philadelphia Quaker population of approximately 1,100. Gary Nash and Billy Smith have calculated the population of Philadelphia to have been 2,100 in 1693;[6] and if one assumes that half the population of the city in its first decade was Quaker, it confirms the estimate of 1,110 Friends in the city. Comparing the 1688 and the 1760 figures for Philadelphia Friends, the population appears to have doubled.

Estimating the Quaker population of early Pennsylvania yields the least reassuring result of the whole effort at tracing Quaker population. Assuming that Philadelphia had 1,100 Friends in and about 1690, and using an estimate by James Logan that city and country Friends were equal in number, we obtain 2,200 Friends in the province.[7] The figure is the lowest of estimates by contemporaries and

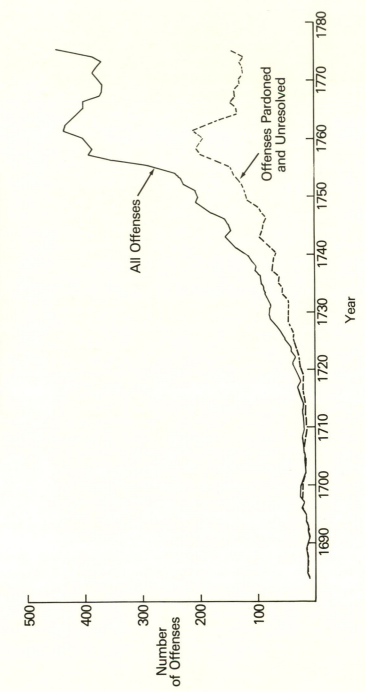

Three Year Moving Averages of Total Offenses per Year
and Offenses Pardoned and Unresolved

Figure 3.

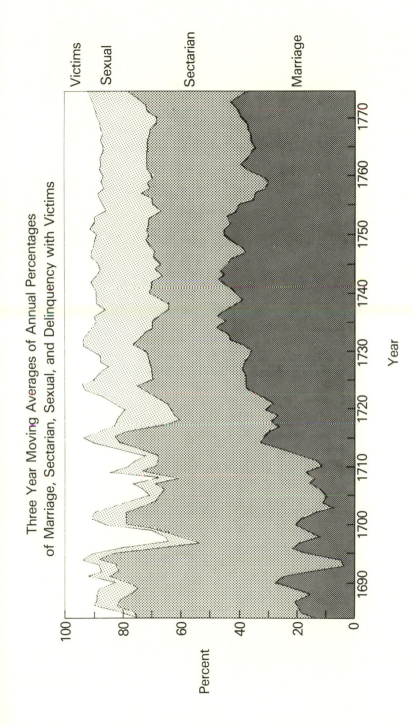

Figure 4.

historians and it is based on the lowest estimate for Philadelphia's population. Therefore, it should be regarded as the minimum figure for Quakers in Pennsylvania in 1690.

For 1760, when the Friends in Philadelphia Monthly Meeting numbered 2,250, we can make a better informed estimate. A way of deducing the populations of other meetings is to calculate them according to the ratio of marriages solemnized in each, from 1761 to 1765, to the marriages solemnized in Philadelphia in the same period. The presumption here is that the demographic influences upon marriage rates operated uniformly throughout the province. The research of Robert Wells on eighteenth-century Friends in Pennsylvania, New Jersey, and New York warrants that presumption, for Wells finds that "regional variations (including rural-urban differences) in demographic patterns could not be identified."[8] Such calculation produces a figure of 12,922 Friends in Pennsylvania in 1760, so that the Quaker population in 1760 was not quite six times greater than that of 1690.[9]

Other evidence that bears upon the question of population increase comes also from the demographic work of Wells. He finds that in his sample from the late eighteenth century, little more than half the Quaker children recorded born ever married (some of them died before marrying, however); that among women living to fifty years of age, the celebacy rate increased dramatically; and that age at marriage rose too, beginning in the early eighteenth century. These trends must produce a decreasing and depressed birth rate, so that before 1750, but especially thereafter, the growth of Quaker population was slowing to a halt.[10]

Converts to Quakerism did not swell the Quaker population either. Records from fifteen monthly meetings show between 550 and 576 admissions to the Society in the colonial period, including children of the converts.

The growth of Quaker population cannot explain the fact that between 1716 and 1745 the annual number of offenses increased eight times over. In seventy years, 1690 to 1760, population increased but six times over. At some point between 1716 and 1745, population growth ceased to account for the increased delinquency, while the number of cases of delinquency accelerated and population growth threatened to stall.

Scrupulosity of some Quaker disciplinarians explains some of the 1716–45 increase too. As we noted earlier, Chester Quarterly Meeting exceeded others in the severity with which it treated delinquency and in the impetus it gave to reformation. That severity and reformism certainly included a scrupulous oversight of the lives of Chester Friends and possibly a degree of concern that antedated that of others. Statistics bear out this contention: in the three chronological periods, Chester Quarter's share of total delinquency rose from 30.9 percent to 49.6 percent, then dropped to 37.7 after 1745. The larger, Philadelphia Quarterly Meeting, having awakened to reform in the 1750s, outstripped Chester in the final thirty years, whereas it lagged behind it by 18.9 percent in the middle period.

The delinquency of the period troubled the eldest of the reformers, John Churchman, who believed that if Friends had lived according to their professions, "the Society would appear more beautiful than at present." Beginning in the 1720s, Churchman labored in Chester County to bring about improvement, and the records of several meetings there indicate that he may be credited with some success in raising the scrupulosity of Friends there. By the 1750s, the preachers of reform subscribed to an interpretation of their church's history that reduced the decades since 1720 to an era of decline, and the Friends of that era to a backslidden generation. Samuel Fothergill repeated to his audiences in Pennsylvania and probably to Friends up and down the Atlantic seaboard that the generation who had reduced the barren wilderness to a fruitful field had let discipline decay and could not instruct their offspring in the statutes they themselves had forgotten. The disciplinary record corroborates much of Fothergill's characterization: a generation had arisen, ignorant of Quaker ethics or content to violate them. The guilty Friends were especially those who married contrary to the discipline.

Marriage delinquency accounted for 41.6 percent of the total for 1716–45. While there were annually an average of 1.7 marriage offenses in 1709–11 and 7.3 in 1714–16, there were 63.0 in 1744–46 and 91.7 in 1749–51. Marriage delinquency was growing two and one-half times faster than delinquency as a whole. From another perspective the trend appears yet more remarkable: in the period 1711–15, only one in eleven marriages was irregular; by 1741–45, one in two was.[11] The Friends who were violating the marriage regulations were likely the first Pennsylvania-born Quakers. Because Quaker immigration to the province was largely complete by 1715 and after approximately twenty years the offspring of immigrants reached marriageable age, the native-born would marry from approx-

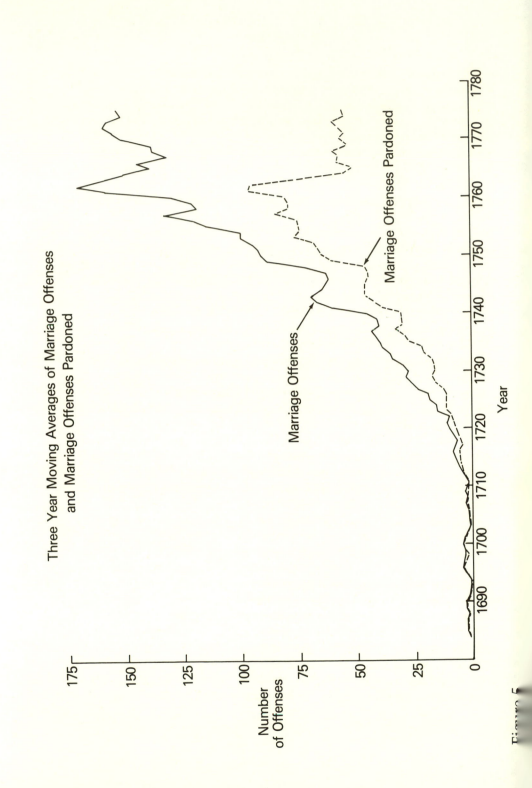

Three Year Moving Averages of Marriage Offenses
and Marriage Offenses Pardoned

Number
of Offenses

Marriage Offenses

Marriage Offenses Pardoned

Year

Figure 5

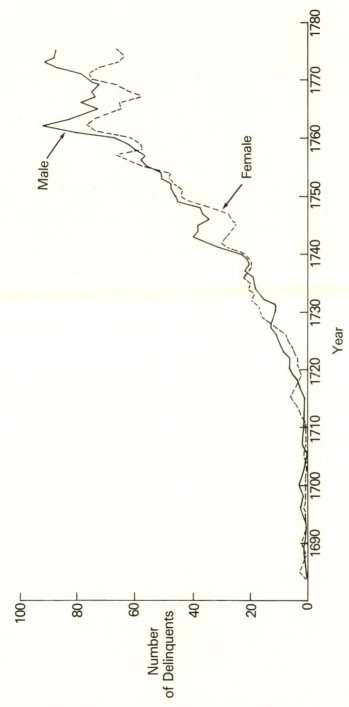

Three Year Moving Averages of Male and Female Marriage Delinquents

Number of Delinquents

Male

Female

Year

Figure 6.

imately 1705 to 1740. If Quaker marriage regulations were to be kept and Quaker respect for them to be tested, the time to do so was after 1705, when this generation came of age. By the standards of the reformers, the generation failed the test, and the blame, said Fothergill, lay with the parents who could not teach their children the statutes they themselves had forgotten.

The private efforts of John Churchman, Samuel Fothergill, John Woolman, the Pembertons, and others to reform the behavior of Friends began to register in Quaker councils in 1755. In September of that year, while the prospect of a French and Indian invasion absorbed most Pennsylvanians, the Friends at Philadelphia Yearly Meeting started a reformation. A committee of fourteen Friends, including Fothergill, Churchman, and Woolman, revised the disciplinary code. That was no novelty, however. The discipline had been revised and amended before without any visible consequences in Quaker behavior. Nor did this committee change the regulations significantly. The novelty was the admonition suffixed to the new edition: "elders, overseers, and all others active in the discipline [are] to be zealously concerned for the cause of Truth and honestly to labour to repair the breaches too obvious in many places that there may be some well grounded hopes of the primitive beauty and purity of the Church may be restored."[12]

The admonition too could have made little difference if the authors and others had not worked to fulfill it. But there was no lack of laborers in the Society. The Yearly Meeting prepared to see that discipline was enforced, and not left to languish after the Meeting dissolved. First, the Meeting appointed a committee of thirty-one to inspect quarterly and monthly meetings to see that they carried out the admonitions of Yearly Meeting. Also, to keep abreast of the meetings, the Yearly Meeting ordered that at least once every three months every single meeting read a list of queries about the behavior of Friends, and that every monthly meeting "distinctly and particularly" answer the queries at every quarterly meeting. Then quarterly meetings answered to the Yearly Meeting. Finally, the Yearly Meeting added a mechanism to check upon the putative shepherds of the flock, the ministers, and elders. It ordered that select meetings of ministers and elders be established in every monthly meeting and that they answer for their own behavior to the quarterly meetings for ministers and elders.[13]

The evidence of industry soon appeared. In 1756, the disciplinarians of the Society discovered 64.1 percent more violations of discipline than they had in 1755. Their finding represented no brief burst of zeal either; for although violations had increased at an average of 200 every five years since 1740, in 1756–60 they increased by 851. They never decreased by more than 5 percent in any five-year period thereafter. The vigor of the reformers appeared also in the conduct of the Society's disciplinary business. Before 1756, the Society spent an average of 6.7 months on a case; after 1756, it spent 4.8 months. More impressive is the fact that before 1756 cases were permitted to drag on; two-thirds of the cases took up to two years to resolve. After 1756, two-thirds of the cases were resolved within seven months.[14]

While the number of offenses and delinquents rose abruptly after 1755, the number of pardons did too (see fig. 3). The campaign to reform the Society did not immediately take so severe a direction that disownments outnumbered pardons; rather it focused on the discovery and the exposure of delinquency.[15] Nevertheless, a roughly constant rate of disownments meant that more Friends than ever were being disowned from a church that was not growing in size because of births or conversions. The church was shrinking and the reformers were aware of this cost of reformation.

The cost increased in the 1760s. In 1763, the percentage of disowned offenders jumped above 50 for the first time to 59.5. It never dropped below 56.7 percent thereafter and in 1775 it peaked at 73.3 percent. From 1763 to 1776, the Society in Pennsylvania disowned 2521 members—271 more than the total Quaker population of Philadelphia in 1760. From the outset of the reformation in 1755 through 1776, it disowned 3157. Using the estimate of Quaker population in 1760, we may deduce that after 1760, the Society disowned 21.7 percent of its members in Pennsylvania.[16]

In the 1770s the reformation spread to New York and New England. New York and New England Friends had ignored discipline to a far greater degree than had their brethren to the south. With the exceptions of several urban meetings, apprehension of delinquents rarely occurred before 1760, and disownments were yet rarer. Although ministers and other Friends from Pennsylvania and England traveled through the Northeast, they did not succeed in immediately reinvigorating the discipline. Their success in Pennsylvania in 1755 points up the crucial presence there of resident Quakers interested in reformation and willing to take up the work that visitors prescribed. In the 1770s, however, the number of disciplinary cases doubled and tripled in various Northeastern monthly meetings, and disownments outnumbered pardons.[17]

The sectarianism and self-consciousness that had originally motivated the reformers was soon felt throughout the Society. Because of the reinvigoration of discipline, Friends who did not adhere to distinctive Quaker behavior were in trouble with the Society. Between the periods 1751–55 and 1756–60, errors involving sectarian misbehavior (other than prohibited marriages) leapt from 301 to 790, and sectarian errors occupied a larger portion of Quaker disciplinarians' time and effort.[18] After 1756, the number of cases of prohibited pastimes and entertainments—such as games, shooting matches, and horse races—increased 4.2 times over what they had been before 1756. Cases of gambling increased 4.6 times; of Quakers attending the prohibited marriages of other Quakers, 2.8 times; of inattendance at worship, 2.7 times. Attendance was demanded especially of otherwise peccant Friends, and inattendance weighed more heavily than any other recorded factor in the disownment of miscreants.[19] The fact that inattendance also began to appear more often as a single offense indicates that it was demanded of more Friends in general and not just delinquents.

The self-consciousness of Friends appeared in the increased number of cases after 1755 where the monthly meetings explained that they acted in order to "clear Truth" or "for the reputation of Truth." These phrases and their variants were venerable and, one might suspect, even hackneyed. However, the increased use of them after 1755, when Friends were rousing their political enemies, suggests that they really did have a function and that they disclosed a Quaker desire to acquit themselves of any misrepresentations. Such was the original purpose of the phrases and the discipline in seventeenth-century England. Pennsylvania Friends had never experienced the kind of persecution that English Friends had, however, and never would. But, after 1755, they came closer to sharing the conditions of their forefathers than they ever had before and they responded as their forefathers had.

The Quaker ethic most often violated after 1756, as earlier, was the complex, sectarian one concerning marriage. It accounted for 36.3 percent of all identified delinquency from 1756 to 1776. The marriage discipline required first, that Friends marry only Friends; for "the Lord saith thou shalt not marry the people of other nations of the heathens or of other religions nor . . . give thy sons and daugh-

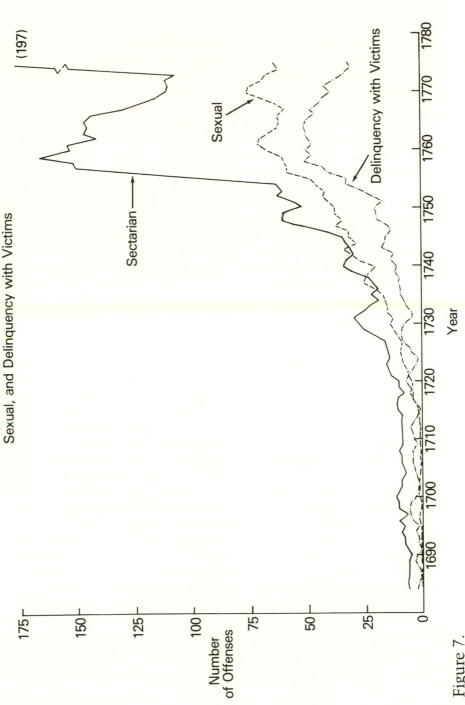

Three Year Moving Averages of Sectarian,
Sexual, and Delinquency with Victims

(197)

Sectarian

Sexual

Delinquency with Victims

Number
of Offenses

175

150

125

100

75

50

25

0

1690   1700   1710   1720   1730   1740   1750   1760   1770   1780

Year

Figure 7.

ters to them."[20] Next, the marriage had to be solemnized by a Quaker meeting. That meant that the intended couple must appear at a monthly meeting to announce their intentions. The meeting then appointed a committee to investigate the two. If it found no irregularity in their pasts, no unabsolved violations of discipline, no objections by the parents, and no previous engagements or commitments, it would recommend at a second monthly meeting that the marriage proceed. A date would be set for the wedding, and two Friends from the monthly meeting would be appointed to attend in order to see that it was "carried on soberly, and that nothing of rudeness or extravagance, or the world's customs be made use of."[21]

Despite the insistence on endogamy and the care the Society routinely took regarding marriages, Friends in eighteenth-century Pennsylvania increasingly ignored the rules, as we have already seen. Friends were quite alive to what was happening and fearful of its consequences for the church. Other than violations of pacifism, no form of delinquency raised as much anxiety in the reformers nor received as much attention.

The Family and the Religious Education of Friends

The reformers believed that a major reason that Quakerism was at a low ebb in the mid-eighteenth century was that the "old hairs," the adults and elders, who should have been leading exemplary lives were not. A church composed of these complacent or resigned members was difficult to reform; such members wished neither to change nor to help change anyone else. Family ties, friendships, and even amicability meant more to them than right behavior—theirs or others'. "Among the many thousands of Israel," complained John Griffith, "there are but few ... who stand quite upright ... who cannot be at all warped by fear, interest, favor, or affection." When pressed to reprimand delinquency and stop the degeneration of the church, these worldly folk complained, "It is my son, daughter, near relation, or friend, that I am loath to offend lest I should suffer in my interest or reputation, or shall gain his or her ill will." The reformers sometimes despaired that any good would come of these temporizing Friends and their generation; they "could not instruct their offspring in those statutes they had themselves forgotten."[22]

If there was a good prospect, it came from younger people, who, the reformers said again and again, comprised most of "the saving remnant" in the church. The future of the church then depended upon cultivating these young people and not letting them be over-born by the proud and intimidating elders in the church. And if improvements were made in the Society, they would be preserved into the following generations by young Friends and the children they reared. The very survival of the Society depended upon them—survival not as a mere association or empty name, but as a living, thriving, unique people. The children would make the difference.

"All that is within me," Samuel Fothergill professed, "is moved when I thus earnestly expostulate with you on behalf of the Dear Children—Suffer me to Entreat you for God['s] Sake, for your own Souls Sake, for the Sake of the cause of Truth 'gather the children.'"[23] To ignore the children was to commit the sin of Eli, John Griffith warned; "consider the fearful calamities which came upon that house; and also upon Israel," in consequence. Friends "wod be speud out & set a side" by God if the parents among them did not teach their children, a mother recorded, having heard George Mason preach so in meeting.[24]

Children were impressionable and malleable, Quaker reformers almost uniformly believed, and so the evil tendencies of children ought to be corrected and excellent lessons taught. "Nip vice in the very bud in . . . Children"; "in youth before the evil root has taken depth, it is more easily plucked up." "You cannot learn religion too soon." "Divine grace and Truth appears to children in early life."[25] No Friend in the late eighteenth century seriously questioned these and similar maxims. Rather, the diarists in the Society (who were numerous) uniformly reported the experiences of their own child-hoods to demonstrate that religious education had or would have made a crucial difference. The question among reformers was never whether education ought to be improved, but only how.[26]

The reformers focused on correcting family pedagogues, the parents, rather than spending their energy upon the miseducated children about to come of age. That focus, however, put the Society in a delicate situation, for its discipline said that "disobedience to parents was death by God's law, and must needs bring death now"; to contradict parents' example to their children would be to belittle parents' authority. But Friends also insisted that "parents ought to be obeyed *next to God*."[27] Because the precepts of the Society and its discipline were regarded as God's revealed will, the authority of parents was not to be used arbitrarily, but rather for the purposes the Society sanctioned. Friends would have heartily approved John Calvin's warning that "if men and women have children, they must understand that there is no subjection due unto them, except they themselves be overruled by God." The family was not to be an autonomous unit within the Society; again, as Calvin wrote, "The family of a believer must be as it were a little church."[28]

The balance the Society struck between supporting parental authority and slighting it in order to correct bad parents involved, first, almost never bypassing the parents to correct small children or minors. The authority of the parents was to be used first and almost always. If the children were adults or approaching adulthood, the Society was less reluctant to interfere with their miseducation at the hands of their parents. And the adult offspring too were treated like any other adult delinquents. Most often disciplined parents were guilty of promoting or abetting the irregular marriages of their children at the least by attending the prohibited wedding ceremonies. When parents, rather than intentionally misleading their children, were insufficiently expert at parenthood or neglected their pedagogical duties, the Society felt that the situation demanded advice or warning rather than interference. Not that it forswore interfering: on infrequent occasions it even insisted on removing the children from the family and placing them in more pious homes.[29]

The tendency after 1755 was toward belittling parental authority. The signal occasion when the Society made the family retreat was in connection with a new disciplinary article on antislavery. By 1776, the Society demanded the abolition of slavery among Friends. Where members, mostly men, but sometimes widows or unmarried women, owned slaves, their obligation was clear: manumit or be disowned. But dilemmas arose with respect to women Friends married to non-Quaker slaveowners: How were these women to be treated according to the abolition minute of 1776? The Yearly Meeting resolved in 1778 that unless the mistresses in such families united with the Society to fulfill the minute, they were to be disowned.[30] What remained unsaid was that the Society was effectively ordering some women to resist the wills of their slaveholding husbands; it was inciting domestic disharmony. Venerable though the station of father might be, it would have to be lowered in order that the Negro be raised from slavery.

The interest of the Society was not entirely philanthropic when it drove a small wedge into the family in 1778. Historians' interest in Quaker philanthropy has partly served to obscure the role of antislavery in the reformation of Quaker morals and specifically its role in the effort to teach Quaker children piety. Friends believed that the dominion of master over slave was no model for Quaker children to imitate. Households with slaves contradicted the lessons which the Society taught and which the Society now expected parents to teach. Humility, modesty, temperance, and reserve were Quaker virtues impaired by the mastery of slaves. It was for that reason Elizabeth Wilkinson, the foremost pedagogue among the Quaker reformers, asked in 1762 that the slaves belonging to a Friend address his children by their names, not "master & miss." It is the reason why Sarah Logan Fisher demanded her brother remove her nephew from Virginia, where "every tender feeling of humanity [was] stifled" by slavery.[31]

After 1755, a spirit of defiance toward parents and family spread, neither sanctioned nor promoted by the Society. Its similarity to war protestors' defiance of political authority suggests that the two were not unrelated. When Francis Parvin, Jr., asked Mary Peisley's advice about refusing to pay war taxes in defiance of parental wishes, Peisley advised defiance. Anne Emlen Mifflin left her parents' home during the American Revolution because they approved the use of Continental currency and disapproved of her boycott of it. She was, she professed, "thus led forth by the hand of an heavenly Parent, from an earthly Parents house for the advancement of his own testimonies."[32] Her estrangement from her parents and the defiant spirit of various young Friends recalls the experiences of Isaac Pennington, Thomas Ellwood, and other seventeenth-century Friends who, in the early years of Quakerism, joined the fellowship against their parents' strictest orders. In some small degree, the spirit of the seventeenth century seemed revived, yet in the context of reform and not of conversion; these objectionable parents were already Friends just as their children were.[33]

Friends came to believe that correcting or disciplining parents who miseducated their children was pretty much locking the barn door after the horse had gone. Action was needed before the life in a home deteriorated to such a degree that parents sanctioned or winked at delinquency. Prevention rather than therapy, Friends realized, was a better way to avoid raising yet another generation of Friends as morally deficient as the present one. Marriage was the proper, early occasion to exercise care for the education of children; parents were necessarily the foremost influence upon character, they being more immediate to the children than the Society's officials, meetings, or parochial schools. "It would be a great and everlasting blessing to children . . . if all parents and heads of families were rightly qualified—as nursing fathers and mothers to bring their children to Christ," wrote Samuel Comfort.[34] The Society felt obliged to exert more influence over the faculties of these little church schools. Obviously, when Friends looked at the epidemic of irregular marriages they understood where to begin to apply a remedy. As long as Friends, either bride or bridegroom or both, solemnized their marriages outside the Society's auspices, Friends did not have opportunity to make inquiries into the couples' qualifications for marriage. When a Friend married a non-Friend, necessarily in a non-Quaker ceremony, the non-Quaker fiancé(e) need feel no obligation to answer to Friends for his or her conduct or history or to make amends for the marriage. And quite obviously this alien, who had no Quaker education, would make a poor educator of their children. If this partner had some sincere concern for Quakerism, he or she would have converted and married in an orderly, Quaker manner. Two believing parents, Friends knew, were necessary to educate children into religion. "When both parents unite in an harmonious labour and fervent concern . . . it could not fail in making a lasting impression on the minds of children and youth. . . . Thus two parents being better than one, and Divine grace forming the three fold cord, which being thrown around the child . . . would not be easily broken."[35] On the other hand:

When two of disagreeing Persuasions in religious Exercises join in Marriage, no Man can reasonably think that their Affection to each other is grounded on, or governed by, Religion; and if not, that it must be some worldly End. . . .

   The perplexed Situation of the Offspring of such Alliances is . . . to be lamented. Attached by Nature to both Parents, the Confusion they are in often renders them unfixed in Principle, and unsettled in Practice.[36]

Friends having confided so much in the ability of parents to educate their children in religion and behavior, and so belittled the prospects of a mixed marriage, it is surprising that for most of the early eighteenth century the Society automatically admitted to full

Table 3
Exogamous Marriages

Date	Delinquents	Percentage of Delinquents Disowned
(1682–1690)	0	
1691–1695	1	100.0
(1696–1720)	0	
1721–1725	3	100.0
1726–1730	4	100.0
1731–1735	8	75.0
1736–1740	11	72.7
1741–1745	17	76.5
1746–1750	19	57.9
1751–1755	38	52.6
1756–1760	74	52.7
1761–1765	107	67.3
1766–1770	98	67.4
1771–1775	125	75.2
Total	503	69.9

Note: Statistics are from eight monthly meetings specified in note 38.

membership the offspring of mixed or exogamous marriages.[37] It treated such children as the equals in every way of children of completely Quaker parents and a superior religious education. By the 1760s, Friends were satisfied that such offspring were decidedly not sturdy members nor the equal of the offspring of completely Quaker parents. And while after 1740 the number of exogamous marriages rose precipitously, and pardons for that error grew similarly, the problem of lukewarm, one-parent birthright members promised to increase for at least the next 25 years.[38] (See table 3.) The indulgence of other alien influences was yet more blatant, although not as common. By the regulations of the Society, the non-Quaker spouses of Friends did not become members by reason of their marriages. In the mid-eighteenth century, however, the distinction between Friend and non-Friend was being dropped. Functions or activities open to members alone were then opened to nonmembers if they had married Friends. Most striking, some meetings were solemnizing marriages between Friends and non-Friends; that is, not only wink-

ing at exogamy but assisting it.[39] Another exclusive Quaker prerogative was attendance at monthly meetings. Yet reformers found
meetings where no one knew for certain who was and who was not
a member. Mary Neale once had some stern words about declension
and discipline to deliver at a monthly meeting and she wanted to
speak to Friends alone; but the meeting in question had so far
declined that when she asked the "ruling members" to clear the
meeting of non-Friends, neither they nor anyone else knew whom to
exclude. The problem arose because Friends and non-Friends were
"so connected in marriage . . . and the discipline being so sadly let
fall."[40] In mid- and late eighteenth-century America, Protestant
churches so commonly disregarded distinctions, discipline, and
prerequisites for membership that these Quaker meetings might be
described as behaving in a typical American Protestant way; that is,
more open, more "denominational," and less sectarian than before.[41]
Also, the meetings appeared to be using or permitting irregular
marriages as a means of recruitment, but all the while recruiting
rather indifferent people into an increasingly formless church. The
reformers utterly condemned such practice. To marry outside one's
faith or to condone such marriages in the hope that a spouse may be
added to the church was "in plain English, no better than 'sinning,
that Grace may abound; doing Evil, that Good may come of it.' "[42]

Miseducation, irregular marriages, and the liberal admission of
offspring together had produced "a motled Generation," hardly able
or willing to cure itself.[43] Until 1755, every monthly meeting in
Pennsylvania had pardoned at least half of the marriage violators.
Radnor Monthly Meeting pardoned every offender for twenty years,
1721–40, while some monthly meetings pardoned every one for five
consecutive years. The situation appeared to improve after 1755
because, like delinquency in general, violations of the marriage code
were more often apprehended. But just as earlier, a large proportion
of the offenders were pardoned. (See fig. 5.) And these pardons
continued to weaken the Society.

In order that any delinquent be pardoned he had to convince the
monthly meeting that he sincerely repented, had reformed his behavior, and had repaired the damage or harm done to persons or property.
But marriages contrary to Quaker regulations presented a different,
more inscrutable case. First, an irregular marriage did not harm
another person or damage his property in any obvious way. Therefore, the meeting could not require the delinquent to satisfy some

victim and thereby prove his remorse. Second, there was no practical way for the meeting to demand that the delinquent quit commiting his error and so demonstrate his respect for Quaker discipline: unlike drunkenness, for example, marriage does not occur often, and the meeting could not practically say, "Stop marrying out of meeting." Neither could the meeting ask the delinquent to divorce the non-Quaker spouse in order to set things aright; the Society of Friends and the province of Pennsylvania prohibited divorce. Quaker meetings were left to make a very subjective judgment about the honesty of the peccant Friend's confession and, thereupon, either pardon him or disown him.

Finally, if the delinquent had violated Quaker marriage discipline by marrying a non-Friend (he could have violated it in other ways), his monthly meeting could ask him to denounce his error. That demand was difficult in marriages where the partners loved each other; it asked one of them to publicly express regret for his or her choice of spouse.[44] On one hand, it was a real test of a delinquent's remorse for his error and his respect for Quaker discipline, but on the other hand, it ironically had an unhappy effect upon Quaker society. Friends wished to create loving, quiet, harmonious households, but denunciations such as these would not help to do so. In cases of exogamous marriage, the Society of Friends found itself in a dilemma when it attempted to pardon and restore delinquent Friends.

By the early 1760s, Friends were obviously unhappy with their disciplinary practice and especially their toleration of irregular marriages. The conduct of a grievous number of Friends who had been judged worthy of reinstatement did not display the reformation they promised when they confessed.[45] Ann Whitall, a very conscientious mother and a disciple of the reformers, left a brief description of a pardoned but impenitent offender: "I think of all that has run away & got married . . . [name erased] is the boldest & most impident that ever I sow . . . She comes & set her self up in meeting & seems proude of what she has dun & will set & sleep so brasen."[46] And worst of all, the violators of endogamy brought their non-Quaker spouses into the family and the community, providing "an Inlet to much Degeneracy, and mournfully affected the Minds of all those who labour under a living Concern for the Good of all, and the Prosperity of Truth upon Earth."[47]

Prompted by Philadelphia Monthly and Quarterly Meetings,

which rued the "pernicious consequences" of delinquent marriages, the Yearly Meeting appointed in 1760 a committee to examine the problem. The next year the Yearly Meeting accepted the committee's unanimous conclusion that "the increase of the breaches of our testimony" occured "too often for want of due care in parents." Parents were not instructing their children in Quaker principles and not keeping them out of the company of non-Quakers who in turn engaged the children's affections. The meeting urged Friends to take more care and warned that if they did not, the community of Friends might intervene.[48]

The next year Philadelphia Yearly Meeting did yet more. Two visiting English ministers, Elizabeth Wilkinson and Hannah Harris, concerned with Quaker marriages and education, brought the subject of "mix'd and clandestine" marriages to the attention of the Yearly Meeting of Ministers and Elders. It, and especially Friend Joseph White, heartily concurred with them and took the matter to Yearly Meeting, where their concern was translated into action. The Yearly Meeting blamed easy pardons and mixed households for many of the Society's problems—these introduced "many inconveniences," and promoted "libertinism, and a manifest deviation from the purity of our profession." Now the Meeting recommended that in the extraordinary case of irregular marriages, Friends ought no longer either solicit or wait for acknowledgments or confessions from delinquents, but speedily disown them. If they volunteered acknowledgments, meetings were to be "well assured, that they proceed from a true ground of conviction in the transgressor."[49] For no other form of error than irregular marriage did the Society discard its policy of waiting months and in some cases years for the acknowledgment and reform of offenders. The uniqueness of the remedy and the haste of the Society proved the Society's anxiety over this delinquency and its effects.

On the same occasion, the Yearly Meeting changed its treatment of the offspring of mixed marriages in order to put a stop to the troublesome effect of admitting them to the Society. It ordered that no longer would they be automatically received as though they were no different from the children of Quaker households. If a Quaker parent asked that the child be admitted, the Society would examine the child's situation to learn whether it had a religious education. Then the child might be admitted. Whether admitted or not, the Society resolved to keep a watch upon all the children of mixed unions; if they acted "scandalously," as might "bring a blemish on the Society," the Society would publicly "declare they are not of us," to correct misapprehensions about the Society.[50]

As in 1756, the response to the new directive from the Yearly Meeting was swift and effective. Although the directive was issued late in 1762, disownments for marriage in the period 1761–65 increased 44.3 percent over the previous five years, and they did so while apprehensions of delinquents increased too, by 22.0 percent. Monthly meetings took an average of only two to three months from learning of the offense to disowning the offender. In 1761–76, 1,426 Friends were disowned because of the persons and the manner in which they married.[51] They amounted to 11.0 percent of the estimated population of the Society in 1760.

The full effect of such discipline upon the Quaker population cannot be fairly described by merely subtracting 1,426 Friends from the prior total. The people disowned had violated the marriage discipline and were young men and women. Robert Wells' research discloses that Quaker women first married at an average age of 22.8 years, and men at 26.5, and that remarriage was not common. Therefore, the disowned were especially people about to start families, whose probable five or six children per wife would have been added to the Society had the parents not been disowned.[52] The Society had maintained its size in the eighteenth century predominantly by natural increase, not conversions. Therefore, after 1762 the Society cut off a substantial source for its regeneration. Through the vigorous use of discipline the Society created a distant as well as an immediate prospect that it would shrink.[53] And yet Friends did it soberly and intentionally, having judged the evils of nominal professors to be greater than the benefits of size.

With the alteration of the marriage discipline in 1762, the Quaker family reached the apex of its importance in the history of the Society. It emerged after 1755 from prolonged decline and decades of neglect, and the significance of its enhanced status exceeds the confines of just the family; it provides an important insight into the very nature of the Society of Friends.

In the 1650s, when the early conversions to Quakerism caused the Society to double and redouble its size, the family was of little concern to the Society. Admissions came as individuals and not families.[54] Offspring of Friends were still too few to pose a problem over the transmission of religious faith to the children. Surely, however, the number of children would grow and the problem would arise—unless Friends adopted celebacy. In the early decades, membership in the Society was *achieved* rather than *ascribed*, to use two broad classificatory terms from the sociology of religion. Achievement includes a host of ways by which a person voluntarily satisfies a requirement for admission, the requirement being almost trivial in some religions and very severe in others. The achievement of early English Friends might be called a severe one—a profoundly wrenching religious experience and change in behavior, plus, after the Restoration, the endurance of religious persecution.[55] Ascribed membership requires no act of will on the part of the person admitted; membership comes automatically and usually by birth to members. Achievement naturally limits admission to adults and some minors and excludes all infants.

In time, when the Society began to regularly discipline members and codified Quaker conduct, the achievement of members came to include a life in accord with Quaker discipline or ethics. A test for membership was a trial of one's conduct to observe its adherence to Quaker precepts. When religious toleration came to England, and respectability to Friends, the ethical life remained as the major achievement for Quaker membership. Meanwhile, the increased number of Quaker offspring required that the Society resolve how the children stood in regard to the Society—which was their parents.[56] How were the children to share in what was in the eyes of their parents the greatest benefaction available to mankind? The historical record is comparatively silent on the question, especially when compared to the thought, debate, and consultation the New England Congregationalists put into the question of children, baptism, and the Half-Way Convenant. It was not until 1737, according to most historians, that the Society broke the silence and officially adopted the policy of "birthright" membership. It apparently meant that children of unions in which at least one partner was a Friend were automatically Friends, or had a right to membership. It seems to be a precise example of ascribed membership, and it discloses that Friends had come a long way from their earlier practice of achieved membership. Richard T. Vann, the most recent and careful student of the problem, revised the picture: No decision upon admission was made in 1737; rather, a decision was made upon the locality of one's membership. Vann does not deny that birthright membership existed, however. It had quietly existed as a Quaker routine since the end of the seventeenth century and perhaps earlier.[57]

Yet, to discover that Friends practiced birthright membership will not permit us to conclude that they changed to ascribed membership for children. Other Quaker practices and changes stand in the shadow of such an apparently simple resolution of the question of children's status.

As early as 1702 in Pennsylvania, when a monthly meeting needed to determine whether a person was a member and whether he should receive the charity and discipline of the Society, the meeting asked whether the person had "had his education among Friends"—rather than whether he was born of a Quaker parent or parents.[58] An affirmative answer indicated a number of possible ways in which the member had come by his education. Quaker parents provided one of the ways; others included living as an apprentice in a Quaker household, attending a Quaker school, or generally associating with Friends. But by far the most common means to obtain a Quaker education was from one's parents or family. Education among Friends then, was nearly equivalent to education by one's Quaker parents. But that is not to equate education with genealogy. Education was an obligation and performance and not intended as a hollow code phrase for a biological relationship. Membership by reason of one's parents' tuition was not ascribed membership but achieved membership. That is, membership in the Society meant knowingly behaving like a Friend; knowledge of Quaker behavior was gained by living among Quaker instructors; the instructors of the vast majority of eighteenth-century Friends were their parents.

Friends presumed a good deal in equating the tuition of parents to the education of children, however. While there is teaching, there may be no learning. Nevertheless, the children were admitted. Therefore, to avoid an unwarranted assumption about the children's achievement, the Society had to oversee both the parents and the children. That oversight was the discipline of the Society, including its effective enforcement. When the Society enforced discipline, it might be reasonably satisfied that parents led lives that served as models of Quakerism for their children and that parents informed their children of the appropriate Quaker behavior expected of them. Once the children reached the age of discretion or their majority, the Society expected them to follow the precepts of their parents and their religion; or else to acknowledge the error of their ways and the wisdom of the rules they violated. The Quaker practice was really a presumption of future achievement, or even an unwritten contract for it. Through church discipline the Society insisted that yesterday's children fulfill their obligations while they enjoyed the benefits of Quakerism. When discipline faltered or languished, as it did in the opinion of eighteenth-century reformers, the birthright became automatic, ascribed admission, and adult misbehavior would little jeopardize one's membership in the Society.

The reformation changed that situation. With severe discipline, the Society presumed that the members understood good and evil behavior as defined by Quaker ethics and that they all would be responsible for their personal records. In 1762, the Society acted to assure that Quaker parents were instructing the children—all of which made membership an achievement whereas several years earlier it had been automatic for most Friends.

While the Quaker family enjoyed a renaissance due to its central role in the perpetuation of the faith, the role of the family in other major American churches was concomitantly declining.[59] The Great Awakening especially caused the decline by exalting evangelism and revivalism. The Awakening focused the energies of the churches upon reaching out to unchurched adults and also to church members deemed to be only nominal Christians; but in all instances, adults. The adults had to testify that they had undergone conversion before they could be counted as Christians. That testimony, however, should not be equated to the relation of one's spiritual condition demanded by seventeenth-century Congregationalists. Standards had changed, and whereas the earlier relation demanded so much of candidates that few deemed themselves worthy of applying, the evangelists invited all to meet the latter-day standard.[60] Few applicants were judged unfit. The religious revival of the 1740s initiated a competition among churches for members which then and thereafter led many churches to equate size and growth with success.[61] Conversions flattered the pride of preachers above all others, and they, like their auditors, became uncritical—except of Christians who did not join the revival. Increasingly little was requested for achieved admission. Because the only persons who could satisfy the depreciated prerequisites were teenagers at the youngest though, children had no immediate role. The focus on conversion belittled nurture; the family as nursery or educator suffered too.[62]

In New England, the family had once stood preeminent as educator of children. The Great Awakening directly contributed to its fall from preeminence by breaking up the parish system in most Connecticut and many Massachusetts towns. The breakup weakened church discipline and put it on the road to extinction.[63] Statistics on the use of discipline show that the decline in use dates from the 1750s, following the Awakening.[64] Without discipline, the churches could not maintain standards for behavior. In Congregational families, parents might increasingly do as they pleased and their children list in whichever direction the winds of secular culture blew them. The church retreated, the family became private, and Christian nurture became voluntary.

The seeds of evangelism and its consequences had lain a long time in the soil of Congregational New England. Conversion, and not nurture, had always been the first concern of the Puritan clergymen, despite their ringing affirmations of family. Since their early careers in England, the immigrant ministers had staked their legitimacy upon their success in bringing souls to Christ. Their vocation and authority, as well as their pride, were bound up in their preaching to adults. And both when the first generation of ministers thrived and enjoyed deference and when the second generation agonized over the decline in conversions and respect shown themselves, the evangelical role remained uppermost.[65] As long as the Congregational Church was tied by covenant to the state, Puritan preachers effectively had a captive audience of settlers, which included more and more unconverted souls. Yet when, after the 1670s, the state declined to play Moses to Aaron, magistrate for the priest, the preachers fretted over the end of their secular helps and spent their energies in attempts to regain them.[66] They would not willingly serve a voluntaristic church until the Great Awakening or later. Meanwhile, the benefit that family pedagogy held for Congregationalism was neglected or dismissed by the ministers. With the perpetuation of Congregationalism so strongly supported by the evangelizing of the preachers and the covenant-based ties to the state, and later by the flood tide of the Great Awakening, it is farfetched to imagine these churches moving toward sectarianism with its emphasis on the family's role in the perpetuation of the faith.

Edmund Morgan, the foremost historian of the Puritan family, first congratulates the Congregational churches on their early escape from narrow sectarianism or tribalism, but he also emphasizes the importance of the family in the Congregational order.[67] He is not contradicting himself—the family can serve an important function in a more or less evangelical situation. His two points prompt one to ask, however, whether the family would not have been still more important within Congregationalism if Congregationalism had taken the sectarian direction. In Congregationalism, the family was not as important as it was in other churches and sects. For example, despite the ministers' and theologians' desire to see Congregationalists practice endogamy, the Congregational church discipline did not require it. Sects do. Friends believed endogamy to be the foundation of Quaker pedagogy, and the foundation for all other ethical behavior and the security of the faith for future generations.

The sectarian family differs from the Church family as educator because it is more likely the exclusive educator. Because Congregationalism escaped sectarianism, it did not insulate itself from secular culture. It continued to be one part of a fragmented world, where it was neither the synthesizer nor the arbiter of culture. It preached, in H. Richard Niebuhr's terms, the "Christ *of* Culture," and not "Christ Against Culture." Therefore, Congregationalism entrusted to the family the transmission of few values that were not already sanctioned and taught by other agents in society—the government, the schools, the business community, and others. The family was hardly the exclusive or preeminent teacher. And the passage of time brought only the loss of functions and curriculum to the Puritan family.[68] Contrariwise, the Quaker family, especially after 1755, taught behavior which often was at loggerheads with the conduct that secular society approved. And it did so because the Society of Friends, as a sect, claimed sovereignty in political, economic, and other matters.

4

The Labors and Faith
of the Reformers

How did the reformers who numbered only a score or so before 1755 manage by 1775 to more than decimate the membership of the Society and to enlist most of the remainder in the struggle for reformation? Whereas the reformers did not represent the status quo at the outset, how did they overturn the Friends who did?

Before 1755, the Society showed little vigor, at least by the reformers' standards. The officers of the church as well as the members shared this fault, partly because of the very indolence and diffidence of the members who were satisfied with or resigned to their officers. Of the officers of the church, George Churchman complained that they were active whenever "it suits their conveniency and does not interfere with their other affairs and is not attended with hardship, not likely to gain the frowns and ill will of their neighbors, and here they come and go like a door on its hinges, from year to year." And what were their qualifications for leadership? That stern critic Anthony Benezet said that it was their wealth, which in the low condition of the church was mistakenly treated as a token "of many Gospel Truths." The English minister William Reckitt put Benezet's criticism metaphorically: "the elders . . . are too much in the outward court, which is only trodden by the Gentiles, or such as are in the spirit of the world."[1] The qualifications for the leaders of the Society, like so many of its other standards, had become those of secular society, complained the reformers. What they did not sufficiently appreciate was that the situation had always been so in Pennsylvania, from the days of Thomas Lloyd through John Kinsey, and that it was part of a problem inherent in William Penn's Holy Experiment.

In a church in which an appreciation of secular attainments and qualifications prevailed, the "true hearted" became diffident and afraid to show themselves, believing themselves to be weak and untalented. They left the really unqualified, complained John Pemberton, to "usurp authority and rule."[2] These true-hearted members were most often young people, a "saving remnant" in whom the reformers confided. The work of reformation had to include changing the attitude of Friends toward the leaders in the church and the qualifications for office, changing attitudes so that reformers themselves would be treated as the spokesmen of the church. Reformers had to hearten and exalt the worthy but diffident members, and if all worked well, finally to overcome the secularly minded leaders who were presently distorting the church's life. Many of these tasks could be accomplished by promoting the single idea of decline from earlier purity. Were Friends to believe that the Society in America had strayed from its historical purpose, and that much of the Society's present character illustrated the error, then changes would appear to be in order.

Persons who had come to occupy positions of eminence within the church, but were not qualified by either their labors on its behalf or their personal characters, were likely to be pushed aside by Friends more vigorous than themselves. Their ascent portended their downfall. Therein lies the clearest and most important reason for the success of the reformers: their energy and labors far exceeded those of their opponents. The opposition did complain and rant. "The libertines, worldly-minded, and opposers of the reformation in themselves and others, cavil and rage," Samuel Fothergill noted in 1756, but, he continued, "the seed is relieved."[3]

On the other hand, the reformers were impressive. Some of the labors in the ministry of John Churchman, William Brown, John Pemberton, and Samuel Fothergill have already been described. But in addition, between 1755 and 1775, thirty-two other English ministers visited Pennsylvania and much of the rest of America, spending up to five years each here. On these visits Americans accompanied the visitors, as when Israel Pemberton spent four months with Fothergill or Benjamin Ferris traveled 1,900 miles with William Reckitt.[4]

Among American Friends, if George Churchman was not the most strenuous laborer, he was certainly the most conscientious diarist. In 1760, he recorded nineteen journeys to Quaker meetings other than his own; in 1761, thirty-seven journeys; in 1762, twenty-five; and in 1763, forty-three. Sometimes the travels were uneventful, but some, like that of March 1765, tested his mettle. On the twenty-third he felt inclined to attend the general spring meeting of ministers and elders in Philadelphia, despite the bad weather. In a heavy snowfall he first made for Wilmington, Delaware, where he attended meeting the next day. Through the second day snow continued falling until it lay three feet deep. Churchman was left to get to Philadelphia by boat, which he did and only in time for the concluding session of the meeting. Yet he found it to be "the last of the feast," which refreshed his spirit.[5]

A slightly different kind of labor which also prospered in these years was the visiting of families. Daniel Stanton of Philadelphia recorded that he and John Pemberton in 1757 began visiting all the families in Philadelphia and the vicinity. By 1760, they had completed the task, having visited over five hundred families in about three years. On these occasions, the visitors might have pointed out vanities in need of reforming; such as owning "large gilded Looking-glass" or "Fine Tea Tacklin & Fine Ceiled Housis," dressing ostentatiously, or acting immodestly. Anthony Benezet appeared too busy to record his works, but Dr. Benjamin Rush recalls having seen him in the streets of Philadelphia in his typical preoccupation: "In one hand he carried a subscription paper and a petition, in the other he carried a small pamphlet on the unlawfulness of the African slave trade, and a letter directed to the King of Prussia upon the unlawfulness of war."[6]

Traveling in the ministry, visiting families, and inspecting meetings were works done by appointment of the Society as well as voluntarily by members. In 1755, 1757, 1762, and 1777, Philadelphia Yearly Meeting appointed committees to inspect all quarterly and monthly meetings and, if need be, report and try to correct their mismanagement of business and discipline. Quarterly meetings, in turn, appointed Friends to inspect monthly meetings, and so on down to families in some districts. In both yearly and quarterly meetings the work continued after the years when the committees were appointed; in Philadelphia Quarter in the 1760s, for example, there was always some person or persons on hand at business meetings, commissioned to keep the reformation moving ahead.[7]

It was the ubiquity of the reformers which initiated the reformation, and more important, kept it from lapsing and becoming little more than a typically brief, eighteenth- or nineteenth-century Protestant revival. The reformers understood the value of their persistence and especially the effectiveness of their travels. John Pemberton observed that at large quarterly and yearly meetings vigor and spirit were easy to come by because of the large number of conscientious and eloquent Friends normally present. But "when friends are scattered and divided to their respective meetings, the living in some places labor under deep suffering and are scarce able to bear up under the sense of death, which prevails through ease and unfaithfulness of many who are called by our name."[8] It was the effect, and probably the intention, of the hundreds of traveling Friends, visitors, and inspectors that the right-hearted in the scattered, small meetings would not be left to labor alone; that the oppressive, dull members (who might not travel to the larger, more comprehensive meetings) be made aware that throughout the Society a change was afoot and that they, and not their critics, might soon be the uncommon members of the Society. John Pemberton had his insight confirmed by John Williams of Shrewsbury, New Jersey, who having heard Pemberton and Samuel Fothergill wrote:

as we Are thus fallen and becom Weak and Poor I rest in hop that Strength and true Riches may be administered . . . by them that are both Strong and truly Rich. . . . What Comes from A Broad Meats with Les opposition and I Could Rejoyce that we Mout be favoured with the Company of Worthy friends . . . in order to Assist us in Restoring the Dissipline in its Primitive Purity.[9]

When David Cooper visited Flushing (Long Island) Yearly Meeting, he discovered that some quarterly and monthly meetings had refused to submit answers to the queries adopted by that Yearly Meeting. He continued, "The subject was now Considered, & so closely Spoak to by Strangers [like himself], that I understood ye next year Answers come from all ye three Quarters."[10] Specific improvements like this one as well as the progress of discipline as a whole confirmed the value of the reformers' method.

Although they did not know it, the reformers were repeating the success of the earliest Friends. Hugh Doncaster and Richard Vann remark that it is difficult to exaggerate the importance of traveling ministers in the first ten to fifteen years of Quakerism. "Mobility, in the basic sense of moving about the country, was a necessity for the origins of Quakerism. . . . the locus of power lay with the traveling ministers." Even though in 1755 and later the context and the purpose of the traveling reformers, mostly ministers, had changed, the method was much the same. Vann is quite correct in remarking that "the Quakerism of 1755 would have seemed in some ways strange to men who had lived through the heroic days of the Interregnum." But then again, they would have been pleased that their successors imitated their methods.[11]

It was a boon to the reformers that some officers of the Society sympathized with them or belonged to their numbers. The difference between London Yearly Meeting and Philadelphia Yearly Meeting, even though a reformation succeeded in both, is illuminating. In London before 1756, the Meeting for Sufferings, London Quarterly Meeting, and to a lesser degree, the Yearly Meeting were usually dominated by the cosmopolitan merchant, banker, and professional Friends of the city. Many of them were intimate with cabinet ministers of the British government. When reformist Friends first checked their influence in 1756, it was partly by the use of blackmail. That is, if the city Friends dared to interfere with pacifist reformers in Philadelphia Yearly Meeting, as they had threatened, the pacifist Friends in England would embarrass them. The English pacifists would duplicate the American Friends' pacifist protest right on the doorsteps of Whitehall.

No such tactic was needed by Friends in Philadelphia Yearly Meeting to prevent Isaac Norris or his like from impeding some Pennsylvanians from protesting warfare, because there was no attempt to impede them,[12] a tribute to the fact that Israel Pemberton was clerk of Yearly Meeting. Furthermore, John Pemberton served as clerk of Yearly Meeting for Ministers and Elders of Yearly Meeting, and James Pemberton clerked the Philadelphia Meeting for Sufferings. Israel and John had few peers as reformers and James, despite an affinity for public office, was sometimes useful to the reformation. Other eminent merchant and professional Friends like Nicholas Waln, John Reynell, Samuel Allison, and John Drinker became conspicuous for their piety and service to the Society. They in turn might ease the way for William Logan, John Smith of New Jersey, the apologist, Henry Drinker, Samuel Wharton, and others who might look askance at George Churchman, John Woolman, Joshua Evans, and other ascetic promoters of reformation.

The higher strata of Philadelphia Yearly Meeting, that is, the quarterly and yearly meetings, were securely in the control of the proponents of the reformation, as proved by the rarity with which an appeal from a disownment succeeded. Even better evidence of their control was the few occasions when the quarterly and yearly meetings sympathized with complaints about queries and accountability, pacifism, abolition, incest rules, and other novel restrictions in the discipline. When expedition was desired and obstructions arose in the lower meetings, Yearly Meeting ordered disciplinary cases removed to quarterly meetings and quick judgment was rendered. The disciplining of slaveholders in 1776, for example, provoked just that recourse.[13] As John Pemberton noted, instructions and labor were needed mostly at the local level, for the Quaker hierarchy was secure.

Before the American Revolution, the Friends who opposed reformation rarely behaved insubordinately. Where insubordination appeared and it was coupled with delinquency, troublemakers were swiftly disowned. It was a different case with otherwise faultless members and meetings who resisted reform. Here the Society responded as forcefully as a peaceable people could, but with the grace of spending immense amounts of time and energy to correct the "misguided" members.

Bradford Monthly Meeting in Chester County proved to be the most obstinate opponent of reform. The committee appointed by the 1762 Yearly Meeting to inspect quarterly and monthly meetings learned that Bradford had refused to answer the standard queries (drafted in 1755) about the behavior and business of Friends and their meetings. It had answered them earlier, and honestly. But when Western Quarterly Meeting told Bradford Friends that it did not like the behavior reported in the answers, Bradford refused to continue answering. That refusal started the trouble, and an inspection disclosed much more amiss at Bradford. Several members who led the opposition also held public offices (very likely constables, justices of the peace, or county commissioners) and were practicing "Conduct akin to persecution, towards some of their Brethren in the County." They were distraining property and possibly even imprisoning Friends who refused to pay taxes that financed the French and Indian War. This was a clear violation of a 1758 Yearly Meeting order that they decline their offices if they had to enforce payment of taxes. The Quarterly Meeting thought they also violated the liberty-of-conscience provisions of Pennsylvania's constitution. They had not been disciplined because they had the support of Bradford Monthly Meeting.[14] All this Bradford refused to report to higher authority once Quarterly Meeting has shown its displeasure.

In February 1763, the committee told Bradford that it was incapable of transacting "the affairs of Truth," that unless it applied without delay to the Quarterly Meeting for help or otherwise "remove[d] the disorders, & maintain[ed] Truth's Authority," Bradford Monthly Meeting would be dissolved and its members distributed among other monthly meetings. That remedy was never applied because the committee corrected the trouble in the reformers' typical way. They discovered at Bradford a "little remnant" of Friends who disliked the behavior of Bradford's leaders and welcomed the intrusion by the Yearly Meeting committee. The committee addressed these Friends, encouraged them to "stand fast," and "earnestly" asked them to do their utmost to turn the meeting around from its present "painful" course. The orderly minority of Friends at Bradford was encouraged and "there was solid reason to believe . . . plain dealing had its use." The change was not sudden. Committeemen from Western Quarter and Yearly Meeting regularly attended Bradford meetings for years, standing by those who were "standing fast" for the discipline. The eventual improvement was remarkable, especially because after several years one of the former leaders of the opposition to the Yearly Meeting became a strong supporter of discipline.[15] Encouragement of the "well-disposed" and a great deal of work had answered the need.

Hempfield meeting, also in Western Quarter, similarly experienced the resoluteness of the Society. It refused to be a part of Sadsbury Monthly Meeting and to attend or report to it. Western Quarterly Meeting resolved that in such a temper Hempfield simply could not meet, and if the members who promoted the contemptuous course of behavior did not obey the Quarterly Meeting and correct their ways, they would be disowned. Hempfield submitted to the Quarter and to Sadsbury, but eventually several Friends were disowned. James and Susanna Wright and their son John were the principal obstructionists. The Wrights were charter members of the political elite of Lancaster County and the arm of the Quaker party there. They had rendered invaluable service to the Assembly and Benjamin Franklin in the gathering of wagons and teams for General Forbes in 1758. After patient counsel, they were disowned.[16] Hempfield was restored to its proper place in the Quaker order.

These two most conspicuous cases and several lesser ones demonstrate that within Philadelphia Yearly Meeting of Friends, its presbyterian organization limited the more renowned Quaker principle of consensus.[17] At least in the eighteenth-century reformation, the progress of the church was not to be delayed or halted because one of its constituent parts objected and resisted. Granted that Friends preferred to use persuasion, tried hard to make it suffice, and usually succeeded, they sometimes coupled their pleading with threats, and to the extent of disowning dissidents, they made good on the threats.

One may also attribute the success of the reformers to the orthodox beginning of the reformation. It began with the enforcement of conventional articles of church discipline such as those prohibiting irregular marriages, fornication, and drunkenness. It was three years in effect before innovations respecting public officeholding and antislavery were introduced and seven years before the change respecting mixed marriages was adopted. For at least those first three years, the patriarchs of the Society were figuratively in the camp of the reformers. The discipline was the codification of their faith and practice; to live in accordance with it was to honor one's forefathers. To justify one's disobedience was to deprecate those forefathers and as much as attest to one's disunity. Reformers needed only to pronounce the implications of the delinquents' protests in order to put them in the wrong and on the defensive. Judging by the number of times that the reformers appealed to precedents and the past, they seemed to have been conscious of their advantage of appearing reactionary. They learned that the role had its disadvantages too, but at the outset, in 1755, it was a boon.

It is likely that while the discipline operated in its historic but thorough fashion for three years, seven years, or even more, and hundreds of peccant Friends departed the Society, the Society progressively liberated itself of the dross that inhibited the progress of reformation. There can be no proof that expelled persons, had they been pardoned, would have repeated their offenses or have frustrated discipline from within Quaker councils; yet it is not likely that they would have advanced the reformation. In uncertain situations, the Society chose to expel offenders and let them apply later for readmission with proof of their personal reformation.

By 1758, the Yearly Meeting was able to amend the discipline regarding public officeholding and the slave trade, and at least one of these amendments operated to hasten reform. The Meeting either could not or, possibly for irenic reasons, wished not to disown office-holders and slave traders. But the sanction it did impose upon them excluded them from the disciplinary business of the Society and thus avoided the risk of their interfering with the thorough administration of discipline, or slowing the eventual accomplishment of abolition and the exit from harmful public offices.[18]

Finally, history seemed to conspire with the reformers. The past teaches the lessons that observers want to discover there; the wars of the 1740s taught nonpacifists very different lessons, for example, from those John Churchman learned and preached. But for those who were willing to lend an ear to the Quaker ministers and reformers, and who believed in a god of history, there was a compelling connection between events after 1754 and the reformers' message.

The Faith of the Reformers

The reformers preached what they practiced—ethics. Often the message was stern and uncompromising. "Our faith is [in] vain," preached Sophia Hume, "if we are found in the breach of the least command . . . for whosoever shall keep the whole law & yet offend in one point he is guilty of all." Winking at "little things," John Pemberton thought, had caused the great faults the Society showed. Many Friends had stumbled and fallen at the very threshold, Elizabeth Wilkinson warned, "by despising the day of small things." Samuel Fothergill believed that one degree of liberty in one's conduct will bring another until "the mind is carried away," and plunged into a state from which it is difficult ever to return. On the other hand, "those who are faithful in a little, shall be made rulers." Vigilance is essential, John Reynell, a merchant, told a colleague. "The Grand Enemy of all our Happiness is seeking by every Method he can our Destruction, and examines us all round to find out where our weak side lies, in Order to make his Attacks there." With an allusion to church history to bolster his warning, Bucks County Friend Joseph White framed the lesson in verse:

> As death among the hedges first begun,
> In little spots, now here, now there, was one,
> Still further spreading year by year, till last,
> The whole reduc'd, and fields became a waste:

> So in the early church declension rose,
> One error these embrac'd, another those;
> Darkness increas'd and vices multiply'd,
> Till purity and Truth were laid aside,
> And a polluted whore was styl'd the bride.[19]

The reformers commended liberty only in the Christian sense of gaining the liberty to attain salvation. "Stand fast in the liberty of Christ," the Yearly Meeting had told Bradford Friends when it meant obey the Society's discipline. "To have our thoughts and actions regulated" by the quest for salvation, the Philadelphia Meeting for Sufferings wrote, "is to be free indeed; to know a happy dwelling in the liberty of truth." Profane liberty, contrariwise, "leads into bondage," and because "true religion . . . sets a bound and limit to the mind," profane liberty was synonymous with libertinism and licentiousness.[20]

The emphasis on small deviations (small, that is, in non-Quaker opinion) from the Quaker code was more common among Friends than the grander and more heroic deeds of some illustrious Friends would lead us to believe. Woolman's, Benezet's, or Pemberton's work on behalf of the larger issues of peace and abolition have obscured hundreds of Friends' preoccupation with such matters as fornication. And yet monthly meetings labeled fornication and other such deeds "henious," "detestable," "gross," and "scandalous," and upbraided meetings that did not treat them as such.[21] From a modern, secular point of view the Friends who worried so much over such errors as these showed a lack of balance and understanding of the difference between venial and mortal sins. What was slaveholding, for example, if fornication was "heinous"? The criticism is appropriate and would be a serious one had Friends not shown an admirable balance through their enormous labors for peace and abolition in all America. But for the membership of the Society itself, ethics were still all of one piece, and no Friend was more scrupulous about the small observances of "Truth" than the heroic John Woolman.

It is also clear that these Quaker men and women did not subscribe to a liberal understanding of human nature and society such as their contemporary Benjamin Franklin epitomized, or as John Stuart Mill did in the nineteenth century, or as many Friends do in the twentieth. To attribute to eighteenth-century Quakers liberal attitudes because they cooperated with Franklin in philanthropies, or because the Quaker city had a reputation for progressive innovations, or because modern Friends are liberal is to err by overlooking what they themselves said and did. They, in fact, showed no significant desire to free men and women of restrictions upon their behavior and character in the expectation that enlightenment, progress, and felicity would result. They preached strict guidance for youths, discipline for adults, conformity and community, vocational education only, and they belittled scores of liberal, centrifugal interests in their people and church. On the rare occasion that they discussed theology, it was often to denounce deism and freethinking.[22]

In a more positive vein, the reformers extolled Christian works above other virtues. "The doers & not the hearers of the Word only were justified." "Being religious in Meetings, without a watchful Circumspect walking out[side] of meetings, and a daily taking up of the Cross will not do." "Religion is a gradual work and must be attended to day by day, for to depend today upon yesterday's exercise will not do." "Neither Education nor tradition would avail in Gods sight"; "I found," wrote Joshua Evans, "I must serve God for myself." "I believe," wrote Anne Emlen Mifflin, "unseparable from virtue [is] a disposition to labour; and without it . . . the mind is in danger of bending its course in the broad road to destruction."[23]

Friends accompanied their instructions in ethics with a metaphor that justified the use of discipline and conformity among Friends. Time and again ministers compared Quaker discipline to a wall around the Society. God would favor a people who conformed to his ordinances and in effect would raise a wall around to protect them. In Nehemiah's concern to rebuild the desolated walls of Jerusalem, wrote John Griffith, much might be found "to show the great analogy hereof with the maintaining of the hedge, or wall of discipline and good order in the christian church." "The ardent concern raised in Nehemiah's mind for the welfare of *God's people* and city; the deep anguish and humble prayer to God; . . . and his whole proceeding in that godly undertaking of raising the walls," deserved to be imitated by all Friends. And as the real walls of Jerusalem protected its people "from dangerous enemies," that figurative wall of discipline would gain God's protection of the Society as surely as stones and mortar. "The same divine power existeth," wrote George Churchman, "which moved upon Nehemiah's heart, & led him first to view the broken walls, & afterwards to build and repair."[24] If the reformation had a patron it was Nehemiah.

When Mary Peisley in 1754 became disgusted at the mixture of Friends and non-Friends, worthies and delinquents sitting in meetings for discipline, she warned that "before one stone can be properly laid on the right foundation," the "unsanctified spirits" must get out of the meeting, "otherwise we believe it will be building [the walls] with the rubbish, which will never stand to the honour of God and the good of His people."[25]

Samuel Fothergill related that in a dream he found himself in America standing in a fine, green pasture walled about, with lambs grazing therein. A pure, clear well fed the lambs; and he was equipped with an axe to guard the well and keep up the walls that protected the pasture. Like most pious Friends of the day, he treated the dream seriously and as an intimation of God's will for him and a commission to teach and protect the purity of the Society.[26]

Just as often Friends used a hedge to describe discipline—

> That hedge, which Fox (divinely taught, and sent)
> In wisdom planted, evils to prevent;
> From rising in the church; . . .

"Our worthy forefathers" erected the discipline, John Pemberton told his brother James, as "a hedge to enclose," and when discipline had been maintained, past Friends found that it preserved the Society. "Divine favor," enabled Quaker patriarchs to maintain discipline "as a Hedge about us," Philadelphia Yearly Meeting assured the members in 1776, when many were anxious that they were defenseless prey for the armed Americans and English. On the contrary, Joseph White maintained,

> Should God see meet with his protecting power,
> To guard our sinking country now no more . . .
> In vain were all our [Americans'] boast . . .
> With carnal weapons to support a fence.

When real hedges died throughout Pennsylvania and New Jersey in the summer of 1776, Friends took it as an ominous sign, and one warned in meeting that "the Lord had taken away the outward hedges, and he would take away the inward hedge"; "destruction" loomed ahead.[27]

Ministers and reformers had proclaimed that discipline and good order in fact called forth God's providential care upon his people, the Friends, as though he had erected a wall and a hedge about them. In one respect a Friend could test that assurance by comparing the worldly fortunes of the Society with those of its enemies. But more subtly, the promise and the metaphor fulfilled themselves. The secular world, including Christianity outside the Society, was described as alien, dangerous, and sinful, whereas discipline or the life of Quakerism was sanctioned by God. To obey the discipline was to refuse to act like others, and acting like others was to sin, degenerate, and resign oneself to spiritual death. Simply conforming to such Quaker testimonies as endogamy, plain speech and dress, and others was to refuse or to wall off the alien, destructive world, and to gain one's reward. To appear like a peculiar people, separate from the "Gentiles," confirmed for one's eyes the existence and truth of the more beneficial spiritual wall.

Straightforwardly as well as metaphorically the reformers insisted upon sectarianism or tribalism, the separation of Friends from others.

As a people we are called to dwell alone [said Anthony Benezet], not to be numbered with the Nations, content with the comfortable necessaries of life; as pilgrims & Strangers; to avoid all incumbrances, as was proposed to Israel of old, to be as a Kingdom of Priests, an holy Nation, a peculiar people to shew forth the praise of him that called us.[28]

As a very pedestrian Friend, James Craft, recalled, Mordecai Yarnall used to preach from the ministers' gallery: "We are gods People, by Creation. We are His by Preservation. We are His by Redemption." "No blending . . . the truth admits of none," George Churchman believed. Children especially had to be separated from the aliens and their customs. "Avoid everything in their dress and address, which might have the least tendency to render them suitable for an intercourse, league, or amity with the children of the land; or of a depraved degenerate world, that wallows in pollution."[29]

This was not the first time that Friends had looked askance at the non-Quaker population around them. In 1719, Isaac Norris, Sr., had blamed the growth of crime in Pennsylvania upon the new people in the province; in 1728, David Lloyd and his Quaker assemblymen had disliked being jostled by city mobs. But their reactions bore only a small resemblance to the reformers' wish to wall off the Society from alien influences. The mistrust of Norris, Lloyd, and their contemporaries was the very conventional one of xenophobes and anxious political and social elites. They belonged with the class of the later New England Federalists, the Know-Nothings, or the Progressives. They were not worried about their own accommodation to the world of politics and secular society, but rather their domination of it or the lion's share of it. They shared the very values of their adversaries and the two camps vied for the same prizes. Observed from a broad perspective theirs was an intramural contest.

But the latter-day Friends were attempting something very different. They had refused the contest with old adversaries because they did not covet the prizes. By the time of the American Revolution most Friends did not seek political powers or office and many mistrusted both. As for secular society, in conspicuous ways Friends turned away from it, provoked its dismay, and wore its abuse like a badge of honor.[30]

Far more often than Friends spoke of the wall of divine protection afforded them by their obedience to their ethics, they rehearsed the misfortune they would suffer or already suffered from disobedience. Quaker pride in their exclusive possession of God's Truth and a share of his benevolence was more than balanced by their sense of special obligation and the extraordinary hazards of error. When John Griffith listed the reasons for practicing church discipline, he specified: preserving the reputation of Friends before the world; preventing evils from spreading in the Society like leaven; but most important, to prevent the Lord from withdrawing his favor from Friends and punishing them as he had Achan and the tribe of Benjamin. Friends could not plead ignorance of the Truth and its obligations. "The ministers of Christ were sent among us from the east and from the west, from the north and from the south, like clouds filled with rain." But, John Hunt (of Burlington, New Jersey) complained, "good sermons . . . were, to many, too much like music to a sleepy man." The Lord was warning Friends as he had warned the Israelites through Jeremiah: "I have sent unto you all my servants, the prophets, daily, rising up early and sending them, yet they [the Israelites] hearkened not unto me." "Some Awful Sensations attended my Mind," George Churchman wrote in 1766, "of a trying dispensation approaching, as a Scourge upon those who 'hold the Profession of Truth, in Unrighteousness.' "[31]

Visiting English ministers spoke even more ominously and threateningly. William Reckitt told American Friends that "unless there was a Reformation & Amendment . . . the Lord would send his Messengers among them, such as the Sword, Pestilence & Locusts." "I am not come the third time into this wilderness country," preached Thomas Gawthorp, "to sew pillows to the armholes of the people. No: I am not come to cry peace, but a sword. There is a bright, polished, glittering sword prepared for this nation." Listeners recalled that Robert Walker "told us [Americans] of the many favours and warnings we had had, and whether we would choose or refuse, the Lord would have a people. That he would call others if we refused . . . that God would be clear and his servants would be clear, and our blood would be upon our own heads." John Churchman had treated Friends in the British Isles to the same kind of ministry. In Dublin, he assured Friends that the Lord's "judgments will overtake, and he will shake his rod, and sweep the wicked with a besom of destruction. . . . Such who continued in their sins . . . would be neither entreated nor warned, it was in the Lord's power to cut the thread of their lives, and appoint their portion agreeable to their doings."[32]

The divinity seemed to collaborate with the Quaker Jeremiahs to fulfill the portents or warnings that Robert Walker had preached. The years from 1755 through 1783 were eventful: there was war, an Indian rebellion, a revolution, several earthquakes, and other, comparatively minor disorders. Samuel Fothergill was in Pennsylvania on 18 November 1755 when an earthquake struck, as though to punctuate Fothergill's criticism of Friends. He spoke to a "vast congregation" of people in the city about this "visitation"; "the subject was awful." "Great is the peturbation of many, and plain the discovery now made, of unprofitable professions many have made of religion. . . . Agitated with fear and horror, they feel their want of a good foundation." In 1763 and 1783, earthquakes again struck the Delaware Valley causing Friends to pause and reflect upon their condition.[33]

The first earthquake occurred while the Indians were attacking the frontiers of the province. The coincidence was not lost upon Fothergill, nor did he permit his audience in Philadelphia to miss its meaning. As the war continued it likewise supplied the preachers with lessons about God's jealousy and justice. "I hope thou are sensible," Fothergill explained to William Logan, a councilor of the province, "the rod hath been laid upon its inhabitants in the counsel of Heaven, in order to revive former zeal for his cause who made your Land as a garden in the Wilderness." "Oh! that it may not happen to us, which was foretold unto Ephriam and Judah," worried John Churchman. "And it is a query with me, whether every step taken for defense by the arm of flesh, do not bring our enemies two steps further within our borders."[34]

Pious Friends discerned the hand of God in quieter events than earthquakes. The hedges died in the summer of 1766. In the summers of 1763 and 1764, worms previously unknown in Pennsylvania spoiled the wheat harvest, an event "sufficient to shew us how easy it was with divine Providence if he saw meet, to eat the staff of Bread, from a forgetful & backslidden People." In May 1774, caterpillars stripped the leaves from the trees until it appeared as though it were winter. The cold winter and spring of 1780 destroyed fodder and grain, cattle died, and bread was in short supply. "These things . . . Seemd to have Something of a Language in them like that of Jonah to Ninevah when he Proclaim'd Yet fourty Days & Ninevah Shall be over thrown." When the people around Nottingham, Pennsylvania, caught an uncommon number of colds in the summer of 1761, John Church-man hinted in meeting "its being a gentle stroke from Providence, presaging a sharper one to come, if people were not aroused to more Spiritual diligence."[35]

"Chastisement is intended for instruction," wrote John Wool-man, and no Friend searched more for God's will and man's obliga-tions in it than Woolman. In the winter of 1759, smallpox struck Mount Holly, New Jersey, and some of Woolman's neighbors died. Woolman reflected:

The more fully our lives are conformable to the will of God, the better it is for us. I have looked at the smallpox as a messenger sent from the Almighty to be an assistant in the cause of virtue, and to incite us to consider whether we employ our time only in such things as are consistent with perfect wisdom and goodness.

. . . this mortal infection incites me to think whether . . . social acts of mine are real duties. If I go on a visit to the widows and fatherless, do I go purely on a principle of charity, free from every selfish view? If I go to a religious meeting, it puts me athinking whether I go in sincerity and in a clear sense of duty, or whether it is not partly in conformity to custom . . . and whether to support my reputation as a religious man has no share in it.[36]

The more ascetic Friends were able to tolerate suffering when they detected in it the means to their own improvement. "We will

sing of thy judgments, as well as thy mercies," wrote George Churchman in a prayer. "The poorest of thy people," he continued,

are helped fervently to pray, that thy hand may not spare them, nor thine
eye pity. . . . we can receive, with thy blessed aid, the bitterest draughts at
thine hand. . . . Thy Rod and Staff, may the one support us, and stay us from
sinking, whilst the other is inflicted for our purification. . . . For thou hast
taught our hearts to believe, and our tongues to acknowledge, that all thy
ways are equal, & thy Judgments just and precious.[37]

Woolman suffered for years from a chronic affliction on his nose and
believed the proper remedy was to eat sparingly, which he did until
he was too weak to travel. In his low and painful condition he was
"favoured" to look to the Lord, "and to feel thankfulness incited in
me for this his fatherly chastisement."[38]

The appreciation of Friends for suffering had several specific origins.
Friends historically had shown a different attitude toward suffering
than had other Protestants. Unlike other dissenters in seventeenth-
century England, Friends actually courted persecution in order to
testify to their faith, prod the consciences of their persecutors and
convert them. The eighteenth-century reformers, well aware of their
inheritance, were not interested in proselytizing, but they showed a
receptivity to suffering that was enhanced by their history. Benezet,
John Churchman, and John Pemberton subscribed to a theory that
suffering was an integral part of church history and almost a prereq-
uisite to religious virtue. In the "first ages of Christianity" and every
reformation thereafter, when persecution and affliction ended, and
the "sunshine of peace prevailed," Christians "lost the sight of the
reason of things & maintained in word, what they contradicted in
practice." Affliction has been "the lott of the Righteous in all ages";
and in this century, they felt those who expect to live nearest to the
Truth have to undergo "as much painful Travel [travail] as any before."[39]
Suffering was also a sure passport to an eternal reward. "It is through
tribulation that the righteous in every age enter the Kingdom," the
Meeting for Sufferings assured Friends during the American Revolution. But rather than promise Friends some delayed gratification for
their good conduct and perseverance, Quaker ministers usually asked
their listeners to understand that sin itself was unpleasant—worse
than God's reprimands. Sin was its own punishment and righteousness was its own reward. If Friends could not grasp that often repeated

homily then they would have to live on in the simple faith in God's inscrutible, "perfect wisdom." "Be assured that the Lord doth not afflict willingly, nor grieve the children of men," and that all things "shall work together for good."[40]

Friends' appreciation of suffering may also be ascribed to the relief afforded by the belief that suffering was historically intelligible and not arbitrarily or gratuitously meted out. At the time of public calamities, Friends enjoyed a private and exclusive historical understanding, in their own eyes, of the purpose of these events. In the wars of the period 1755–83 many Friends found solace or comfort in being able to discover God's retribution for irreligion, avarice, mistreatment of the Indians, and slavery, while their neighbors suffered and wondered why.

Special knowledge suggested that Friends were a special people—as Benezet, Yarnall, and some others had explicitly said. Misfortunes that struck the Society or individual Friends could be interpreted as God's election of Friends: he corrected them alone because he cared for them alone. When Friends were harried because of their pacifism, for example, some went away from the experience convinced that God had vouchsafed to them the revelation of his will. Their punishment was God's correcting them for their past bellicosity or urging them to extraordinary testimonies on behalf of peace.

But at the same time, election—the belief in a special relationship to God confirmed by misfortunes—was difficult to sustain in any systematic way. No Quaker theologian or historian ever attempted it. The great obstacle to any systematic exposition of Quaker election was the heterogeneous nature of Pennsylvania. The Holy Experiment was never intended to be an exclusive religious community like Massachusetts Bay, and when misfortune came to the polyglot province, it was impossible to say who was the offending party. However much Friends revered the Hebrew prophets and likened their history to that in the Old Testament, they did not formulate any religious covenant resembling that of Abraham or the Federal theologians.[41]

It disgusted the Quaker prophets that some Friends and others did not heed the instructions administered in personal and public calamities. When a man, purportedly a Friend, asked John Churchman what caused wheat rot to chronically destroy the grain in the vicinity of Boston, Churchman retold the common story that God had cursed the land because its inhabitants had executed Friends in

the seventeenth century. His listener retorted "with an air of jest-
ing," that he believed nothing of that explanation. Churchman replied
that if the man believed the sacred writing of the Old Testament, he
would know "that the Almighty sometimes manifested his displeasure on a people or nation, by famine, sword, or pestilence, for their
transgressions." You are a "narrow" man, the listener accused. Now
Churchman discerned what sort of man he was speaking to; he was
a deist and did not believe that God worked through nature and
history nor could he give any credit to the Old Testament. Churchman cut off the conversation. "It was very difficult to reach those
low freethinkers, who exercise themselves in the wisdom which is
from beneath."[42]

When the Indians attacked in 1755, Samuel Fothergill railed that
"resentment, anger, and destruction to their enemies" was the response
of Pennsylvanians, instead of "a strict inquiry, 'Is there not a cause?' "
When the earthquake followed in November, he saw more of the
same stupidity. People tried to dispel "any awful impressions" by
attributing natural causes to the event, "lest the Lord of nature should
be . . . inquired after." God "commanded the subserviency of the
elements to himself," and holds them ready "to execute his purposes
of chastisement and reproof." The language of nature to its Creator
is "My Father, shall I smite them? Shall I smite?"[43] Focusing upon
any particular misfortune and its causes was foolish; the misfortune
was merely coincidental to a transcendent plan. "Enemies of one
kind or another will have dominion." The attention of men and
women had to be raised from the historistic level, or from the particular and immediate conditions of history, and they had to stop
attempting to escape or avoid history. For Friends, history was theo-
phany, a visible manifestation of God. "The empires and kingdoms
of the earth are subject to his almighty power; he is the God of the
spirits of all flesh, and deals with his people agreeable to that wisdom
the depth whereof is to us unsearchable."[44]

"Prophecy," observes Garry Wills, "looks simultaneously backward and forward, assigns men fresh tasks with an urgency born of
ancient obligation."[45] Wills' characterization fits the eighteenth-
century Quaker prophets. In assigning tasks to their brethren, they
disclosed that their greatest motive was probably their feeling of
obligation to the past. In their every mention of reformation they
proclaimed an awareness that the past exceeded the present in right-

eousness and the future must measure up to the past. In John Woolman that sense appeared most profound, its having been one of his
earliest recollections. "From what I had read and heard," he wrote of
his childhood, "I believed there had been in past ages people who
walked in uprightness before God in a degree exceeding any that I
knew, or heard of, now living; and the apprehension of there being
less steadiness and firmness amongst people in this age than in past
ages often troubled me while I was a child." In the years that followed,
Woolman often thought with a profound sense of gratitude of the
Christian martyrs and their sufferings. To his mind, the history of
the Christian church showed a long, painful emergence from darkness and the widening of a channel for the freer ministry of the
Gospel, all secured by the faithful at the cost of "their liberty and all
that was dear to them of the things of this world!" This "great work
of God going on in the world" bore fruit in the liberty of conscience
that Christians presently enjoyed—and this, wrote Woolman, "hath
not appeared [to me] as a light matter."

A trust is committed to us, a great & weighty trust, to which our diligent
attention is necessary. Whenever the active members of this visible gathered
church use themselves to that which is against the purity of our principles,
it appears to be a breach of this trust, and one step backwards toward the
wilderness; one step towards undoing what God, in Infinite Love, hath done
through his faithful servants, in a work of several ages, and appears like
laying the foundation for future sufferings.

   There is a gratitude due from us to our heavenly Father. There is justice
due to our posterity. Can our hearts endure, or our hands be strong if we
desert a cause so precious; if we turn aside from a work under which so
many have patiently laboured?[46]

The objects of Woolman's veneration were more catholic than those
of most reformer Friends. George Churchman was more typical when
he "was favour'd with a degree of lively Faith concerning the exalta-
tion of the Standard of Truth in time to come; Edward Burroughs &
others of our primitive Friends were brought into memory, with their
unshaken Zeal & Valour for the good Cause, may we not hope that
it will yet rise with Eminence?" "Oh that a thorough care might
more generally prevail, to return to your first love and to your first

Works," urged Fothergill, "then would the Lord of all power plead your cause."[47]

Three historical eras particularly stirred the spirit of the reformers: early Christianity, the Protestant Reformation and especially the rise of Quakerism, and the founding of Pennsylvania. Henry Drinker recapitulated the Quaker outlook in describing to James Thornton the Yearly Meeting's epistle to its members:

It gives a short account of that Godly Simplicity into which the primitive Christians were led & out of all vain & corrupting amusements. Their decline from ancient purity in these respects is related, & then the revival of the Light of Truth in the Reformation & the dawning of the Gospel day in our worthy Ancestors.[48]

By 1750 the founding of Pennsylvania was well along to becoming the icon that Edward Hicks painted in the nineteenth century, and it, in turn, moved its celebrants to achieve more than the sometimes shabby reality of early Pennsylvania deserved by way of homage. One Englishwoman, Elizabeth Wilkinson, recorded her feelings after a visit in Pennsylvania during which she "went to Pennsbury to see the mansion House of that great, good man William Penn whose name is honoured to this day by the Indians & others. The thoughts of the degeneracy of his descendants . . . made me feel sorry." Anne Emlen Mifflin had similar thoughts: "The notion of just and constitutional Government is a joke, for all Governments that have existed on Earth . . . originated in fraud and force with one excpetion; . . . the Government of Pennsylvania," which was "entirely without the latter." But it too became vitiated, she added, by the degeneracy of succeeding generations of Friends and the admission of peoples who did not profess Quaker principles of peace; so that when Quaker politicians lost their offices, it merely signified their unworthiness as heirs to the founder.[49] The object of the Quaker reformers was as much the restoration of an Arcadian past as it was the creation of a utopian future, and the belief that such a righteous community had existed only shortly ago moved them to labor more effectively than did the dream of an unprecedented future.

A sense of obligation grew too out of a belief that a providential blessing upon early Pennsylvania had yet to be requited. In 1759, the Yearly Meeting wrote to all Friends:

If we carefully consider the peaceable measures pursued in the first settlement of the land, and their freedom from the desolations of war which for a
long time we enjoyed, we shall find ourselves under strong obligations to the
Almighty, who, when the earth is so generally polluted with wickedness,
gave us a being in part so signally favoured with tranquillity and plenty, and
in which the glad tidings of the gospel of Christ are so freely published that
we may justly say with the Psalmist, "What shall we render unto the Lord
for all his benefits?"[50]

Quaker abolition had one of its origins in the Quaker sense of divine
benefaction, as Woolman showed in his renowned work *Some
Considerations on the Keeping of Negroes:* "When we trace back the
steps we have trodden and see how the Lord hath opened a way in
the wilderness for us, to the wise it will easily appear that all this
was not done to be buried in oblivion, but to prepare a people for
more fruitful returns, and the remembrance thereof ought to . . .
excite us in a Christian benevolence towards our inferiors."[51]

Even sleeping or in reverie, Quaker reformers and prophets did
not escape their temporal obligations. They treated their dreams as
divinely inspired visions and messages. While Friends did not tolerate any form of occult divination or prophecy, they labored over the
Christian interpretation of their own dreams and visions. The dreams
were mostly nocturnal allegories of their daytime concerns and
teachings, or so Friends construed them upon waking. Elizabeth
Wilkinson recorded a dream that simply incorporated an allegory
she and others commonly repeated while preaching. She saw a row
of young, green trees unprotected by a hedge, one of them growing
out of line, inclining toward the highway. It was being damaged by
the shadow of a large but withered old tree. She enclosed all the
young trees with a hedge. Two days later, she conferred with John
Churchman about the meaning of the dream, and not surprisingly
they agreed that the young trees represented Quaker youths and the
old tree, the ministers and elders. She ought to have "spiritualized"
further upon her vision, Churchman advised. A year earlier, in 1761,
Churchman had drawn a similar moral about Quaker youth from a
somewhat different vision. In his dream, a large company of children
dressed in beautiful, uniform apparel of dove-gray color approached
in even steps. It signified to Churchman the advance of the church
from its backsliding and its unfaithfulness to "our Worthy Predecessors in the last Century and in the fore part of the Present." Although

Churchman did not comment upon it, the uniformity of dress and behavior of the children in the dream suggests the uniformity being impressed upon Friends through discipline at the time, or the desirability of uniformity among Friends.[52]

Samuel Fothergill repeatedly saw a vision of the last judgment in which a host of people dressed in white were called to ascend. Some did, whereas others remained behind on the earth, perplexed and afraid. "Why are we left behind?" they asked. They were answered by an earthquake which shook off their white garments, revealing iron chains fastening them to the earth. This vision Fothergill related for the benefit of those who were "too much Glued or rivetted to the Earth."[53]

John Woolman recorded more dreams than any other Quaker diarist (seven of his own and two of other Friends), and they illustrate Quaker concerns and his reform interests especially. Two dreams treated war and peace, two treated slavery, one, frugality and the death of the profane will, and two, clairvoyance. Some of them suggest that, as with Wilkinson and Churchman, the cares of the day pursued Woolman after he had retired to bed. Yet a few others seemed more spontaneous and to generate an interest rather than reflect or confirm one. In February 1754, before the French and Indians had clashed with the English and before fear of such a clash was common, Woolman dreamed a vision of a storm of fire approaching him, followed by a new scene of red streams stretching from the horizon across the firmament, and of military men drilling, who scoffed at him and taunted him. Although Woolman did not comment upon his vision, he could have concluded that the war and his role in opposing it confirmed his presentiment—or that his future behavior ought to conform to the role he was commissioned to perform by this divine inspiration.[54]

Friends believed in a gift of clairvoyance in religious matters generally, including not just Woolman's premonition of war, but knowledge of the religious states of people and of mortal death as well as spiritual. Woolman "saw the different states of the people [in England] as clear as ever he had seen flowers in a garden." In England, Churchman remarked about his penetration, asleep or awake, beyond the professions of Friends and into their actual spiritual states; and moreover, he believed that his judgments were confirmed by facts he later learned. At a Yorkshire meeting, a Friend at Churchman's left side stood and extolled the religious bliss of the moment. Yet

Churchman knew it was a false profession, for in an earlier dream someone at his left rejoiced like David before the ark, while a voice from the right protested that the ark had been removed by the Philistines because of the sins of the people. Churchman told the Yorkshire meeting that they mistook their own condition and that death reigned there. After he said that, further conversation was "shut up." Later, a local intimate of Churchman told him that the meeting had withered and that one member had married several of his children to non-Friends, explaining that he had thereby contributed to the growth of the Society, and that the meeting ought to forbear disciplining his family lest they offend the non-Quaker spouses.[55]

The dreams and reveries of Friends did not afford much respite from the work of reformation. Dreaming and meditation have been classic means of escape from earthly ties and of transcending one's perplexities. They were not such things for Friends. Their dreams and visions were ones of commission. They dreamed about this world and history, sin and righteousness, decline and improvement, and not about paradise, rest, or safety. The world mattered, and the reformers were turned back into it by their brief exits from it. The author of their dreams made them into prophets, not mystics.

Ironically it may seem, these Friends showed at the time a lack of concern for the world and their life in it. That unconcern also arose from a sense of divine commission and religious obligation. Because of it, the success of their work or their effect upon the world did not ultimately worry them. They did not select their labors or their methods with the effects and success in mind. Unlike secular reformers, they did not believe that the result was everything, or even the main thing. Rather, it was the fulfillment of an obligation; it was not their place, who were indebted to God, to regret their efforts or to judge their effect. Much of the persistence and fortitude of Quaker reformers and philanthropists can be credited to that disregard for obstacles and odds. "Travelling up and down of late," wrote Woolman, "I have had renewed evidences that to be faithful to the Lord and content with his will concerning me is a most necessary and useful lesson for me to be learning, looking less at the effects of my labor than at the pure motion and reality of the concern."[56] Although Woolman would not have said so, his and other Friends' success may be attributed to their unconcern for results.

5

The Fruits of Reformation: New Testimonies

There is a common assumption among historians of Quakerism that there has been a line of continuity in the social concerns of Friends that extends from the seventeenth century to the present. The fact that some variety of pacifism and an uneasiness about slavery had always existed among Friends added to the likelihood that Quaker abolitionists and notorious pacifists of the eighteenth century would be regarded as natural successors to the seventeenth-century leaders of the Society of Friends. Yet, as historian Richard Vann observes, "one of the remarkable things about Quakerism is that none of the 'testimonies' with which it has come to be identified—penal reforms, abolition of slavery, and pacifism itself—were typical concerns of the earliest Friends."[1] It is a mistake to assume that the social concerns of Friends existed continuously or that they grew steadily since the seventeenth century. An era of Quaker complacency separated seventeenth-century Quaker leaders from the eighteenth-century reformers and severed the later Friends from the reformist impulse that had existed in the earlier age. When innovations appeared after this hiatus, they had their own causes in a different milieu than the lost seventeenth-century one. The history of religious sectarianism shows scores of sects that have prospered in secular terms while they shucked off their original character and became content with a profession of religion that hardly distinguished them from their nonprofessing neighbors. That was happening with Friends too. If new or reinvigorated testimonies were to appear after such a lapse, a religious revival was needed to generate them. That revival occurred and from it came those philanthropies for which modern Quakers have become renowned.

Wealth

Quaker reformers of the late eighteenth century bolstered their arguments by citing earlier criticism of wealth and its unwelcome effects. The foremost expositors of Quaker doctrine from George Fox to William Penn had understood that property and transcendent religious values competed for men's loyalty. Robert Barclay, the seventeenth-century systematizer of Quaker doctrine, stated that "the chief end of all religion is to redeem man from the spirit and vain conversation of this world, and to lead into inward communion with God."[2] But neither Barclay nor any other Friend demanded that their brethren discard property or not accumulate it to begin with, so that they might pursue undistracted that inward communion or the "Light within." Quite the opposite, the founders of the Society, like other Protestant reformers, insisted that Friends not retreat from the world to monastaries and other sanctuaries and not forsake wordly vocations. And so they immersed themselves in the world's business while trying to have, or professing to have, only a transient interest in it.[3]

They prospered mightily in the world—the Barclays, Gurneys, Hanburys, Cadburys, Lloyds, Logans, and Pembertons—and accumulated enormous estates. That was proper too, for nothing the founders said prohibited Friends from having wealth, having it in decidedly unequal amounts, and spending it according to the size of their estates and their social rank. "Our principle leaves every man to enjoy that peaceably, which either his own industry or his parents, have purchased to him . . . for we know, that as it hath pleased God to dispense it diversely, giving to some more, and some less, so they may use it accordingly." "I am sure 'twas to enjoy Property with Conscience that [Protestantism] was promoted," wrote Penn, who enjoyed more of it than he could afford.[4] And so, the Quaker attitude toward wealth and its hazards was an equivocal one, similar to the equivocal one that Friends were also taking on slavery. Both were possible evils and a danger to religion, but when used properly, and even extensively, they were unobjectionable.

The change that occurred in the late eighteenth century brought wealth itself, and not just its possible effects or misuse, under severe criticism. The reformers did not neglect the effects, however; never had Friends scrutinized the consequences for spiritual values and humanity as closely as these reformers did, nor specified so clearly their role in the decline of the Society of Friends. In addition, for every Friend who criticized wealth specifically, there were two or more who harangued the brethren on the contrariety of "the world" and "Truth." Unlike the abolitionists' success, the critics of wealth never succeeded in simply prohibiting wealth or private property. They appear to have had no objective or plans for curtailing or sharing property. Instead, Anthony Benezet prophesied that someday a people, not necessarily Friends, would arise who would live modestly and share property. And George Churchman marveled at the communal arrangement of property among Nantucket Friends. To curtail wealth, Friends would have to define wealth and measure it; and that was a considerably more difficult job than requiring, for example, that all slaves be freed. Moreover, wealth had its undoubted philanthropic uses, as Friends proved at that very time in their support of the Pennsylvania Hospital, the Friendly Association, schools for Negroes, and other charitable institutions. The effect of the new criticism of wealth was the proscription of the pernicious effects of wealth or its misuse. Friends emerged from the reformation a more modest, plain people than they had been before 1750. In the post-Revolutionary era, the economic elite of Pennsylvania hardly appeared among the leaders of the Society. The age of Quaker "grandees," to use Frederick Tolles's term, had ended, even though Quaker wealth did not.[5]

Wealth, or the pride it supported, had insinuated itself into the church and weakened it, the reformers believed. In a moving retrospection on his times, John Smith of Marlboro, Pennsylvania, an octogenarian minister, told Friends that over the decades "marks of outward wealth and greatness appeared on many in our meetings of ministers and elders"; the movings of the Holy Spirit were overcome by a fascination with property, making the Society spiritually barren. Self-seeking, wealthy men had become leaders in the meetings, Benezet maintained, and they enjoyed an unquestioned reputation for discerning "Truth." The temple is filled with buyers and sellers, and moneychangers, complained John Pemberton, and they ought to be driven out. The rich fancy that they honor Quakers if they condescend to be called by that name and to be seen in Quaker meetings. And the other folk fear their frowns and desire their smiles. Delinquent women sat up proudly in meetings as though their costly dress hid their faults. Slaveholders ignored their error out of the pride that they could afford slaves and others could not. Friends who prospered at their professions "were attributing to their own industry."[6] Unless they committed an error, the discipline availed little against these proud, wealthy members. Attitudes first had to be changed in order that wealth might figure less in the life of the church; and so the reformers preached against wealth as no Friends had ever done.

Anthony Benezet was the most strident Quaker critic of wealth. He was a complete reformer, renowned for his abolitionist labors, but he was also interested in pacifism, the American Indians, education, prohibition of alcoholic beverages, and the poor. In most of the evils he fought, he found the common denominator to be avarice and wealth. "The great rock against which our society has dashed," he wrote, is "the love of the world & the deceitfulness of riches, the desire of amassing wealth." Wealth was to him simply irreconcilable with Christianity. If every tittle of the law has to be completely fulfilled, he asked, how can we flout the plain, unequivocal injunction of the Gospel against wealth, which tells us to love not the world and to lay not up treasure on earth, and which asks how shall those that have riches enter the kingdom of heaven? "I cannot look upon the love of the world & giving way to desire for riches . . . as a pardonable frailty," he wrote, "but rather esteem it a depearture [sic] from the divine life, which must either kill all religion in the Soul, or be itself killed, by it." The Gospel and getting wealth "will no more unite . . . than iron will unite with clay." Benezet was not persuaded either by rich men's apologies that they were philanthropists. If that were true they would hire a clerk whose sole business it would be to search out worthy objects of charity and give all the money away.[7]

George Churchman felt that the Friends of Philadelphia especially deserved advice and caution about their wealth and he wrote to James Pemberton that city Friends were covering their religious lights "with that wide mouthed bushel which they use constantly measuring to themselves the honors, profits and treasures of this world . . . and but rarely are they heard, either in words or thoughts concerned for the posperity [sic] of truth and beauty of Zion."[8]

On a visit to Nantucket in 1781, Churchman came as close as

any reformer of this generation to discovering a Utopia—and a Quaker one at that. Most of the seven or eight hundred families on the island were Friends and their interest, farms, and pastures were pooled "in a kind of joint Commonwealth." Little law was practiced there; few differences over property arose. Annually they distributed the increase according to every person's share of the whole. At meeting for worship, some fifteen hundred attended and Churchman observed more moderation in dress than he had ever seen before. It was "a Social, friendly & commendable way of living" which would be more generally practiced if men permitted religion to regulate their lives, Churchman concluded.[9]

Less strident than Benezet and Churchman was John Woolman, who wrote more about wealth than either of his colleagues. He collected most of his thoughts on wealth in his essay *A Plea for the Poor*, subtitled *A Word of Remembrance and Caution to the Rich*.[10] In this essay and in some of his other works, Woolman presented what is a more reasoned and systematic criticism of wealth than anything written by other Friends. Woolman discovered the evil effects of avarice among the most pressing problems of his day, including wars, slavery, racial prejudice, usury, exorbitant rents, drunkenness, debility, and cruelty to animals. Woolman calculated that many of these oppressions might practically be eliminated were men content to limit their property to their physical needs. But in the essay there was as well the biblicist insistence that a rich man can no more enter heaven than a camel pass through the eye of a needle. Although he might argue the evils of wealth from it economic effects, Woolman, no less than Benezet, shared the belief that wealth disqualified the Christian. All of the woes of the wealthy were not deferred until the afterlife, however. Woolman went on to explain ontologically how wealth and avarice served as their own punishment in this life as well, and the ascetic spirit of Christianity was its own reward. Calmness of mind and a spirit at rest was for Woolman the complement of a perfect resignation to God's regulation of one's life. It was simply impossible for a greedy and selfish man to be resigned. The selfish "have their portion in that uneasy condition 'where the worm dieth not, and the fire is not quenched.' " And the poor, when they envy the "outward Greatness" of the rich, "murmur in their Hearts because of their own poverty, and Strive in the Wisdom of this World to get Riches for themselves and their Children; this is like wandering in the Dark." Poverty was no torment where a poor man understood the truth of the promise that "as the sufferings of Christ abound in us, so our consolations aboundeth by Christ. II Cor. 1:5."[11]

Wealth disturbed most Friends for sectarian reasons. It was too clear to the reformers that the motive for certain matrimonial matches was the gaining or the enhancing of an estate, and not religion. When the Society could interpose, the couple or their parents often took the marriage outside the Society for solemnizing. When it could not, it helped to produce another nursery for profane values and desires. Parents would hazard disownment in arranging their childrens' marriages "if there is but money in the way," complained Elizabeth Wilkinson. To find dowries and estates, they did not confine their search to the brethren in profession. Some Friends, even Quaker ministers, "join hands in Marriage with people, which, had they not been rich, they would . . . not even 'have put with the dogs of their flock,' " complained Benezet. The ministers profess that their newly acquired wealth helps free them to work in the ministry. They forget, Benezet railed, that the Gospel has been spread mainly by the poor— but rich in faith—who did not go to Egypt and Babylon for help.[12]

It bothered Friends even more that wealth corrupted the children as well as their wealthy parents. The children might never know the simpler life that their parents had at least at one time experienced. In their youth, the watershed of their lives, these children would be exposed to most of the snares of the world. It was a profound disservice for rich parents to inflict those hazards upon susceptible children. The parents did inflict them, however, out of a sense of duty— or so they professed. They quoted Scripture, said Fothergill, to prove that he was worse than an infidel who did not provide for his family. The Meeting for Sufferings and others warned Friends against this subtle delusion that in amassing wealth they were fulfilling a religious obligation to their offspring. "By buying cheap & selling dear," wrote Benezet, they "get possessed of such an heap, which might answer the Sober wants of hundreds . . . & finally, leave it solely . . . to his heir or heirs, to the gratifying their idleness & pride, & every other noxious passion of the human mind, this appears to me to be an atrocious degree of vanity."[13]

Despite Israel Pemberton's services to the Society, his estate, the largest in Pennsylvania, disturbed some Friends. It was not that his wealth suffocated his own better instincts, but that his children, and especially his oldest son, showed little of the father's religious bent. The father's estate would someday feed the children's profane appetites. Benezet had so often warned Pemberton of the danger that Pemberton grumbled, "It's tiresome to hear Anthony always saying the same thing." The English minister Samuel Neale wrote to Pemberton, "I love thy children. I believe they will be tried with one of the greatest trials, worldly riches." They will succeed "into fullness and worldly glory as at one step, by which they are raised as with a torrent from the little footing they had." In the end, Pemberton ignored their advice and left £60,000 or £70,000 to his children, and according to Benezet, not a farthing to charity. As Benezet had predicted, the inheritance provided "wings for his Children & Grand Children to flutter, if not fly off above Truth."[14]

The two wars in the years 1755–83 came as a relief to Friends who were sorely troubled about wealth corrupting the Society. Even the earlier war, King George's, had its lessons for alert Friends. James Logan and Samuel Chew had then candidly argued that Quakers' wealth obliged them to modify or discard their pacifism in order to protect their property and other people's. And indeed, after 1744, Quaker legislators began to behave as though there were some wisdom in the advice. To reformers, however, the essays of Logan and Chew proved only that property was a prime cause of wars and needed all the more to be deprecated.[15]

In the French and Indian War, the tension between property and Quaker ethics appeared much more clearly. The lack of a militia and wagons and teams for an army could have caused some Friends near the frontier to loose their homes and other property to Indian attacks. An effective Quaker boycott of wartime taxes, far-fetched though that was, might have inhibited the progress of the militia and regular armies, but far more likely, it would have had no effect upon the war. Rather, those who did not pay their taxes would have suffered mainly from the distraints the sheriffs made upon their properties. During the war, an awareness that property inhibited Friends' religious impulses in wartime was communicated to the members. At Chester Quarterly Meeting in 1758, the three hundred Friends in attendance were urged "to be particularly careful to have our minds redeemed from wealth . . . that so no temporal concerns may entangle our affections or hinder us from diligently following the dictates of Truth . . . in these days of calamity and distress, wherein God is visiting our lands with his just judgments." The Yearly Meeting epistle of 1759 observed, "Many parents were concerned for their children and in that time of trial were led to consider that their care to get outward treasure for them had been greater than their care for their settlement in that religion which crucifieth to the world and enableth to bear a clear testimony to the peaceable government of the Messiah."[16]

Before the end of the French and Indian War, Woolman had probably completed his *A Plea for the Poor.* In two chapters of his essay he attributed the genesis of wars to selfishness and wealth: "selfishness hath been the original cause of them all." The spirit which loves riches, he explained:

is like a chain where the end of one link encloses the end of another. The rising up of a desire to attain wealth is the beginning. This desire being cherished moves to action, and riches thus gotten please self, and while self hath a life in them it desires to have them defended.[17]

The war passed, leaving little damage to Friends' estates because so few lived on the frontier and so few protested the taxes. Whatever sense of humility and sacrifice the war had fostered was forgotten even before it ended, when the colonists spent exorbitant amounts of money on imported goods, enhancing their standard of living as never before in the eighteenth century. These flush times continued until interrupted by the American Revolution.[18] Americans remarked at their own or their neighbors' profusion and some complained of the spectacular indebtedness that accompanied it. Friends indulged too, and the critics among them recognized the evil in it. In the years before the American Revolution, remarked John Hunt (of New Jersey), "excess and superfluity of almost every sort, in houses, furniture, and dress," seemed to be growing fast. He continued:

In the time of great prosperity, when the fatness of the earth was showered down in a plentiful manner upon us, we were too much like the brute animals, who eat the fruit under the tree, and look not from whence it comes. . . . "Their idols were upon their hearts, and upon their cattle; the carriages were heavy laden—they were a burden to the weary beasts"—as the prophet Isaiah expressed in his day.[19]

For Friends like John Hunt, the Revolution came partly as a relief. Benezet naturally tried to use the occasion to improve Friends. The war will "bring us to ourselves," "bring our wants and desires into a much narrower compass," and "teach us . . . to live more agreeable to our profession"; because this war, he predicted, will not be brief "like a passing storm" or remote, but will affect all Friends and "come heavier upon those who are most loaded and encumbered with the clay of this world." Its destruction will be "greater upon those whose possessions are most expensive, and have been at the greatest pains and expenses in adorning their pleasant pictures."[20]

Reformers expected that the Revolution would amplify their protest rather than drown it out. Certainly the stirring and heroic language the reformers and the Society used in propagating its message would have sounded affected without the war as its setting. And whereas in peaceful and prosperous times, wealthy Friends might dismiss Benezet as a crank, the war undoubtedly moved some to listen when they saw their property disappear and the prophets confirmed.

Abstemiousness and Simplicity

Drunkenness is another instance in which the Society had historically prohibited the abuses but not the agent. Unlike the effects of selfishness and profusion, however, the ill effects of alcohol were easily detected and regularly prosecuted. Indeed, drunkenness was the third most common violation of the discipline and the most intractable problem among Friends.

In order to maintain temperance in early Pennsylvania, the Quaker government strictly regulated the number and operation of inns, taverns, public houses, and their patrons. Governor Thomas Lloyd reputedly visited taverns late in the evening and ordered people home from them. The Society periodically cautioned and disciplined its members for dispensing rum at auctions and for incontinence at weddings and burials. Despite these efforts, drunkenness grew and the problem became "scandalous." Drunkards appeared at every level of the Society: the clerk of Chester Monthly Meeting was repeatedly drunk, and a drunken minister from Concord rode around the countryside preaching and "craving for" liquor. The son of the eminent minister Mordecai Yarnell, when not yet 18, was continually drunk and was carried off the streets of Philadelphia to Pennsylvania Hospital.[21] Drunkards were notorious recidivists. Drunkenness was "an inlet to many other evils" too: 1,033 drunken Friends committed 809 other offenses. They cursed and swore, quarreled and fought, stopped attending worship meetings, got too deeply into debt,

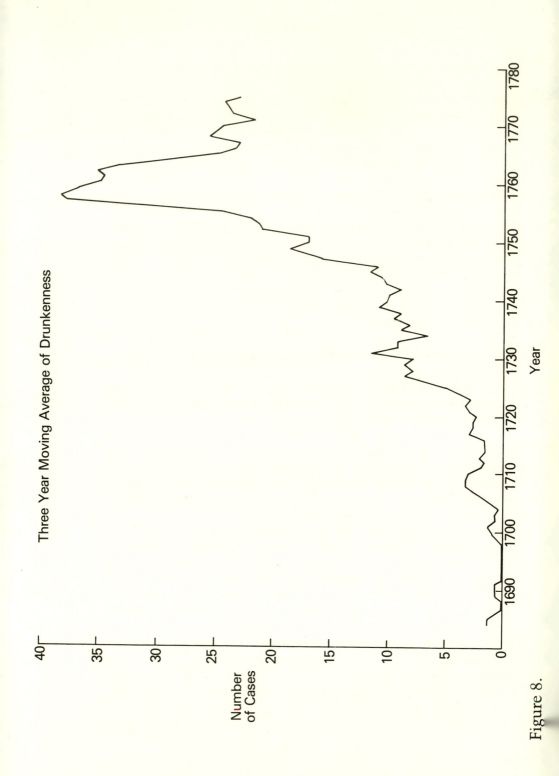

Figure 8.

neglected their families, and in some cases, abused their families physically.[22] It was natural that after 1755, when Friends tried to perfect behavior in other respects, they would pay close attention to the very conspicuous problem of drunkenness.

The Society never devised in this era a means of rehabilitating the chronic offender. Disownment remained the outcome in most severe cases.[23] The Society moved increasingly toward a policy of encouraging abstinence or prohibition and continued in that direction into the nineteenth century. Again, John Churchman and John Woolman were the earliest Friends in this era to become alarmed at the pernicious effects of alcohol. In 1761, Churchman told his friends of his disgust at the abuse of the body caused by consuming alcohol. It was the custom to supply rum to harvest laborers, who were often severely taxed to harvest a crop before weather or other hazards damaged it. Churchman believed that the practice showed that Pennsylvanians had declined from the standard of health and strength of the abstemious founders of Pennsylvania. In *A Plea for the Poor*, which Woolman was composing at roughly this time, he discussed alcohol. He too was disturbed that it perverted the true nature of the body and mind, even when taken moderately but regularly. And the drunkard is "further removed from that frame of mind in which God is acceptably worshiped." Woolman traced the evil back to its source in avarice and superfluity. These desires required unnecessary labor in order to gratify them, and to sustain their hard-pressed bodies, men, and especially agricultural workers, consumed large amounts of rum. In his journey in 1769, Woolman noted the intimate link between rum and the slave trade. To consume the former was to patronize the latter.[24]

On his farm, Friend Joshua Evans stopped supplying rum to his laborers at harvest. In his experience, when he supplied it the laborers got drunk and caused waste, rather than being refreshed and strengthened. Moreover, in order to get rum for their hired hands, he and other farmers shipped the choicest grain from Pennsylvania to the West Indies. Because in at least these two respects the poor went without bread for the sake of this unwise custom, Evans stopped it and paid his laborers the difference in money. He discovered he had just as many laborers as before. Still he was criticized because rum reputedly prevented men from collapsing from their toil; Evans jeopardized the lives of his men, the neighbors said. And so he told his men not to hurry, even if a rainstorm threatened the crop. His policy proved effective, Evans concluded, but he would have followed it anyway because he was certain the Lord had required it of him.[25]

The whole Society began to move toward abstinence after 1762, by dissuading Friends from keeping public houses. Philadelphia Friends especially had become alarmed over the proliferation of the houses and they complained to the Assembly about them. The Assembly, in turn, blamed the Proprietors because they licensed public houses in Pennsylvania. Quaker disgust with drunkenness and the whole range of social disorders that it promotes became a political issue in the 1760s and one of several motives for some Friends who wished to see the proprietary charter dissolved. Throughout the province monthly meetings began to admonish members who undertook tavern-keeping, although they did not discipline these people. The excuses of the admonished members usually appeared legitimate—physical inability to follow a trade, for example—and they were accepted. But when a Philadelphia woman who drank to excess got a license to open an ale house, Philadelphia Monthly Meeting disowned her.[26]

In the 1770s, the growth of whisky distilleries in Pennsylvania caught the attention of the Quaker reformers. In a pamphlet entitled *The Mighty Destroyer Displayed*, Benezet attacked the manufacture and use of whisky for much the same reasons rum had been attacked: The stuff corrupts morals; it devastates the body, and it, more clearly than rum, turns perfectly good foodstuffs into an evil commodity. Men get drunk while the poor lack bread.[27]

At the very lively, reformist Yearly Meeting of 1777, the Society moved against trade and use of spirits among Friends. Friends from Philadelphia Monthly Meeting and Western Quarterly Meeting asked that the Society do yet more to discourage the use of alcohol. The Yearly Meeting gratified their request by ordering that Friends must not enter the manufacturing or vending of liquor and those who were already a part of those trades were to desist. Neither were Friends to partake of the liquor made from grain nor to sell their grain to anyone who used it for distilling. In this instance, as in others, war proved a fillip to reform—a war within only miles of the Meeting—for the Meeting declared that the distilling of liquor had added to the sins of the nation, for which God was now punishing it.[28]

A crucial difference between Quakerism in the 1730s and after 1755 is the Society's treatment of eccentric, reformist members. For example, Benjamin Lay, an abolitionist the Society disowned in the

1730s, was eccentric for more reasons than his disorderly protest against slavery. He was also a strict vegetarian, lived in a cave, and refused to drink tea and to wear the wool of any animal.[29] In his day, Lay was disowned and regarded as less than sane, whereas John Woolman, whose testimonies resembled Lay's (although his temperament did not), became a model for his contemporaries two decades later. The tolerance and sympathy of Friends for unusual religious testimonies which most Friends did not adopt, grew immensely in twenty years.

Woolman appears to have initiated most of the more unconventional personal testimonies of late eighteenth-century Friends. He wore undyed homespun clothes, refused to use sugar and silver tableware, and sometimes traveled on foot to distant places.[30] Woolman's motives were various. Several of the testimonies served his profound respect for simplicity—"true wisdom" he called it. The use of dyestuffs shortens the life of clothing, Woolman and his imitators believed, and serves not much purpose other than to gratify pride and support hypocrisy. Dyes only hide dirt; it is better to wash clothing really clean. Silver plate is pure superfluity and is unworthy of men's exertions to get it. Woolman refused sugar because it was one of the products of slave labor in the West Indies. Some Friends similarly refused tea because sugar normally accompanied it. Woolman, beginning in 1766, made four journeys in the ministry on foot so that he might "have a more lively feeling of the condition of the oppressed slaves, set an example of lowliness before the eyes of their masters, and be more out of way of temptation to unprofitable familiarities."[31]

While Woolman was obviously protesting against slavery by these testimonies, he was at the same time displaying his respect for simplicity and economy. The labor that men performed to get unnecessary, fashionable clothes, silver, and sugar all oppressed human bodies beyond the tolerance the Creator had intended. Prudence, "true wisdom," and religious "Truth" were all confounded. It happened that for sugar, the bodies were black and the chattel of white men. The oppression for pride's sake appeared too in the drunkenness of the farm laborers, the brutalizing conditions of sailors who freighted superfluities from shore to shore, the freezing postboys of England expediting trivia, and the woebegone draft animals pushed to death for the teamsters' profit.[32]

Although pride and selfishness damaged that spirit which desired

communion with God, and the drunken man was completely incapable of worshipping God acceptably, we would misrepresent Woolman if we concluded that worship was his sole consideration. There
was in Woolman the appreciation of asceticism because it helped
men to approach God more easily. Yet that was not a neo-Platonic
depreciation of mortal life and flight from it. Woolman had a profound
appreciation of life and health—other men's as much as his own;
and "true wisdom" completely complemented life and health. The
mortal condition was not to be escaped by religious devotions or
asceticism, but enhanced and truly experienced.

Woolman started something. Whether through personal acquain-
tance with him or not, other Friends imitated him. Joshua Evans was
the most notable. Like Woolman, he dressed in undyed homespun,
but he also let his beard grow. Shaving, he felt, was a human contriv-
ance "authorized through pride." Almost all Friends disagreed. Evans
was a vegetarian, but he was accused by David Cooper of being an
inconsistent one because he drank broth and gravy. Evans's reply to
Cooper was that others after him would further the reformation.[33]
When Evans requested permission to walk to New England in the
ministry and his meeting refused him a certificate to travel, he
defended his request using George Fox's well-known odd costume
and John Woolman's example to argue the case on behalf of Quaker
tolerance. Ten years after the Revolution, Evans was pained at the
thought of paying a tax on salt because it helped to retire the revolutionary war debt. Avoiding salt was uncommonly difficult, but
Evans resolved to eat bread and water in order to avoid the host of
foods requiring salt.[34] Anne Emlen Mifflin curtailed her use of butter,
believing it was corrupting. Warner Mifflin, her husband, quit smok-
ing because it "shakles" the soul with "improper burthens." Numerous Friends adopted a boycott of all products of West Indian slavery.
Quaker women dyed bedspreads with walnut leaves rather than use
indigo, even redying older spreads which were already blue. One
Quaker host was amazed to discover the bed of his Quaker guest
untouched at morning. When asked why he had not slept in the bed,
the guest replied he could not be free to sleep in bedclothes dyed
blue. He had spread his coat on the floor and slept there, despite
the very cold weather.[35] In the reformed Society, some of these
characters were venerated and some were merely indulged, but
none was disowned.

Abolition

Friends were the first community of people in Western history to corporately espouse and practice the abolition of slavery. If there is an extraordinary event in their past—or in modern history—it is their adoption and promotion of abolition. Slavery had been practiced in the West beginning with the ancient Hebrews, and although the institution had its critics, none of them changed the minds of their slaveholding fellows or inhibited the institution. Indeed, with the expansion of Western Europeans into the New World, slavery experienced a grand revival that perpetuated it for another three centuries and more. To ask why the institution did eventually fall into disfavor and decline is to address a singularly momentous change in history. Any answer must treat Friends for they were the first abolitionists in practice as well as profession.[36]

Abolition was no part of the Quaker consensus until the mid-eighteenth century or later. The fact that Friends criticized the institution from the time of George Fox did not make Fox or his successors different from other Western critics of slaveholding. Friends as well as non-Friends kept their slaves and later bought more. On the other hand, it is equally true that the legacy of criticism by Fox and other past critics of slavery could and did affect later practicing abolitionists. The crucial question is not whether past criticism contributed to eventual abolition—it did—but rather what necessarily intervened later to transform ages of occasional criticisms into effective abolition?

As for Fox, in 1657 he cautioned Quaker slaveholders in America and asserted the equality of man. He advised that Negroes be treated like white bondsmen and freed after a term of service. Although his advice was not taken, the considerable community of Quaker slaveholders in Barbados did heed the advice of Fox and William Edmundson to Christianize their slaves and to treat them kindly. These marks of consideration gained them banishment, fines, and other loss of property; yet they persisted.[37] Even while Friends continued holding slaves, there was this small testimony to their willingness to be regarded as troublemakers and to suffer on behalf of Negroes rather than go along with the times.

In Pennsylvania, there existed an obvious tradition of Quaker discontent with slaveholding. Just as clearly, these discontented Friends represented a minority view in a church which respected uniform behavior and discouraged passionate criticism of the brethren. Six years after the founding of Pennsylvania, the first protest against slavery in mainland America appeared—written by Germantown Friends. From then until 1738, Pennsylvania Friends periodically prodded the Yearly Meeting to espouse antislavery, but with no success. Chester County Friends authored four orderly petitions to the Yearly Meeting, which established their preeminence as champions of abolition in Philadelphia Yearly Meeting. But all the petitions were politely dismissed and the authors cautioned to forbear reflecting upon slaveholding brethren. Clerk Isaac Norris disliked the disturbance of the otherwise serene meeting of 1715: It "was large and comfortable, and our business would have been very well were it not for the warm pushing of some Friends, of Chester chiefly, in the business of Negroes." After the schism of 1692 and the endemic rancor it fueled in the following twenty-five years, Norris understandably was apprehensive of dissenters, even orderly petitioners from Chester. Any conservative Friend would not have regarded antislavery as an altruistic cause, because the first protest to follow the Germantown one was authored and published by the Keithian schismatics in 1692. George Keith criticized Friends for owning slaves and he prohibited the practice among his short-lived group of Christian Quakers. As he had also done with pacifism, Keith tainted the espousal of abolition with heresy and caused conservative Friends to distrust abolitionists for years thereafter.[38]

But just as important, the leadership of the Society from 1710 on was not congenial to abolition. Norris was one of the principal importers of slaves in Pennsylvania. He and some of the wealthiest and most eminent Friends in early Pennsylvania had immigrated from Barbados and Jamaica where they had owned slaves. In Pennsylvania, they maintained their ties with slaveholding Friends in the islands.[39] Furthermore, the behavior of Norris and his colleagues during the depression of the 1720s and the anxiety of James Logan and others over their property in the colonial wars left little likelihood that the Society would champion such a threat to property as abolition. Abolitionists would require new leaders with very different priorities before they could get a hearing.

Some of the Quaker abolitionists were disorderly individuals, and they got shorter shrift than Chester Friends. William Southeby was disciplined in 1716; John Farmer was disowned in 1720; and Ralph

Sandiford was disowned in 1731. The most notorious protestor of them all, Benjamin Lay, sounded a note in 1738 that would often be repeated by the reformers after 1750: "I know no worse or greater stumbling blocks the devil has to lay in the way of honest inquirers than our ministers and elders keeping slaves; and by straining and perverting Holy Scriptures, preach more to hell than ever they will bring to heaven by their feigned humility and hypocrisy." He urged that these "old rusty candlesticks" be removed from their church offices; but that did not begin to happen for another twelve years. Lay also practiced a severe asceticism that John Woolman, Joshua Evans, and later, some other Friends took up. He might have served them as a model. His writings and Sandiford's display the strong sense of obligation, guilt, and divine justice in the case of slaveholding which appear so often in the preachings of the reformers and in their denunciations of slavery. But in Lay and Sandiford's era, no one listened. The Society disowned Lay in 1738.[40]

The silence that followed appeared to represent a proslavery triumph; Quaker abolitionists appeared exhausted and dispirited. Yet in a way so unobtrusive as almost to escape notice, antislavery sentiment survived: In Pennsylvania and New Jersey, some Friends acted upon their private unhappiness with slavery by manumitting their own slaves in the 1740s.[41] These Friends represented a younger generation than those "old hairs" who had disowned Farmer, Sandiford, and Lay. From their cohort came the prophets of the 1750s who would finally prevail. When antislavery activism reasserted itself in the 1750s therefore, it had a constituency, albeit untested, upon which it could call. And second, it had a tradition of the patriarchs' misgivings about slavery, which could be employed upon cautious Friends, as well as the record of antislavery martyrs to inspire later prophets to fulfill the promise of the past.

David Davis has pointed out that "whether a man is considered a saint or a troublemaking eccentric depends largely upon circumstance." Southeby, Farmer, Sandiford, and Lay were disowned or disciplined for espousing abolition, but John Woolman was treated like a saint within his own lifetime for doing so. Quakerism had changed, and had done so in less than twenty years. Considering this, the important point according to Davis "is that by the mid-eighteenth century, Quakerism provided a cultural setting in which hostility to slavery could become something more than individual dissent."[42] Davis, like Sydney James and others, specifies the French and Indian War as the cause of a crisis within the Society of Friends which suddenly prepared the way for antislavery. But the way to antislavery was prepared just as much by the new leadership in Philadelphia Yearly Meeting, the vigor of the reformers, including Woolman, the root-and-branch correction of Friends' lives, the disownment of hundreds of members, and the symbiotic effect of new testimonies like pacifism and asceticism. All these influences made up the new sectarian cultural setting which afforded abolitionists a hearing and a following.

The story of the changed climate begins with Woolman. Among reformer Friends he was the first to record his antipathy to slavery. In 1742, he felt oppressed because he had consented to write a bill of sale for a Negro. By 1746, he had resolved to take a journey to the South to learn more about slavery. The fruit of that journey was his famous pamphlet, *Some Considerations on the Keeping of Negroes*, which was not published for another seven years. When Woolman finally took his pamphlet in orderly fashion to the Society for its imprimateur, the temper of the Yearly Meeting had changed, especially because of its new leadership. The Yearly Meeting had the pamphlet printed and distributed at its own expense. One of the censors for the Yearly Meeting was the abolitionist Anthony Benezet and another principal Friend among them was the minister and reformer Michael Lightfoot. And at the head of Yearly Meeting stood the Pembertons, instead of Norris or Kinsey. Excerpts from Woolman's pamphlet appeared in the Yearly Meeting's 1754 annual epistle to its members, before the pamphlet was published.[43]

These messages amounted to advice, although of a most eloquent kind. In 1755, the Yearly Meeting acted against the slave trade among Friends, and more important, its orders were carried out. According to the Yearly Meeting, any Friend who imported or bought slaves domestically was to be dealt with by his meeting; if the purchaser proved obstinate, however, no sanctions were to be applied.[44] In light of the fundamental resolution by the Yearly Meeting of 1755 that the entire discipline be reexamined and enforced, the progress of antislavery that year appears more natural. Previously, the Yearly Meeting's cautions against purchase of slaves (in 1716 and 1730) had simply been ignored. One may assume that the Meeting did not mind, the cautions being largely a sop to Chester County Friends. But after 1755, monthly meetings did apprise purchasers of slaves that the Society disapproved.

The more vigorous meetings brought the purchasers before them for scrutiny. Goshen thus queried two purchasers and excused them after they promised not to purchase slaves again. Philadelphia Monthly Meeting, once a center of proslavery sentiment, vigorously admonished purchasers. By 1757, Philadelphia had become dissatisfied with the limits upon its ability to discourage the slave trade.[45] That year the Meeting called four purchasers before it and instead of dismissing them with an admonition, it suspended consideration of the four until it questioned Philadelphia Quarterly Meeting about how far Friends could disoblige their behavior. The question was transmitted to Philadelphia Yearly Meeting in 1758 for a more definite resolution. There the slaveholders and their spokesmen turned out and a spirited debate occurred. Because the defenders of slavery labored under the Quaker tradition which was critical of slavery, none of them openly justified the practice. Instead, they pleaded for Quaker unity and community, qualities which few Friends could gainsay; but that tactic was the bugbear of the reformers on many fronts. The proslavery speakers rued the "uneasiness" the reformers would cause their brethren, and asked the reformers to be patient in the assurance that God would "in time to Come" open an easier way for the deliverance of Negro slaves. Woolman gave their plea little credit. If these apologists would put away their self-interest and their desire to accumulate wealth, they would immediately find the way to abolition open. Avarice, not a respect for Quaker unity or harmony, was the obstacle. He urged the Yearly Meeting to oppose "friendships which do not stand on the immutable foundation." Finally, he warned that where a duty was clear, to ignore it was to warrant "that by terrible things in righteousness God may answer us in this matter."[46]

The facts of the slave trade in Philadelphia corroborate Woolman's characterization of his Quaker opponents and their motives. The French and Indian War had interrupted the flow of indentured servants from Europe and had enticed servants already in America to enlist in the British army there. Merchants and tradesman in the city became hard pressed for laborers and turned to Negro slaves to supply their needs.[47] In the decade of the 1750s, slave imports at least tripled, and in 1762 they peaked at close to five hundred. By 1768, they were down to the level of the early 1750s, some thirty annually.[48]

Philadelphia Friends were as guilty of buying these slaves as anyone else in the city, and maybe a bit more so. Quaker slaveowners amounted to 10.4 percent of the city's total while Friends were 9.9

percent of the city's population.[49] When Woolman pressed the Yearly Meeting in 1758 to act against slave trading, he was pitting Quaker benevolence against Quaker ownership and avarice. Quaker abolitionists and reformers had preached that Friends were, or ought to be, redeemed from the world's evils. But the Quakers in Philadelphia behaved much like everyone else about slave ownership. The leadership of Philadelphia Monthly Meeting had joined the reformers in pushing for a change, but the "laity" in the Meeting were resisting and succeeding in forestalling the day when full abolition would come to the Society.

In 1758, the Yearly Meeting gave the reformers only part of what they wished. It did not threaten the Friends who already owned slaves, nor did it apply its fullest sanction to future traders. It answered Philadelphia Monthly Meeting's request by ordering that any Friend who purchased or sold a slave could not participate in the business of the Society, including discipline, unless he showed satisfactory repentance for his action and was pardoned. For the nominal Friend and slave trader that meant little; it might even be a benefit, because the Society also refused to receive his financial contributions to the Society by the same 1758 minute.[50] For the Society, however, it was a means to help relieve itself of the drag that slaveholders put upon its progress toward reformation; they were not out of the Society, but they were quieted. In 1758, as in 1755, the antislavery discipline complemented other reforms. The same sanction of partial exclusion was passed in 1758 against Quaker officeholders who prosecuted Quaker pacifist protestors. These protestors had refused to pay taxes levied for the French and Indian War.

Application of the 1758 Yearly Meeting antislavery directive varied among monthly meetings. Some followed it perfunctorily while others showed an interest worthy of its authors. The responses of the offenders varied too, from regret and amendment to prevarication, evasion, and astonishment. For twelve years Gwynedd Monthly Meeting applied no sanctions and just accepted offenders' expressions of regret. At worst that meant, for example, pardoning a purchaser who desired "Friends to pass it by" because he would not purchase another slave. Radnor, which together with Gwynedd was the most lenient of meetings in many other respects, excused a purchaser in 1771 after merely telling him to consider Friends' testimony on slave trading.[51]

In extenuation of their errors, offenders alleged their extraordinary circumstances: The Negroes were disobedient, unruly, unmanageable, or thieves and had to be sold. I. R. explained that by selling his thieving slave outside the city, he "prevent[ed] his being brought to an untimely end"; yet, he said, he was convinced slavery was wrong. For nine months, Philadelphia Monthly Meeting suspected M. R., who, although warned, sold two slaves because they were "wicked" and unsuited for freedom, she said. T. Y. explained that he had to take a Negro in consideration for a debt or else lose his repayment.[52] Three Friends were proved to have lied to their meetings about their reasons for having slaves. One Friend alleged that he only hired Negroes, but was discovered purchasing them. The two others claimed they had purchased Negroes for benevolent reasons, but they later sold the same Negroes into deprived conditions.[53] Other offenders were candid and surprised at the Society's prosecution of them. Five from Abington found nothing reprehensible about buying slaves. One from Wrightstown angrily refused any response to the Meeting which was annoying him about his "innocent" purchase of a slave. James Pemberton complained in 1763 that the most troublesome way in which Friends came to own slaves was by inheritance. The heirs to this human legacy protested that they were comparatively blameless. At the same time their good fortune provided an inducement to other Friends: These others rationalized that they should be forgiven for purchasing slaves they could not inherit.[54]

Leniency was not the rule in Pennsylvania. Philadelphia, where slaveholders were concentrated, accounted for 47 percent of all the offenses prosecuted under the 1758 minute. Philadelphia Monthly Meeting condemned under the 1758 minute or else disowned twenty-five of its forty-four offenders and pardoned twelve from 1758 through 1774. Throughout Pennsylvania in those same years, Friends condemned or disowned forty-nine of one hundred offenders and pardoned thirty-six.[55] Again, the vigor of Philadelphia Monthly Meeting shows the incongruity between the leadership of the Meeting and the "laity." Slaveholding delinquents from all over the province appear to have been nominal Friends by one standard: As many as 56 percent of them were recidivists (both before and after the slavery offense and for offenses other than slave trading).

In ways not anticipated in 1758, some meetings increased the rigor of their sanctions against slave trading. In 1763, when J. C. brought his marriage proposal to Goshen Monthly Meeting, it denied him permission to marry because he had purchased a slave. Goshen was improvising in this case because the denial of permission was a disability ordinarily placed only upon full delinquents, and J. C. had only been condemned under the 1758 minute. However, J. C. did not appeal and Goshen was never overruled. As early as 1759, Buckingham Monthly Meeting demanded that a slave purchaser free the Negro he had bought. Philadelphia did likewise in 1764. It became dissatisfied with a purchaser's promise of manumission and his later written agreement to manumit because he omitted both the name of the slave boy and a condemnation of the institution of slavery. The Meeting finally pardoned the purchaser after a year, when all the arrangements and papers were satisfactory. The demand of manumission became more common in the early 1770s. Chester demanded that a purchaser educate the Negro he had acquired and execute a written instrument manumitting him which bound the offender's heirs as well as himself. Two years later, Chester demanded that another purchaser, who had freed his slave, also compensate the Negro for his service.[56]

Sales of slaves were much less common than purchases, but were more grievous errors than purchases. When a Friend sold a slave, the Society lost its oversight of the support and the vocational and religious education of the Negro. Also, the prospect of manumission, which was becoming more common, disappeared with each sale. Moreover, the Society had an obvious way to test the goodwill and religious profession of someone who purchased a slave; but this too disappeared with a sale. In almost all cases of sales, the Society apprehended the offense after the slave was sold. In the 1760s, it was customarily satisfied with the pretexts the offenders gave for selling. But later, Friends occasionally demanded that the seller repurchase and immediately free the slave.[57] These demands or sanctions, especially manumission, were extraordinary and were not called for by the discipline. Yet the quarterly meetings and the Yearly Meeting never reversed the impositions; rather, they seemed silently to acquiesce in the practice. Without an amendment to the discipline, abolition was becoming the object of many meetings and of many Friends in the early 1770s. Whereas in 1758 the inertia of slaveholding custom and the opposition of hard-pressed city merchants had slowed the prosecution of slaveowning, and the discipline outdistanced the enthusiasm of many Friends, by roughly 1770, enthusiasm and prosecutions commonly exceeded the demands of the discipline.

Ministers, committeemen, and private Friends were especially painstaking in their promulgation of antislavery doctrine. No one was visited more often than the slaveholders, especially in the 1760s. Slaveholders were made to feel guilty and out of unity with the Society. David Ferris told a Quaker minister and slaveholder "that as the Gospel had not in the Fullness of its Dawning taken place in [the slaveholders'] Minds, it was not likely such could be Ministers of a covenant they themselves were never brought into." George Churchman grew angry at slave-dealing members who presumed to sit in business meetings despite their partial disownment. One of them, a proud woman, "being more wealthy than some of her neighbors . . . could scarcely stoop to the Strictness of discipline."[58]

The ministers saw the evils of slaveholding being proved to them through the misfortunes that overcame Friends and Pennsylvanians and that might continue until they liberated their slaves. Slaveholders, warned Woolman, "incur his heavy displeasure whose Judgments are just and equal, who exalteth and humbleth to the Dust as he seeth meet." When John Churchman attended the general meeting of ministers and elders in Philadelphia in the spring of 1756, in the company of Samuel Fothergill and Catherine Payton, he witnessed a grim spectacle. Two or three bodies of frontier inhabitants were carted through the streets to incense the people against the Indians and stimulate the war effort. People followed the bodies cursing Indians and Quakers. The sight was "very afflicting," Churchman recorded, and "I said within myself, How can this [calamity] be? Since this has been a land of peace, and as yet not much concerned in war; but as it were in a moment, my eyes turned to the case of the poor enslaved Negroes. And however light a matter they who have been concerned in it, may look upon the purchasing, selling, or keeping those oppressed people in slavery, it then appeared plain to me, that such were the partakers of iniquity."[59] In the succeeding war of the Revolution, Friends harangued American leaders with jeremiads pointing out the current awful consequences of slavery in America.

By 1773 at the latest, abolitionist Friends had become unhappy with the minute of 1758 and especially with its indeterminateness. Falls Monthly Meeting queried Bucks Quarterly Meeting in 1773 about how to treat a member previously convicted of slave purchasing when he committed a subsequent, different offense. In 1774, a Friend from Wilmington, Delaware, came to Philadelphia Monthly Meeting with a certificate attesting to his membership insofar as a slave seller could be a member. His case impelled Philadelphia to ask Quarterly and Yearly Meeting to reopen the question of slavery, revise the 1758 minute, and bolster Friends' testimony against a practice "so evidently contrary to our Christian profession, and principles and common rights of mankind." In response, the Yearly Meeting resolved in 1774 to completely disown any Friend who bought, sold, or transferred slaves. Also, any Friend owning slaves suitable for freedom who did not free them had to appear before Yearly Meeting for questioning; all owners had to educate their Negroes for eventual liberty, instruct them in religion, and keep them no longer than white bond servants were obliged to their masters. If they did not comply, they were to be excluded from the Society's business and disciplinary meetings. Now even the most listless meetings showed some spirit on behalf of abolition. Gwynedd reported in 1775 that of eight members who owned slaves, five owners had agreed to manumit ten of them.[60]

In view of the strong minute of 1774 providing for gradual emancipation and its enforcement, it appears as no surprise that Philadelphia Yearly Meeting in 1776 resolved to disown completely Quaker slaveholders who refused to manumit. Yet there was a feeling of urgency in the 1776 Meeting. A committee on emancipation reported that progress was too slow, that too many Friends refused to give up their slaves. This "awful and alarming dispensation" of war, said the committee, reminds Friends of their obligations to grant justice. The resolution to use the strongest sanction against slaveholders, disownment, was not all the Meeting required, however. In a new query to subordinate meetings, it asked whether Friends "use those well who are set free and necessarily under their care, and not in circumstances, through nonage or incapacity, to minister to their own necessities?"[61] The Society did not intend to permit callous slaveholding Friends to escape the burden of supporting aged and infirm Negroes by emancipating and forgetting them.

Although slaveowning officially became a disownable offense at the 1776 Yearly Meeting, Quaker slaveholders had been disowned before then. Since 1758, delinquent slaveholders had been ousted from the Society because they had committed offenses in addition to slaveholding. Between 1758 and 1776, fourteen of eighteen slaveholders who committed an additional offense were disowned. Twenty-one others were disowned for recidivism, or for violating the discipline in some way other than slaveholding. In comparison to the whole body of delinquent Friends, slaveholders were an exceptionally unfaithful lot. They had a rate of recidivism of more than 50 percent, whereas all delinquents had a rate of 10 percent.[62]

After 1776, Anthony Benezet and other Friends labored to persuade
Friends to manumit their slaves rather than suffer disownment, and
then assisted in the arrangements for manumission. In Philadelphia
Quarter, which contained most of the slaves owned by Pennsylvania
Friends, 343 were emancipated between 1772 and 1790. In the Delaware River precincts of Philadelphia Yearly Meeting slavery was more
common, and so too were manumissions. Duck Creek Monthly
Meeting members manumitted more than 600. Warner Mifflin,
husband of Anne Emlen Mifflin, indefatigable abolitionist, and a
member of Duck Creek, liberated 21 and persuaded his father, Daniel
Mifflin, to liberate almost 100. Ironically, when Daniel Mifflin was
fined for not serving in the Revolution and refused to pay, the sheriff
seized a Negro boy and sold him for the fine. The boy had earlier
been emancipated by Mifflin.[63]

Before Philadelphia Yearly Meeting resolved for complete abolition of slavery from its ranks, some Friends were promoting the end
of the slave trade in the province and beyond. After the success of
abolition within the Yearly Meeting, the abolitionists were free to
direct more of their energies outward. In the larger realms of the new
state and nation and in the international commerce in slaves, Friends
quickly set to work and sometimes proved effective.[64] All told, the
abolitionist work was Quakerism's greatest philanthropy.

Abolition and the Context of Quaker Sectarianism

A necessary and critical condition for Friends' adoption of abolition
was their coeval withdrawal from secular society. These two features
of Quaker history from 1755 to 1776 were not merely coincidental,
discrete aspects of the reformation, but rather complementary developments. Before the revolutionary war, the effect of sectarianism on
abolition is especially marked in the synchronous withdrawal from
government and the adoption of abolition measures. In 1758, the
Yearly Meeting placed the first sanction upon officeholding Quakers
(ones who enforced punative laws against pacifist protestors); it
bolstered advice to withdraw with partial disownment of Friends
who refused.[65] The same year the Meeting laid the same sanction on
slaveholders. In 1776, the Yearly Meeting began disowning completely
all Friends who stayed in public offices and also all slaveholders who
did not agree to free their slaves.

As early as 1748, some reforming Friends indicated disenchant-

ment with the uses to which public power was being put. But it was
the decisions of Quaker officeholders made against the background
of the approaching war with France in 1754 that alienated Quaker
reformers. The behavior of the officeholders then and thereafter typi-
fied the concerns of American Whig politicians. The Pennsylvania
Assembly was engaged in a controversy with the Penns which originated early in the 1740s. The clash was an exemplary case of the
tenacity and the success of American Whiggery. Quaker reformers
believed, however, that the holding of political office often jeopardized Quaker testimonies, and found their suspicions confirmed
after 1753. For them, politics and government became not the way
to save America first from proprietary oppression and later from
British oppression, but more likely the way to impose oppression on
one's conscience and on one's brethren. The Whig concerns of American politicians increasingly occupied them after 1763 and drew them
into a consuming insistence on the tyranny of Great Britain. Were
the Society of Friends to have shared this insistence and joined the
Revolution, their other concerns, particularly for abolition among
Friends and all other Americans, would have suffered—just as church
concerns had suffered before 1750 from Quaker leaders' absorption
with politics.

Since the antislavery movement is often said to have thrived in
the revolutionary era and abolition to have succeeded in the Northern states in the following forty years, it may appear implausible that
the war effort competed with the abolition movement for the attention or energies of the revolutionaries. With a common interest in
freedom, did each not succor the other? But the prosperity of antislavery sentiment in this era is more apparent than real. First, as the
historian Donald Robinson points out, "between 1765 and 1780, no
leading politician was brooding much about Negro slavery, or seriously at work on plans to loosen its hold on the nation's life."[66] They
were fighting a war and, at best, had postponed other concerns. From
the drafting of the Declaration of Independence onward, considerations of political and military expediency obliged the revolutionaries
to compromise with the existence of slavery. And once the Revolution was won, new "imperatives" arose which required that abolition
be further postponed, especially for the sake of national unity. Politics functioned to secure compromise and maintain harmony.

Moreover, the sentiment for abolition did not encompass enough
American voters to generate any radical change in the institution of

slavery or to spur political leaders to abolition. In the two Northern states where slavery existed in considerable degrees, New York and New Jersey, gradual abolition came only after 1798 and was so permeated with fraud and evasions that it was as much sham as real.[67] As for the South, the expectation that antislavery would bear fruit focused on Virginia and North Carolina. In Virginia, the ideals of the Revolution supposedly quieted defenders of slavery or converted them to the wisdom (but not the practice) of antislavery. But actually there were masses of vocal, belligerent, proslavery citizens who were untouched by revolutionary enthusiasm for abolition. In North Caro-lina, as we will see, antislavery also had a limited following.[68]

The existence of manumission societies in both the North and the South has helped to enhance the misleading impression of the popularity of abolition. The trouble is that there was a great deal of redundancy among abolition groups: In all states having abolition societies, except for Connecticut and Kentucky, "Quakers were the chief organizers and most active supporters." Three-fourths of the most active members of the Pennsylvania Abolition Society were Friends; one-half in the New York Manumission Society. In the South, North Carolina accounted for 37 percent of Southern antislavery organizations, and in these, Friends comprised as much as 80 percent of the members. These organizations were subsidiaries of the North Carolina Manumission Society, and writes John M. Shay, "its membership, leadership, and philosophy were overwhelmingly Quaker."[69] The Quaker members were especially immigrants from Pennsylvania and New England.

Other churches that had shown a heartening interest in aboli-tion—Methodist, Baptist, and Presbyterian—had retreated into silence by 1795. Of Baptists in the South, Shay says that they failed as abolitionists because they were "like other major Protestant denom-inations . . . Southerners first and Baptists second." Unlike Friends, their every reaction was not shaped by their religion, their world view not determined by it.[70]

The plight of a minority of zealous abolitionists in an unsympa-thetic democracy has been treated most thoughtfully by Aileen Krad-itor in her work *Means and Ends in American Abolition*. Her subject is William Lloyd Garrison and the American Anti-Slavery Society, but her comments upon them apply to earlier, Quaker abolitionists too. Kraditor uses the insights of philosopher George Santayana to illuminate the abolitionists' situation and to defend radicals like

Garrison from the critics who condemn Garrison's scorn for the customary methods of democratic politics. According to Santayana, democracy presupposes that "all concerned are fundamentally unanimous, and that each has a plastic nature which he is willing to modify." In such a political system, "all questions at issue must be minor matters; fundamentals must have been silently agreed upon and taken for granted when the democracy arose." Truly inestimable things will never be risked in an election. "To leave a decision to the majority is like leaving it to chance—a fatal decision unless one is willing to have it either way.[71] Neither the Garrisonians nor Friends were willing to rest with the matter either way; neither were plastic and neither easily fit the American die—nor were slaveholders malleable respecting their peculiar property. The Civil War and the following struggles over civil rights prove that slavery and racism were in no sense minor matters in the American ideology that could be subject to negotiation within the political mechanisms of American democracy. Slavery was assured from the outset; antislavery was foreclosed. "The Northern states adopted us with our slaves, and we adopted them with their Quakers," pronounced Congressman William Smith of South Carolina in 1791.[72] In view of the general acquiescence in slavery, radical methods like Garrison's were reasonable; conventional politics would never have got abolition to the ballot. The question regarding Friends is not, however, whether their methods were radical and unwise, but whether they would have become abolitionists at all had they not withdrawn from American government. According to Santayana, they would not.

Santayana describes the kind of people who can espouse radical changes. He mentions specifically Christian martyrs and Protestant reformers, but his description also fits reformist Friends: "they were not plastic and would never consent to lead the life dear or at least customary to other men"; "they insulated themselves from society around them"; they "live a jealous, private, unstained life of their own."[73]

Sydney James accounts for Quaker involvement in abolition by suggesting that through their philanthropy Friends attempted to acquit themselves with Americans, serving causes that Americans respected.[74] That explanation is inconsistent with the fact of the Quaker isolationist sentiment described earlier in this book. But more important for the history of abolition, the premise is wrong: Americans did not share the sentiment that would have permitted

Friends to ingratiate themselves by becoming abolitionists. The history of the Connecticut Society for the Promotion of Freedom is instructive in light of the motive that James attributes to Quaker abolitionists. According to James Essig, this weak reed of abolition existed mostly as a means for Connecticut clergy to overcome estrangement between themselves and the laity. Abolition was to be a cooperative enterprise of clergy and laity to help the clergymen reestablish their leadership and status among respectable laymen. It may have done that, but it did almost nothing for abolition.[75] Had Quaker-led abolition societies existed for similar reasons, we might expect that they would have been as ineffectual and barren as the Connecticut Society. They were not; and one reason for their effectiveness was that they existed truly for abolition and not for establishing liasons with respectable non-Quakers.

If abolition advanced in the revolutionary era, it did so mostly because Friends criticized the priorities and postponements of American leaders and themselves took the lead. Had Friends remained at the political center in Pennsylvania (or in the United States) as they were before 1755, it is not to be presumed (as Daniel Boorstin does) that they would have championed the most severe reform in American history or that they would have championed it so long and doggedly. It is unlikely that Quakers in the line and mold of Isaac Norris, Sr., and John Kinsey would have been friendlier to abolitionists than Norris or Kinsey had been to Southeby, Farmer, Sandiford, and Lay. Before the church welcomed abolition, it first moved away from political concerns and toward the periphery of American society. There it did not need to compromise with people whose values it disparaged and whose membership it did not court. By becoming less a party to society, it became, as Reinhold Niebuhr describes the church, "that place in human society where men are disturbed by the word of the eternal God, which stands as a judgment upon human aspirations."[76] Were the Quaker church to have remained as much a twin of the state as it had been in early Pennsylvania, it is doubtful that Friends would have been so acutely disturbed by slavery and even more doubtful that they would have judged severely the priorities of their countrymen at the birth of the nation.

The new emphasis on asceticism and simplicity had an effect too, for the promotion of abolition. Friends believed that avarice was perhaps the foremost reason that men had slaves. While emphasizing that race prejudice specified Negroes as fit for slavery, Woolman argued that avarice foreclosed the possibility that a slaveholder would impartially examine his faulty reasoning for enslaving Negroes. The corrective was for him to forego the advantages that slaveholding brought to his making his livelihood, specifically, to give up the prospect of gaining more property. If Friends were made ascetics, according to Woolman, the problem of abolition would largely disappear. Second, avarice and licentiousness had led to slaveholding, but slaveholding in turn reinforced these and other personal evils. Here was a cycle of evil. Having complete mastery over other human beings undoubtedly fosters pride and a host of cardinal sins—sexual license, indolence, egregious appetites, and conspicuous consumption—which need more wealth in order to be satisfied. In this condition, a Friend could not attain essential Christian meekness and humility. Slaveholding, avarice, and pride disabled Friends as parents and pedagogues and jeopardized the continuance of the church. The concern over protection of property and the dread of any interruption in accustomed styles of life quashed the pacifist inclinations of wealthy Friends. To adopt a metaphor from Woolman, these testimonies were links in a chain, each serving the other and creating the strength of the whole.

The symbiotic effect of this mix of religious testimonies appears all the more certain because of the appearance of such testimonies and their similar effect among American evangelicals at approximately the same time. A number of social critics appeared among the Baptists, Methodists, and Presbyterians of the late eighteenth century. They included several of the most eminent clergy in American religious history, including the Methodists Francis Asbury and Thomas Coke. Like Friends, these men were pronounced ascetics for preaching humility, simplicity, and meekness, and for glorifying poverty and decrying avarice. They were grave and serious, cursed by Southern gentry for their puritannical criticism of life in the South. They would have ended gaity, drunkenness, gambling, horse racing, and cursing among Southern gentry had they had their way. For them, as for Friends, *the world* was a term for alien values and danger. Like Friends, they saw slaveholding as the effect of avarice and the cause of most of the other evils they decried. In the condition of the slaves they saw something of their own humble lives reflected. They shared with the slaves the same persecutors.[77]

From the 1760s through the 1790s, these evangelicals labored to put their respective denominations behind the cause of emancipation. But they quickly learned that to champion abolition, they and their churches would have to forego the dearest prospect of their lives—the addition of thousands of converts to their ranks. For Methodists and Baptists especially, the harvest of souls would likely occur in the South. It would not occur, however, if the churches required converts to manumit their slaves or discouraged brethren from their dreams of a future made comfortable by the wealth that slaves afforded. By the end of the century, the issue had been resolved by these evangelical abolitionists, or for them: Their churches would neither espouse abolition nor insist upon it. Instead, they assimilated American slavery with its accompanying evils. Aggrieved consciences were salved with the thought that although slaves were still enslaved, their evangelized souls could be freed from the bondage of sin.[78]

What the Society uniquely displayed was the resoluteness to insist upon abolition from its members. Individual Friends would not be allowed to ignore Quaker abolitionist strictures—as Southern Methodists ignored the orders of their General Conference.[79] Nor would Quaker meetings shift to accommodate the balky members, as the Methodist Conference did. Stern discipline cost the Society of Friends hundreds of members and afforded little prospect of attracting many converts. It also stimulated envy and anger. All this is saying once again that Friends chose a sectarian course for themselves, knowing that if they did not cut as large a figure in American life as they had done in William Penn's day, they could at least preserve their integrity.

Methodism and Baptism grew marvelously in America after the Revolution and were reckoned to have prospered. Quakerism shrank and suffered in the South. But because Friends did not define the prosperity of Christianity in an evangelical or democratic way, and because they more often thought of suffering and servanthood when they looked for evidence of Christian progress, they were content with their chosen lot and especially with their abolition.

Conclusion

Quakerism changed considerably between the seventeenth and eighteenth centuries; new testimonies against slavery, war, and other oppressions accounted for much of the change. Despite these very considerable and obvious differences, the Quakerism that emerged in America after 1755 revived some of the spirit of the seventeenth-century while forms changed. It was a reformation in the sense that it was a return to original character, a re-forming of it. Seventeenth-century Quakerism had supported a host of eccentric, holy men and women—in the opinion of many Englishmen the whole Society was a set of eccentrics. For at least half the Society—the women Friends—Mary Maples Dunn believes, "It is possible that the Quakers became a closed, withdrawn society in part so that the women could live more comfortably with a social role that was not universally accept-able."[80] But as time passed, toleration in England increased and the behavior of Friends became merely quaint and routine. Then, within the Society, the eccentrics were not tolerated; they were an embar-rassment to Friends. In that era Quakerism was planted in Pennsyl-vania and grew, and toleration within the Society fared none the better for the divisions and worldly prosperity among early Pennsyl-vania Friends. But after 1755, when Friends discovered they were less and less appreciated by their contemporaries, the old spirit of inno-vation and of eccentricity reappeared and flourished, almost it seemed, measure for measure with secular society's dislike of Friends. As the Society of Friends gravitated away from the center of American soci-ety, it became a greater sanctuary for odd, holy men and women. Eccentrics were no longer cut off in order to redeem the reputation of the whole church with secular society; instead, the church supported or indulged them. In this, the most important respect of all, the reformers were true heirs to the founders.

THE POLITICAL
REFORMATION

6

Prologue to Reform,
1739-1755

Quaker Hegemony: The 1740s

Whenever the date that Quakers decided to withdraw from the government of Pennsylvania, it would mark the close of an epoch. To many Americans and Europeans, Pennsylvania was almost synonymous with Quakerism—deservedly or not. Benjamin Franklin, a deist, found that because he came from Pennsylvania, in France he was presumed a Quaker.[1] Once most Quaker politicians renounced public office after 1756, the Society of Friends could still not avoid being credited with either the blame or the praise for whatever happened in the province. Pennsylvania was the Quaker province and whenever Friends renounced their leadership of its government, it would punctuate a renowned era in the minds of many Westerners.

When Friends did make their exit beginning in 1756, the time was extraordinary beyond the mere fact of change or abandonment of an originally Quaker enterprise. It came at a uniquely Quaker period in the politics of the province and at a time of unprecedented need by Quakers for their continued control. Friends had always had the predominating hand in the government of Pennsylvania. For most of its provincial past, Friends did not preside at the apex of the executive branch of the government—the governors or lieutenant-governors were not Friends, with one exception. The sons and heirs of William and Hannah Penn, proprietors of the province, also were not Friends in spirit or, later, in name. But beyond that, the executive branch or magistracy of Pennsylvania was Quaker in large part. The Assembly was Quaker-led and Quaker-controlled before 1756, and the members were mostly Quakers. The judiciary and the law codes were Quaker or bore the marks of Quaker authorship. The question therefore remains, What distinguished the time of the Quaker exit from a past of uniformly Quaker leadership?

First, never before the 1740s had Friends in Pennsylvania been politically united. The greatest single blot on the history of the ambitious Holy Experiment is the internecine fighting that sprang up among Friends within seven years after the founding of Pennsylvania.[2] The fighting did not cease until 1711. In the preceding twenty-two years it contributed to a schism in the Society of Friends and the temporary loss of the province to royal control (1693–94). By 1721, the factionalism was reborn. Only in 1726, when a few Friends realized that the provincial constitution and Quaker hegemony were completely jeopardized by Friends' myopic quarreling, did the internecine feuding subside.[3] After a hiatus in the 1730s, when political affiliations and contests hardly existed, a unique feature in Pennsylvania's politics appeared—the Quaker party.[4] Here was a party behind which almost all Friends united, whose uppermost concerns included the maintenance of the Quaker quality of Pennsylvania government, and whose leaders were overwhelmingly Quaker. With turnovers in personnel and despite minor setbacks, the party dominated provincial politics until 1770. The name Quaker stuck to it long after most Friends had departed it. But never did the party experience greater success and unity than in its first decade, the 1740s, when it was unmistakably the Quaker party, pursuing Quaker objectives.

The second unique feature of the 1740s was the threat to Quaker politics. Quaker governance had been threatened and forfeited before— in 1693 and 1694. But the similarity between the 1690s and the 1740s is superficial. In the 1690s, the move to replace the provincial charter and repress Quakerism was sparked by royal officials and a few Anglicans in America, using their influence in London.[5] The animus against Quaker government in the 1740s was far more widespread and indigenous to Pennsylvania. Rivals to the Quaker leaders searched for some purchase upon Quaker control. Indeed, they felt entitled to supercede Quakers, for they shared few of the presumptions about the peculiarly Quaker quality of Pennsylvania governance and they knew well how small a portion of Pennsylvania Friends

comprised in 1740. Unlike the 1690s, Quaker voters could not overcome any other group at the polls; allies were a necessity. The Penn
family could no longer be counted upon to defend Quaker politics;
the sons of William Penn were among the enemy. And English
government, the great hazard in past eras, was as likely to be counted
among the enemies as among the friends of Quakerism. Therefore,
the list of Quakers' enemies was longer than ever before while the
old sureties of Quaker government were diminished.

The desire of the Quakers' detractors in the 1740s was to oust
Friends from the Pennsylvania House of Representatives. They
attempted it in two ways. They tried to have the king or Parliament
order Friends out, and they tried to vote Friends out at the polls.
Lieutenant-Governor George Thomas was the first to approach the
British government with the suggestion that it oust the Friends. Quaker
power in Pennsylvania was intolerable, he complained to the Board
of Trade, and it jeopardized the security of the empire.[6] Thomas's
complaints arose from the unwillingness of the representatives to
follow his advice that Pennsylvania assist Great Britain in its current
war with Spain—the War of Jenkins' Ear. Thomas requested a provincial militia, enlistments in the regular British army, and supplies and
appropriations. He got none of these in satisfactory ways or amounts.[7]
Thomas became enraged and concluded that being Quaker, regardless of a man's incumbency in the House or his politics, was reason
enough for disqualification from public office. He was specifically
attacking the Society of Friends, and not just a political party. He
suggested to the Board of Trade that it must somehow disqualify
Friends from office.

Others shared Thomas's enthusiasm for disqualifying all Friends.
In the fall of 1741, a year after Thomas's complaint to the board, a
petition to the board was prepared and signed by 265 Philadelphia
merchants and professional men. The petitioners rehearsed the supine
situation of Pennsylvania in the current war and blamed it on Quaker
legislators, whose religion allegedly stopped them from defending
Pennsylvanians. Thomas Penn carried the petition to the board, the
Penns' legal counsel prosecuted it, and the Penns lobbied on its behalf.[8]

Against this concert of their enemies, the Friends in Pennsylvania
(with the inestimable assistance of their English brethren) triumphed
completely. In May 1743, the Privy Council Committee on Plantation Affairs (parent body to the Board of Trade) decided that the king
had no authority to alter the electoral system in Pennsylvania. He

might advise Parliament to alter it, but he should entertain that notion only in grave circumstances. The situation in Pennsylvania, the committee concluded, did not constitute a grave danger to the lives and property of Englishmen, despite the representations of the governor and 265 petitioners. Friends were elated with the decision. Their opponents were despondent and divided, attributing to each other the failure of their cherished scheme to rid themselves of their Quaker nemesis.[9] The Philadelphia petitioners produced a second such petition in 1744, but it fared even worse then the first, dying of inattention in London.[10]

The other means to oust Friends from the legislature was the ballot box. In the October 1740 Assembly election, when the controversy over defense was old enough that issues, Quaker partisans, and their opponents were identified, the Quaker party won a gratifying victory. The voter turnout was the greatest in Pennsylvania to that date and Friends took it as validation of their policy. The next year, while the defense controversy raged and the petition to the board was being prepared, all was calm in the House. The members were of one mind in almost all matters, Isaac Norris II reported. The opponents of the Quaker party had not one man in the House. They could not even learn what was happening there, so tight-lipped were the Quaker party representatives.[11] (The sessions of the House were closed to the public, as they had always been.) They were left wringing their hands and guessing what mischief the assemblymen would next spring upon them.

The election of 1742 was one of a half-dozen most notable ones in colonial Pennsylvania. The Quakers' antagonists, usually identified as the Proprietary party, drafted candidates and made up tickets, courted voters, and generally prepared to give the Quakers a "warm" challenge. They believed that their complaints against the Quakers had such obvious merit that the voters might well turn the tide of Quaker power that had been running strongly since 1739. They failed. The Quaker party triumphed in all the counties, but attention focused on the city where a riot occurred at the polling place.[12] Blame for the riot was effectively put on the Proprietary party and censure was heaped upon it from many quarters. The result, almost forgotten in the recriminations over the riot, was the defeat of the Proprietary party ticket. Together with the failure of the petition in the Privy Council committee, the failure to vote Friends out of office chastened the Proprietary party. It did not mount another election chal-

lenge for the next twelve years. In effect, there was only one party in
Pennsylvania then, the Quaker party. The opposition was a dispirited, bickering number of individuals.

From 1741 through 1750, there were no more than eleven non-
Quakers among the fifty-two men who sat in the House. Only four
of these non-Quakers sat in the tempestuous years before 1745. But
the religious affiliations of the eleven made no political difference,
for they all voted like Quakers.[13]

War was the stimulus to this partisanship in Pennsylvania and
the lever that Quakers' enemies tried to use in London and Pennsylvania to pry the Quakers out of office. With the arrival of international peace in 1748, Quaker politicians were well satisfied with
their policy and record in that decade. They had refused to create a
militia in Pennsylvania, to assist the enlisting of Pennsylvanians
into the regular army, and to prepare a naval defense of Philadelphia
and its shipping. Occasionally, they even criticized the details of
British military planning. Their hegemony in Pennsylvania was secure
and nearly unchallenged. Their popularity was proven and reproven
each October at the polls. Their concerns for the interference from
the king and Parliament was allayed by the clear success of the
Quaker lobby in London. Greater success and security cannot easily
be imagined. H. L. Osgood, historian of the colonial wars, writes,
"One can imagine the serene content and contempt with which the
Quakers viewed the costly and futile plans [of the British mili-
tary]. . . . The peace of Pennsylvania had not been disturbed except
by rumors of war, and in view of the issue as a whole, who could
have desired a more complete justification of the Quaker argument?"[14]

These were the circumstances of a people who in the next pitched
encounter with their political adversaries voluntarily decided to leave
public office. It is not surprising that the most useful argument of
Quakers who resisted leaving office was the wisdom and popularity
of Quaker governance, proven in the 1740s to all but the most partisan opponents of the Quakers and to a coalescing group of Quaker
reformers.

While Quaker reformers of the 1750s venerated the memory of
William Penn and other earliest Pennsylvanians, they showed little
filiopietism toward succeeding generations of provincial politicians.
In their own day, rather than being proud, they became deeply skep-
tical of the merits of Quaker governance. That judgment was colored

by their understanding of the intervening generations. Whether their low estimate of Quaker performance was correct or not is moot; they nevertheless held it strongly.

These Friends did not espouse abandoning government in order to escape being tainted by the world beyond the Society of Friends. Instead, they had a vision that more might be done for society, or its suffering members, from a private station and in a philanthropic way. Their choice provoked disagreement in their own time and thereafter about whether these Friends had chosen correctly—the private means over the public.[15] Again, the question is moot.

The Wages of Whiggery

For a pacifist, nonviolent people like Friends, occupying executive and judicial offices in government raised inherent problems. Magistrates had to sentence criminals to punishments including death. The history of the province is sewn with enemies and gadflies of Quakerism who pointed out the inconsistencies between profession and practice.[16] Friends could not avoid such challenges. Did any degree of complicity with such magisterial duties violate Quaker nonviolence? If not, how deeply involved might a Friend become?

Wars raised less subtle problems.[17] Friends positively could not serve as combatants or command and direct armies and navies. For that reason, only one Friend ever served as governor of Pennsylvania, because the office obliged him to defend the province in case of war. Less exalted officials of the province might well escape any complicity with warfare and, in fact, almost always did. Until 1754, England's wars were remote from Pennsylvania.

Pennsylvania's Quaker legislators would seem to have been less likely to jeopardize their ethics than would other officers of the government. Passing criminal laws might not taint a Friend's nonviolence in the way or degree that enforcing the law would. Wartime situations need not conflict with a legislator's pacifism either. Yet however innocuous a legislator's office might appear, his jeopardy would depend upon the demands of his historical situation and the exact confines of Quaker pacifist ethics. In the 1750s, his historical situation was a complicated one and the reformers in the Society attempted to make his pacifism even more confining.

Quaker pacifism prohibited Quaker legislators from enacting laws that raised and equipped armies or navies and directed their use—though it was unlikely for a legislator to have to make laws directing their use. No Quaker-controlled Assembly in Pennsylvania ever violated that prohibition. However insensitive some Friends in the Assembly may have been to the finer points of pacifism, the majority never seriously contemplated so gross a breach of their ethics. To these Friends belonged the credit that no Pennsylvanian was conscripted and no Friend, Mennonite, or other pacifist ever had to have his pacifism tested by a draft. For their refusal, the legislators suffered the abuse of nonpacifist detractors. When they did not measure up to the demands of their ethics and the expectations of their more scrupulous brethren, it was on a finer scale of pacifism that their breaches were measured.

When the Quaker ethic on pacifism prescribed that Friends must not equip armies, it meant that administrators and legislators must not get involved in any details of accoutering, paying, housing, or feeding the combatants. Because nonpacifist Englishmen and Pennsylvanians found this disability so sweeping, Quaker legislators were hard pressed at times to defend their participation in government. They would surely have declined their offices or been forced out had it not been for a recourse available to them in their ethics. The legislators could raise and contribute money to all the functions of war as long as they did not specify what bellicose need the money was intended to satisfy, and did not themselves spend the money for warlike uses. Friends believed that a Christian could ethically supply money to his sovereign even when the sovereign—a non-Quaker—used it to prosecute wars. That was the construction that seventeenth-century Friends put upon Jesus' response to the Pharisees in Matthew, chapter 22: "Render therefore unto Caesar the things that are Caesar's and unto God the things that are God's." The precept required all Quaker private citizens to pay their taxes to their sovereign without protest. By extrapolating from the individual taxpayer to the Pennsylvania Assembly, where Friends predominated, the Society required that Quaker legislators supply the king or queen's demands for money. Historically the monarch rarely demanded money from the colonial legislature and then only in wartime. Sometimes the monarch asked explicitly for supplies or the payment of troops. All the Friends ever gave was money "for the King's (or Queen's) use." The king or queen was well satisfied with the money.[18]

Thus far no ethical problems arose for Friends. It is only when a yet undisclosed allegiance of the Quaker assemblymen enters the picture that Friends encountered trouble. Then the assemblymen angered their more scrupulous brethren, their proprietor, king, fellow Pennsylvanians, and many English Friends. In almost all of the American colonies assemblymen had waged a protracted contest with the executive over power and prerogatives. These contests were the most pervasive and distinguishing single feature of colonial politics. Pennsylvanians had fought their contest with the executive for local assembly power as well as any colonists and better than most. By 1701, with William Penn's grant of the "Charter of Liberties," Pennsylvania had gained a degree of local self-government that was the envy of most colonists. Even so, the Pennsylvanians continued to enlarge upon the Charter's concessions.[19]

When wars coincided with these contests, assemblymen might bargain for power with their king, proprietor, or governor, who needed the colonists' assistance against foreign enemies. Friends had no ethical problem in so bargaining except when the power they desired was the exclusive control of expenditures. In peacetime they could ethically exercise total control; but in wartime they would violate their pacifism if they used such power. Their option was to relinquish the power of expenditure to the executive, and perhaps never get it back again. Thus, they would reverse the direction of colonial political development, the growth of assembly power. It was a high price to pay for one's pacifist scruples. Their pacifism clearly handicapped them in a wartime contest for power with king, queen, royal governor, or in Pennsylvania in the 1750s, with proprietor Thomas Penn and his lieutenant-governors.

In the 1750s, an ongoing contest between the Quaker Assembly and Thomas Penn reached a white heat while an international war broke out in the very province of Pennsylvania. At this juncture the pacifism and abnegation of Quaker legislators was tested as never before. In 1748, Penn had vowed to stop the erosion of this power. Particularly, he wished to secure his control over the amount and use of provincial paper currency and appropriations. Whenever the Assembly's bills on these subjects displeased him, he would veto any and all of them.[20]

Penn's vow was bound to stir up the anger of the assemblymen because they already mistrusted Penn. In the 1740s, he had tried to have the British permanently exclude Friends from public office in

Pennsylvania. In a province which many Friends considered their country and its government their patrimony, such an exclusion was scandalous. That the son of William Penn would so dishonor the memory of his father encouraged Friends' worst suspicions about him. Having earlier failed to exclude Friends from office, Penn appeared ready to render them powerless in their offices in the 1750s.[21] From 1751 to 1754, Penn exhausted whatever goodwill he had left as he and his lieutenant-governors vetoed the Assembly's money bills one after another. His sphinx-like posture and the lame excuses that his governors gave for their vetoes fueled the assemblymen's worst suspicions about Penn's guile and malice. Without being a myopic, radical Whig, a Quaker assemblyman could discover to his satisfaction a pattern of jealousy and deceit in Penn's behavior since 1741. In this time of impending war, the question for Quaker legislators was how far could they go in attempting to stop Penn?

In February 1754, His Majesty's Secretary of State ordered that if the French encroached upon Pennsylvania, Pennsylvania must prepare to repel them and the Assembly must supply the armed force.[22] In Quaker parlance, that was Caesar speaking. The Assembly could not refuse money without offending the English government and violating the Quaker obligation to render unto Caesar. But the secretary's order brought a welcome prospect as well as a problem. The Assembly could draft an appropriations bill but one that was so self-serving, so carefully constructed to leave with the Assembly all power for deciding how and when any money would be spent, that it would be almost useless. If Penn again tried to stop such mischief, he would have to veto the appropriation, but at the same time risk the crown's anger for obstructing the defense of the empire. Penn might escape the crown's anger if only he could explain to the English that the Assembly equally obstructed the defense by its clever, aggressive bill. The Assembly was out to control the appropriations process almost regardless of the effect upon imperial defenses. In sum, Penn and the Assembly would both have to wage a press campaign at Whitehall and Westminster to let the English learn as much or as little about the obstructions in Pennsylvania as benefited one or the other's case.

In May, Lieutenant-Governor James Hamilton transmitted to the Assembly intelligence from George Washington about the strength of the French at Ft. Duquesne on the Ohio River. Quickly the Assembly sent to Hamilton an appropriation bill loaded with self-serving provisions. Hamilton tried to delete the provisions, but the House would not have it. It told Hamilton that the means, time, and terms of raising and spending money was its right, always had been, and always would be. He had no right to interfere upon any pretext whatever. Hamilton vetoed the bill.[23]

Two months later, the French drove Washington and his Virginians out of western Pennsylvania. The Assembly registered the shock, and tacitly its obligation to act, by voting to emit £35,000 of currency, only £15,000 of it for the king, and the rest for itself. Hamilton vetoed the measure because of the £20,000 difference. In December, the secretary of state unconditionally ordered Pennsylvania to help provision two regiments of the British army en route to America. Instead of attending to the secretary's order, the exasperated assemblymen resolved to petition the king against their governor's and Penn's behavior—in order, they said, to preserve their civil and *religious* liberties.[24]

When the assemblymen claimed to be protecting their religious liberties, they were forcing a false analogy with the 1740s. In the 1740s, the Penns and their collaborators in Pennsylvania had tried to exclude Friends from the legislature because of their very religion. In 1754, no one had threatened or attempted to oust Friends. Penn and his governors had vetoed appropriations bills, but that did not threaten religious liberties. The assemblymen were badly confusing their religion with politics, and confessing that they had come to treat Pennsylvania government as a Quaker prerogative. To attack the Assembly was not to abuse any religious denomination.

The petition that the Assembly drafted did not explicitly claim that Thomas Penn had violated their religious liberties. However, there was an undertone of religious grievance throughout the whole document. Without informing the king of its final constitutional objective—the exclusive control of expenditure—the House fully informed him of the constitutional obstruction to the exercise of that power—Penn's vetoes. If the ministers at Whitehall thereupon blamed Penn for the impasse in Pennsylvania, they might insist he approve whatever appropriations bill the House offered him. The House would win the contest. Also, to disarm an accusation sure to come, that the assemblymen would not or ethically could not help to defend the empire, the petition informed the king that the House had contributed *on its own* £5,000 to the war effort. It was clever scheming, but it was also unethical.[25]

The £5,000 the House had laid out to ingratiate itself with the crown was entirely controlled by the House. It authorized seven of its members including Speaker Isaac Norris and James Pemberton, Israel's brother, to spend the sum on provisions for the king's troops.[26] The assemblymen were not rendering to Caesar; they were Caesar. Their violation of Quaker ethics opens the whole question of their motive: If the assemblymen's premier concern was to preserve their civil and religious liberties under the charter, why did they violate the religion they professed to revere?

None of the assemblymen's consciences pained them then or in the next three months, because after the three-month lapse, the Assembly, in April 1755, answered a request from Massachusetts by supplying £15,000 "for the King's use." The money was real, but the form was sham. The Assembly gave the money not to the king and not directly to Massachusetts, but to a committee of seven appointees to purchase provisions.[27] Yet by using the language "for the King's use," the Quaker legislators had acknowledged that they knew ethics were involved.

In January 1755, Isaac Norris and other legislators had tried to have the Society of Friends officially enter the contest on their behalf. Norris and William Callender wrote to the London Meeting for Sufferings asking it to help support the Assembly's petition to the king. Nothing less than the destruction of the charter of Pennsylvania was at stake in the current confrontation between Penn and the House, they asserted. Also, James Pemberton asked Henton Brown, a merchant member of the Meeting, for the same favor. "In every part of their conduct towards the people of this province for some years past [the proprietors] appear to be aiming to subvert the . . . charters from King Charles," Pemberton wrote. "We can no longer pretend to . . . being . . . freemen"; the proprietors "seem bent on enslaving us."[28]

In the 1740s, the London Meeting for Sufferings had done a superlative job of defending Pennsylvania Friends against attempts to oust them from the provincial government.[29] Naturally, the Pennsylvanians looked again to the London Meeting to "defend" them. At first glance a request might appear appropriate, but heads not turned by Pemberton's fustian prose would discover that the request was improper and possibly unethical. The Meeting for Sufferings was an official organ of the Society of Friends and operated on behalf of patently Quaker concerns. But in this case no one was attacking the Society of Friends and obliging the Society to reply. Rather, some

Pennsylvanians were asking the Society to defend their legislature's power. In this request the petitioners had lost sight of the difference between a religious body and a government. In what was probably his most percipient moment ever, Isaac Norris summarized the whole inclination of the Assembly since 1739: "we [assemblymen] have very much thrown our dispute from being a Quaker cause, to a cause of liberty."[30]

At Whitehall Penn routed the Quaker Assembly so deftly that it hardly appeared a contest. At the end of King George's War, Lord Halifax, the sternest president of the Board of Trade since the early eighteenth century, set about reducing the autonomy of the colonies.[31] Penn cultivated Halifax unflaggingly and discovered how neatly his will for Pennsylvania complemented Halifax's reformist program. The whole Cabinet Council knew of Penn's resolve to best the Pennsylvania Assembly. Not an Englishman could be found there or elsewhere in the government who faulted Penn.

Penn relished the spectacle of the Assembly forging its way to Whitehall and defeat. He helped the Assembly inflate the dimensions of the international crisis because he knew that the blame would accrue to the Assembly: Press the House constantly for money, he told Lieutenant-Governor Robert Hunter Morris; if it adjourns, recall it; "in the most pathetick Manner beseech & conjure them to consider the impending Ruin to themselves and their Country." "The more indecent their behavior is[,] the better." When Penn told the secretary of state that the assemblymen were going to complain to the king about himself and Morris, the secretary asked whom they would complain to, the king of England or the king of France? "I despise all their representations to the last degree," Penn sneered.[32] It was such anger and determination as this that colored the Pennsylvania Friends' opinions of Penn and propelled them to overrun their ethics in order to chastise Penn.

English Brethren and Dubious Friends

Before 1755, London Friends had not been privy to the grievances of the Quaker brethren in the Pennsylvania Assembly nor had they figured in the Pennsylvanians' stratagems. With no knowledge of Pennsylvania political history and no first-hand experience with Penn's provocations, English Friends were not likely to have responded enthusiastically to the request that the Pennsylvanians pressed upon them. The Americans had sent off their request in high dudgeon, but the Londoners, who did not read it in a like mood, discovered its errors and fatuity. The Meeting for Sufferings immediately recognized the impropriety of their receiving a letter from Norris and Callender and passed the letter on to Richard Partridge, the province's agent in England: political requests to political lobbyists. A deputation from the Meeting visited Penn anyway and came away doubly convinced that the contest between Penn and the Assembly was not its business.[33]

For reasons unknown to the Pennsylvania assemblymen, the Meeting for Sufferings was not the willing collaborator against Thomas Penn that they had expected. Without doubt, the Meeting had acted correctly regarding Norris's request and the Assembly petition to the crown; but some eminent members of the Meeting had improper motives for denying assistance. Since 1751, at least two members had been collaborating with Penn and the British government to protect the Ohio River Valley and to speculate in Ohio lands. The foremost of these Friends was John Hanbury. He was the premier Englishman among a number of speculators, mostly Virginians, who had organized the Ohio Company. With Capel and Osgood Hanbury, he controlled the tobacco trade with Maryland and conducted a large part of that trade with Virginia. His ties to Virginians were numerous and long standing. In England, Hanbury enjoyed access to the members of the Board of Trade, privy councillors, the secretary of state, and to Thomas Penn, among others. To gain the support of such powerful officials for his land venture, Hanbury explained to them that the Ohio Company's interest complemented the public interest. By settling the Ohio country, he and the Virginians would raise a barrier against the encroaching French. With Penn, Hanbury promoted the construction of a fortified trading post on the Ohio River. In 1751, Penn agreed to contribute more than £400 to the construction of the fort—but only if the Pennsylvania Assembly would commit twice as much to it.[34]

No one needed to alert Penn that the Quaker assemblymen would balk at constructing a fort, and so he made a concession to their pacifism. He would purchase the arms and ammunition and leave them free to apply their contribution to the project as they saw fit.[35] However, the distinction that Penn proposed—between the supply of weapons and nonweapons—was Penn's invention and no part of Quaker ethics.

Although Hanbury never urged any Quaker to vote or plump for the fort, he was an author of the plan to induce the Quaker Assembly to help construct it. Because John and Capel Hanbury were members of the London Meeting for Sufferings, it was their responsibility to help protect Friends from the harm that might come their way because of their religious profession. In past decades, the Meeting had labored assiduously to have the government tolerate Friends, then tolerate their nonjuring, and to reduce the penalties laid upon Friends who chose to suffer rather than violate their consciences in various ways.[36] Now, at least one of the Meeting members schemed at defensive war and in a way that induced his brethren to violate their faith.

Friends in Pennsylvania appear never to have learned of Hanbury's role in Penn's request to them. Even if they had, they could have accused Hanbury only of conspiring to violate Quaker ethics, because no fort was erected on the Ohio River until the British army did so in 1758. When Governor James Hamilton urged the plan for a fort upon the assemblymen in 1751, they politely reminded him of their religious persuasion and for the most part kept silent.[37] The project languished. The Ohio Company persevered. By 1754, the French unmistakably threatened the company's interest and Penn's. More than ever before, the company needed a speedy response to the French encroachments and desired to see the British and Pennsylvanians raise and equip an army to oust the French. The delays from the statehouse in Philadelphia were exasperating.

Demagoguery

While Penn and the Quaker assemblymen maneuvered against each other in 1755, a stranger to the contest, the Reverend William Smith, appeared on the scene and dealt a blow to both the Quaker politicians and the whole Society of Friends as well. Smith was a Scottish Anglican priest, the first provost of the College of Philadelphia, and a projector of several educational and cultural institutions in America.[38] When Pennsylvania was only a prospect in his future, he memorialized the Society for the Propagation of the Gospel in Foreign Parts to educate the Germans in Pennsylvania. He meant Anglicize them. The "Society for Propagating Christian Knowledge among the Germans settled in Pennsylvania" was founded in London to advance Smith's proposal. The Reverend Dr. Samuel Chandler, the eminent Presbyterian pastor at Old Jewry in London and a friend of the Church of England, became its secretary.[39] In Pennsylvania, friends of the proprietors became the trustees of the Society. Benjamin Franklin served too because as yet he was not identified as a partisan of the Assembly or the Quaker party.

In early 1755, Smith anonymously wrote a pamphlet entitled *A Brief State of the Province of Pennsylvania*, which purported to explain to Englishmen why the French were succeeding in western Pennsylvania. He laid all the blame on the province's Quakers and Germans. The Quakers criminally mismanaged the government and the German voters—"ignorant, proud, stubborn Clowns"—kept them in office. Smith explained that most Quakers were pacifists and therefore would not permit the province to be defended. Those Quakers in the Assembly, however, were greedy hypocrites who would not defend the province because the military establishment they would have to create would become a hostile political organization as well. If a militia were created, its officers and enlisted men would ultimately oust the rival Quaker party from the legislature. And so, whether Quaker were faithful pacifists or backslidden politicians, they were alike the bane of the province, according to Smith. Smith prescribed an old remedy for the trouble: Make the Quakers swear oaths of allegiance (an impossibility for them) in order to sit in the House, and perhaps add an oath to defend the country. As for the German voters, they ought to remain disenfranchised until they became "educated"—which would take about twenty years, Smith estimated.[40] Because Smith attacked all Friends and not just the current legislators, he had legitimized a response from the Society of Friends.

Smith's patron, Thomas Penn, did not conspire with him to produce the pamphlet. Penn disliked involving the public in politics. But about the same time the pamphlet appeared in London—February 1755—Penn began to suggest that the government disable all the Quakers in Pennsylvania from occupying public office. When Penn found that few people in the government were paying his suggestion any attention, he urged some Pennsylvania sympathizers to petition the government to act, thereby forcing it to respond. To Penn's gratification some persons hinted to the London Friends that if their Pennsylvania brethren did "not act a rational and dutiful part," they would not be suffered to stay in the Assembly.[41] While Penn thought the prospect for disabling the Quakers was modest, the London Friends began to feel otherwise.

In the spring of 1755, the London Friends worried about the growing number of enemies arrayed against the Society. There was Penn and the author of the *Brief State;* but also, reported Dr. John Fothergill, "a torrent of invidious reflections . . . are propagated industriously by a set of men who . . . [made] martyrs of some of our ancestors." Fothergill named two sets of enemies: Lord Halifax and others at the Board of Trade, "who would be very glad to crush every appearance of liberty abroad"; and the Presbyterians, among whom Chandler was a principal. The Board was hunting and even provoking indiscretions by Pennsylvanians in order to find a pretext to strike down the Assembly. The Presbyterians in Pennsylvania were relaying every prejudicial fact about Quakers to London, where their party incessantly repeated them in order to have Friends excluded from the Assembly.[42] While the Friends in the Assembly were working up some of their most ingenious mischief against Thomas Penn, the London brethren felt chastened and advised caution.

William Smith's pamphlet, printed in London, appeared in Pennsylvania late in April 1755. It did not chasten most Quaker assemblymen then or later. An informed Pennsylvanian could see that the pamphlet was desperately partisan and grossly untrue in places. The assemblymen were, contrary to the author's claim, paying large sums to General Braddock and to the Massachusetts expedition against Crown Point. They were cutting a road to Ohio, and assemblyman Franklin had gathered wagons and teamsters to transport Braddock's immobilized army. Because at this same time Governor Robert Morris was weekly maligning the assemblymen, the *Brief State* looked like just one more of his attempts to discredit them. The assemblymen treated it like all his "mockeries," harassing him all the more in return.[43]

Friends outside the Assembly registered considerably more apprehension, as Smith noticed, and slightly less pugnacity. As early as 5 May, Philadelphia Quarterly Meeting had completed an address to the London Meeting for Sufferings. The spirit of Norris and Callender's earlier letter pervaded most of the address, although none of the signers was an assemblyman. The address contained accusations of artifices and designs against liberty and the charter, and a novel claim that in recent decades the Penns had gradually and willy-nilly wrung concessions from the people, greatly adding to the Penn's "Power & Treasure." The Whig outlook of the assemblymen seemed to be shared by the leadership of Philadelphia Quarterly Meeting.

Compared to the accusations in the Meeting's letter, the remedy the Meeting sought revealed a great deal more patience on its part. The authors wanted London Friends to help moderate the difference between them and the Penns. The Londoners should explain to the Penns how Governor Morris had embittered Pennsylvanians' feeling toward Penn. They must convince Penn that Friends abhorred rumors then circulating that they would oblige the Penns to give up the colony to the crown. If a friendly interposition with the Penns failed, however, the Meeting for Sufferings should join the Assembly agent in London in defending Friends from the attacks leveled at them.[44]

Conscience Stirs

One remark in the letter was signally out of character. The Meeting said that some Friends declined to serve in the legislature and the executive offices of Pennsylvania "as they found themselves incapable of preserving the Peace and Tranquility of their Minds & steady maintaining our Christian Testimony in all its Branches" while serving.[45] Still other Friends would have preferred not to serve, the letter said, but had to because they could not find a sufficient number of replacements who could be trusted to preserve Quaker liberties. The refusal of some to serve was the first evidence that conscience was stirring amid the anger, anxieties, and rationalizations that flourished among Quaker politicians.

Israel Pemberton later explained that specifically the House's appropriation of £15,000 upon the request from Massachusetts had caused him to question the legislators' altruism. However, he kept his doubts largely to himself because he felt that as long as the Assembly paid the money out of its own coffers, it was not exactly the Society's business. Also, shortly after the appropriation, he was distracted by Smith's *Brief State* as well as by the Assembly's address to the king. While the *Brief State* helped to convince Pemberton that Pennsylvania Friends had some genuinely virulent enemies, the Assembly address angered him because of its aggressiveness toward Penn. Those were not complementary attitudes and it appears that Pemberton was torn between an inclination to be irenic and a Whiggish fear for the rights of Pennsylvanians and Friends. In the following year, Pemberton's disgust at the ever more bellicose behavior of the House would resolve for him his dilemma over his proper course of action. That spring, however, he and Philadelphia Quarterly Meeting both were indecisive. Some Friends and contributors to the Meeting's letter, said Pemberton, resisted the slightest inclination to align the Meeting with the Assembly, while others wished to explain fully to English Friends the ominous designs on Pennsylvania's liberties.[46]

The London Meeting for Sufferings, the respondent of both the assemblymen and Philadelphia Quarterly Meeting, discovered the difference between the communications and the attitudes of the two bodies. It tried to assist both, but it especially welcomed the Meeting's proposal for conciliation. Why then were the Quaker assemblymen so aggressive? And moreover, the Assembly had recently sent a message to Penn in which it had not spared him any of the blame for the clash between them; "low and malicious," "most unjust and wicked," Penn called it. That message, the Meeting for Sufferings told Philadelphia Quarterly Meeting, "has plac'd our hopes of succeeding in a friendly Mediation with the Proprietaries at a greater Distance."[47] Why did Pennsylvania Friends inflame Penn on one hand while they wanted to parley with him on the other? The answer was that the Meeting was hearing from two different groups of Friends with different attitudes—an unprecedented event. Neither the Meeting nor Penn knew enough about the differences that were emerging between Quaker officeholders and Quaker churchmen to understand the mismatched letters from America. The Meeting was just confused, whereas Penn concluded that the different approaches to him were more Quaker trickery.

The Friends who were unhappy with the Assembly and wanted peace with Penn had very likely been listening to Quaker ministers Catherine Payton, John Churchmen, John Woolman, and perhaps others. Payton, in March 1755, asked some weighty Friends to arrange an interview between her and the Quaker assemblymen. She felt obliged to tell them how difficult it would be for them to satisfy the people's expectations on the eve of war and still maintain their own Quaker ethics. She got the interview and delivered her warning. She spoke generally about pacifism and accused no one in particular of any explicit transgressions of his ethics in the past three months. Yet her generalities were no reason to disregard her; she seemed to be asking that Friends not serve in the Assembly at all.[48]

By the end of March the ministers of Philadelphia Yearly Meeting added their warning to Payton's and were as general and sweeping as she had been. Their warning was contained in a letter addressed to all Friends and not just the assemblymen.[49] The spirit of the letter promised to make a good deal of trouble for the legislators if the authors followed it up with actions. Nothing less than the with-drawal from government would seem to satisfy the ministers. "Mortify that which remains in any of us which is of this world," they advised; discard "the surfeiting cares of this life and [be] redeemed from the love of this world that no earthly possessions nor enjoyments may bias our judgments or turn us from [an] . . . entire trust in God." "Cease from those national contests productive of misery and blood-shed"; the kingdoms of men and the earth are "as the dust of the balance."[50]

The average Quaker assemblyman who read the advice must have wondered whether it was intended as throwaway pieties or real policy. Were the assemblymen really supposed to trust God to "plead our cause for us"? Was that the way Penn's aggression would be stopped and the Assembly would secure its right to spend Pennsylvanians' money? What exactly did the ministers have in mind when they warned that God might "give us to taste of that bitter cup which the faithful ones have often partook of"?[51] Did they expect the assembly-men to look resignedly on if the proprietors or the French gratified their desires at Pennsylvania's expense?

By the summer the ingredients of a crisis were present: The Quaker Assembly and Proprietor Thomas Penn were estranged and intransi-gent; the impatient British government was expecting speedy obedi-ence from Pennsylvania; William Smith and others had fixed the blame for inaction upon all Friends; and while many Friends were slighting their pacifism, others were exalting it. The defeat of General Edward Braddock's army would soon throw these contrary characters and courses into a whirl that some would not escape.

7

Withdrawal from Government, 1756

While Thomas Penn and the Pennsylvania Assembly were exploiting the French menace to the British Empire in order to bring the wrath of the British government down upon each other, the defeat of General Edward Braddock's army in July 1755 should have been sufficiently grim to cause the two rivals to desist. Nine hundred and seventy-five British were dead or wounded, the survivors were in flight, and the French and Indians were masters of the West. Yet the defeat did not resolve the political contest. It did, however, mightily help to resolve the future of the Society of Friends in government.

When the news of Braddock's defeat reached Philadelphia, the consternation in the city was hardly to be expressed, one resident recorded. Suspicion that Roman Catholics composed a "fifth-column" caused a mob to arise and threaten to demolish the only Catholic church in the city. Friends defended the Catholics, insisting that the Catholics were protected by Penn's charter as much as anyone else. The magistrates managed to disperse the mob and the Catholics escaped harm. For almost two months the Pennsylvania frontier remained curiously quiet. Then on 16 October, the Delawares and Shawnees attacked. In November, the Indians crossed the mountains and the Susquehanna River and there drove out the Germans at Tulpehocken who thirty-three years earlier had supplanted the Indians. By December, the Indians had reached far to the east to attack the Moravians at Gnadenhutten. Throughout the autumn and winter the Indians continued to strike when they pleased. Ironically, the discontents which had provoked the Indians to attack were largely land frauds and abuses by the Pennsylvania government. Eminent Friends had been party to these abuses, and their complicity justified the reformers' low esteem for the generation of Quaker leaders preceding themselves.[1]

In the winter of 1755, the Pennsylvania frontier collapsed. Settlers fled down from the mountains to Shippensburg, Carlisle, York, and Reading. Some of the inhabitants of the towns in turn joined passing refugees and fled on toward Philadelphia. In the city, the eminent merchant Thomas Willing, "almost crazy" with anxiety over the safety of his family, contemplated moving to England. Rumors circulated in Philadelphia that eighteen hundred French and Indians were but seventy miles away and still advancing.[2]

Indians still friendly to the province fled from the frontier too, but they found no sanctuary anywhere. The whites cursed and damned all Indians without distinction, called them murderers, and threatened to mob and kill them. Friends found themselves in the company of the Indians when haggard refugees and others appointed the blame for their suffering. In Reading, some men were barely prevented from burning down the houses of the few Friends there. The calamity was "all owing to the influence of our Quaker Meeting," Thomas Willing believed; "may God destroy their Seed forever, & root 'em from the Face of the earth."[3] In their anger, the real and imagined victims of the Indians falsely concluded that the province was undefended because the Quaker legislators were pacifists. No amount of argument or evidence that the legislators were even then violating their pacifism was likely to shake their belief in Quaker villainy. Demagoguery had splendidly succeeded.

After Braddock's defeat, but before the Indian reprisals, Governor Morris asked the House to speedily appropriate a large sum of money for defense. Presumably the province was so menaced that the House might have desisted in its contest with Penn and abandoned its obstructive demands. Instead, the ingenious House offered Morris an appropriations bill that included an unprecedented tax upon the Penns' lands. Now it became Penn's and Morris's turn to approve or deny the province money, and forestall the war effort. Pacifism did not figure in these machinations at all.[4]

Morris and the Assembly hectored each other more now than before. The assemblymen, understanding that they were liable to be called unpatriotic and even seditious, paid out some money for defense. In August, they put £1,000 in the hands of members Norris, John

Wright, Joseph Fox, who were Friends, and Franklin and Evan Morgan, who were not. Although the House resolution read "for the King's Use," the phrase obviously meant nothing with regard to the users; by now this pretense was commonplace when Quaker legislators violated their ethic. The next month the Assembly resolved to solicit voluntary contributions up to £10,000 total, for Norris and Fox, plus four non-Friends to expend. Finally, it drafted a bill for £50,000, which, if it became law, would violate Quaker ethics. The bill commissioned Norris, Fox, Franklin, and Morgan, together with exgovernor Hamilton, to expend the £50,000. Once again, Friends would be unethically prosecuting a war.[5]

Nothing came of the £50,000 bill before the Indians attacked in the fall. In October, when Governor Morris informed the assemblymen of the attack on Great Cove, they passed a £60,000 appropriation much like the earlier bill for £50,000. Yet despite the deaths on the frontier, the bill did not become law because Thomas Penn would not tolerate its tax upon his land. To most observers of this contest, Penn seemed to be the obstructive party.[6] But Penn had already found a way to shift the blame to the Assembly. Late in October, the Assembly learned that Penn had volunteered £5,000 of his own to defend the province. Quickly the Assembly dropped the objectionable tax on Penn's lands and passed the remaining bill. Penn's gift, petitions begging the Assembly to defend the province, and a visit from three hundred Germans (ready to tear the legislators out of the House, chuckled William Smith) had so clearly made the assemblymen look niggardly and blameworthy that they could no longer equivocate and dissemble.[7] Now all Pennsylvanians would be taxed for the war and Friends would be a party to the use of the money for war.

Some Friends became increasingly restive over the Assembly's behavior even before the tax became law. At the annual convention of Philadelphia Yearly Meeting in late September they opened a discussion about the ethics of paying taxes that financed war. John Woolman, one of their number, reported that they were uneasy about paying such taxes. Since he did not qualify that expression of uneasiness, he apparently meant *any* taxes, and not just those that Friends expended. Their grievance was so general it could shake the basic presumptions of Quaker statesmen, Quaker ethics, and provincial politics. At the 1755 Yearly Meeting a committee was appointed to consider the difficult question these Friends had raised; no answer was even remotely in sight.[8]

James Pemberton, whom the voters returned to the House in the 1 October election, reported that he and several other members were reluctant to sit, and were made all the more uneasy by Isaac Norris's reprehensible conduct—exactly what, he did not say.[9] Whereas the violations of the pacifist ethic had begun ten months earlier, Pemberton's discomfort, like that of the colleagues for whom he spoke, appeared tardy. And moreover, he had been one of the legislators appointed in January to spend the House's £5,000 for the war. It is reasonable to suppose that in the nine-month interim, Friends like John Woolman had pointed out to Pemberton and other legislators their ethical errors. Even so, conscience did not get the better of Whiggery; these legislators kept their seats in the House for political reasons.

Israel Pemberton and some other Friends were so disgusted at the record of the Quaker House that they refused to vote (even though Israel's brother was running) and counseled other Friends to do likewise. But their boycott made little difference at the polls; Friends succeeded in being elected just as they always had, despite some organized opposition from the Presbyterians in Chester County, who "covenanted" to support an opposition ticket. Samuel Fothergill so mistrusted this new Quaker Assembly that he asked John Churchman to go to Philadelphia to attend the opening session. "My mind has been pained Day & night . . . lest a Breach incurable be made, by the Assembly's enacting what many tender minds cannot comply with."[10]

The watchdogs of the Assembly shortly had their grievance. On 6 November, the bill for £60,000 passed that body. Samuel Fothergill and four other Friends spoke privately to Speaker Norris and other Quaker assemblymen. Apparently unsatisfied, the protestors decided they had to publicly address the whole House. Now twenty in number, they delivered their address the next day.[11]

The protestors told the assemblymen explicitly how they had violated Quaker pacifism: they had raised money and put it into the hands of a committee that used it for war. And the twenty cast the assemblymen in a role that they had not even remotely imagined for themselves. The protestors accused them of destroying Quaker religious liberties and the charter of the province. This accusation against men who had touted themselves as the saviors of the charter and the liberators of the province from proprietary slavery! Two of the protestors, Israel Pemberton and John Reynell, had even paid the assemblymen that same compliment within the past ten months.

And insofar as Pemberton and Reynell were indicting past errors, they ought to have remembered their own past Whig zeal. If the accusation of these protestors did not disturb the assemblymen, the recourse they announced must have: they promised that they would refuse to pay the tax, preferring to suffer the consequences of violating the law.[12]

The House replied to the twenty protestors by scolding them for insinuating that they spoke for any Friends other than themselves and it accused them of haste, indiscretion, and ignorance. The twenty did not understand, it said, that in 1711 the Quaker Assembly had levied a tax in order to grant £2,000 for Queen Anne's use. In fact, 1711 was irrelevant; the twenty had accused the Quaker Assembly not of levying a tax for war but of putting the revenue into the hands of *its* commissioners, who then used it for war. In 1755, the Assembly was not rendering to Caesar, but to itself, and the money was not explicitly for the king to use. There was simply no analogy between 1711 and 1755 to excuse the present Quaker legislators. Some of them did not know the difference, some did not care, and at least five who did—James Pemberton, Joshua Morris, William Peters, Peter Worral, and Francis Parvin—voted against the tax.[13]

Israel Pemberton complained bitterly of the pride and callousness of the Quaker assemblymen. They did not, Pemberton maintained, have to bring division and suffering upon the Society by a tax that made all Friends accomplices to their misuse of the revenue. They could have raised the money some other way, but any alternative to the property tax "would not gratify their Darling Scheme of gaining some advantage over the Governor & Proprietor, for the sake of which every other Consideration seem'd to be little regarded."[14] Yet when Penn's gift and other developments foiled their scheme to tax his lands, the assemblymen persisted with the tax!

With the tax on the statute books, Friends who could not comply with it felt obliged to alert their brethren in Pennsylvania to the ethical implications of paying the tax. In December, two important committees that the Yearly Meeting had created in September were scheduled to meet jointly "to consider some things in which the cause of Truth was concerned," said John Woolman.[15] At the meeting, which Woolman described as "the most weighty that ever I was at," the committeemen labored over the differences among them— while outside in the streets the bodies of two dead, scalped men were carted about to arouse the wrath of the people against the Indians.

As time wore on, Friends who felt easy about paying the tax left the meeting, and the twenty-one remaining members drafted their message to their brethren. In their message, "An Epistle of Tender Love and Caution to Friends in Pennsylvania," they did not urge Friends to boycott the tax; instead, they principally recounted their own apprehension about the tax and the course they were prepared to take. But that was enough; the division between Quaker assemblymen and the protestors would shortly be complemented by a similar one in the Society as a whole.[16]

Trouble other than the split between Quaker assemblymen and Quaker protestors was inevitable. The tax law had to be enforced by constables and justices many of whom were Friends. They faced the dilemma of punishing their brethren, or suffering for not doing their official duty. Or, they could resign from office and give up the political power that Friends wielded in the three oldest counties of Pennsylvania. If they decided to enforce the law they would become persecutors in the eyes of the protestors and enemies of religious freedoms guaranteed by the charter of Pennsylvania.

In yet another way the Quaker Assembly added to the suffering of conscientious brethren. It had given up a handsome sum of money without taxing the Penns, but the grant did not satisfy the public. "The Assembly have sold their testimony as Friends to the people's fears, and not gone far enough to satisfy them," Samuel Fothergill observed.[17] And so, to meet the increased clamor of the people, the Assembly went further. It passed an act for a volunteer militia, the first such act in Pennsylvania's history. By it, no one violated Quaker ethics except the Friends in the House who voted for it and any Friends who volunteered to serve. The damage appeared limited, but as Israel Pemberton observed, these bellicose acts would convince the world that all earlier expressions about Quaker ethical restraints were a sham to hide a simple appetite for power—much as the pamphlet A Brief State had explained. Why was there no militia earlier to save lives, the English ministry very angrily asked when it learned of the act? Getting Friends to provide for war seemed merely a matter of pushing them hard enough. And when pushed, hypocritical Friends would not for conscience' sake suffer bodily or in their estates. That seemed to be the reasonable construction to put upon Quaker behavior. However, Pemberton knew that some Friends would in fact suffer rather than pay what was demanded, and that they would suffer all the more because their hypocritical brethren had provoked the government to treat all Friends roughly. Men "who formerly were deaf to their [Proprietary partisans'] Lies," about Friends will now listen and believe, demand more from the House, and get it. In the end, Pemberton despaired, our enemies will "oblige Men of our own Choice to subject us to the Difficulties we feared from [our enemies]."[18]

Pennsylvania Abandons Its Native People

When the "Epistle of Tender Love and Caution" alerted Friends that the assemblymen would use their taxes for purposes inconsistent with Quaker pacifism, the authors probably never foresaw how dreadfully accurate they had been. In April 1756, five of the eight legislators and others who had been commissioned to expend the £60,000 asked the governor to declare war upon the Delawares and offer bounties for their scalps. Among the commissioners only Isaac Norris and Franklin did not join the request. Quakers John Mifflin and Joseph Fox, who had long treated Quaker pacifism cavalierly, signed it along with three non-Friends. They were disowned by the end of the month. The commissioners were doing what the public wanted; "The general Voice of the People calls aloud for a Proclamation offering Rewards for Indian Scalps," Richard Peters observed. The Iroquois allies approved of the measures. Thomas Penn thought scalp bounties were "the only proper method" to stop the Indians, although he found bounties on Indian women rather repulsive. Among all Pennsylvanians, only some Friends protested.[19]

In the most fraternal address ever to the Assembly, these Friends begged the Quaker legislators "by the Profession you make of being the Disciples and Followers of our Lord Jesus Christ, the Prince of Peace," and for "the Honour of God," stop the proclamations of war and bounties. But the Assembly did nothing more than discuss the request. The Council, when asked, summarily rejected it, and on 14 April, the governor proclaimed war and offered on behalf of the commissioners $130 for every scalp of a male Delaware and $50 for a female. The province had licensed a pogrom.[20]

Perhaps nothing in the lives of this generation of Friends staggered them as much as the two proclamations. Friendship with the Delaware Indians had mythic importance to the pious Friends of the mid-eighteenth century; the "Peaceable Kingdom" was as real to them as Edward Hicks later portrayed it on canvas.

The Settlement of this Province was founded on the Principles of Truth, Equity, and Mercy and the Blessing of Divine Providence attended the early Care of the first Founders to impress these Principles on the Minds of the Native Inhabitants, so that when their Numbers were great and their Strength vastly Superior, they received our Ancestors with Gladness, relieved their Wants with open Hearts, granted them peaceable Possession of the Land, and for a long Course of Time gave constant and frequent Proofs of a cordial Friendship, all which we humbly ascribe to the infinite Wisdom and Mercy of God.[21]

Although Friends, beginning that April, learned that the course of honest friendship with the Indians had been shorter than James Logan and other brethren had led them to believe, the original peace between William Penn and the Delawares remained for them an icon without a crack in it. These Friends did not begin to regard the Delawares as aliens and savage enemies once the Delawares attacked. The Indians were not devoid of understanding and a sense of justice, the Friends told the Assembly, and it therefore behooved the assemblymen to inquire whether the Indians had been mistreated. These Indians were original constituents of the community, less aliens than the Scotch-Irish and other parvenue Indianphobes. To pay "bloodthirsty Presbyterians"[22] and others to scalp these ancient friends was to dishonor a solemn commitment to them and to deny the best part of the Quaker past. It would also "lay a foundation for a general Warr." "The Burden thus brought on the Faithful is great," Israel Pemberton lamented; "It had seem'd as tho' the prophet's words would be literally verify'd among us, 'the Leaders of the People cause them to err & those who are led of them are destroy'd.' "[23]

Politically minded critics like Pemberton faced the dilemma whether to correct the government's Indian policy using public offices and power or using private means. Several months earlier, in November 1755, the Assembly had replied to Morris's views about Delaware attacks by proposing to inquire what had provoked the Delawares, and that proposal was reason for Friends to take heart in the good offices of others. But amid the quarrels with Morris, the inquiry was forgotten, and now the House had collaborated in scalping. There was little reason to expect pacific behavior from any part of the

government that spring.[24] Pemberton's efforts to restore peace with
the Delawares therefore would not depend upon the government.
Pennsylvania might abandon its own original people, but Friends
would not. The way of withdrawal, which pious Friends urged upon
the brethren in all aspects of their lives, was the method Pemberton
employed to remedy the public problems. He would not reenter public
office or the electoral process on others' behalf. He worked privately
and philanthropically.[25]

The fruitless attempts in the spring of 1756 to persuade the House
to change its aggressive policy exhausted the hope of some Quaker
legislators. On 4 June, six Friends resigned from the House. They
could not, they felt, concur with the business of the House or change
it by their votes; yet their very presence in the House contributed to
the quorum that permitted the distasteful business to be done. They
could no longer be accomplices to their brethren's errors, or appear
by their presence to condone them. And so they resigned.[26] That day

began the slow exodus of Quakers from government which, by fits
and starts, led twenty years later to the complete divorce of the
Society of Friends from the state.

Many Friends who were heartsick at the behavior of the Quaker
Assembly nonetheless remained uneasy over the hazardous consequences of discarding public offices and power. But the most reform-
minded Friends pronounced the withdrawal a boon to the Society.
Anthony Benezet, for example, observed:

Friends begin to see what they might long ago have seen, if the God of this
World, the deceitfulnes of wealth & Honour had not blinded their Eyes viz.
the impossibility for us, as a People . . . in times of War . . . to maintain the
Government & be honest & true to that noble, evangelike Testimony which
God has given us to bear as a people.[27]

Suffering might be the hazard of leaving the government, but just as
surely "we are in the Lord's Hand whom, we trust, will cause all
Things to work together for good."[28]

Arraignment in London

Friends had little or no political credit left at Whitehall. Two months
before Braddock's defeat the Board of Trade had censured the Quaker

Assembly. William Smith's *Brief State* had prepared a Quaker scape-goat for Braddock's debacle and the subsequent losses. And Penn and the Presbyterians were urging the ministry and Parliament to oust Friends from the Assembly. The twenty tax protestors added the first of many ironies to the decline of Quaker polity by affording Penn and other enemies an opportunity to damn the Quaker politicians out of the mouths of the brethren themselves. Penn got the copy of the protest pirated by the disloyal Assembly doorkeeper and passed it around to everyone from the Duke of Cumberland, the king's brother, to the members of the Board of Trade. The protest against a war tax nicely complemented Smith's allegation that Quaker pacifism, together with Quaker greed, prostrated the province—while it also obscured the £55,000 being expended for weapons, forts, and scalps by the Assembly. Later in 1756, Smith got a copy of the "Epistle of Tender Love and Caution," prefaced it with some damning observations, and sent it off to London to be printed up and circulated. It gave "great disgust at Court," an English Friend reported.[29]

British belief in inflexible Quaker pacifism and selfish sectarianism was unintentionally bolstered by some London Friends in February 1756. The king had appointed a day-long religious fast during which the public was supposed to quit its usual business and profane activities. The discipline of the Society forbade Friends from observing fast days and all other forms of contrived or forced worship. While most Friends had obliged the king and willingly violated the discipline, several in London refused to close their shops. Then the magistrates, therefore, shut the shops, whereupon some of the Friends reopened them. Mobs arose and attacked the reopened shops, and newspapers praised the behavior of the mobs. These few Quaker protestors "immediately exposed [all of] us to the general resentment," complained one merchant member of the Meeting for Sufferings, Henton Brown.[30] The current situation of Pennsylvania Friends compounded the discomfort of the trimmers in London: already-angry Englishmen doubly reviled Friends because of their unpatriotic brethren in America. And Englishmen who had not so far been exercised at the Pennsylvanians now were because of their anger over the London protestors. Brown complained to James Pemberton that because of the demonstration by some few London Friends, the defense of Pennsylvanians at Whitehall would probably fail.[31]

Early in 1755 Penn had induced William Allen to join the campaign against Quaker legislators by petitioning the king to oust them from the Assembly. Braddock's loss to the French and the frontiersmen's suffering lent immense gravity to the partisan petition. It went to the Board of Trade where the president, Lord Halifax, welcomed it in February 1756. Although the success of the petitioners was hardly in doubt, the petition received a full hearing with solicitors, counselors, the Assembly's agents, and Friends in attendance.[32]

The petitioners depicted the province as utterly defenseless because of the machinations of Philadelphia Yearly Meeting and the scruples of the Quaker legislators. The assemblymen, they argued, had and would cling to their pacifist principles, whatever the effect upon Pennsylvania; Quaker pacifism was vigorous, pervasive, and uniformly respected. It was the sort of scrupulosity which would have heartened pious and reformist Friends. On the contrary, the respondents argued ironically with greater truth than the petitioners, the Assembly had defended the province. They flourished before the Board the appropriation of £55,000 and its applications, and the act for a militia.[33] They—Friends describing other Friends—were making a case for Quaker patriotism and the bellicosity of Quaker legislators! But the board would not or could not believe that Friends were inconstant pacifists. The board members had stereotyped Pennsylvania Friends as pious people, yet selfish too. And the board had evidence to support some of its mistrust: "It is most manifest," the petitioners had argued to the board, "from the insolent Address . . . by 20 Quakers, that this Assembly is led by the Nose, by that illegal Caball, called their Yearly Meeting, & their Quarterly Meeting." It appeared to be of no consequence to the board that a pacifist protest necessitated bellicose Quaker legislators, or that there might be some distinction between the Assembly and the Society of Friends. The board was satisfied that it was right, and it reported as it had in May 1755, that the Assembly had no intention of using revenues to support a war and that its militia act was a sham. As in 1742, however, the board was powerless to grant the petitioners the relief they desired; only Parliament could exclude Friends.[34]

Prior to the hearing at the Board of Trade, Penn, Halifax, Chandler, and the Presbyterians were preparing the way for Parliament to disqualify Friends from sitting in the Assembly.[35] It was no difficult job. "Scurrilous invectives . . . had raised such a general indignation against you [Pennsylvania Friends] that no measures so violent could have been proposed, but many of all parties, persuasions & interests would have joined in supporting them," John Fothergill discovered; the dislike for Friends was stronger than at any time since the Restoration. Misinformed or partisan ministers and members of Parliament reviled Friends: "You owe the people protection & yet withhold them from protecting themselves. Will not all the blood that is spilt lye at your doors?" The critics swore not to "sit still and see the province in danger of being given up without endeavouring its rescue." Even though it violated the provincial charter, they vowed to oust Friends from the Assembly. What did a charter matter compared to the desolation of the province?[36]

Penn and the Board of Trade drafted bills to disqualify Friends and the government supported them. The situation of Quaker assemblymen appeared lost. The Quaker lobby called upon the men "in considerable Stations, who had been our firm Friends [sic]," but now they "seemed . . . to be either wavering . . . or disposed to join in the popular cry against us." Still, the Meeting—and especially Henton Brown and John Hanbury—was "moving heaven and earth" to save their Pennsylvania cousins. They discovered one remaining friend in the government. He was Lord Granville, president of the Privy Council, who in 1742 had helped Friends in similar need.[37]

The very best concession that Granville could obtain for Friends would oblige Quaker legislators to voluntarily resign their seats for at least the duration of the war. Granville persuaded the government to agree to pass a law only dissolving the Pennsylvania Assembly. The Society, or Meeting for Sufferings, would vouch that no Pennsylvania Friends would stand for one or more elections following the dissolution.[38] To this the Meeting agreed without hesitation. Had Granville not interposed and the Meeting accepted his compromise, "you [Pennsylvanians] would 'ere this time [3 April 1756] have been incapacitated . . . from ever sitting in any assembly in America," Fothergill warned the Pennsylvanians. Now "we [members of the Meeting for Sufferings] stand bound for your good behavior"; "the Honour & Reputation . . . the well being of the Society" have become the collateral in this bargain, Fothergill and Brown emphasized to them.[39]

Parliament never passed an act to dissolve the Pennsylvania Assembly, but nevertheless Friends were obliged to remove their members from it, presumably by the election of October 1756. London Yearly Meeting chose two Friends—John Hunt and Christopher Wilson—to travel to Pennsylvania and secure compliance from the Pennsylvanians.[40] Scepticism was common both in the government and in the Society over whether the Pennsylvanians would comply.

Hunt and Wilson's instructions to the Pennsylvanians commanded them to withdraw from the House, and also to pay their taxes. The tax protest to the Assembly and the "Epistle of Tender Love and Caution" had deeply embarrassed English Friends at the time when they were most politically vulnerable. Having suffered a loss of prestige at Whitehall through no fault of their own, they committed themselves deeply to the effort to retrieve the fortunes of their Whiggish Pennsylvania brethren who had caused their loss. Then they witnessed Pennsylvanians, by a tax protest, jeopardize their effort and give the lie to Friends' apologies to the government. Yet the English Friends both in and out of the Meeting for Sufferings had more interests at heart than the political career of their American brethren. John and Capel Hanbury were, of course, interested in the defense of the Ohio River Valley, along with Thomas Penn. John Hanbury, together with John Tomlinson, non-Quaker, had served as paymaster and commissary to the British forces of General Braddock. David Barclay, the Quaker merchant and banker, was procuring a thousand muskets for Penn. He was also William Allen's business agent in England and transacted the financial business connected with Allen's petition against the Quaker legislature.[41] Each had at least one reason, large or small, for wanting the tax protest ended.

The London Friends were not deliberately callous and certainly not without charity. But the kind of lives they led did not quicken their appreciation of the pious and stiff ethical behavior of some of their brethren. As Bucks County minister Joseph White observed, they were so involved "in almost every branch of trade, and in commerce and conversation that there [was] scarcely time for the busy and active part . . . to reflect . . . on the condition" they were in, and how they were "involved and unavoidably led into . . . a martial spirit." Although they refused military service and did not hire substitutes, at least not directly, they were nonetheless "more nearly attached to private interest than to the truth" and went "exceedingly near the brink of the precipice in fanatic illuminations . . . and in closing their shops." Their behavior grieved "honest minds," and what was worse, increased some Friends' sufferings. These eminent English Friends, like their American counterparts, probably never even knew that when they balked at their Quaker testimonies, magistrates and mobs harassed more than ever the humbler members who kept the testimonies. To those outside the faith, the behavior of the wealthy Friends defined orthodoxy and licensed the harassment of more constant Friends who appeared to be mere eccentrics. "For my part I can make no other distinction between them and other people than barely refusing to bear the sword," White concluded about the Londoners. "But for what reason they refuse let the impartial judge."[42]

At the convocation of London Yearly Meeting in June 1756, some Friends wanted to censure explicitly the "Epistle of Tender Love and Caution" and to load "the authors with blame to the utmost of their power."[43] These indignant Friends claimed to have been provoked by the heterodoxy and pride of the Americans. The Americans' refusal to pay on the grounds that payment violated their ethics and offended their consciences implied that English Friends were and always had been violating Quaker ethics and silencing their own consciences.[44] But this indignation, if genuine, was based on ignorance of the difference between the situations of English and Pennsylvania taxpayers. As John Fothergill clearly understood, "it was not altogether the payment of the tax but that the tax should be raised, directed and the use allowed by an assembly the major part whereof were of our profession that gave the offense." Fothergill must have tried repeatedly to drive home that simple distinction to his angry city acquaintances. The refusal of these intelligent men to admit the distinction, and therefore the legitimacy of the tax protest, surely helped to convince him that something other than ignorance or dullness fueled their anger at the Americans. While many of them professed to have the good of the Society at heart when they condemned the protestors, "private reasons operated on a few," Fothergill concluded.[45]

Samuel Fothergill returned to London that same summer and the critics of the protest appeared to have been lying in wait for him. As he recounted to John Churchman, when he went to a meeting in London:

I had a continued chain of hard labor and principally toward those who ought to be the head, but are the tail. I found in almost every mind a secret displeasure against the friends who signed the Epistle of caution and advice; and fully expected to be tried by the Meeting for Sufferings for being concerned in it. . . . I was repeatedly attacked in private; to some tender minds I gave good satisfaction, but to others who are devoid of any sense of the purity of our Testimony, and act upon worldly principles . . . it was labor lost.[46]

The Friends who wanted to censure temporarily had to be satisfied with less—the order sent by Hunt and Wilson that Pennsylvanians must pay their taxes. The order was peremptory and it unmistakably conveyed the pique of the Meeting for Sufferings as well as that Meeting's belief that the tax boycott insidiously reflected upon English Friends. Appended to the order were five London Yearly Meeting minutes and seven acts of Parliament dating from William and Mary through 1732, all to prove that Friends had paid taxes when they knew the taxes were *"for carrying on a War."*[47] The situation the order so emphatically addressed, however, was obviously not that of Pennsylvania Friends. Any recipient of it might justifiably dismiss it.

Hunt and Wilson could just as well have stayed in England for all the assistance they rendered the Meeting for Sufferings. All the Friends who withdrew from the Pennsylvania Assembly did so before Hunt and Wilson arrived in Pennsylvania, and most withdrew for very different reasons than London Yearly Meeting had for wanting them out. If the emissaries convinced any protestors to pay their taxes, there is no record of it. Rather, the two began to doubt the rectitude of their instruction. What they accomplished was no part of their commission at all; namely, they helped to reconcile the divisions among American Friends.

Six Friends had resigned from the House in June 1756 because they could no longer countenance its behavior nor be accessories to its acts. At the special elections held to replace them, six candidates of the Assembly or so-called Quaker party ran unopposed. In the city of Philadelphia and in Philadelphia County at least, Friends "very unanimously declined voting." For Penn, the heralded event only changed the situation for the worse. "The hottest headed of all denominations" will fill the Assembly hereafter, Peters lamented, "and Franklin will rule them. . . . the Anti-Proprietary party will reign sole Arbiters of the [October] Election, and your plagues and Vexations encrease."[48]

Because Hunt and Wilson had a slow passage to Pennsylvania, they were prevented from applying the order from the Meeting for Sufferings at the October election—or the earlier special one. As in the June withdrawal, the pious Friends unintentionally did the Meeting's work for it by trying to discourage Friends from participating in the election in any way. In October in Philadelphia County, "Very few of the Sober Sort Voted at all," William Logan observed. But others less sober ran, and "too many" Friends voted. No arguments could prevail with these many Friends to abstain, James Pemberton told Samuel Fothergill. Hunt and Wilson learned of all these attempts only after the election, and in their report to London, they absolved the Society in Pennsylvania of any complicity in the election results. The two Englishmen appeared surprised at the popularity of Friends in Pennsylvania. Friends were being boomed for the Assembly without their approval or even their knowledge. Had they shown any inclination to serve, the public would have elected a great majority of Friends to the Assembly, "so strongly were the Publick disposed to have Friends for their Representatives." Having credited the misrepresentations of Pennsylvania politics that William Smith, Penn, the Presbyterians, Halifax, and others had circulated in England, Hunt and Wilson were understandably surprised. In the end, out of a total of thirty-six members, twelve "under the name of Quakers" were elected.[49] For the first time in the history of the province, there was no longer a Quaker majority in the Assembly.

Five days after the election, when Hunt and Wilson reached Pennsylvania, they took up the task of persuading the remaining Quaker legislators to resign. These Friends were interviewed and the "expediency" of resigning urged upon them. Four consented almost immediately; the rest refused "to shake off their Raggs of Imaginary honour." The two emissaries spoke to Isaac Norris first, on the assumption that if he resigned the remaining Friends would do so. But they failed; the Speaker was too anxious about the security of the Assembly and about his own political career to step down.[50] In his opinion the Friends who had protested his and other brethren's behavior in the Assembly were "mostly very weak men."[51]

There was a clear difference between the motives of these four who resigned in October and the motives of the six who had resigned in June. Whereas the six could not condone the unethical behavior of the Assembly, the four apparently could. They specified that they were resigning because of the order from the Meeting for Sufferings; that is, because the British government would oust them if they did not go voluntarily.[52]

Like the six who had resigned earlier, the four assemblymen were replaced by antiproprietary men and the politics of the province continued without a hitch on the course taken since 1739. As a knowledgeable politician from the province could have told the Penns, the ministers at Whitehall, and the Presbyterians, the Quaker assemblymen were only a scapegoat and the exclusion of Friends was no panacea. Friends had no monopoly on Whiggery in Pennsylvania. But despite this revelation, Penn did not fault his own tactic; rather, he accused Friends of going back on their commitments. To his mind, they had committed themselves to the election of "moderate" men who would turn provincial politics to a course more agreeable to him.[53] But they had made no such commitment. The pious Friends wanted little or nothing to do with electioneering and the Quaker political activists worked for Penn's antagonists.

As for the second part of Hunt and Wilson's mission—their instruction to make Pennsylvania Friends pay war taxes—Israel Pemberton had learned of the Meeting's order before Hunt and Wilson had their commission in hand. Before the two left England, Pemberton, clerk of Philadelphia Yearly Meeting, had warned John Fothergill that there would be trouble if the two tried to enforce the payment of taxes.[54] They nevertheless tried. There is no way of knowing how many contrary minds they changed: probably not many, because before they left America in late 1757, even they themselves had come to disagree on the question. Those who refused to pay probably continued to refuse; it was "a scruple so fastened upon the minds of many Friends that nothing moved it," Woolman recorded.[55] In any case, surprisingly soon after Hunt and Wilson arrived in Pennsylvania, the whole matter of the implementation of the order by the Meeting for Sufferings disappeared from conversation.

Because Hunt and Wilson were failing to extinguish the tax protest, and because the problem of a Quaker-dominated legislature was solved largely without their help, they were free to devote their energies to a problem that English Friends were hardly aware of. The Society in Pennsylvania was badly divided over the behavior of the Assembly and the Friends still remaining in it. Some Friends talked as though schism lay ahead. During their year in Pennsylvania Hunt and Wilson tried with a large measure of success to mediate the differences between the two camps. They won the gratitude of such Friends from differing camps as Isaac Norris and John Churchman.[56] Their "steady & prudent" conduct, it was said, was "instrumental to prevent some affairs of the Society from being thrown into confusion."[57]

When Hunt and Wilson returned to London, they reported nothing to the Meeting regarding their obligation to bring the Pennsylvania protestors into line; it must have seemed dated to them. Instead, they advised that the subject of taxes ought not to be discussed publicly. "The provincial tax . . . had not produced [in Pennsylvania] such an opposition of Minds . . . as to destroy that Love & Charity which ought to subsist amongst Brethren." The two men concurred completely with the Philadelphia Yearly Meeting that Friends everywhere should "be Quiet in their Minds, and not enforce their Sentiments one upon another."[58]

Hunt and Wilson's advice was not acceptable to a number of English Friends, mostly Londoners. In the previous year, while the two were off in Pennsylvania, these London Friends were too restive to let their emissaries work out a solution or obtain compliance. At either London Yearly Meeting of 1757 or the Meeting for Sufferings, "some whose Kingdom is of this world," wrote Samuel Fothergill, wanted to send the Pennsylvanians an epistle "which would have Kindled a flame," but they were forestalled. John Griffith, formerly of Pennsylvania, warned John Pemberton that "most of the London Friends censured those much who made a stand against the payment of the tax, and would have sent amongst you such epistles as in all likelihood would have done you great disservice."[59]

The Londoners had consented to Hunt and Wilson's mission partly because it was more seemly to induce the Americans to pay the tax than to censure them. When the two returned without the compliance and with unwelcome advice, the Londoners did not swerve from their resolution to have their own way. Samuel Fothergill and others foresaw that the Londoners would raise the issue of taxation in London Yearly Meeting, presumably because they expected the Meeting to censure the Pennsylvanians. Fothergill knew, however, that they had presumed too much. Since the time that city Friends had harangued Fothergill upon his return from America, Fothergill had sounded out other Friends about their sympathy for the American reformers and their agreement with Hunt and Wilson's advice. Fothergill discovered a body of well-wishers large enough to foul the plans of the Londoners. "There are many here [in England] pain'd with our Land tax [which supported war], & anxious to go forwards towards Perfection in faith & practice." With the knowledge that he could muster quite a protest in England, Fothergill went to the impatient Londoners several months before the 1758 Yearly Meeting and warned them that if they forced a discussion of the Americans at the Meeting, they would witness a tax protest right at home. That would be a novelty indeed, whereas there were no Friends in Parliament who had legislated the English land taxes or used the revenues for war. Fothergill's warning was sufficiently sobering to make the Londoners "guard against every thing, or measure, which might bring [the tax] to public discussion."[60]

The Yearly Meeting in 1758 proved to be a debacle for the London enemies of reform in still other ways. Since at least 1754, London Quarter had resisted the changes that Samuel Fothergill, John Griffith, Mary Peisley, and others had promoted. For example, unlike all other Friends and meetings in England, the London Meeting of Ministers and Elders refused to answer queries about the state of the church in its precincts; and London meetings refused to visit, or inspect, families, just as they had refused for the past sixty years. Finally, London contested a recent disciplinary article which required Friends to refuse the "overplus" of property taken in distraints for tithes.[61] The elitism of London Friends was not confined just to politics and practiced only in the Meeting for Sufferings; it embraced procedure and administration, religious testimonies, and commonplace morality. But in 1758, the exceptions which London had made for itself were withdrawn from it by the Yearly Meeting, and the Londoners were proved "unequal to the weighty Body of Friends in the nation." "A memorable time" Yearly Meeting was, John Griffith recalled, "the power and virtue of truth wonderfully attending and the weakness of the opposers [of reform] and the emptiness of their reasoning easily discovered."[62]

The check upon the authority of London Friends had ended as well the probability that they would ever dictate the behavior of American Friends.[63] Friends other than the tax protestors were determined not to suffer London Yearly Meeting ordering them about.[64] Had the Londoners proceeded to censure Pennsylvania's protestors, Pennsylvania Friends of various stripes would have ignored it. Such a confrontation would have severly strained the Quaker community and enhanced the possibility that it might divide at its Atlantic axis. But that danger was averted and all Friends were left with the less volatile difference between Quaker reformers and Quaker conservatives.

8

Perfecting Pacifism, 1756-1758

In the French and Indian War, Quaker pacifism shook off the torpor of at least half a century. In the decades preceding the war, Friends in England and America increasingly had come to regard their pacifist ethic like an article of law, to be followed in a precise way, yet with an indifferent spirit. The precision of the ethic derived from Quaker construction of biblical texts which had been passed down to eighteenth-century Friends by their predecessors. Until the 1750s, nothing was added or altered. A casualty to this conservative mentality was the enthusiasm and optimism that seventeenth-century pacifists had injected into their testimony.

In the late 1650s, George Fox and several other Quaker patriarchs said they had come to their pacifist beliefs by the movings of the spirit of Christ within them. They did not allude to biblical texts as their inspiration or limit their testimony to the letter of the Gospels. And whereas they expected that within the foreseeable future Quakerism would embrace all mankind, their pacifism carried with it an ecumenicity that disappeared in the eighteenth century. A later generation of seventeenth-century Friends—David Barclay, William Penn, and John Bellers—living after the expectation of a Quaker apocalypse had died, maintained the ecumenicity within the pacifist ethic for new reasons. They argued upon secular and humanitarian grounds that war was ultimately destructive to all belligerents. They were not content to shrug off warfare as the just deserts of the unconverted part of mankind. Finally, in the late seventeenth century, Friends began to allude to New Testament texts to demonstrate the incompatibility of war with the principles ordained by Christ.[1]

In the eighteenth century, the sources of Quaker pacifism underwent a revaluation which ended the ecumenicity in it. The textural emphasis prospered while arguments of a humanitarian, philanthropic nature nearly disappeared. With pacifism as with other Quaker testimonies to the unconverted, the stirrings of the Spirit disappeared. What remained was an overweaning concern about Quaker *complicity* with warfare, rather than about war itself.[2] It was a demonstration of sectarian exclusiveness which ironically prospered while many of the marks of Quaker exclusiveness—endogamy, dress, speech—were declining. In Pennsylvania, the Quaker pacifist concern had historically been more narrowly focused upon complicity than it had in England. For whereas English Friends might still be concerned about militia duty and the naval press gangs, Pennsylvanians, living under the panoply of Quaker legislation, had only to worry about their legislators' complicity with warfare. The Pennsylvanians needed to see that their legislators not levy, direct, or immediately pay for warfare. But pursuit of war by the non-Quaker state or magistrate ("Caesar") using Quaker money was a fact that Friends not merely abided but increasingly defended. Few Friends stood sufficiently removed from this orthodox "script" to appreciate that the Quaker demand for loyalty to the state in the eighteenth century overbore a languishing sense of the Spirit within and of humanitarianism. By 1756, their pacifism was becoming, to use John Milton's words, a "fugitive and cloistered virtue, unexercised and unbreathed, that never sallies out and sees her adversary."

Not until well into 1756 did tax collectors in Pennsylvania begin to demand payment and test the resolution of some Friends not to pay. When refused, the collector might bring in the constable to distrain the goods of the protestor, sell them at auction, keep the amount of the tax plus reasonable charges, and return the surplus, if any. If there were no goods to distrain, the constable might jail the protestor. A protestor who resisted or failed to cooperate with the law officers paid double fines.[3]

By the end of the year, ten or twelve protestors appeared in Nottingham Meeting in Chester County. But that meeting was extraordinary, for there were only some thirty protestors in all Chester County. From time to time between 1756 and 1764, tax collectors distrained John Churchman's property—cattle, household goods, and clothes. He estimated his losses at £15.[4] In Philadelphia, there were "many more non-conformists than was expected," Israel Pemberton reported. "Our ministers," he added, "are all of one mind both great and small" in supporting the protest. "Many" Friends, therefore, had goods distrained; some were threatened with jail. A constable took the two sons of James Estaugh off to jail, but he shortly let them go. The constable was satisfied with distraining the tools of their trade. The value of the tools exceeded the fines they owed, and moreover, the lack of tools left them unable to pursue their livelihoods. Yet such harassment was uncommon in Pennsylvania as a whole, Pemberton observed; the number of Friends who refused to pay was small compared with those who not only paid but censured those who refused. If the protest had any value, it was that it might make others think.[5]

It was not the loss of goods that grieved Friends as much as the discovery that the magistrates, especially the county commissioners, who prosecuted protestors were fellow Quakers. It was a harsh fact that the protestors could do little about. Their protest was a private act and not sanctioned by the Society. Officeholding, on the other hand, was perfectly ethical—although serving in the Assembly was temporarily inexpedient. And so, if it were ethical for Friends to pay taxes for war, and ethical for Friends to make and enforce the law, what could the protestors argue against Quaker magistrates? If it were appropriate that the lawmakers be disciplined by the Society for abusing brotherhood out of respect for the state, then it might be considered equally appropriate that those who refused to pay taxes be disciplined for slighting their Christian obligation to the state and embarrassing their brethren who did not.

The protestors tried to point out that it was really not relevant to speak of balancing obligations or violations: The legislators had *unethically* levied a tax, the magistrates were enforcing the unethical law, and they, the protestors, were laudably disobeying it. But that argument was so much labor lost. The opponents of the protestors harped, "Render unto Caesar . . . Render unto Caesar," oblivious of its irrelevance.[6] Because so few members joined the protest in its first ten months, the protestors planned not to press the Yearly Meeting to champion their cause and discipline their Quaker persecutors. Like seventeenth-century Friends, whom they consciously imitated, they would rely upon the example of their suffering to soften the will of their persecutors and prick the apathy of the uncommitted. Yet it was ironic and sad that they should use this means not to reach "gentiles," as the Quaker patriarchs had, but their own people. They were reformers and not evangelists, and they were acutely aware of the difference.

At the Yearly Meeting in September 1756, "many seemed to come prepared for war," Israel Pemberton reported. But if they relished the prospect of war between tax protestors and others, they were disappointed; the Meeting chose not to discuss the tax problem. The time was not "seasonable." Israel accounted it a victory not to have the problem brought up: "The mouths of the gainsayers were stopped," he cheerfully recorded. "The Lamb's spirit was victorious."[7]

When enough Quaker legislators—and six were enough—had resigned that the Assembly became a non-Quaker body, the tax protest lost much of its purpose. And when the £55,000 in taxes was all collected, the protestors would lose what remained of their grievance. Because of the ethical nice points and several conditions of the protest, it was bound to become dated and limited in its significance. For the future, only at the unlikely juncture of a Quaker-controlled legislature levying taxes and appropriating the revenue for war would the protest of 1755 and 1756 have any application. But rather than quit protesting after six or ten Friends resigned, the reformers broadened their concern.

On 23 March 1757, the Assembly and Governor William Denny enacted a tax of £100,000.[8] One would expect that the protestors would pay the taxes levied by the act because they had earlier objected to taxes levied and directly expended by a Quaker-dominated Assembly for war; now the Quaker majority in the Assembly was gone. Some paid without hesitation; others kept on refusing. "We think something more than a testimony against our apostatising brethren is required and do not find ourselves at liberty to pay," wrote Israel Pemberton.[9] From reforming some unorthodox brethren in public office, these Friends had moved on to a resolve to reform the Society itself, or its ethics on war. Now they were not merely pointing an accusing finger at some individuals; they were disapproving of the whole institution of war. They had begun by accusing Quaker lawmakers of being errant and unorthodox; now, by broadening their protest, they had assumed the role of the unorthodox. Now they could be scolded, disciplined, or even disowned: "Where any in the Church of God pretending conscience or revelation," stated the discipline of the Society, "shall arise to teach and practice (however insignificant or small in themselves) . . . principles or practice . . .

contrary to such as are also received as true . . . those who have a
true and right discerning may . . . condemn and judge such things,
and their doing so will be obligatory upon all members . . . because
they will see it to be so and submit to it."[10]

From the beginning there had been evidence that orthodoxy had
never been the first priority of the protestors and that war alone
aggrieved them. Nine years earlier, John Churchman, first of the
protestors, addressed the Quaker-dominated Assembly when it was
debating whether to erect naval defenses for Pennsylvania. On that
occasion he did not specify that the Assembly had erred by appropriating or spending money. He merely warned the members about
"warlike preparations" and recommended instead a "humble trust"
in God. He may have objected to war under any circumstances. The
"Epistle of Tender Love and Caution" did not quibble explicitly over
who expended revenues for war or over the composition of the
Assembly; the authors stated simply that the money was "intended
for purposes inconsistent with our peaceable testimony." Of all the
Quaker reformers, John Woolman left the most extensive account of
his reasons for protesting, and he clearly explained that a concern for
orthodoxy was not one of them. "It equally concerns men in every
age to take heed of their own spirit," Woolman concluded. He had
been reading about Thomas à Kempis and John Huss, and he copied
into his journal Huss's words: "This I most humbly require . . . that
I be not compelled to the thing which my conscience doth repugn or
strive against"; "I refuse nothing[;] . . . this only one thing I except,
that I do not offend God and my conscience."[11] Although Friends
professed to be guided by the "spirit within" and to have escaped the
errors of confessional Protestantism, the past weighed heavily upon
them too. The discipline was, in fact, the hand of the past restraining
the freedom of the present. Woolman and other reformers, understanding as much, respected discipline and preached it. Therefore,
they were caught in a dilemma when the obligations from the past
crowded their pacifist inclinations. They decided finally for freedom
to heed their consciences.

These Friends were restoring to Quaker pacifism the element of
humanitarianism that had been missing for some fifty years, and
some, like Woolman, were listening for the Spirit more intently than
Friends had for an even longer period. They were not troubled merely
or mainly by the fact of Quaker complicity in war. They were
troubled by war itself, beyond whatever effect it had on Quaker lives

and souls. Paying taxes to war helped to destroy people's lives and property—that was undeniably true and an insupportable burden on some consciences. The proof texts from Matthew and Romans on taxpaying were no balm. And so these few Friends did not pay. Although the world might punish them for their refusal, the world also knew immediately why they suffered—which was more than could be said for the world's understanding of Quaker grants "to the King's use."

For the radical pacifists, who had given the conservatives of the church legitimate reasons for disciplining them, the Yearly Meeting of 1757 was a time of "close probation and exercise." Some were "willing to have the matter opened, & if we [pacifists] were to be thrashed, [we were] willing to bear it." Israel Pemberton, with uncharacteristic patience, hoped that no one in the protestors' camp would rashly raise the issue; time was needed for their example to work upon the unconvinced—even as he himself had only gradually discovered the merit of their cause, he admitted.[12]

The issue did arise and the Yearly Meeting appointed a large committee of forty-three members to consider the tax question and report back. On the committee were the most prominent ministers and reformers—Churchman, Woolman, William Brown, Joseph White, Anthony Benezet; only one assemblyman or former assemblyman; and five English Friends including Hunt and Wilson. The committee unanimously recommended that because of the diversity of sentiments about taxes it was improper for Friends to discuss the matter publicly. "We are one in the Judgment," they said, and "it is highly necessary . . . that Friends every where endeavour earnestly to have their minds covered with fervent Charity towards one another."[13] The Yearly Meeting adopted the committee's report. Considering the unorthodoxy of the radical pacifists' protest, that was a victory for them. They could continue their delinquency and hope that in time Friends would consider it a virtue.

The French and Indian War tested Friends in a less equivocal way than taxing them had. In 1756 and 1757, Governors Morris and Denny and the mayor of Philadelphia proclaimed days of fasting and prayer when, as in England, citizens were to abstain from labor.[14] Unlike the matter of paying taxes, no Friend had a choice about observing the fast day; all were obliged to ignore it. Unlike Friends in London, the Pennsylvanians became indignant at the pronouncement of these observances. The Meeting for Sufferings and Philadelphia Monthly

Meeting protested that these fast days constituted an unprecedented violation of the religious liberties guaranteed by the provincial charter. They protested to little or no avail. The proclamation remained, and in 1756 many Friends observed the first fast. Some even held a religious meeting, to the dismay of other, more conscientious members. The Society made the celebrants acknowledge their error. Because the celebrants seemed to have erred from ignorance as much as from indifference, the Yearly Meeting printed two thousand copies of instructions to Friends, to guard against any more innocent violations.[15]

The Society's remaining wartime troubles came from the Assembly. While Friends yet controlled it, it passed an act for a volunteer militia, and Governor Robert Morris, beset by frontiersmen, signed the act. Thomas Penn, however, loathed the act because of its democratic features. With little effort, Penn induced the Privy Council to nullify it. He then demanded a new, satisfactory one from the Assembly, which at the time contained only a minority of Friends. Quakers were not to be conscripted, Penn made clear, but they were to pay for substitutes.[16] He congratulated himself on his estimable solicitude for Quaker pacifism when in fact he gave them merely what he found convenient. Quaker principles required them to suffer rather than pay for substitutes, but Penn was not going to concede that point of conscience.

That Penn should demand from the Assembly a militia act prejudicial to Friends should not have unduly alarmed them. There was normally a great disparity between what Penn demanded and what the Assembly supplied. The fate of Friends really depended upon the Assembly's disposition toward them. Seven or eight Friends were still members, one of them the speaker; but whether they could be depended upon to protect the Society was questionable. Neither the Friends nor the other assemblymen were likely to conscript Friends but neither were they likely to show Friends any additional consideration. The whole group was more united in their political outlook than divided by their differing religious professions.

At its 1756–58 session the Assembly largely divided its attention between the appropriation of £100,000 for the war and a new militia act. The militia bill that it drafted and then passed in March 1757 contained a new hazard for Quakers—"an equal and considerable Fine . . . laid on every Person capable of bearing Arms" who did not serve. The Assembly touted the justice of the provision—its equal operation upon all people: "every Congregation have the same Liberties [to escape military service] upon paying the Fines for Non-attendance on the Military Duties."[17] But the equality was in the eye of those who did not scruple at paying fines; to Friends, who did, it was a violation of their religious liberties, and much the same as Penn's insistence that they pay for substitutes. The plain language of the Charter of Privileges and the laws of the province protected Friends and others from the very thing the Assembly had ordered. And, Friends added, the history of the province from 1682 to the volunteer militia act of 1755 certified these rights and immunities in the law and impeached the actions of this Assembly.[18] As some Friends might have understood but preferred not to say, before 1756 the parties to the charter, laws, and history of Pennsylvania, except for the king, had been Friends or mostly Friends. Now they were mostly outsiders. The lesson seemed to be that the Quaker sanctuary depended not upon the constitution and laws, but upon Quaker government; and as many Friends warned, withdrawing from the government was fraught with dangers for the Society. It was no wonder that altruistic as well as proud and vain Friends balked when reformers asked them to leave their public offices.

When the Meeting for Sufferings protested to the Assembly against the militia bill, the Assembly paid the protest "little or no notice." The House even suspended its normal procedures in order to avoid the petition.[19] Speaker Norris told Friends that they were tardy in coming to the House—the bill had already gone to the governor for his signature. He also made it clear that he would be no party to their effort, and that they should not presume upon his membership in the Society as Friends had done with other Quaker legislators in the past seventy-four years. But the representatives of the Meeting for Sufferings corrected him: the bill would be returned to the House with the governor's amendments and then there would be an opportunity for the House to consider the Friends' recommendations. But the Friends did not win the opportunity to amend the bill; Norris and the House continued to ignore them. They then turned to Governor Denny, but he recommended that they appeal to the House. They already had, they replied. Go to the House anyway, he repeated, for he had sent the bill there with his amendments. Following Denny's injunction, the Friends returned to the House, only to learn that it had adjourned.[20]

Some Friends were enraged by this runaround; others were dispirited. The legislature had not even shown the petitioners the courtesy any citizen had a right to expect. And they were not just an odd lot of citizens or even of Friends, but were the representatives of the whole Society. The pride of many of them must have been wounded because never had the Society been so patronized by an Assembly of the province. We are the descendants, the Friends reminded the House, of the "pious, sober & substantial People . . . called Quakers," who had come to this place and improved a wilderness in order to enjoy the religious rights granted us.[21] But having to remind the legislators of that fact was a humbling exercise in itself and an admission that Friends' situation had gravely declined. It is ironic that while this group of Friends was being harassed and snubbed by the legislators, Englishmen still believed that the legislators were Friends and ciphers of Philadelphia Yearly Meeting![22] How much did Friends have to suffer from their representatives before Englishmen discovered the difference between the representatives and Friends?

The militia act that the Assembly and governor passed in 1757 was still too democratic for Penn but it was the only act the Assembly was willing to give him. Consequently, Pennsylvania remained without a militia for the rest of the war and Friends escaped the trials they had anticipated. The Whiggish behavior of Pennsylvania's legislators for once returned the Society a benefit.

From a different consideration, however, it was not an unmixed benefit that Friends escaped the suffering a militia law would have brought. If the Society of Friends were to be reformed, the members who preferred their ease to everything else ought to have been discovered, and separated from those who would suffer or sacrifice their ease on behalf of the church. The discipline of the Society operated to separate persons who were really committed to the Society from nominal professors, and when the reformers revived discipline they were "winnowing" the members.[23] Self-imposed trials or reform, however, created considerable acrimony within the church, divided brethren, and opened the reformers to accusations of sanctimoniousness and insensitivity. Even Friends who were themselves willing to suffer disliked contriving tests for others. But if, instead, the Society were to be dealt an imposition from an alien quarter, no one in the Society who counseled resistance and suffering could easily be accused of cruelty or of causing the suffering of their brethren. The trouble before 1758 was that the imposition upon the Society—taxation for war—was an equivocal threat to Quaker religious standards and did not come from an alien, or entirely alien, quarter. It was no great boon to reformers like Samuel Fothergill who hoped the tax would "be finally conducive to the glory of the ever worthy Name, if it issue in the winnowing of the people." Instead, it was likely to bring merely "such a breach and division as never happened amongst us since we were a people."[24] The reformation appeared deadlocked, certainly as far as its political side was concerned.

With no better test than the tax, Friends in 1758 encountered unforeseen demands which were temporarily useful in discovering slackers and relieving the deadlock. In 1758, the government raised a new expedition, commanded by General John Forbes, against Ft. Duquesne. In the 1756–57 session, the Assembly passed an act regulating the hire of wagons or horses to be used to transport military supplies. Any owner of wagons or horses who was asked by a constable to hire them out was obliged to comply. Noncompliance was punished by a fine of between twenty and forty shillings, as was any other act that obstructed the services demanded by the law. Any protestor who refused to pay his fine would have his goods distrained and sold at auction.[25] In 1757, the act made little difference because no military expedition existed. But in the spring of 1758 and later, General Forbes's expedition created a great demand for transport, and Friends, among others, were obliged to supply.

Many Friends complied with the demands of magistrates to lease their wagons and horses, but at the same time most of them were uneasy about the morality of supplying an army and being paid for it. Because there was no dearth of Quaker magistrates ready to reassure the vacillating owners that supplying wagons and teams violated no Quaker precept, most of them complied.[26] The Quaker magistrates spoke only for themselves. Some monthly meetings believed, on the contrary, that supplying the army did violate Quaker discipline, and they proceeded immediately against the putative delinquents. That action provoked officeholding Friends to complain, and in their meetings they controverted such proceedings—as they had opposed every measure intended to promote pacifism or maintain discipline. In Chester County, controversy arose in Quarterly Meeting and the Meeting in turn asked for a judgment from Yearly Meeting. The less scrupulous Friends did not want the Yearly Meeting's advice; the query (together with one about keeping Negro slaves) was something "not worthy of noting" they protested. But it went to Yearly Meeting anyway.[27]

At Yearly Meeting a committee of twenty-nine Friends unanimously resolved that leasing wagons and horses was a military service
in violation of Quaker pacifism. With little debate, the Meeting
adopted the report and ordered monthly meetings to work with the
violators to convince them of their error and to secure their promise
not to repeat the error. As for the Quaker magistrates who facilely
advised their brethren to commit the error, they were to resign from
any public office that obliged them to demand from their brethren
"any act they [the brethren] may conscientiously scruple to perform."
Nor were the Quaker magistrates to demand compliance from non-
Quakers who could not conscientiously comply with the law. Forcing compliance from *anyone* was "Essentially repugnant to that
Liberty of Conscience for which our Ancestors deeply suffered" to
obtain and preserve. If magistrates persisted in their "repugnant"
conduct after being warned, they were to be denied admission to the
Society's meetings for business and discipline and excluded from all
"the Affairs of Truth." They would not be disowned, but they would
be removed from influence in the Society.[28] Because of their behavior
outside of Quaker councils, these public men might no longer continue
to obstruct the progress of pacifism and discipline within. From
another demand the government laid upon Friends had arisen a prospect that reformation might proceed.

It "affords great satisfaction," remarked James Pemberton,
reviewing the work of the Yearly Meeting, "that when Friends are
Collected the holy standard hath been lifted up & so generall a Consent
appears to fly to it that the Spirit of Libertinism is kept under."[29]
When collected together, Quaker reformers could indeed direct the
higher councils of the Society and rather easily put down the opposition. But when the reformers dispersed to their local meetings,
success did not come as easily as at Yearly Meeting. Most opponents
of reform—men of public affairs—did not turn out in large numbers
at quarterly and yearly meetings in order to direct the business; they
committed their time and energy to the Assembly and other public
institutions. By comparison, their commitment to the church was
nominal. But when this nominal affiliation demanded some real
compliance from them in their public lives, they resisted and denied
the reformers an easy execution of the Yearly Meeting orders.

Chester Quarterly Meeting found that several or even most
monthly meetings in the Quarter were ignoring the orders. Later, in
1759, it discovered that Friends who had supplied wagons and horses

in 1758 and had been reprimanded were doing it again and defending their behavior.[30] The demands of the military had not ended with the Forbes expedition; by fits and starts such demands continued until the end of the French and Indian War. Consequently, the enforcement of the Society's order became a long-term labor.

Delinquents, unabashed at their errors and recidivism, joined other Friends in criticizing the disciplinarians as draconic, uncharitable, and dangerous to the unity of the church. Pacifism was not the only ethic the disciplinarians were enforcing at the time; they vigorously pressed the whole code of the Society upon the attention of the other members. Even so, the complaints of the "libertines" most often specified the pacifist demands upon them. Their recourse when the hierarchy of the Society looked askance at them was to suggest that the disciplinarians were driving Friends so hard that they would provoke a schism. Not that these discontented members threatened to leave the Society; that would have been hard driving on their own part. Members would have seen that the complainers were using the prospect of schism to manipulate the church. Rather, the discontented wished to appear like advocates for some nameless, disconsolate members, overborne by the disciplinarians. And their ploy had its successes.

In January 1759, James Pemberton believed that "A spirit of Destraction, Confusion, and Division was never at so great a height among us as now."[31] The dissidents had scared up an advocate in John Fothergill, who warned Israel Pemberton that

From what I hear some amongst you are straining at gnats and swallowing camels. Rigorously insisting upon points which are disputable . . . whilst rancour, animosity, and fiery ignorant zeal is tolerated, nay commended. . . . it is hardly possible to be in such a state and yet maintain Christian charity. There is scarcely anything that can occur which can justify disunion.[32]

Even Anthony Benezet, who had signed the unanimous report to prohibit assistance to the military, began excusing the delinquents, extenuating their errors, and criticizing the disciplinarians: "we should be more backward in picking up Stones, for it's very hard for persons in trade not to be, even inadvertently, more or less engaged in Matters that border very near, if not exceed the Waggon affair."[33]

In its report, the Yearly Meeting committee of twenty-nine had anticipated objections that pleaded for unity and charity. It wrote that when the Society cannot correct friends who violate the liberty of conscience which the earliest Friends suffered to establish, *"true Unity cannot be maintained."*[34] In a treatise on disciple, the reformer John Griffin criticized:

those whose principal view is only maintaining the form or outward character in religion, feel very little or no pain on account of the disorderly practices of their fellow-members, and therefore they can easily daub with untempered mortar, and smooth all over, crying peace . . . ; and all this done under the specious pretence of charity and christian tenderness.[35]

Really, both the pacifists and their opponents were promoting liberty and curtailing it as well. The pacifists desired the liberty to violate the law without having their fellow Quakers prosecute them. Their opponents wanted to be left at liberty to prosecute law-breakers without having the Society discipline them or make them leave public office. As for unity (or "true Unity"), when the pacifists used that ambiguous word they meant uniformity within the Society, and specifically, uniformly pacifist behavior. Their critics espoused a unity or consensus that permitted diversity of opinions and behavior about war and pacifism—daubing over differences. Finally, the disciplinarians suspected that when charity was urged, it was likely some self-indulgent Friends pleading for their own comfort while only pretending to care about others.

If draconic enforcement of the 1758 Yearly Meeting order was ever anything but a fabrication of the more bellicose Friends, it was very short-lived. Only thirty-two Friends were disciplined between 1758 and 1764 for supplying wagons and horses, whereas the contributors were far more numerous—Chester Quarterly Meeting boggled at the labor required to treat all the delinquents in its precincts.[36] Instead of bringing contributors before the monthly meetings, recording them, appointing a different committee to treat with each one, and requiring a public disavowal of their error, they were visited privately and reprimanded or counseled as the case required. To extrapolate from records about the thirty-two who did go through the formal disciplinary process, most of the others probably pleaded ignorance of the 1758 order, blamed Quaker magistrates who had cajoled them into complying, and ended by promising to obey the order—all of which was taken as a satisfactory response. No magistrate was disowned from the Society or excluded from its business meetings, although two (included in the thirty-two) were disciplined and forgiven. Whether the disciplinarians were fearful of schism and proceeded cautiously or were simply lenient, they in any case relied upon persuasion rather than coercion.

Year in and year out between 1758 and 1764, reformist Friends visited delinquents and meetings, tirelessly advising, cautioning, and correcting them.[37] George Churchman in his extensive journal described these labors which were only summarily noted in the Society's records. At James Moore's home near Lancaster, Churchman and two other ministers had a "serious Conversation" with a regular member who was a magistrate and for some years an assemblyman.

I felt easy [Churchman recalled] in a gentle manner to put him in mind (tho' an elder Brother) of the Concern and united Sense & Judgment of our Yearly Meeting, expressed in one or more minutes thereof ... and to consider whether it was not safest for those who craved to experience the Unity of the Body, to pay a due regard to the Sense of the Body. . . . I had . . . satisfaction in that conference, believing the Spirit of Truth owns even small motions rightly begotten.[38]

The three preferred to speak to officeholders privately, because when they addressed them in open meetings, other members occasionally rose to defend the officeholders against the advice and emissaries of the Yearly Meeting and of quarterly meetings. The committeemen felt weak at Chester Quarter, Churchman said, because so many active members of the Society justified their magistrates.[39]

On 3 February 1763, Churchman and other committeemen rode to Middletown Monthly Meeting in Bucks County through deep snow.

The meeting was painful & heavy; by reason of a Spirit of Opposition, especially in two elderly men of their Active Members; who appear'd averse to matters they accounted new, and to regulations different from what had been in practice among them. (One we found was a Commissioner for laying that called the King's Tax). This was truly an exercising Season; yet we were favour'd with Ability to communicate our Sentiments pretty fully.[40]

That summer Middletown and adjacent Wrightstown Monthly Meeting wanted the 1758 Yearly Meeting minute revoked insofar as it required Quaker magistrates to decline offices in which they had to prosecute their brethren. After Bucks Quarterly Meeting referred the request to Yearly Meeting in September, the Yearly Meeting resolved that its order stood.[41]

While it labored with Quaker magistrates and lesser officials, the Society did not forget its premier recidivists, the assemblymen. Every year since 1755 they had appropriated additional sums for the war and raised them by taxes. Altogether these appropriations amounted to £460,000.[42] The assemblymen were notoriously bellicose, "From holding Principles of nonresistance we are become a People valiant for war," wrote Edward Shippen, Jr., a non-Friend, "and a thorough Quaker is scarce to be found among our people in power."[43] Consequently, the Meeting for Sufferings in 1760 appointed a committee to visit the Quaker assemblymen and Speaker Norris.[44] In seven visits during five months, this committee reminded the assemblymen that all that Quaker legislators could ethically do was appropriate money for the king's use; then it read to them a bill of their errors since 1756 which terminated with their refusal to leave office when their public duties had obliged them to oppress their brethren.[45]

The indictment sounded conclusive, but the assemblymen had an alibi. Just as they had since 1755, they refused to admit that the appropriations acts demanded anything a Friend was forbidden to give: "Render unto Caesar," they canted. The laws demanding wagons and horses were a different matter. The assemblymen agreed that the laws oppressed Friends and they tried to excuse themselves from any blame by telling the delegation that sometimes they had voted against the acts and had asked that their nay votes be recorded. The House had denied their request, however. Despite the legislation prejudicial to Friends and the overruling of the minority of the House, the Quaker assemblymen assured their visitors that the House was in fact "well affected" toward the Society and would relieve Friends' suffering—which made the punitive effects of their laws sound like mere inadvertence.[46] That relief never came.

The Friends refused to resign their seats in the Assembly. Their presence there, they averred, was not due to their own exertions or even their desires. Without solicitation they had been drafted by the people. They talked as though they were the flotsam of democracy, carried into the House on the popular tide. They resented suggestions that they resign. They saw themselves as performing awesome duty in the legislature: namely, preventing Thomas Penn from subverting the charter of Pennsylvania and depriving the people of their constitutional rights.[47] They very likely missed the irony in their proud statement of their mission, even though the Friends from the Meeting for Sufferings had read one-half of the irony to them only minutes before. Whiggism preempted their capacity to worry about religious rights, and their violations of religious liberties guaranteed by the charter hardly registered with them. They were unable, as John Woolman would say, to make someone else's situation their own.

The different rights that Quaker legislators and Quaker reformers defended illuminated much of the history of the province and the Society. The legislators were the successors of Thomas Lloyd, David Lloyd, and John Kinsey, who like these earlier Friends worried over the loss of their public power to aliens like governors of the province, immigrants, and the Proprietary party. In the 1750s the Quaker legislators assailed Penn's instructions to his deputy governors with the very brief that David Lloyd had drafted in 1725. They held on to their seats for the same reasons that Friends in the 1740s had refused to give up the legislature to the Proprietary party. The former and present Friends had in common a concern for powers and rights which, with few exceptions, had no necessary connection with Quakerism. Substitute Baptists or some other denomination for Friends and the substitutes could aptly argue the same case. Substitute a political party for Quakers and in most cases, the same arguments would serve the party as well as they served the Quakers. It was not as a suffering church, but as an embattled political party or oligarchy that most of these Friends had resisted alien threats. Their Quakerism was largely coincidental and the desire for power and place essential to their careers. By 1755, or even 1744, Quaker politicians had become less sensitive than their predecessors to what was genuinely Quaker about their political mission, until at last they denied their brethren's religious rights in order to more easily secure their own political powers and careers.

The reformers, on the other hand, served mostly as a foil to this history. They did not ask that any public powers or offices be preserved for Friends. They were no political party. In relation to the government, they were subjects only and supplicants pleading for their right to live without being oppressed because of their religious ethics. Ironically, they were asking to be granted the very liberties that William Penn and other Friends in 1682 had expected to grant to all who would come to Pennsylvania. But because Quaker government had taken a different course, after 1755, the Friends who paid attention to these religious liberties appeared as reformers.

Friends had been a minority among Pennsylvanians since the turn of the seventeenth century, but not until the French and Indian War did they behave like a self-conscious religious minority. The more reformist and ascetic Friends in Pennsylvania understood their minority status and the comparative weakness of the Society; however, they prized this status and discovered in it the Society's deliverance from its decline. "Our Connections with the Powers of the Earth are reduc'd to small Bounds," the Meetings for Sufferings confessed, yet we fervently desire that this circumstance "may have the proper Effect to establish the Church in Righteousness, & fix our Trust in the Lord alone for Protection & Deliverance."[48] When a complete reliance upon Providence became the foremost qualification for a Friend, they could interpret their ouster from government and their disfavor among the public as the interference of Providence on their behalf. Seeking to reassert Quaker power and recreate Quaker connections, on the other hand, betrayed a lack of faith. This amounted to a transformation of Quaker values greater than the transformation of their station in public life. The lesson was so foreign to their political experience that it was very difficult to teach; and no wonder that the pedagogues from the Meeting for Sufferings failed with many assemblymen. "The Lord said 'resist not evil,'" Anthony Benezet preached. But Quaker officeholders objected that if Benezet's advice prevailed, they would all become prey to their enemies. "I grant that," Benezet replied, but suffering "is no cause of grief. . . . We must give up our interest, and suffer matters to go contrary to our judgment."[49]

For numerous Friends, the humbler status of private citizen and the single dependence upon God would not be their lot by choice; and the French and Indian War was withal not punitive enough to force them to a humble station and to faith alone. Even the more stalwart members of the church occasionally betrayed too great a reliance upon worldly prospects. Israel Pemberton, for example, "raved like a mad man," when he learned that his candidate for governor had not received the office in 1756.[50] But despite these and other outbursts of the old spirit, humility gained ground in the Society and in Pemberton too. At the end of 1758, probably the most frenetic year of his life, Pemberton's meditation on his own experiences pretty well described the tendency of the whole Society:

Infinite wisdom is directing us to a more inward, self-denying Path than we or most of our immediate Predecessors have trod in. It seems at times as if our Enemy were employ'd to instruct us in this lesson, at least their unjust Treatment should serve to impress it on our minds, & tend to alienate us from the desire of seeking the Friendship or honour of Men.[51]

9

Reformation Stalled, 1763–1765

After 1763, public attacks upon the Society of Friends frustrated the reformers' plan for the withdrawal of all Friends from government. Quaker politicians and their like-minded brethren were not entirely, or even mostly, unreasonable and callous men. Feeling the need to protect Friends and believing that, when beset by enemies, one must resort to power and public schemes, they were unwilling to forgo power. Reformers had to admit the dilemmas of the times and the attractiveness of using power to solve them, even though they doubted the ultimate wisdom of the solutions. It was especially painful for them to admit that they might be abandoning the Indians of Pennsylvania to official and public indifference and hostility. Withdrawal from government seemed to conflict with another aspect of reformation—philanthropy. The governor and Council had declared war upon the Delawares and the Assembly had conspired to pay men to scalp them. Now who would restore the peace and provide justice for the ancient friends of William Penn and the original Quaker settlers? How would Friends now fulfill the solemn, benevolent promises made in fabled meetings under an elm on the shores of the Delaware? Was the peaceable kingdom forfeit?

In 1756, some Friends resolved to use their private influence and wealth to aid the Indians. No other form of Quaker philanthropy except abolition followed so soon after the Quaker shift to sectarianism. The effect of this philanthropy upon the future of almost all Pennsylvania Friends was profound. It was far greater than the immediate outlay of Friends' time and money and the abuse and disappointments returned to Friends. Because the fear of Indian attacks was uppermost in the minds of most Pennsylvanians, to physically aid the Indians and politically defend them was to do little short of committing treason in the eyes of some. The Indian menace would eventually recede, but the animosity against Friends would not disappear like its original cause.

The Perils of Philanthropy

By late 1757, some Philadelphia Friends had fully organized to assist the Indians—giving their organization the name the Friendly Association for Regaining and Preserving Peace with the Indians by Pacific Measures. The members were all Friends, mostly wealthy, overwhelmingly from the city, politically aware, and sympathetic to the reformation of the Society—although most were not active reformers. Israel Pemberton, James Pemberton, John Reynell, Abel James, Isaac Zane, William Callender, and Jonathan Mifflin were the foremost members and officers. From beginning to end, Israel Pemberton dominated the Association's activities.

The Friendly Association was intended to restore the Indian policy of Pennsylvania to its historic, peaceful course; that involved investigating the Indians' grievances and correcting any legitimate complaints or injustices. In doing so, Friends were presuming to inject themselves as the principal intermediary between the government and the Indians. That activity raised a political uproar, and from many quarters returned more reproach than applause.[1]

From 1757 through 1762, the Friendly Association and Israel Pemberton shrilly averred that the Delawares had been defrauded in the Walking Purchase of 1737.[2] The Friends assigned the blame for the war so unequivocally to that fraud and to the Penns that the Penns made no distinction between these new antagonists and their old nemesis, the Assembly. Likewise, most Pennsylvanians, uninformed about the differences within the Society or the ongoing reformation, lumped the Assembly and the Friendly Association together. They attributed the worst motives of the assemblymen to the privately active Friends. If a critic already disliked the Assembly or the Society, he damned both in the same breath.

Admittedly, there were reasons for the public's confusion. The Assembly and its Indian commissioners had private or selfish reasons to repeat the charges that Friends made against the Penns; assemblymen expected that the Assembly's good name and power would grow from any embarrassment of the proprietors. The Friends in the Association really had philanthropy at heart, but they got little credit for it, thanks in part to the Assembly. It seemed rather that all Friends conspired to run Pennsylvania just as they always had and that Israel Pemberton meddled in executive affairs much the same as he had in the 1740s.

The successes of the Friendly Association were few.[3] For the Society, the effects of those efforts was momentous. The Society already had a reputation for obstructing the defense of Pennsylvania early in the French and Indian War. Now many Pennsylvanians linked the whole Society with the Friendly Association's patronage of the Delawares and the more than £5,000 it expended on their behalf. And well they might; most Friends trusted the Delawares more than they did vocal frontiersmen and other antagonists of the Indians. The mistake of the frontiersmen was not especially to link all Friends to the charity shown the Indians, but to damn the Indians out of hand and all Englishmen who helped them.

In 1763, when the Friendly Association's activities substantially ended, its impact upon the Society substantially began. In the northwest, the Ottawa chief Pontiac was rallying the Indians of the area to rebel against their new overlords, the English. In the spring of 1763, the Indians attacked and took every British fort in the northwest except Detroit. In June, they took the forts in Pennsylvania except Pitt, which they beseiged.[4] In July, together with the Delawares, they struck east of the Allegheny mountains. As in 1755, the settlers fell back to the towns of the east; Carlisle, Shippensburg, and Lancaster again swelled with refugees. That the Delawares, long cultivated by the Friendly Association, were killing colonists, confirmed the frontiersmen's prejudice against Friends. They did not require evidence of any Quaker complicity in the attacks in order to damn Quakers, just as they did not ponder the Indians' motives before damning them.[5]

Winter brought a hiatus in the Indian attacks, but the beginning of the colonists' revenge. When rumors of the Indian attacks reached eastern Pennsylvania, fanatics there were ready to embellish the stories and fire up local prejudices against Indians—any Indians. Threatened with death, innocent and peaceful Indians from Northhampton County fled to Philadelphia where Friends mustered to welcome them.[6] The killing of twenty Conestoga Indians at Lancaster became a cause célèbre in the politics of the period.

On 14 December, a band of some 50 men from Paxton Township

near Harrisburg rode to Conestoga Manor near Lancaster and murdered 6 of the Indians. Fourteen Conestogas who escaped (because they were away peddling brooms and baskets) were lodged in the Lancaster jail for their own safety. And yet, on 27 December, Paxton men returned, broke into the jail, and killed the 14. The Paxton men reportedly swore that next they would get the 140 refugee Indians in Philadelphia.[7] Giving full credit to this and similar threats, the government shipped the doleful Indians off to New York and safety. David Cooper, a Friend who helped the Indians in New Jersey, discovered many people were enraged, calling "for having ye whole [red] Colour Destroyed as ye Jews destroyed ye Canninites, without regard to fd. or foe." One drunken zealot from the neighborhood came after Cooper with sword and gun.[8] The governor of New York would have nothing to do with the planned sanctuary for the Indians and stopped them at the Hudson River. Back across New Jersey the Indians trekked, arriving at Philadelphia on 24 January.

The return of the Indians angered the Paxtonites, who prepared to march to Philadelphia. Word reached the city on 4 February that they were coming on, prepared to "put to death all the Indians," surround the Quaker meetinghouses, and demand that Israel Pemberton be turned over to them. Pemberton sent his family away from the city immediately and shortly thereafter followed them. His flight embarrassed some Friends and relatives.[9] The frontiersmen regarded Pemberton as an aspiring quisling. He had agents and spies circulating among them, they averred; he had caused fur traders to be killed by the Indians. "The[y] spar no pains for to make thee look as black in the ies of the wereld as men . . . cin invent," a Lancaster County Friend furtively wrote to Pemberton. "I wod have thee bestor [bestir] thy self," he urged, for they will do you "all [the] meles [malice] lys in thir power."[10] Pemberton had already bestirred himself.

The whole city bestirred itself. No alarm since Braddock's defeat, if even that, had so galvanized its inhabitants. Infantry and artillery mustered; redoubts were put up. The distant report of guns provoked the firing of cannon in the city on the fourth of February. On the night of the fifth, church bells rang, streets were illuminated, citizens emerged from their beds to take up arms. It was no false alarm; the Paxton men were indeed coming. But the Paxtonites (approximately 250 of them) stopped at Germantown, their aggressions cooled by a rainstorm and the knowledge of a warm welcome awaiting them in the city. Franklin and six other officials and citizens went out to Germantown and conferred with the Paxtonites.[11]

After the conference, the conflict shifted to a different mode, pamphleteering. Never had Pennsylvanians seen such a profusion of pamphlets as those that were published about the march and the Indian rebellion—sixty-three in about eight weeks.[12] Friends were mentioned in almost all of them.

In the press, Friends were accused of the deaths of the frontier inhabitants, and judged every bit as guilty as the Indians. "In many things change but the Name, / Quakers and Indians are the same," went one piece of doggerel. It continued:

never spare
To give yur Indians Clothes to wear; Send 'em good Beef, and Pork, and
    Bread,
Guns, Powder, Flints and store of Lead,
To shoot your Neighbours through the Head; . . . Encourage ev'ry friendly
    Savage,
To murder, burn, destroy and ravage.[13]

Several authors explained that Israel Pemberton and other Friends had perversely and falsely persuaded the Delawares that they had been defrauded in 1737. He taught them to despise white men and gave them "a rod to scourge the white People." And when the Quaker strategems worked and the Indians attacked, the Quakers "secretly rejoyc[d] when . . . [they] hear[d] of whole Settlements murdered and destroyed."[14]

It did not matter that Friends had befriended woebegone, weak, or Christian Indians, some of them defrauded of their land. All were guilty. "They are all Perfidious," and the ostensibly peaceful were only spies for the rest.[15] Whatever Friends had done to help any of them made them accomplices of all. And the Friends' lack of generosity to the frontiersmen, compared to the £5,000 given the Indians, incriminated them still further. The Indianphobes presumed that men segregated according to color, religion, and civilization, and that Friends had violated these bonds by assisting heathen, savage redmen in preference to their own kind.[16]

The motives that the pamphleteers and others attributed to the allegedly evil Friends appeared lame. Israel Pemberton and other friends were supposed to be profiting from a monopoly of the fur trade. George Bryan, the Presbyterian and future revolutionary leader, observed that his fellow Presbyterians and Scotch-Irish believed that the Quakers were unhappy at their minorityhood and did not mind that the Indians reduced the numbers of their rivals. One pamphleteer wrote:

> Of Scotch and Irish let them kill
> As many Thousands as they will,
> That you may lord it o'er the land,
> And have the whole and sole command.[17]

Quakers resisted frontier petitions for reapportionment of the Assembly because the Society, predominant in the three southeastern counties, would lose its alleged control of Pennsylvania's government. Pamphlets also explained that Quakers had posed as ombudsmen for the Indians only in order to contrive another excuse for attacking the proprietors.[18] Whatever the particulars, the pamphleteers basically asserted that Quakers constantly lusted for power and had won it by hook or crook and despite the contrary appearances of their retreating from public offices.

More incriminating in the eyes of Scotch-Irishmen, when the Paxton men approached Philadelphia on 5 February and the city mounted a defense, two hundred or so young Quaker men took up arms and busied themselves in the preparations. Well-wishers and antagonists of the Society alike were astonished at the sight, but the antagonists recited the episode tirelessly, whereas the well-wishers and Friends had little to say in reply. It was the linchpin for several arguments in pamphlets like *The Quaker Unmask'd*. Because of the undisputed fact that the Friends were armed, specious charges were printed and read. "When their King and Country call them to Arms, they plead Conscience," wrote David Dove, but when his countrymen vex a Quaker "then see the Quaker unmask'd, with his Gun upon his Shoulder . . . thirsting for the Blood of . . . his Opponents."[19]

Such were the returns for Quaker philanthropy to the Indians. Friends judged that it was wisest not to reply; their credibility had been too severely compromised and the opposition literature was too profuse in the winter and spring of 1763–64. The Society issued only one statement, and that to the governor in order to answer the accusations the Paxton men had presented to him and the Assembly. "Truth will gain ground," John Hunt wrote from England, "not by open contests and reasoning, but by humble resignation and Suffering. The great Cause of Religion never lost by Suffering."[20]

Their silence, however, did not mean that Friends were not worried.

The Paxton episode gave Friends good reason to believe that old fears were warranted. They knew that Presbyterians had joined Anglicans and the Penns in 1755 and 1756 to help oust Friends from government. John Fothergill had ominously warned at the time that old enemies were reviving, and that through Samuel Chandler's efforts, Presbyterians on two continents were synchronizing their efforts to harry Friends. Now, seven years later, the spectre of Presbyterian malice reappeared. Old accusations were being repeated at Whitehall and St. James's: Pennsylvania Friends were helping to cause the Indian depredations. And in America there appeared to be no end to the difficulty the Presbyterians could create with their numbers and violent character. As far as James Pemberton could see, the prospect was cheerless. "The old envious persecuting spirit" of the seventeenth century was alive again, and history appeared about to repeat itself.[21]

A considerable number of Quaker party members and other Friends subscribed to a more convoluted explanation of the winter's events. For them, the march of the Paxton men was no simple frontiersmen's rebellion that flopped. Their suspicions were aroused by the fact that the magistrates at Lancaster had not exerted themselves to prevent the murder of the Conestoga Indians; that the frontier magistrates sent no intelligence of the Paxton men to Philadelphia; that Governor John Penn had not interrogated two representatives from the Paxton gang at Germantown; and that the executive branch appeared slow in prosecuting the murders at Lancaster. Add to these oddities the fear among Philadelphians that another march was in preparation, and one had reasonable motive to suspect that the episode had not ended and that a conspiracy was still afoot in the spring of 1764.[22]

The more mistrustful observers concluded that the Proprietary party had manufactured false evidence, commissioned the march or riot, and even hired idle soldiers to join it in order to drive the Quaker party into submission to the proprietors. The Presbyterians were, as in 1756, only the cat's-paw of the cunning Penns. James Pemberton, while a believer in conspiracy, could not credit this full-blown version. He believed the Paxton massacres and march had their independent and obvious causes, but that once the Presbyterians were making mischief, the Proprietary party gladly turned whatever advantage it could from that mischief.[23]

In March, Governor Penn imposed a novel condition upon the Assembly before consenting to a £50,000 appropriation. The assemblymen concluded that they had just been given a ransom demand: Accede to his condition and the governor would expedite the money needed to assuage the frontiersmen's wrath and forestall another march upon the city. The assemblymen were enraged, especially in view of the genuine inequity of Penn's condition. They answered not by conceding but by resolving to give Pennsylvania its sharpest turnabout ever. They planned in earnest to have the proprietary charter repealed and royal government introduced into Pennsylvania. To their minds, the new regime could not help but improve the mercenary rule of the Penns. Therefore, the Assembly deputized Franklin to go to London to lobby in behalf of the change; and in Pennsylvania it instigated a press campaign to gain popular support and signatures upon petitions for royal government.[24]

Discipline Defeated; Reformation Stalled

The march of the Paxton men and the effects it generated in the press and government severely wrenched the Society of Friends. Friends were embarrassed by the two hundred young members who took up arms on 5 February. Little that the Society could do or say would have quieted the glee of the Presbyterians and others at this apparent show of hypocrisy, and the Society did little enough.[25] In March, Philadelphia Monthly Meeting appointed a special committee to investigate the men who had turned out on 5 February, and to separate the contrite from genuine nonpacifists. Almost every month for the following three years the committee reported its progress with the delinquent young men. In April 1765, the committee dismissed the penitent men and some thirty-two others who were minors, but continued with the unrepentant for another two years. Six are recorded as publicly condemning their errors.[26]

The excuse that the unrepentant delinquents offered to Philadelphia Monthly Meeting for their misdeeds focused upon the Paxton men rather than themselves. The enormity of the frontiersmen's offense and their danger to the province justified the bellicosity of these Friends. The government had been incapable of stopping the insurgents or apprehending them for their earlier crimes. No government could long exist that permitted such a large number of men to defy it, argued Edward Penington—a socially and economically prominent Friend who allegedly had led a whole company of men in arms.[27]

Penington's statement is interesting because he did not excuse himself on the more pardonable ground of self-defense or some fear of his life, but out of concern for the government and law. Penington was hardly conscious of his sectarian affiliation, but rather affiliated himself with the old political order, which needed defending. In concluding, Penington told his judges that he felt the Society was liberal enough to overlook his behavior and others' like it.

Penington had judged the Society correctly. The exceptional fear that the Paxton men had excited, together with Friends' belief in the venal origins of the march and Friends' involvement in a remedy for it—royal government—led many to extenuate the error of the unrepentant delinquents. They treated the delinquents as victims of the Proprietary party's machinations, who did not deserve disownment. In the end, they were not disowned. Excusing them was a signal failure of discipline between 1755 and the American Revolution. Because the public as well as the Friends understood what was at issue in the debate, discharging the delinquents fueled the many allegations that Friends were hypocrites.

The dismissal of the delinquents by Philadelphia Monthly Meeting in 1767 caused a dispute in the Society; not everyone was ready to truckle to the city Friends who sympathized with the delinquents' response to the Paxton men. The non-Philadelphians wanted additional treatment of the offenders and they succeeded in having the transactions of Philadelphia Monthly and Quarterly meetings laid before Yearly Meeting and debated. But Yearly Meeting resolved to let the affair rest and be satisfied with Philadelphia's handling of it. William Logan and, very likely, other Friends who had been most threatened by the Paxton men were pleased by the outcome.[28]

Also embarrassing to the Society were fourteen or sixteen remaining Quaker assemblymen in 1763–64, who "subjected the Society to a load of defamation and Calumny."[29] Out of the whole Assembly of thirty-six members, Friends comprised only a minority and could not control the House as their protagonists claimed. Yet the Paxtonite pamphleteers did not use even the equivocal title Quaker party, but just Quakers or Society when they referred to their opponents. In the press of 1764, the distinction between fourteen or sixteen, and a majority of Quaker members was too nice a one to register among the readers who were being treated to scalpings, conspiracies, revolts, and other sanguine episodes. The Society did not attempt to correct the distortions in the press, but it did resolve to get Friends out of office. In 1764, Yearly Meeting ordered quarterly and monthly meetings to redouble their efforts to have Friends resign legislative and executive posts, and to report the following year on their progress. Additionally, Friends were not to run for office, promote the candidacy of any Friend, or vote for him. As much as protecting its own reputation from the pamphleteers, Friends were equally concerned that Quaker assemblymen had "laid waste" to the pacifist testimony "in return for which Providence may have permitted Confusion to come upon us."[30]

The assemblymen had passed a property tax and appropriated money for war, were deliberating upon a militia, and had given tacit consent to scalping.[31] They were persecuting Friends who would not pay taxes for war. When they flouted their pacifism, who could blame Presbyterians and others for overlooking the mass of steady Friends and suffering tax protestors, or for dismissing the whole lot of Friends as hypocrites? When they supplied too little defense too late to really help the frontier, who could fault the frontiersmen who cried that not ethics but religious and ethnic prejudice had stopped these Quaker cynics from voting adequate and timely aid to save Presbyterian lives?

Despite the burden the Quaker assemblymen put upon the whole Society, the Yearly Meeting did not change the minute of 1758 to flatly exclude all Friends from office and disown those who disobeyed. Too many Friends still anticipated that the Society might benefit from legislative action (if not from this current class of Quaker legislators), so that the Society should not yet withdraw categorically from government. In the 1763 Yearly Meeting, while Indians were devastating the Pennsylvania frontier, Friends from Bucks County had even asked that the 1758 minute on officeholding be repealed. The effort failed. When, the following year, Friends came to suspect a conspiracy of Presbyterians and Penns, the time appeared opportune to return to office to foil the conspiracy. The Society nevertheless stood by its 1758 policy. No great change was to be expected in the Quaker quota of officeholders, however, as long as eminent Friends equivocated on the conditional testimony on officeholding. James Pemberton—former clerk of the Meeting for Sufferings and clerk of Philadelphia Yearly Meeting through most of the 1760s—after a hard fought contest, won a seat in the Assembly in 1765 in order to keep out an "Envious Presbyterian, George Bryan."[32] Too often, Pemberton rationalized, the Society had suffered from its inattention to the business of government and from officials who were unmindful of Friends' concerns.

Friends Divide: The Campaign for Royal Government

The effort to bring royal government to Pennsylvania formed the long epilogue to the Paxton scare; Franklin, Joseph Galloway, and other members of the Quaker party did not give up the scheme completely until 1768.[33] Meanwhile, this campaign divided Friends into supporters and opponents of the change. It was a grave matter among Friends—a genuinely religious issue and not just a politician's trifle. Any Friend who appreciated his religious liberty understood that to change the provincial constitution was to tamper with the guarantee of that liberty. The stakes were high, but the wisest course of action to secure them was by no means clear. Most Friends understood as much and appreciated that the uncertainty involved should temper their criticism of Friends who chose the opposite course. It was not a difference, in other words, that threatened schism, nor was it a matter of discipline.

The events of 1763 and 1764 impressed upon Friends their minorityhood in Pennsylvania and the hostility that masses of Pennsylvanians felt toward them. In these circumstances, the civil and religious liberties of Friends took on unprecedented importance. Numbers alone would not protect Friends. Who or what would? Some Friends, alarmed by the Paxton march, the most ardent suspecting conspiracy between Presbyterians and proprietors, trusted in the prospect of royal government. A second group, more phlegmatic than the first, trusted in the proprietary regime, the Charter of Liberties, and the laws securing those liberties. To their minds, the Paxton threat had not made tatters of these sureties. They also suspected that royal government might bring an established Church of England, tithes, curtailment of free speech, and other disabilities. The touchstone of Quaker politics had been the Charter of Liberties and those friends saw no good reason that it should not continue to be. A third possible group were the most pious of Friends. They believed that whoever threatened them and whatever the hazard, Friends must forgo expedient, worldly schemes to save themselves. They must confide in divine providence. That attitude usually meant that they numbered themselves among the Friends who wanted to rest with the old charter. The distinction between the second and last groups was not a sharp one.

The division among Friends which the campaign for royal government created appeared most spectacularly within one family and between two clerks of Yearly Meeting. Israel Pemberton opposed the campaign whereas James Pemberton labored in its behalf. In March 1764, James appeared very distressed by the Paxton march, the signs of Proprietary conspiracy, and the prospect of Presbyterian predominance in the province. Yet he spoke of the incipient campaign as though it were other people's business. At the October 1764 election for the Assembly, Israel went to the courthouse and urged Friends to forgo voting, as he himself had done for ten years past. James, learning of Israel's performance, went to him and persuaded him to come home.[34] The election became the hinge upon which James's behavior turned. Benjamin Franklin and Joseph Galloway lost their House seats in that contest which was the greatest defeat the Quaker party ever suffered at the polls. James was incensed at the results. The opposition had used "scandalous artifices," "calumny," "subterfuge," and demagoguery to oust Franklin—a man of "great abilities and long experience," motivated only by his "spirit of patriotism free from views mercenary or self-interested." "No man in this province has been so instrumental in promoting the public good," James felt. Now he and others had to work on Franklin's behalf because Franklin's "great modesty and aversion to controversy makes him negligent of care or labor in obviating the reproaches" of his enemies.[35]

Israel shared few of James's opinions, which is remarkable and praiseworthy, considering that the Paxton men had reportedly sworn that when they got to Philadelphia they would avenge their comrades' deaths upon Israel. Israel could have heard himself cursed up and down most of the frontier. But yet, after his brief flight from the city in February, he showed admirable composure and an irenic spirit toward the Presbyterians. "There are some of us whom no resentment of the most injurious treatment could sway to . . . retaliate it by joining in these measures" to replace the charter government of Pennsylvania, Israel wrote to David Barclay. Pennsylvanians simply enjoyed "the best frame of government that ever subsisted." Franklin, contrary to Israel's cool example, had let his ego and passions get the better of his judgment. "Some of us who know his fixed aversion to the proprietaries and their government," Israel continued, apprehend that if he can advance himself by the scheme for royal government, he will pursue it despite the benefits of the present constitution. Israel did not trust Franklin any more than he had in 1756 when Samuel Fothergill denounced Franklin as a foe of the Society equal to the Presbyterians. Unlike his brother, Israel also perceived that among Pennsylvanians "the desire of preserving our constitution on its original basis is so deeply fixed that they would rather submit a little longer to . . . inconveniences . . . [than] risk the loss of it."[36]

For having abandoned the Quaker party and opposed Franklin's plans for royal government, Israel became something of a pariah among his former colleagues. A Franklin sycophant and self-appointed apologist for Friends specified that "It was the Folly and Rashness of *one Man* [Israel Pemberton], that furnished [the Presbyterians] with the Means of giving their Misrepresentations of the Conduct of the Assembly the Appearance of Truth." And Israel had sullied the reputation of the Society of Friends as much as he had that of his former party. "Reciting all the Mischiefs which [Israel] has brought on the Society, the Disgrace he has, and is continually subjecting [Friends] to [and] . . . the Numbers his absurd Conduct has driven from the Society . . . would take up more Time than I can at present spare," the author harangued. One of Franklin's oldest Quaker friends, Hugh Roberts, professed to see "pernicious points" beneath Israel's "outward appearance of humility." Roberts deduced from Israel's example that some of the "most cunning and meanest" people find religion the best screen for dishonorable behavior.[37]

The split within the Pemberton family was just the most spectacular example of a division in the Society. William Logan, having had an unpleasant confrontation with the Paxton men at Germantown, understandably favored royal government, whereas his brother, James, Jr., defended the present Proprietary system. Henry Drinker, a merchant whose services to the English got him into trouble in the 1770s, marked the beginning of his interest in politics at the Paxton march. By their collusion with the Presbyterians the Proprietors intend to "reduce us to a State of Vassalage," he believed; if Pennsylvanians did not resist them "we should soon be reduced to as much a State of Slavery as the Subjects of a German Prince."[38] It was a measure of the gap between pro- and anti-royal government partisans that beginning in 1764, some anti-royal government partisans would use the same language as Drinker's against England. In the Assembly, unreformed party men like George Ashbridge from Chester County never balked at their party's plan to revoke the charter, whereas other country representatives and Friends disavowed any intention to revoke it.[39]

The convocation of Yearly Meeting at the end of September and the annual election on 1 October disclosed the strength of the royal government partisans in the Society and in the province. Three months before the Yearly Meeting convened, the Meeting for Sufferings became distrustful of the campaign for a change of government—out of its anxiety over the fate of Quaker religious liberties—but it took no position. In early September, the Meeting became more assertive and told the London Meeting for Sufferings not to appear at Whitehall in support of the royal government petition.[40]

The uproar of the past year brought a host of Friends to the Yearly Meeting late in September. Members from the more distant meetings of the province traveled to Philadelphia anticipating that important matters would be discussed and perhaps resolved. When everyone had spoken to his satisfaction, it appeared unquestionably clear that most Friends disapproved of the campaign for royal government, including the signing of petitions for it. The campaign was not, as some urban Quaker allies of Franklin had objected, a purely political matter of no concern to the Society of Friends. The free exercise of religion, and especially religious ethics like pacifism, depended upon the constitution of the province. Very few Friends from the country had signed the petitions and now, in convocation, they could make their opinions heard. They gladdened the heart of Israel Pemberton, who for months had felt beleaguered by the Quaker partisans of Franklin who lived in the city.[41]

The Yearly Meeting resolved that the Society would not support the campaign, but rather "be still & quiet" in "this time of probation." It appeared to be an especially gratifying resolution for the reformers, who were preaching less involvement in politics and greater dependence on Providence. But an equal consideration was the graceful exit it gave the partisans of royal government, whom it did not positively rebuke. The minutes and epistles of the Meeting were carefully drafted to avoid stirring up rancor in the Society. Quaker legislators, however, were not among the royal government partisans who were humored; the Meeting wanted them out of office. It tacitly said that these legislators, who passed a war tax, were neither very faithful to their religious profession nor very wise in protecting the free exercise of it.[42] But in the new post-Paxton era, the legislators were not about to abandon power.

The October provincial election showed that sentiment among Pennsylvania Friends represented rather well the sentiment among Pennsylvanians generally. A majority opposed a change of government.[43] Franklin spent most of 1765 in London unsuccessfully attempting to negotiate with the Penns a solution to the Assembly's complaints—using the petition for royal government only as a bluff.[44] In the 1765 Assembly election, Franklin's cohorts got out the vote for the largest election in Pennsylvania to that date and avenged the setbacks of 1764. James Pemberton ran for Assembly and at first tied the "City Champion" of the Presbyterians, George Bryan, then defeated him in a November rematch. Franklin took the election as a referendum and the victory as a vindication of his scheme; he rushed the petition for royal government to the Privy Council. There it utterly failed. Franklin nevertheless persisted with it until 1768 and succored the hopes of the party faithful at home. But Friends' expectations of his success declined and also their anxiety over the constitutional protections they enjoyed.[45]

Political Aftermath

Some of the foremost antagonists of the Society of Friends disregarded most Friends' disapproval of royal government. They fit the campaign into an alleged Quaker conspiracy against the frontier. Henry Muhlenberg, a leader among the German church folk (Lutherans and Reformed) reported that the campaign was a Quaker ploy to distract attention from the grievances of the frontiersmen.[46] Presbyterian George Bryan too equated the campaign with Quakerism. The Quakers' "tottering cause" required "some new clamor be raised, some popular bustle be made" to divert public attention from the frontier. As Quakers had shown in the French and Indian War, it was a venerable trick of theirs to shift the clamor of the people away from the "Quaker" Assembly to the alleged usurpations of Thomas Penn. In the war, the Quakers had treated Penn amicably while they maintained in Pennsylvania the fiction that they were engaged in a formidable struggle with him.[47]

Muhlenberg and Bryan held the minority view in Pennsylvania, however. The principal effect of the campaign for royal government was to spare the Society some of the abuse it had suffered in the press and out-of-doors during Pontiac's Rebellion. Franklin's leadership of the campaign drew upon him most of the anger of the Pres-

byterians and other erstwhile foes of Friends.[48] The campaign awakened many persons to the difference between the Quaker party and
the Society of Friends. Israel Pemberton, twenty-five years an adversary of William Allen and the Proprietary party, put aside the memo-
ries of half a lifetime and welcomed Allen's overture to jointly protect
the old charter.[49] Pemberton had already proven himself an ally, having
for three years opposed Franklin, and among Friends recently
denounced his fellow Quaker Galloway "as a weak & a bad Man."[50]

The campaign for royal government produced another notable
reconciliation, this one within the Society of Friends. Isaac Norris,
long the head of the Quaker party and even longer the speaker of the
House, could not abide the idea of royal government, and in 1764 he
broke with Franklin, Galloway, James Pemberton, and the rest. Old
and ill, he could not muster much opposition to Franklin; his lieu-
tenant, Joseph Fox (disowned by the Society in 1756 for supporting
war with the Indians) succeeded him as speaker in October 1764,
after a furious row in the House with the Franklin party. Fox, now
political kin to most Friends, defeated the bona fide Friend, George
Ashbridge, for the post. Now the old rivals Isaac Norris and Israel
Pemberton found themselves in the same camp together with an
apostate.[51]

In the context of the severest threat to Quaker liberties yet, some
old personal and political wounds had been healed. But despite that,
the primary effect of Pontiac's Rebellion and its aftermath was to
remind Friends that they were an increasingly outnumbered and
powerless minority in Pennsylvania, dependent upon the protection
tendered by the precious Charter of Liberties of 1701. Their precariousness and now clearer loss of mastery over public affairs enhanced
the teachings of the Quaker ministers and prophets that Friends
must depend finally upon Providence and not upon worldly prospects.[52] But at the same time, other Friends took their perilous situation as reason for redoubling their public activity, in pursuit of the
power that would make them and other Friends secure. Although a
minority of the Society, they were stalling the reformation by their
persistence in office. They comprised one of the two divisions in the
Society born of the Paxton episode. And while the Indian issue receded
from public consciousness in the 1760s, the division persisted in the
Society, fueled by an emerging controversy with Great Britain.

10

The Exhaustion of Quaker Politics, 1765–1775

In the minds of important Quaker politicians, the Paxton riots had installed the Presbyterians (or Presbyterian henchmen of the Penns) as the premier menace to Quakerism and liberty in Pennsylvania. Their remedy for the menace was royal government. But because of such actions by Great Britain as their taxation of the colonists after 1764, royal government was becoming a very unpopular concept. If a Quaker did not disengage himself from a possible obsession with the Presbyterians and Proprietors, he might find himself in the unfortunate and embarrassing position of being a proponent of British authority at the very time that Britain was alienating Americans. Unless he came to his senses before 1775 or 1776, he might be branded a Loyalist. The hazard would be great for Friends who did not rise above such provincialism. Regrettably, however, the hazard would be shared by those Friends who did rise above it.

A majority of Pennsylvanians never came to share the view of Franklin, Joseph Galloway, and many assemblymen that royal government was a solution to their problems. Nevertheless, Franklin and his colleagues went on their own proud way, pursuing the change of regime regardless of the people's will. British taxation did not jibe with Franklin's picture of her maternal concern for American liberties and property. But rather than admit that Britain had embarrassed his plan and party and quit his project, Franklin persisted until 1768 in trying to change Pennsylvania's constitution. Rather than fall into step with the majority of Americans who resisted taxation and regulation by Britain, Franklin, Galloway, and others temporized and then muffled opposition from Pennsylvania.[1]

The significance of this policy for the Society of Friends was that a number of very vocal and conspicuous Friends supported Benjamin Franklin and shared in his embarrassing obliviousness to British intrusions and American reactions. These Friends were especially the political incumbents whom reformer Friends wanted out of office, the ones who for at least two years had been stalling the political side of the reformation. At the hands of these important Friends, the conservative record of Quaker politicians after the Paxton riot was melded with Tory attitudes toward American revolutionaries. Public impressions of the Society were more often obtained from the behavior of these politician Friends than they were from what reformer Friends said and did.

Franklin's Foes and Friends

Reformer Friends had long mistrusted Franklin. He first made them uneasy with his scheme for a militia in 1747. By 1756, reformers regarded him as one of their enemies. Richard Peters observed that the Quakers are "afraid of the Presbyterian influence, and much more so of Franklin." In a public meeting with Franklin and Governor Robert Morris, Samuel Fothergill "poured out" reproofs upon Franklin and passionately denounced the Assembly party. Morris was so disquieted by Fothergill's tirade that he interfered to spare Franklin, his nemesis, further upset.[2] Franklin's campaign for royal government only hardened the hostility of many Friends toward him.

But Franklin also had Quaker admirers: wealthy, urban Friends who helped to draw up their party's tickets, financed election campaigns, and published partisan newspapers and broadsides.[3] They were the Friends whose names appeared in the press. They were the dry goods merchants upon whom the success or failure of American resistance to Great Britain—through nonimportation—would depend. And they were conspicuously wealthy. The whole Society would share in their profile or caricature, and after 1770 share the aspersions heaped upon them. These Friends had the effect of linking all Friends to the alleged evils of Franklin's scheme and with Toryism. The problem of public opinion and the false propinquity of party and Society was no considerable one before 1770. But the reputation and record which Franklin finally shook off after 1768 would prove to be a continued burden for the Friends who had labored for Franklin. Regrettably, it would be an immense burden for Friends who were innocent of any part in Franklin's scheme.

Among the Quaker supporters of Franklin, the most important for the Society's reputation were James Pemberton, clerk of Yearly Meeting and the Meeting for Sufferings, and Joseph Galloway. Galloway was second only to Franklin in the party and its local strategist after 1764, when Franklin was in England. Other Quaker supporters were Thomas and Samuel Wharton, who were brothers, import merchants, and land speculators in partnership with Franklin and his son, William. With Joseph Galloway, Thomas Wharton established the *Pennsylvania Chronicle* in order to promote the views of their party among the voters. Hugh Roberts was a former Quaker assemblyman and longtime friend of Franklin. Joseph Richardson, Abel James, and Henry Drinker were prominent dry goods merchants. James, Thomas Wharton, and another Friend, Cadwalader Evans, heavily financed the activities of their party. Finally, of the twenty supporters of Franklin who organized in 1764 to promote the party's fortunes at provincial elections, twelve were Friends.[4]

Fear of Presbyterianism and disorder was the great motive of Franklin's partisans. In this decade, while many Americans throughout the colonies grew apprehensive over the Church of England and the prospect of an American episcopate, these Friends cheered the news of the growth of Anglicanism.[5] Unlike numbers of their brethren, they viewed the church not as the historic oppressor of the Society, but as the worthy rival to the Presbyterians for precedence in America. To their minds, only the church held out a fair prospect for containing the growth, power, and malice of Presbyterianism. I "could wish to see that Religion [Anglicanism] bear the Reins of Government throughout the Continent," Thomas Wharton wrote to Franklin.[6] Fears of Presbyterianism definitely clouded the political vision of James Pemberton. After his 1765 election to the Assembly, his obsession with Presbyterianism became central to all other issues—royal government, the Stamp tax, and elections. Pemberton persisted in his Ptolemaic error until the Revolution, well after Franklin and others were rid of it.[7]

Resisting Revolution

Because James Pemberton believed that the Stamp Act of 1765 would not be burdensome or objectionable, it is not surprising that he looked askance at the tumult it raised in America and doubted the patriotic and constitutional motives that the protestors professed. Pretending to be "actuated by a spirit of Liberty & Patriotism," wrote Pemberton, the Presbyterians (not all Americans) were by their protests actually forging a union, preparing for the day when they would take the reins of government into their hands.[8] That would be an "oppressive & dangerous" day indeed, he felt. The Stamp tax was, in his view, merely a pretext for action, and patriotic professions were a cover for dishonorable party motives. The violence of Presbyterians appeared most clearly in New England—Pemberton and other Friends did not distinguish between Congregationalists and Presbyterians— while Pennsylvania remained calm in 1765. Nevertheless, the disposition to be violent existed among Pennsylvania's Presbyterians as it did in New England's; it merely failed in effect because the locals were too weak to act outrageously.[9]

Franklin had regretted the tax and advised the Grenville ministry against it, but finding the ministry determined to have it, he pragmatically extracted some profit from it. He had his friends appointed stamp distributors in Pennsylvania, New Jersey, and Maryland.[10] After the August 1765 riots in Boston caused the distributorships to be no posts of honor or profit, the opponents of Franklin used his nominations as another means to link him to the acknowledged evil of royal government. They even suggested that he wrote the tax law. In the press, they urged the voters to oust every Franklin supporter from the Assembly. To James Pemberton's jaundiced eye, this attack upon Franklin was exclusively a "wicked" artifice to gain office and power, and no expression whatever of genuine indignation over Franklin's complicity in the sale of unconstitutional stamps.[11]

A month after the Stamp Act riots in New England and on the arrival of the news of George Grenville's resignation from office, Franklin's adversaries in Philadelphia celebrated uproariously—the debut of the "Sons of Liberty" in Pennsylvania. But in addition to making speeches, ringing bells, and lighting bonfires, the crowd threatened to level the houses of Franklin, John Hughes (Franklin's nominee and a distributor of stamps), Galloway, and Samuel Wharton. Nothing came of it, or of later threatened riots, because Galloway had as many as eight hundred ship's carpenters and mechanics patrol the streets and forestall riots.[12]

James Pemberton believed that Presbyterians had planned and executed both the aborted riots and threats to John Hughes. They were following the tactics of their New England brethren after being prodded to riot by the Proprietary party—just as the party had prodded them in the Paxton riot. The Stamp Act marked no new departure in colonial politics for Pemberton; he regarded it, rather, as another scene in a familiar, local drama. In February 1766, after the potential for violence had dissipated, the Meeting for Sufferings advised Pennsylvania Friends to avoid any public tumults—advice that probably arose from Quaker ethics and good motives, but which nicely complemented the policy of the Franklin party and the prejudices of the clerk of Yearly Meeting.[13]

Philadelphia was not entirely quiescent nor were all the city's Quakers supine in face of the Stamp tax. Some four hundred "merchants and traders" signed a nonimportation agreement in late October and November 1765. Of these, more than eighty were Friends and included eight members of the Meeting for Sufferings. James Pemberton, Thomas Wharton, Abel James, and Henry Drinker were among the prominent Quaker merchants and signers who also backed Franklin and the petition for royal government. Other Quaker signers like Israel Pemberton and John Reynell did not belong to the Franklin party. Some Friends admitted that public indignation at the Stamp tax obliged them to sign.[14] Yet Friends honestly rued the Stamp tax— few Americans did otherwise. The distinctions among Friends, like the distinctions among other Americans, arose from the ways in which they were willing or not willing to oppose British impositions. As for signing petitions and joining other orderly forms of protest, few Friends would refuse. Mobbing and even more pallid extralegal protests were out of the question, however.

The city merchants appointed eleven men to enforce the nonimportation agreement and to secure more signers. Of the eleven, five were Friends. The Friends probably had not pondered the effect of their agreeing to enforce the articles of nonimportation on their Quaker nonviolent ethic. Also, in a second action, the merchants composed and sent a memorial to the merchants and manufacturers of Great Britain who traded with America describing the economic grievances of the Philadelphians because of the tax and labeling it unconstitutional. The signers included eighty-five Friends, members of the Franklin party as well as its opponents.[15]

Most of Franklin's supporters found nothing objectionable in nonimportation and the memorial, but their local captain, Joseph Galloway, and James Pemberton did. Galloway thought the boycott was just another Proprietary party measure. He dismissed the attitudes of his own colleagues who had joined it, and he reproved them as though they were mindless adolescents. Pemberton called the behavior of the merchants violent when all they had done was express indignation.[16]

Next, many of these same Whiggish merchants met with the future revolutionary, Charles Thomson, in order to demand the resignation of their fellow party member and Presbyterianphobe, John Hughes. But Galloway imposed his will upon his wayward flock; he had his carpenters and mechanics attend the meeting and hiss the speakers into silence.[17] The phobias of the conservatives like Galloway, James Pemberton, and Hughes bowled over all contrary evidence. While some members of their own party displayed ungovernable ire over the Stamp tax and professed reasonable motives, the conservatives belittled the members and refused to believe that local Presbyterians and Proprietary party members could share those same reasonable motives in protesting taxation.

The conservative Friends burdened the whole Society with their own increasingly illiberal reputation. The future revolutionary Benjamin Rush complained that Philadelphia was cursed with "a set of men who seem resolved to counteract all our efforts against the Stamp Act, and are daily endeavoring to suppress the spirit of Liberty among us. You know I mean the Quakers."[18] John Pemberton told his brother James that James's service in politics led the public to question his altruism.[19] More important, it led the public to question the altruism of Friends like John Pemberton, who had foregone politics and public office.

A celebration was warranted when news of the repeal of the Stamp Act reached Philadelphia on 19 May 1766. But Galloway's minions were in the streets again, preventing any raucous behavior. Some show of joy had to be allowed the people, and so the city was illuminated. Galloway remarked that it was the Proprietary party that did it. James Pemberton noted that he did not see a single Friend's window illuminated.[20] Since King George's War, Friends had usually not joined in such celebrations.[21] Now their sectarian practice complemented the Franklin party's wish to present an agreeable face to Great Britain.[22]

In 1766, at the close of the first chapter of American resistance to Great Britain, the great majority of Friends still had no indelible Tory record to burden them, while many had actively assisted in the repeal of the Stamp Act. But the next episode would change the policy of the Society and the reputation of many Friends.

Tory Ethics

When Parliament taxed Americans anew in 1767, Franklin's scheme for ingratiating Pennsylvania with the crown and installing royal government still lived. At the time, Galloway, Thomas Wharton, James Pemberton, and others of their party were, as earlier, more concerned about Presbyterian lawlessness than taxation. "We have [in Pennsylvania] Laws without being executed. . . . We have Offenders but no Punishment. We have a Majestracy but no Justice; And a Governor but no Government," Galloway ranted.[23] Galloway welcomed the Townshend Acts as a harbinger of royal government in Pennsylvania which would finally establish law and order.[24] As he understood it, his responsibility in these times was to speed the advent of royal government by still permitting nothing offensive to the crown to occur in Pennsylvania. He surely found the behavior of Philadelphia's merchants in 1767 and 1768 encouraging.

When the merchants of Philadelphia were invited to join their counterparts in other colonies in a nonimportation pact, they declined. The Pennsylvania Assembly complemented the merchants' rejection by tabling the Massachusetts Circular Letter. Secretary of State Hillsborough threatened to dissolve any American assembly that entertained the letter, but even that show of British contempt did not arouse the Pennsylvania Assembly. Then, after so much bowing and scraping in the direction of the crown, came a calamity. In August 1768, Franklin informed Galloway that his efforts to obtain the royal charter were fruitless and at an end.[25] The cynosure of Pennsylvania politics had disappeared; the cement of the Quaker party had dissolved. The news left the party with little more than its anxiety and its envy of its opponents to sustain and guide it. The emotions and habits of the past five years were too intractable to overcome, and yet they were not the means to resist an incipient revolution. Slowly at first, then quickly after 1770, Galloway and many of his colleagues lost their mastery of the political scene, including the streets and crowds of Philadelphia, as they adhered to their old ways and cherished their old enemies.

Despite the loss of this rationale for conservatism, late in 1768

James Pemberton continued to feel gratified with the conservatism of Pennsylvania and its merchants. The Assembly and the merchants had ignored clamorous proposals craftily masked with a "pretext of patriotism." They had instead authored "decent" petitions to the king, Parliament, and British merchants, which had an added benefit of shutting up the extremists who had touted more severe measures. Nevertheless, Pemberton recognized that the comparatively conservative merchants were becoming restive and would adopt more severe measures like nonimportation if their decent petitions failed to bring some relief.[26]

Galloway could not give into any proposal he attributed to his political rivals. Furthermore, to him, even a deaf Parliament did not justify a nonimportation agreement. Nonimportation, he felt, was simply mob violence. The Presbyterians held the patent on that too.[27]

Despite the misgivings of Pemberton and Galloway, nonimportation came to Philadelphia in March 1769, with the cooperation of Quaker merchants. Eight Friends were chosen to serve on the committee charged to implement the nonimportation agreement formulated by the merchants. John Reynell was its chairman.[28] In July, the resolution of the Quaker committeemen (and perhaps of the Quaker signers) to enforce the boycott was tested. A cargo of malt from Yarmouth, England, arrived in Philadelphia aboard the ship *Charming Polly.* Amos Strettel—either the ship's master or the owner of the malt—called upon several unidentified members of the committee who told him that he might land the cargo. But when the whole committee met, many members protested the decision of the few, and the committee resolved to settle the question at an open meeting of Philadelphians. The crowd that assembled at the State House for this purpose decided that any person who bought or assisted in unloading, storing, or selling the malt would be deemed "an Enemy to his Country."[29] These resolutions, like similar ones to come, indicated that an extralegal nonimportation compact could be enforced only by popular discouragement of noncompliance. At most, that might mean the use of force and violence against importers.

Conservative men thought these meetings threatened anarchy. To keep the compact at this cost—intimidation and force—meant to Friends like James Pemberton that they join the likes of the Paxton men. From careers of promoting law and order in Pennsylvania, it appeared to these Friends that they were being asked to disavow the law and their political record.

Philadelphia Monthly Meeting advised all its members, but espe-cially the eight who had volunteered to administer the nonimporta-tion agreement, to withdraw completely from the committee. In September, the Meeting for Sufferings advised all Pennsylvania Friends to beware of the nonimportation agreement. After interviewing the eight, the Monthly Meeting reported that once they understood the gravity of enforcing the agreement they appeared "fully convinced" of their error in having volunteered for such duties. Several of the eight had been named to the committee without being consulted beforehand and without being present at their nominations. Both meetings specified that they especially disliked the nonimportation committees presuming to call a popular meeting. For one thing, they added gratuitously, the "greater part" of the people were "incapable of judging on a matter of so great importance."[30]

Friends also went to considerable trouble to protect their reputa-tion as they understood it, which meant to cultivate a very decorous image. Members from Philadelphia Monthly Meeting met with the captain of the *Charming Polly* before he returned to England in order to persuade him not to confuse Friends with the men who had enforced the boycott against him and "to remove any prejudice [against Friends] he might go away with." Friends had to avoid, they said, criticism from their superiors and to acquit themselves "in principle and prac-tice dutiful affectionate and loyal Subjects to the King."[31]

In the past, London Friends had several times importuned the Pennsylvania brethren to behave in a decorous and even submissive manner. Not so in 1769. Quite the opposite, John Fothergill sent James Pemberton some damning characterizations of the king's ministers, which declared in effect that the crown did not deserve the respect it was legally entitled to and which Quakers were ethi-cally obliged to give.[32] But Fothergill's pessimism did not penetrate the hard-coated prejudices of its recipients, mostly because it was beside the point. Pemberton and his collegues did not favor the crown from any profound appreciation of royal government or feelings of obligation. They were fearful of unruly masses in Pennsylvania and the crown was the best available port under an ominous sky.

Because many American patriots later accused the Society of Friends of the uttermost partisanship, it appears that Quaker pronouncements reflected the conservative influence of such men as Pemberton and Galloway, and not that the Society was hewing to an orthodox ethical line in the Anglo-American confrontation. True, despite having made so much of Friends' religious obligations to the crown, the Meeting for Sufferings and Philadelphia Monthly Meeting were not fairly applying Quaker ethics. When the Meeting for Sufferings warned all Friends against participating in the boycott of British merchants and manufacturers, it acted without religious grounds. Not to buy or consume was not breaking any law nor was it disloyalty or sedition. It certainly was not violence. Therefore, when the Meeting pointed to Friends' obligation to obey the government, it was bending an ethical rule to meet political ends. Earlier official pronouncements had been quite in order—that Friends avoid the mobs and public tumults. But the pronouncements of 1769 showed a Tory bias. The American Revolution would finally make these finer points of ethics irrelevant; but in 1769, before anyone foresaw a war, the Society was advising its people to quit the resistance movement before it became violent and their participation unethical.

The orders given to the eight committeemen were more specific than those for all Friends. Here the Society stood on firmer ethical grounds. By agreeing (or being appointed) to enforce a boycott, the eight would likely violate their nonviolent ethic since physical force was their only real sanction if someone violated the boycott. And only if the eight were serving as magistrates enforcing the law could they have ethically commissioned or used force. The Meeting correctly warned them to resign.

Because mention of the use of force made all the difference between whether the Meeting's orders were legitimate discipline or whether they were simply a show of political bias, it is odd that neither the Monthly Meeting nor the eight said anything specifically about force, or even about extralegal combinations. What the eight offered in explanation of their resignation was their respect for "the rights of individuals"—in this instance, one's right to join the boycott or not.[33] The eight seemed to presume that the nonimportation agreement entailed depriving someone of his freedom of choice. If that was true with the eight (and with the Meeting, which was satisfied by their professions), they showed commendable respect for civil liberties. But the promotors had an equally commendable motive. Most of them did not relish curtailing Americans' freedom of choice; they came to it, rather, in the process of protecting Americans' freedom solely to tax themselves. Their dilemma, and Friends' too, was that means conflicted with ends, and freedom must suffer one way or another. The Whigs favored freedom from taxation and Friends the freedom of choice. The most important fact for the future of Friends was that in 1769 they chose the less popular liberty.

The decisions of the summer and fall of 1769 marked the critical period for Quaker involvement in the Revolution. Thereafter, the policy of the Society of Friends never favored or condoned involvement in the Revolution. Almost certainly the Society would have come to that same decision or taken that course at a later stage of the struggle with England—and for increasingly defensible reasons. Seventeen sixty-nine did not mark the only juncture in Quaker history when Friends could have turned away from the resistance movement. The date was more important because it was early or premature for the Society to have become so severely critical of the American resistance to Great Britain. Most of the credit for the haste lay with the political activists in the Society who had since 1763 contracted a phobia of their opponents. But also the dry goods merchants in the Society were to blame. Nonimportation became the principal weapon in the American Whigs' armory, and that required the merchants to be the lever on Britain. In 1769, the Quaker merchants—Pemberton, the Whartons, James and Drinker, and possibly others—decided they would not oblige the more impatient Whigs in that way, and the Society prohibited compliance with nonimportation too. In trade, in politics, and in the Meeting for Sufferings and the Philadelphia Monthly Meeting, much the same group of conservative Friends reappeared. Not unlikely, they believed that the men who envied their policy and party in politics, who pressed them to boycott Great Britain, and who had abused Friends were all the same crowd—Presbyterian and proprietary partisans. They could not be trusted or credited with genuine Whig motives. After the Townshend episode had ended and resistance subsided throughout the colonies, James Pemberton reasserted yet another time that those who had spoken most loudly of liberty had "given proofs of the most tyrannical disposition."[34]

Quakers as Plutocrats

After Friends and some other dissidents resigned, the nonimportation committee came under the control of more forceful and enthusiastic men. For one year, nonimportation was enforced in Philadelphia, with encouragement from Franklin in England.[35] When, in July

1770, the merchants of New York discarded nonimportation in that city, Philadelphia merchants resolved to do likewise. The local enforcement committee, not sharing the discontents of the restive merchants, determined to resist any efforts to dissolve the nonimportation agreement. The upshot was primarily a debate in the newspapers over the wisdom of ending nonimportation. In the debate, the dry goods merchants supported an end of the boycott.

A new note appeared late in these debates. In the campaigns against Great Britain so far, Philadelphia had heard little or nothing made of class, economic, or vocational differences in the city. The credit for that silence belongs mostly to Franklin and Galloway, who had tied the artisans and mechanics to their party and their policies. Now a division arose between the workers, who supported the boycott, and the dry goods merchants, who opposed it.[36] At the same time, Franklin, the idol of the workingmen, was abandoning Galloway, the merchants, and their archconservative politics.

On 12 September, sixteen merchants, nine or ten of them Friends, announced a plan for polling opinions on nonimportation—as New Yorkers had done when they ended that city's agreement. Knowing that the poll was intended to end nonimportation, the nonimportation committee opposed it. But the merchants succeeded and the committee angrily resigned.[37] The merchants had beaten the committee, but they did not seem to have mastered the battleground. They complained that Philadelphia appeared out of control. Thomas Gilpin, a Friend whom the revolutionaries would exile to Virginia in 1777, complained of the "intemperate violence" of the past several months: "We have had summonses by ballots, town meetings, hasty resolutions made and repealed, proclamations and measures carried by clapping, hallooing &c."[38] It was also election time, and while the merchants were prevailing over the nonimportation committee, they were losing the contest for the electors. Beginning in the fall of 1770, newspapers and pamphlets railed at the merchant grandees who had long been accustomed to running the party—Quaker merchants like Joseph Richardson, Abel James, and the Whartons. Galloway attracted more abuse than anyone else by far. Writers called the public's attention to the "greatness and Opulency" of the merchant politicians and the disparity between their fortunes and those of the mechanics. The politicians allegedly sponsored laws that positively harmed their lower-class constituents. These "gentlemen" ought not be elected, "A Brother Chip" told his fellow mechanics; when we add power to their wealth, he complained, we make lords and masters of them and slaves of ourselves.[39]

In the election of 1770, the mechanics and carpenters abandoned Galloway and the "Old Ticket"; they went over to the "Presbyterians," Galloway fumed. All was in confusion, he complained, and he was being publicly abused. After that fall the old coalition was never again reassembled. Galloway had only the gentlemen left as constituents, and Franklin had abandoned him. Although speaker of the House for years to come, Galloway had to be elected from a safe district in Bucks County. All the while the invective against the merchant gentlemen—the "old corrupt Junto"—continued: These men will "make Merchandise of you and your Liberties forever," "A Citizen" warned his readers.[40]

In the press, the champions of the mechanics had never accused Friends per se of indifference to the mechanics' welfare or of favoring Britain. Yet Friends were a majority in the groups the mechanics and radical Whigs attacked. They were a majority of the ten or so major dry goods importers who alone could bring off or scuttle a nonimportation pact, a majority of those who resigned from the enforcement committee in 1769, a majority of the sixteen protestors who ended nonimportation in Philadelphia in 1770, and a majority of the leadership of the "Old Ticket." What appeared necessary to cement the connection between Quakerism and hostility to the revolutionary movement was an official Quaker pronouncement against radicalism or the resistance to Great Britain. The 1769 advice from Philadelphia Monthly Meeting and the Meeting for Sufferings was not of that sort, but the necessary pronouncement would come in time. When it did, there already existed in the press and in the minds of some Pennsylvanians a caricature of Quaker plutocrats. That caricature would then be applied to all Friends, and not just those who fitted it.

The Exhaustion of Quaker Politics

After a three-year hiatus in the opposition to Great Britain, the East India Act stirred up the American Whigs again. The Society of Friends remained true to its recent record when opposition to the India Act appeared. Friends were advised to avoid any role in extralegal organizations promoting resistance to Britain, to have nothing to do with committees, mass meetings, conventions, and the like.[41] That is not to say, however, that all Friends obeyed the admonitions. Some joined the resistance movement in order to promote boycotts, congresses, and defense; others joined in order to stop those very things. Until 1775, neither was disciplined by the Society.

The Quaker policy of discouraging from the beginning any participation in extralegal bodies had an immediate look of impartiality or neutrality about it. The Society advised the politically moderate Friends as well as the more radical ones to give up their political activity. But the appearance was misleading because the Society did not advise Friends who agreed to sell the East India tea to quit their commissions. As if to confirm the caricatures of the workingmen radicals, Abel James—defeated by the workingmen's vote in the 1772 Assembly election—agreed to sell the tea. He was joined by his partner Henry Drinker. Long-time party warhorse Thomas Wharton was another tea commissioner, making Friends three of the six commissioners in Philadelphia.[42] On the face of it, their commissions were business matters, not politics. Yet that was hardly the whole truth, for they necessarily became the means of taxing American tea drinkers. Still the Society chose to treat their activity as a private matter of a business nature; it never so much as mentioned them in its records. Since the Society's reason for prohibiting Friends from joining committees was the unconstitutional and extralegal nature of these bodies, it would have been only consistent of the Society to stop the Quaker commissioners from collecting unconstitutional taxes. Friends had agreed since the Stamp tax that taxation by Parliament was unconstitutional. The inconsistency of the Society was obvious.

In September 1773, a month before news of the Tea Act upset Philadelphians, articles in the press implored the workingmen to vote against the Galloway party, which, it said, had "tread upon mechanics' necks." The articles singled out the "House of Wharton" for special attention.[43] By mid-October and the official news of the Tea Act, broadsides and articles called the public to resist the new legislation. A meeting of some seven hundred people at the State House on 16 October appointed a committee to meet with the commissioners of the East India Company to get them to resign. At first, all the Quaker commissioners resisted the demands. Then Thomas Wharton resigned, while Abel James and Henry Drinker waited more than a month, expecting the agitation to die down. When the agitators did not quit but began to talk about violence, the other two capitulated in a surly manner.[44]

In late December 1773, the radical Whigs forced the ship *Polly* to return to England with its cargo of tea. James Pemberton labled the act an arbitrary breach of law and justice, and he demanded restitution for the "suffering" merchants. Former commissioners James and Drinker could not bring themselves to credit the radical Whigs with any real concern for liberty. Men with a real concern, according to the two, would never have interfered with merchants' liberty to do business, sell tea, and refuse a boycott. No, the Whigs were simply "wicked." Pemberton had shortly before professed that Friends "are not insensible of the Incroachments of powers [by Great Britain] & of the value of our Civil Rights."[45] That was true, but the complete truth was that the city Friends, at least, worried more about the interference with their own freedom to do business than with Americans' freedom from parliamentary taxes.

At the earliest sign "of a ferment rising among the people," the Friends of the three monthly meetings in the city convened and decided that Friends must forego any protests against the Tea Act and the commissioners. But the decision amounted only to admonition and not discipline. The Quaker convocation was well timed because a public meeting at the State House was announced for the following day. The response of Friends to the Society's caution must have been heartening, because as far as James Pemberton could discover, no Friends "of any Account" appeared among the seven hundred at the meeting.[46]

Also early in the tea episode, Friends became fearful of the mass meetings and crowds. After 16 October, Philadelphians periodically met together out of doors, and these crowds continued to make Friends wary of the resistance movement. On 27 December, some eight thousand Philadelphians gathered to protest the landing of the tea. Two or three hundred people met in May 1774; twelve hundred in June. That fall popular committees spring up in townships and wards across the province.[47] The Society boycotted them all. It found no wisdom in the plan of some Friends to join the new groups in the hope of containing the hot tempers of some participants. Instead, it felt Friends should keep to their homes, off the streets, off the committees, and out of power.

While the Society watched power and authority drain away from the constitutional bodies in Pennsylvania in 1775 and 1776, it did nothing to gain a voice in the new irregular ones that accumulated power. Although the Society had, since 1756, counseled Friends to get out of public life, and especially out of those offices that jeopardized Quaker ethics, it had equivocated at enforcing its judgment. The clerk of Yearly Meeting had served the Franklin-Galloway party in the Assembly. But when confronted with bodies and parties they distrusted—ones run by agitators, workingmen, and Presbyterians—the city Friends pushed the admonition immediately and heartily. The distinctions that these Friends made seemed to be more political than ethical.

Not all Friends obeyed their monthly meetings. In 1774, the Boston Port Bill, the Coercive Acts, and a call to assist Massachusetts provoked new committees and meetings. Both moderate and radical Friends took these opportunities to join committees, for their respective reasons. When Paul Revere arrived in Philadelphia on 19 May with a proposal for nonimportation, Speaker Galloway refused to assist any such scheme for intercolonial cooperation. At the same time, he distrusted the popular organizations that sprang up in lieu of the Speaker's or the Assembly's leadership.[48]

When about three hundred people met on 20 May, even Thomas Wharton joined them to select a committee of nineteen men to respond to Boston and to formulate other plans. The committee was decidedly moderate in its composition and contained such Quaker moderates as Edward Penington and Jeremiah Warder, Jr.[49] Under pressure from radicals, the nineteen consented to the creation of a larger committee in June. Again the moderates determined to control this new body of forty-four members and they succeeded. Eleven Friends sat on this committee. They included Thomas Wharton, who said that he joined in order to keep "our city within the limits of moderation and not indecent or offensive to our parent state."[50] Even though James Pemberton attended no organizational meetings, his friends selected him for the committee too. He immediately refused to serve or to let his name be used by the committee, even for the sake of moderation. Pemberton complained that all such committees were unknown to the charter and laws of Pennsylvania and were therefore to be rebuffed.[51] The Philadelphia Meeting for Sufferings believed that the committees in the city, and the new ones springing up in rural areas, threatened the province with "anarchy" and the loss of Friends' "Civil, & Religious Liberties."[52] In light of their current moderate composition and record, the committees did not deserve that impulsive judgment. Nevertheless, the Meeting for Sufferings stayed with its judgment and advised the Quaker committeemen to resign.

The committee of forty-four, reduced to forty-three by Pemberton's resignation, was the last extralegal body in which Quaker moderates participated. The committee passed out of existence in November 1774, when it was replaced by a popularly elected committee of sixty-six. Five Friends sat on the larger body, all of them radicals who were later disowned by the Society. The five reflected the nature of the whole committee, for it represented the end of moderation in Philadelphia and an abrupt disjunction with the past.[53]

Before the advent of the committee of sixty-six, the moderates had suffered losses from other quarters. Realizing that the Assembly was likely to be a more amenable body than any of the extralegal committees, Joseph Galloway reassumed the effective leadership of the Assembly in July 1774. Plans for the Continental Congress were afoot and Galloway felt obliged to see that Pennsylvania helped to moderate that body's behavior. First, he ignored instructions about the Congress which an ad hoc provincial convention sent to the Assembly in June. He did the same to the convention's nominations for Pennsylvania's delegates to the Congress. Instead, the Assembly named Galloway and four of his associates.[54]

Galloway failed signally. The Continental Congress rejected his "Plan of Union," the bright hope of the moderates and conservatives at the Congress. The defeat precipitated the end of his political life in Pennsylvania too. The October election for Assembly had gone badly, and when the representatives convened they voted Galloway out of the speakership.[55] Galloway succumbed completely to the prejudices he had long contained and began ranting about a Presbyterian conspiracy that had undone him. In December, the Assembly endorsed the radical doings of the Congress, among them nonintercourse with Great Britain. The Meeting for Sufferings, upon learning of the Assembly's endorsement, sent a delegation to the Quaker assemblymen to reprimand them for either assenting to or condoning the motion. The delegation was to lay before the assemblymen "the trouble & Sorrow they brought on their Brethren."[56] The sorrow was all the greater for the constitutional way that Pennsylvania was brought to this radical juncture—through its Assembly's actions.

The strategems of the moderates and conservatives had come to nothing and in the least likely arena.

For several months after December, James Pemberton hoped that the Assembly might recant; but that hope was a slim reed, and the news of Lexington and Concord ended it completely. For many prominent members of the Society of Friends, the last hope for security from radicalism and licentious Presbyterians pretty much disappeared at the end of 1774.[57]

Isolation

The isolation of the Friends increased. On 1 June 1774, the radical Whigs—the Presbyterians according to James and Drinker—proclaimed a fast day in honor of the hardships of Bostonians. The religious denominations of the city supposedly sponsored the fast, Friends excepted. Friends' long and unpleasant experience with such fasts aggravated their misgivings about the radical Whigs, and Friends' noncompliance confirmed the Whigs' suspicions about them.[58] Before there was in fact any oppression of Friends by the radicals, the Yearly Meeting, in its annual epistle to members, dwelled upon the persecution of Friends and its precedent, the sufferings of the early Christian church. The epistle pressed upon Friends the same disdain for "Plots, Insurrections or Conspiracies" that Quaker patriarchs showed at cost of their lives and property. It spoke of Pennsylvania's Charter of Liberties like a landmark receding from Friends' view. The epistle seemed clearly devised to prepare Friends for some ominous future or a return to a dark era in their history.[59]

Amidst all the talk of liberty in America, the Society testified that it was the king to whom Friends were beholden for their religious liberties ever since the founding of Pennsylvania. At least a year before Tom Paine raised for Americans the question of their loyalty to the king, many Friends in their own minds had narrowed their options to loyalty and gratitude to the king, or sedition and revolution.[60] For some time it appeared that confiding in the king's government was the expedient course as well as the obligatory, ethical one. The king would be their sanctuary from their local oppressors.[61] But that prospect failed in 1775, much like the protections afforded by the Pennsylvania charter.

In early 1775, John Fothergill and David Barclay were attempting to mediate the difficulties between the colonies and Great Britain. But they found little reason to think they would succeed. The British were deaf and bigoted, "as regardless of the happiness of American as the mandarines of China." "Had our greatest Enemy's the direction of our councils," Fothergill wrote to James Pemberton, "they could not drive us to a more dangerous precipice." The ministers in Lord North's government were more of the absolutists who had appeared in every reign since James I and who, like their predecessors, denied the people's civil and religious liberties. In these circumstances, "Mind your own business," Fothergill ordered the American Friends; do not "court unworthily the favor of your superiors on this side nor oppose with vehemence the party which steps forward in the protection of your liberties which are all at stake." This advice tempered some rather obsequious language and unwarranted hopes that the Meeting for Sufferings had used and nourished toward the king's government.[62] At the same time, Fothergill's news almost completed Friends' isolation: The American Whigs were long suspected of tyranny and now the British appeared little better.

In the years after 1765, the political side of the reformation—the exit from government—seemed to be in eclipse. Friends with an inclination to trust in power and public office failed the test of the prerevolutionary decade of repressing their felt need for worldly security in the face of their enemies. But the great irony of these ten years is that in a positive sense they belonged to the history of the Quaker reformation. The worst outcome for a reformed Society of Friends would have been for Friends like James Pemberton to have found their trust in power confirmed and rewarded. Instead, they failed in their strategies for Pennsylvania. The lesson they were left to learn—from the reformers who would tell them as much—was the futility of relying upon power and politics, of wanting more security than a serious Christian knows to expect. Whether the political Friends ever took the lesson to heart or not, they were definitely out of office and without power. The reformation had advanced. What remained was to have Friends, the pious as well as the political, pay the cost of retreat from the world and of neutrality in the Revolution.

11

Beleaguered Quakers, 1775–1782

While conservative Friends were discovering for themselves the futility of relying upon royal government, the king, and the Pennsylvania provincial constitution for their salvation, they saddled the Society of Friends with a reputation of Toryism or Loyalism. Since 1769, premature and biased statements from Philadelphia Monthly Meeting and the Meeting for Sufferings were widely taken to represent the sentiments of all Friends. In 1775 or 1776, when resistance turned into war, first for the restitution of Americans' rights and then for independence, Friends of whatever political stripe had to disavow the movement. Further, they were ethically obliged to remain loyal to the king. Whatever their true sentiments might be respecting the belligerents and despite the precious little they might actually do for the king while being loyal to him, they were not free to repudiate the king and yet remain Friends. To their historic American antagonists, the single course open to Friends seemed to confirm suspicions of Quaker Loyalism. The evidence of Quaker Tory attitudes since 1769 was obvious. The misfortune for many or most Friends was that while the Tory record was compiled by a number of city nabobs, all Friends would have to suffer for it. Perhaps Friends would have suffered as much merely by persevering in their pacifism and their practical neutrality. Either course would, however, have brought the same response from the reformers: Suffering has been the fate of true Christians in every age and if rightly understood, a boon to reformation.

Sealing Friends' Fate

In the three months of 1775 before the revolutionary war broke out in Massachusetts, the Society made some crucial decisions. In January, the Meeting for Sufferings met long hours, day after day, and resolved that monthly meetings must discipline Friends who participated in the Continental Association or any other groups fostered by the Continental Congress. If members disregarded the admonitions, they were to be disowned. The Meeting for Sufferings accompanied the order with a public declaration of the Society's hostility to the Congress and the consequences arising from it—which the Meeting called "Insurrections, Conspiracies & illegal Assemblies." The declaration also professed Friends' loyalty to the king and his government.[1] This was the first and very conspicuous occasion for the public to tie Quakerism to the Galloway party or clique.

The orders were promptly enforced. Even before the war broke out in April, active and prominent Whigs like Thomas Mifflin, Benjamin Marshall, Owen Biddle, and Joseph Wetherill were called before meetings to be admonished, and finally they were disowned. As common as disownment was after 1755, it never attracted as much attention as in 1775, when it was imposed upon these and other Quaker members of the Patriot party. Some non-Friends grew angry at the Society out of an illogical attitude that the Society had no right to disown—as if the Society were some public body and not a private, religious denomination. Other critics talked as though it were prohibiting a man's freedom of expression and association. For their past political behavior and these disownments, Friends got into nasty arguments in the coffeehouses and streets of Philadelphia. James Pemberton called several Friends and others rebels because they supported the Congress. A Patriot later threatened Pemberton in public that "If there was blood Shed here [in Philadelphia] he was the first that should go to pot."[2]

The timing of the Friends' sanction upon Whigs was impolitic. It did not coincide with the outbreak of war, conscription, fines, taxes, or a declaration of independence. Nothing occurred in January 1775 that could be understood as a forthright challenge to Quaker ethics and pacifism. Why then did they act in January, three months before the war and its difficulties appeared? Very likely the decisions of January were the belated effects of Quaker despair that was two months old or more.[3] The Continental Congress, Pennsylvania's approval of it, and the Continental Association primarily produced the order to discipline. The association was destined to become a quasi-military organization, and James Pemberton early suspected that mobilization was the objective.[4] But nothing, not Congress, the association, or Pemberton's premonition, could permit Friends to put a good face on their decisions of January.

The radical Whigs had more plausible motives to attribute to Friends. It appeared that Quaker moderates, who had lost their ability to slow the progress of radicalism in the province late in 1774, had joined conservatives like James Pemberton and permitted the Society to discipline political activity, since the only political activity in the province was radical. This inference may have been wrong. It is regrettable, however, that the timing of the Quakers' behavior fit the inference.

Quickly the publications of the Society brought it public attention. According to rumors in Philadelphia, the publications had convinced the British ministry to resist conciliation with the Americans. The ministry was emboldened by this purported evidence that a substantial number of important Americans opposed the Congress and its association. A second rumor held that English Friends were angry at the decisions of Pennsylvania Friends. Both rumors contained a grain of truth. David Barclay had written James Pemberton that some people at court gossiped that American Friends positively approved of British policy. The publications of Pennsylvania Friends sounded partisan and calculating, and not like a religious manifesto, Barclay complained.[5]

Rejoinders to the Quaker publication attempted to discredit the Meeting for Sufferings and disassociate it from the Society of Friends. One pamphleteer claimed that the Meeting was an unrepresentative, illegitimate, partisan, and meddlesome body. "The mark of Cain be upon [the Meeting for Suffering]!" the author cursed; "but let the Society be held guiltless."[6] This author and other Pennsylvania Whigs were vying with the hierarchy of the Society for the loyalty of the members.[7] They were trying to divide the church and carry off a large number of its constituents—or even better, capture the whole church for the radical Whigs. Some Whigs anticipated their success by exaggerating the Quaker enthusiasm for the war. Whereas less than three score Friends in Philadelphia had volunteered for military duty by May, rumor had it that the whole Society approved of the war.[8] Wherever it prevailed, this misrepresentation of Quakerism could help to recruit impressionable men. A contest between rumor and fact began and although it subsided after 1776, it never died. It caused the Society to become very self-conscious, like earliest Friends, and to attempt by discipline and publication to distinguish itself from the falsehoods.

Circumstances that completely warranted a statement from the Society and a dialogue with the radicals first appeared in May. Citizens and Committees of the Military Association began petitioning the Assembly for a salary and supplies, among other things. On the last day of June, the Assembly resolved in favor of such aid and laid a tax on all estates.[9] For Quaker traditionalists as well as reformers, the tax was one they could not pay. The advanced scruples of the reformers stopped them from lending any support to war. Traditionalists had no such scruples, but they would not pay taxes on behalf of an insurrection. That would not be rendering to Caesar but overthrowing him.

A greater danger, and one that had no precedent in Pennsylvania, was conscription or militia service, or a payment in lieu of service. The expectation that Friends and other pacifists ought to serve first appeared in a violent way in a natural place. In Lancaster County on 1 June, the volunteer militia came down to Lancaster for drill. Instead of drilling, they marched to the courthouse and demanded that the County Committee force all male inhabitants to join the militia. The angry militiamen had heard that the County Committee had been bribed by pacifists to except them. The Committee—a conservative group of men led by the Shippen family—turned down the demand and, furthermore, resigned and stood for reelection in order to demonstrate their authority. Most were vindicated.[10]

Then the Continental Congress sparked the campaign to make conscription part of provincial law. In July, it resolved that all ablebodied men sixteen to fifty years old, excepting pacifists, should join the militia. As soon as the Assembly convened in September, it began to receive petitions for conscription.[11] The petitions recited the volunteers' hardships and their contributions to the community—loss of time, neglect of livelihood and family, and others. It was inequitable, they complained, that they should support these burdens while the whole community reaped the benefits—security or protection, the safeguarding of liberty, and others. "Where the liberty of all is at Stake, every Man should assist in its Support, and that where the Cause is common, and the Benefits derived from an

Opposition are universal, it is not consonant to Justice or Equity that the Burdens should be partial."[12] It was an old argument, long used to rationalize the expropriation of property or the labor of unwilling persons. In the Revolution the Quaker response to this argument was simple: "We profess to be redeemed from the causes of War, and therefore . . . we desire not the Protection of it."[13] They wanted no part of this alleged community of beneficiaries, and therefore, of obligees either.

On 20 October, when two committees from the city requested a militia law, the Meeting for Sufferings protested to the Assembly within a week. Citing the Laws Agreed Upon in England and the Charter of Privileges, the Friends maintained that their protection "was not limited to the Acts of public Worship only." Rather, they and all Pennsylvanians could not be compelled "to do or suffer any other Act or Thing contrary to their religious Persuasion," in the words of the charter.[14] The very province was founded by Penn and settled by Friends for this clear purpose of protecting religion and conscience. To accede to the militia request would be to repudiate the most venerable fact about Pennsylvania. And too, it would produce religious persecution and suffering, the Friends warranted.

The address of Friends to the Assembly brought howls from the Patriot side. The parts of the charter quoted by Friends in defense of their pacifist exception "relate only to an Exemption from any Acts of Uniformity in Worship," the Military Association officers wrote, "and from paying towards the Support of other Religious Establishments." To bolster their case these respondents pointed out the powers that Charles I put into Penn's charter for levying war, appointing officers, and commanding them. How did these square with a province for and of pacifists? Much less to the point, the respondents brought up the subject of taxes for war. Had not Friends always paid these and had they not been levied without any exceptions for religion?[15] The answer was yes, but the question was not relevant because Friends were not objecting to taxes but to militias. The fact that no exception existed for any taxpayers did not prove that no religious exceptions of any kind existed, especially since there had never been any militia law before.

The respondents repeated the divisive allegations made earlier against the Meeting for Sufferings and its orders. Feigning astonishment, one committee told the legislators, "We are firmly persuaded that a Majority of that Society have too much Sincerity, Candour and

good Sense to be influenced by such [pacifist] Principles." And a
second reminded the legislators of the "mischievous Consequences
from a former Production said to have come from the whole Body of
the People called Quakers; but which, as we have reason to believe
. . . flowed from a *few* Individuals."[16] All the military committees
making these accusations contained Friends, many of whom were
being disciplined at this time. These delinquents refused merely to
shrug off being rebuked and they contested the very authority of the
Meeting for Sufferings. They attempted to discredit the Meeting and
to pose as true spokesmen of Quakerism. Through the military
committees they were able to vent their discontents and jealousy.

Friends' wealth did not escape the attention of the committeemen. The first petition of the fall claimed "that People *sincerely* and
religiously scrupulous are but few in Comparison to those who upon
this Occasion, as well as others, make *Conscience a Convenience.*"
Wealth, the petitioners suggested, was the true motive. "A very
considerable Share of the Property of this Province is in the Hands
of People professing to be of tender Conscience in military Matters."
These wealthy men were willing that the associators risk their lives,
while the wealthy volunteered none of their property. Patriots defended
property, while the Quakers engrossed it. And if the Patriots lost,
they lost their lives, whereas the wealthy would forfeit nothing. The
British might even promote them to high offices, which "they seem
to desire and expect."[17] Quaker wealth supplied the Society's critics,
as it had since King George's War, with the means to deprecate its
ethics and question Friends' professions. The new petitions were
extrapolations of the pamphlets published since 1770 attacking the
plutocrats of the Galloway party. Wealth was the biggest common
denominator. Given the Patriots' anger and their knowledge that
some Friends were devoted to their property, wealthy Friends could
expect to have their distinct attachments to wealth or to peace tested.

In November, the Assembly acceded to the petitioners' wishes
and obliged all male citizens, sixteen to fifty years of age, to join the
military associations. Nonassociators would be charged two pounds,
ten shillings.[18] But within three months, the associators were
complaining to the Assembly that it had treated the nonassociators
too leniently. The nonassociators were "the Lazy, the Timid and
Disaffected," who taunted the volunteers, saying they rated their
lives at fifty shillings a person. The nonassociators were plainly the
"Enemies to the Liberties . . . of America," and they ought to pay for

their mischief. The associators recommended that men over the age of fifty be obliged to pay, especially because they held the largest estates in the province. Charges or fines on everyone should be increased. Berks County associators (frontiersmen) wanted field officers instead of elected county commissioners to judge appeals from the fines. The men from Berks were loath to admit the premise of their petition, which was that patriotism was not producing enough volunteers, and so they couched it in the subjunctive: "The great Advantage given to the Non-Associator [a small fine] . . . would entirely defeat the Association, if the People in general were not actuated by a patriot Spirit." But rather than give them a hypothetical penalty for the hypothetical lack of patriotism, the Assembly raised the fine on nonassociators.[19] Throughout the war it continued to be the same, long story: the volunteers never quit putting a premium on their services or a ceiling on the fines they recommended against their opposites.

Friends could not pay these penalties or fines for nonservice. Some dissident members argued the orthodoxy of paying them in lieu of service, but the point was never really a doubtful one. The payment of the fines was no more orthodox than paying tithes to the Church of England; nor could Friends pay the fines if the government imposing them were legitimate and not revolutionary. "A time of suffering seems likely to be our Lot," John Reynell concluded when the fines were legislated;[20] either that, or, as Reynell did not remark, a time of defections.

In January 1776, Tom Paine broached for all Americans the question of their loyalty to the king and Great Britain. In "a style hitherto unknown" Paine repudiated the king, made light of him, extolled treason, and invited Americans to do likewise.[21] His statement, *Common Sense*, became immensely popular, but maybe least so in Pennsylvania, where the prophet lived. Paine confirmed the fears of Friends that American belligerents sought revolution and independence, not the redress of grievances. The Meeting for Sufferings issued what we might call the third Quaker manifesto (the others being that of January 1775 and the address to the Assembly on militia). The Meeting prefaced this epistle with a stately recapitulation of God's providential care for Pennsylvania. The present war proved that the people had declined, had offended God; for " 'When a mans ways please the Lord, he maketh even his Enemies to beat peace with him.' " In the past "the Sins and Iniquities of the people subjected them to grievous sufferings. The same causes still produce the same effects." What have we done to offend God? the epistle asked; then suggested a dozen actions that ranged from enslaving Negroes to profaneness.[22]

The revolutionaries were not inclined to listen to Quaker jeremiads. For them, the Revolution proved the virtue of Americans, just as Paine had written. It was the recommendations in the Quaker epistle rather than the prologue that attracted their attention: here the authors hoped that the bond with the king and his government would not be broken. Friends themselves, the authors ordered, simply could not assist in "setting up and putting down Kings." "May we therefore firmly unite in the abhorrence of all such Writings and measures, as evidence a desire and design to break off the happy connection we have heretofore enjoy'd with the Kingdom of Great Britain."[23]

Paine was livid; the Quaker piece was objecting to him and *Common Sense* in all but name. He took up his pen and composed a letter which subsequently appeared as an appendix to *Common Sense* and made Friends infamous among Patriots. Some parts of what Paine asserted in his letter were true, much of it was not new, and all of it, colored by his passionate sarcasm and verve, attracted readers. "Ye [Quakers] appear to have mistaken party for conscience," Paine wrote. The understandings of the authors of the Quaker epistle "were darkened by the narrow and crabbed spirit of a despairing political party." "You [the Meeting for Sufferings] are not to be considered as the whole body of Quakers, but only as a factional and fractional part thereof." The Quakers were hypocrites too. It is "exceedingly difficult for us to give credit to many of your pretended scruples; because we see them made by the same men, who, in the very instant they are exclaiming against the mammon of this world, are nevertheless hunting after it with a step as steady as time, and an appetite as keen as death."[24] It was a sentiment that Quaker reformers shared and that they in fact, rather than Paine, were the authors of.

These were the preliminary digs at Friends in the pamphlet. Paine focused his criticism on Friends' avowed rationale for opposing independence and called their behavior inconsistent with it.

[Your principles] instruct you to wait with patience and humility, for the event of all public measures, and to receive that event as divine will towards you. . . . Wherefore, as ye refuse to be means on one side, ye ought not to be meddlers on the other; but wait the issue in silence. . . . The men, who, in the very paragraph before, have quietly and passively resigned up the ordering, altering and disposal of kings and governments, into the hands of God, are now recalling their principles, and putting in for a share of the business.[25]

Paine had made a clever, sophistical argument. What the Meeting for Sufferings had done by way of dictating behavior in the January epistle was to remind Friends of their religious obligation to be loyal to the king and to continue their traditional and orthodox acknowledgments of his authority. For Paine to censure this part of the epistle as partisan "political testimony" was to misconstrue it. If the "silence" he desired from the Meeting meant not reminding Friends of their obligations, or still more, overlooking the breach of their obligations, Paine was encouraging Friends to disregard their ethic and meddle on his revolutionary side. Citizenship has its positive obligations which Friends understood to be religious obligations too. To disregard the obligations is not to be neutral but to disavow one's citizenship, the king, and to commit sedition or treason. And for Friends to quit these obligations was to be irreligious. If the obligations were nonpartisan, then the reminder of them, in the January epistle, was too.

On the other hand, Paine had detected the political moralizing that the Meeting for Sufferings had put into the epistle. To ask Friends to follow their ethic was one thing, but to ask their "abhorrence" of all writings like *Common Sense* and to characterize the connection with the king as "happy" was passing judgments on the historical merit of loyalty and revolution. Friends ought to be loyal to the king regardless of the merits of his rule, or whether it was "happy." Happiness or unhappiness was irrelevant, and to put it in was political advocacy. Paine rightly excoriated the Meeting for it. English Friends had already disapproved of it.

Attention to the Quaker ethic on loyalty lapsed, while the exasperation and the jealousy of the Patriots continued to focus on their wealth and avarice. The Reverend Henry Muhlenberg, an eminent Lutheran, claimed that the Quakers "laughed at the Associators, and meanwhile raised the price of all necessities and amassed money for their tender consciences." Gossip spread that English Friends had gained from the crown "security and indemnification" for the estates of Friends in America, if ever they suffered from the Patriots. With insurance like this, of course the Quakers could swagger in face of the Patriots' impositions.[26] These Tories, wrote Paine in *The Crisis*, "have voluntarily read themselves out of continental meeting, and cannot hope to be restored to it again, but by payment and penitence." They "have endeavored to insure their property with the enemy, by forefeiting their reputation with us, from which may be justly inferred, that their governing passion is avarice." Paine had a prescription for avarice though: "The only cure of toryism of this cast, is to tax it. . . . Make them as much afraid of losing on one side as the other, and you stagger their toryism; make them more so, and you reclaim them; for their principle is to worship any power they are most afraid of."[27]

Friends were being taxed and penalized already, but the Assembly was not as hostile to Friends as Paine and much of the public desired. It was not using taxation to make Friends fear it or stagger their presumed Loyalism. Difficult though it was for Friends to appreciate the leniency of the government toward them before July 1776, they would soon experience a government in Pennsylvania that would show them a difference.[28] The Assembly, under the leadership of John Dickinson, was perhaps the most conservative in the American colonies in resisting the movement for independence. Radical Whigs like Paine, Timothy Matlack, Christopher Marshall, James Cannon, and Benjamin Rush—the first three being former Friends—chafed under this conservatism and resolved to replace the Assembly, including the charter or constitution of the province—the whole regime—with a new system.[29] It amounted to a domestic revolution in the midst of an anticolonial one. Its significance for Friends is that this coup abolished the constitution that had often been their inspiration, and lately their protection, and it left them at the mercy of their greatest detractors. The coup began in earnest in mid-May and succeeded by the end of the summer.

A foretaste of life under the new regime was afforded Friends on 17 May, when the Continental Congress appointed a day of fasting—in order to facilitate the scheming of the radicals in Pennsylvania. Friends publicized their refusal to observe the fast by, among other things, refusing to close their businesses for the day. A mob of young people walked the streets with clubs on the seventeenth to assure that Friends closed down too, and the Friends who resisted them "were compelled by stones to listen."[30]

In June, the Committees of the Association convened a conference to lay plans for a constitutional convention. Of the delegates at the conference from Philadelphia, Bucks, and Chester counties, 30 percent were disowned and disciplined Friends, a majority of them for offenses having nothing to do with the Revolution. The city committee, which had plotted the coup from the inception of the idea, was laced with former Friends.[31] As Paine had already showed the way, Friends would suffer some of their hardest blows in the Revolution from persons who had been Friends and either left the sect or been disowned. For some radical Patriots, the Revolution may have offered a way to avenge their disownment or discipline by their former church.

In July, the projected constitutional convention met, modeled a new regime for the state, and with surprising ease, dispatched the old charter government into history. American independence had been declared earlier in the month—it seemed pallid to many Pennsylvanians when compared to their provincial revolution.

The new regime compounded Friends' reasons to alienate themselves from the times; *their* Pennsylvania was now twice removed.[32] At the Yearly Meeting in September, Friends resolved that any member holding a public office of any kind was violating the oldest professions of Quakerism and must resign the office or be disowned. Also, Friends must not elect any person, Friend or otherwise, to public office.[33] This was a novel prescription, far more rigid than those since 1758 that treated public service. The uneasiness about holding public office, which the reformation had brought to Friends, had never completely weaned them from the Holy Experiment, or, on the other hand, their enjoyment of public power. Never had the Society flatly proscribed officeholding, but only warned of the hazards possible in some unspecified public posts. This new order did not equivocate, but demanded a complete exodus from public life. By it Friends discarded one whole aspect of secular life. The reformation had advanced by the handiwork of the Society's foes.

The new regime in Pennsylvania had assured the same effect as the Yearly Meeting ordered. In order to hold public office under the new constitution, a prospective official had to take a religious oath. In order to vote a citizen had to swear an oath or affirm that he disavowed the king and supported the new constitution of Pennsylvania.[34] Friends could do neither and were therefore excluded from the political process in the state—like thousands of others whose conservatism alone disqualified them.

By the end of 1776, the Society had established some points that may have been in doubt the previous two years. First, the Society had not been persuaded or cowed into silence or inaction. Both its prescriptions for its members' behavior should there be war and its sanctions upon them had offended the revolutionaries. But despite the attacks upon Friends for their discipline, they did not discard it. Friends did not realize it in December 1776, but in the previous twelve months they had disowned more members than they would in any subsequent year of the Revolution. The total for 1776 was 190 men who assisted the Revolution, mostly by military service.

Enforcement of the prohibition on military service should not be taken for granted. In the Revolution, military service was more than just another article of discipline; it became a very special case historically, for which exceptions conceivably might have been made. The Society had finessed an exception on behalf of its young men who had mustered to meet the Paxton men; perhaps it could do so again, when they mustered to meet the British. Or, like the Moravians in the French and Indian War and the Revolution, Friends might just have candidly discarded most of their pacifist ethic.[35] They did neither. The rigor of the discipline in the past twenty years and the belief that Friends' adversaries in this revolution were their old adversaries from 1763 kept them to the pacifist and neutral line. Before 1776, Friends had prepared an affirmative answer to the question that the revolutionaries put to them in 1776: Will you suffer your church to be reduced in numbers and power through your persistence in your unpatriotic, sectarian way? Still, the threat that Paine had made remained unfulfilled and it remained to be seen whether Friends, when punished in their property, would adhere to their pacifism and loyalism.

The second fact that emerged in 1776 was that the Society was not suffering from a schism. Most Friends did not treat the orders of the Meeting for Sufferings as the expressions of a "fractional and factional" number of Friends. Philadelphia Yearly Meeting in 1776 ratified the course the Meeting for Sufferings had taken and the Yearly Meeting was the largest ever to that day and free of rancor.[36] As for the 190 or more Friends disowned, none stepped forward to protest against the Society's discipline. They appeared to be content with the idea that a religious denomination could set standards of behavior and expel the members who violated the standards. Many probably did not care about the Society one way or another. There was anger surely over Quaker pacifism or loyalty, but the angry revolutionaries did not seriously accuse their opponents of being pseudo-Quakers. Rather, they let Friends keep their name and hoped to make it infamous.

While there was no schism, there clearly was a defection from the Society: 948 members in Pennsylvania were disowned for behavior associated with the Revolution. The most unequivocal nonpacifists among them were those who volunteered for military service—specifically to bear arms. A description by Kenneth Radbill of the background of 420 of these volunteers, those from southeastern Pennsylvania, permits some inferences about the Society, the reformation, and also the Revolution.[37]

First, like the great majority of middle-class Americans who enlisted, most of the 420 enlisted in 1775 and 1776. Like other enlistees, these Friends were caught up in the flush of patriot enthusiasm—the "rage militaire"—that characterized the early years of the Revolution.[38]

City Friends were clearly overrepresented among the armsbearers. Whereas Philadelphia had 17 percent of the Quaker population of Pennsylvania, it had 37 percent of the armsbearers.[39] The wealth of the volunteers who appeared in the tax lists of the city of Philadelphia and Philadelphia County was much less than that of other Friends. The two lowest of nine economic brackets contained 68 percent of all volunteers, but contained only 29.9 percent of other Friends.[40] Clearly age explains the low economic status of many volunteers. One hundred of the 194 volunteers in the city and county of Philadelphia do not even appear on the rolls, indicating that most were dependents and minors. In Chester and Bucks counties, too few volunteers appear on the rolls to even warrant an analysis.[41]

In Philadelphia city, the mean age of the volunteers was 30.0, and for Chester and Bucks counties, 25.6 and 29.5, respectively. In Philadelphia Monthly Meeting, the modal age was 21.[42] To gain a perspective on age, Robert Wells found that the average age of first marriages among Quaker men in his study was 26.5. Marriage normally indicates ownership of sufficient property or establishment in a trade sufficiently to support a family—and this is especially true of Friends.[43] The occupations of the volunteers in Philadelphia County were as much as 86 percent artisan. In Chester and Bucks counties, the largest group was farmers, at 37 and 72 percent, respectively, with millers, carpenters, and smiths also common in Chester.[44]

Kinship and acquaintanceship appear to have influenced the

volunteers in their decisions to enlist. Of 140 volunteers in Philadelphia whose genealogies could be determined, 41 had brothers (or half-brothers) who had volunteered, and 13 (who include some men in the previous category) had fathers or sons as volunteers. A total of 73 of the 140 were related in ways no more distant than first cousins or uncles. Family ties were more pronounced in Chester County, where 91 volunteers were related and 63 unrelated. Bucks County showed the fewest kinship connections.[45]

As for acquaintanceship among volunteers (beyond kinship), records exist from thirty individual Quaker meetings—which are meetings of record for business whose membership is the same as a meeting for worship. It is at this level that Friends worshipped together, lived within convenient distances of each other, and most often shared their experiences. Of the 198 volunteers from these thirty meetings, 100 came from only six meetings.[46] Evidence, therefore, seems to indicate that volunteers inclined others toward their course of behavior or reinforced each other's decision to enlist. Or, in the contrary situation, if a young Friend pondered enlisting, he might more easily have rejected the thought when no relative or colleague supported him as he brought the Quaker community's censure down upon himself. And similarly, Quaker volunteers living in urban centers, like Philadelphia, could more easily find approval of their course from nearby non-Quakers and patriots than could an isolated, country Friend.

The fact that 77.9 percent of the volunteers were disowned only for armsbearing and had no prior violations of discipline indicates that they were obedient Friends by and large. (Yet since they were young, they had not yet spent many years under the discipline of their meetings.) Because they were apparently content with Quakerism in most respects other than pacifism, and because the war passed (and early on turned into an unromantic episode), we might expect a substantial number of these Friends to return to the fold. Few did—only thirty-one, or 7.4 percent. Had they been jealous of the Society and wished to punish it, they might well have joined the Free Quakers. As we will see below, the Free Quakers contained some of the preeminent enemies of the Society and the Free Quakers as a body harried the Society of Friends in Pennsylvania. Yet only thirty-seven disowned volunteers joined the Free Quakers and never constituted more than 37 percent, and usually about 20 percent, of the Free Quakers.[47] In general, disowned, armsbearing Friends were indifferent about the Society and probably had been indifferent, but not irregular, Friends before the Revolution.

In sum, whereas the youth, urban residence, kinship ties, and acquaintanceships of these Quaker armsbearers seem to have encouraged them to enlist, the influence that wealth and occupation had upon their enlisting appears unclear and confused by their youthfulness. Reformers said little about these defectors; they worried much more about retrograde persons still within the Society. After twenty years of sectarian reform, a substantial number of Friends had succumbed to a mass, secular movement—republican Revolution or "rage militaire"—and been swept out of the "enclosed" community. Some Friends said during the Revolution—for other reasons—that the city of Philadelphia seemed to be a weak spot in the world of reformed Quakerism. But the reformers did not despair; rather, they believed that their precepts needed only more application.

By the summer of 1776, most Friends had not yet felt the oppressiveness of the Revolution. Those who had volunteered had gone willingly. The testing that Tom Paine and others had recommended for Friends really began with the new, radical state government in Pennsylvania.

The constitutional convention of the summer of 1776 exceeded its proper business in many ways and one of them was by "legislating" the first ordinance against nonassociators and pacifists. Every nonassociator sixteen to fifty years of age had to pay twenty shillings a month until the new legislature met. And every nonassociator over twenty-one was assessed four shillings per pound annually on the value of his estate.[48] Six months later the first House of Representatives under the new constitution passed a militia act that fined men eighteen to fifty-three years old for not mustering. The House provided for exemption from militia service only by the hiring of substitutes. The exemption was not acceptable to Friends.[49] By 1777, the House became more vindictive. It amended the previous disabilities on pacifists by doubling the tax levies upon them and fined each one £40 or imprisoned him four months for not mustering.[50] With that, the pattern for the treatment of pacifists was nearly complete; only the amounts of the fines increased thereafter. In 1779, the fine rose from £40 to £100, and later that year, from £100 to £1000. Violation of other aspects of militia laws brought a six-fold increase in fines. The gross increases reflected more than vindictiveness, however. Paper currency depreciated enormously and to stop the fines from becoming nominal, they had to be increased enormously.[51]

In a second way the radical revolutionaries tested Friends' attachment to Great Britain and to their property. The constitutional convention had erected several oaths for voters and public officers after July 1776.[52] That was no problem for Friends, who voluntarily refused to vote and serve in office. But in June 1777, the legislature created an oath or affirmation of allegiance for the common citizen, making it impossible for Friends to evade. The penalty prescribed for nonjurors and nonaffirmers inhibited their ability to do business and manage property, among other things. They could not sue for debts, buy, sell, or transfer lands, tenements, and hereditaments.[53] In 1778, the penalty had increased so that upon first tender of the oath, a nonjuror was fined £10 or jailed. Upon second tender (mandatory), his refusal brought the forfeiture of his estate and chattels and his exile from the state. Nonjurors practicing certain vocations who did not desist from them were to be fined not less than £500.[54] The last provision and an amendment to it in 1779 troubled Friends exceptionally. It prohibited them from maintaining their private schools, because schoolmasters, tutors, professors, and trustees were among those whose vocations were proscribed if they did not take the oaths. Friends believed that since their schools were parochial, the laws inhibited the propagation of their faith and practices and infringed upon their religious liberties. They believed that the lawmakers regarded the Society as an adversary political party and that the intent of the law was to encourage disaffection from that party.[55] From the lawmakers' point of view, as Tom Paine had said in print, Quakers had overstepped the bounds of *religious* ethics and taken a political stance (with their pacifism and rejection of revolution), for which reason the propagation of their "politics" deserved no protection under the law. What had begun in 1776 as an attempt by the provincial government to have nonassociators contribute the equivalent of a volunteer had become an attempt to compel allegiance to the new Commonwealth or suffer the consequences, including the extinguishing of one's church.

The amounts demanded from Friends, as well as other pacifists and nonjurors, do not satisfactorily describe their losses.[56] The Society required that Friends refuse the services that the law demanded, refuse the monetary equivalent of the services, and refuse to pay the penalties that their disobedience brought. The last of these Quaker obligations was an old one in new dress. English Friends had long been obliged not to pay the penalties laid upon their refusal to pay tithes to the Church of England. Instead, they were to permit the magistrates to distrain their property and sell it for the taxes or tithes owed, and not take any surplus which the magistrates might return to them.[57] Had all magistrates been kindly and conscientious, Friends would ordinarily have lost no more than they would by volunteering the amount of the penalty. Instead, magistrates took more goods than necessary, from a mean spirit or laziness.

In the Revolution, the same practice appeared; magistrates distrained more than the laws required and were rarely corrected. Elizabeth Drinker, who had much property to lose, kept a good record of the excesses of the magistrates. For a fine of 13 shillings, magistrate Pickering in June 1779, took a looking glass worth 40 to 50 shillings, six pewter plates, and a pewter basin. In September, Jacob Franks and the son of the auctioneer took, in lieu of the militia tax and penalty, a walnut dining table and six walnut chairs, a mahogany tea table, a mahogany-framed looking glass, and two pewter dishes. In May 1780, Jeremiah Baker took a mahogany table worth £3 or £4 for an 18-shilling tax. Next month, Adam Lapp confiscated a dining table, five chairs, a pair of andirons, and £18 sterling. He was back next month for six walnut chairs, a walnut tea table, another pair of andirons and two brass kettles.[58] The Drinkers were one of the wealthiest families in the city, and one whom the revolutionaries deeply suspected of being Loyalists. Their situation and sufferings may not have been typical of that of most Friends. Fortunately, the Society kept records of the losses of all Friends and tabulated them, thus providing an insight into the sufferings of most Friends. In rural Chester County, one monthly meeting with 120 families lost £6,109 from 1777 to 1781, or more than £25 per year per family. In 1790, the average Quaker and Mennonite farm family of five in southeastern Pennsylvania produced £40 of disposable income. If their income was as great in the Revolution, which was not likely, they lost 60 percent of it to the revolutionaries. The liklihood that such losses were partly due to illegal and excessive distraints is supported by an act of the legislature in 1789 providing relief from such abuses by magistrates during the Revolution.[59]

A Friend who had suffered from the abusive magistrate might presume that he was losing more property for the sake of the Revolution than was the average American Patriot. But was he really? Was

Paine's threat to make Friends pay exorbitantly fulfilled in the laws? According to the calculations of Arthur Mekeel, Pennsylvania Friends lost £38,550 in the Revolution.[60] How much did Patriot Pennsylvanians contribute? It is not possible to specify the sum, records being far short of what Friends kept and the experiences of the revolutionaries being more varied than those of Friends. Still, there is a way to make a comparison. That is to ask what part of the Quaker losses arose from their refusal to share the average citizen's responsibility in the Revolution, and what part was extraordinary and a penalty upon their refusal to cooperate by supporting the new government.

Mekeel has broken down the losses of Friends into categories.[61] They show that 41.6 percent of Friends' losses arose, first, from fines upon their refusal to muster, provide substitutes, or otherwise assist the armed forces, and second, from fines upon their refusal to take oaths. Assuming that the lawmakers fined Friends and other pacifists only the equivalent of their militia obligations, then Friends did not really suffer in that area more than average Americans. But by not taking oaths, they suffered extraordinarily, because the revolutionaries did swear. Unfortunately, there is no statistic on the amounts lost for refusing oaths and no possibility of dividing the 41.6 percent into its two components.

All but 1.2 percent of the remaining 58.4 percent of the losses arose from requisitions of property by the American armies and distraints and fines for not paying taxes to the state government. Non-Friends escaped the first of these losses by accepting the commissary certificates the government issued in exchange (although the value of the certificates varied wildly until 1790). Friends were forbidden to accept compensation for what the armies took from them. At times that refusal could be used punitively. For example, in 1777, out of pique at the Society's order that Friends refuse the oath of allegiance, the Committee of Safety ordered that all the soldiers who came to Philadelphia be billeted upon nonassociators.[62]

The fines for not paying taxes affected Friends and not the revolutionaries. We know therefore that although measurement of the burden borne by Friends is imprecise, it was considerable, and it is aptly a measure of their suffering. And as for Paine's threat, the man who cherished his property, upon examination of the laws and their enforcement, should have joined the revolutionaries and discarded his Quakerism.[63]

Imprisonment was a hardship that comparatively few Friends had to undergo. Imprisoning the large number of Friends who kept their testimonies on oaths, allegiance, and pacifism would have caused a great logistical problem. When imprisonment of Friends did occur in Pennsylvania, it seems often to have been the result of personal dislike or old political animosity. One of the most famous cases of imprisonment illustrates frontier antipathy toward Friends and the violence common to the revolutionary frontier. The revolutionaries apprehended Moses Roberts, a Quaker minister from Berks County, summarily shackled him, and sent him down the Susquehanna River. They put Roberts in Lancaster jail until he could post £10,000 bond to leave the county for the duration of the war. He was accused of trafficking with Loyalist Indians. He had chosen to remain at his frontier home the past two years despite the flight of most of the inhabitants in the face of Indian attacks at Wyoming. Roberts's pregnant wife had remained at home with the children, but after two months a band of men from Sunbury warned her to get out. With what she could hastily pack up, she fled to the Quaker community at Maiden Creek and left behind for their oppressors the house, furniture, livestock, grain, and mill. Greed and religious envy were the motives of these Patriots, the Meeting for Sufferings unequivocally pronounced.[64]

The Meeting for Sufferings labored hard to free Roberts, especially by petitioning Chief Justice Thomas McKean for relief. But McKean showed a cold contempt for the Quaker petitions. He took the occasions of their petitioning him to harangue them. In a different case, he jailed two Friends for not performing the offices of constable while the law prohibited them from holding office. Roberts was finally freed, but not by McKean.[65]

The most famous case of imprisonment by far was the exile of seventeen Friends (and five others) to Winchester, Virginia, in 1777 and 1778,[66] another incident that revealed old antagonisms in the community as well as the nervousness of Patriots in the heat of war. Once already, in the winter of 1776, the British had threatened to invade Pennsylvania, and the Continental Congress had fled to Baltimore. While many radical Americans prepared to flee like the congressmen, they remarked about Friends' contentment with their station in Philadelphia and their apparent resolve to stay. That fed the suspicion already circulating that Quakers had an understanding with the British and had insured their property with them.[67]

Nothing came of that British approach toward Philadelphia, but the following summer the British attacked in earnest. In August,

General William Howe's army had landed in Maryland and moved north toward Philadelphia. Anxiety filled the Congress and suspicions about defectors arose again with the belief that the city had become an asylum for crypto-Loyalists. John Adams, remembering well his clash with the "priest and Pemberton-ridden Quakers," recommended to Congress, along with William Duer and Richard Henry Lee, that eleven Friends—"persons of considerable wealth"— be apprehended. The Friends had shown, by the epistles they had published and by their general behavior, that "there is no doubt it will be their inclination, to communicate intelligence to the enemy, and in various other ways, to injure the councils and arms of America."[68] The Supreme Executive Council of Pennsylvania was happy to implement this resolve of Congress. It added thirty other men to the list. Twenty-six, out of a total of forty-one, were Friends. The Friends could have eased their condition if they had agreed to affirm their allegiance to the Commonwealth of Pennsylvania and to restrict themselves to their homes. But they refused to give their word and instead protested the violation of their rights. While the Council prepared to exile them to Virginia, they obtained writs of habeas corpus from Chief Justice Thomas McKean—a rare lapse from his customary hostility toward Friends. The Council ignored the writs, and within forty-eight hours the House passed a law suspending habeas corpus.[69]

The most radical Pennsylvanians dominated the executive and legislature of Pennsylvania at the time and continued to do so until 1780. In 1777, these old antagonists of the city Friends were venting the anger that the Quakers had roused in them as early as 1770. Anxious about invasion and doubtful of the neutrality of Friends, they moved against them in a hasty, summary way.[70]

The Quaker prisoners believed that their prosecutors or persecutors held them incommunicado and exiled them in order to encourage young Friends to join the Revolution; without leaders, Quaker youths could be lured away from their pacifism.[71] That was not a silly inference in light of the youth of the Quaker volunteers in 1775 and 1776. And the behavior of defecting Friends and the Whig propaganda supplied the exiles with other good reasons to credit that motive. The revolutionaries had tried to co-opt much or all of the Society. What some of the exiles overlooked was the envy that their own past political partisanship, insensitivity to Whiggery, and wealth had created in their oppressors.

The suffering of Friends in exile varied according to their age and physical constitution. None was closely confined or deprived of the necessities (which they often purchased by themselves or received from Virginia Friends).[72] On the way to Virginia, all were subjected to the threats and rage of rural Pennsylvanians, particularly at Reading and Harrisburg. The Friends were worried that these shows might turn into violence. They did not. The final sufferers among the exiles were the aged and infirm John Hunt (from England) and Thomas Gilpin, both of whom were exiled despite their infirmities. They died in Virginia. Israel Pemberton died at home the following year at age sixty-four. According to John Pemberton, he had been weakened by the exile and despite his release, he had continued to decline.[73]

The exiles were returned to Pennsylvania and released at Shippensburg. They wished to be delivered to their home, Philadelphia, which was then in the hands of the British. In the refusal of the Supreme Executive Council to deliver them there, the exiles believed that they had again taken the measure of the radicals' resentment of them. The House had passed a law confiscating the estates of persons crossing lines to enter British Philadelphia. If Friends wished to be reunited with their families, they would have to violate that law. Their jeopardy appeared very contrived. They crossed the lines anyway, as Friends often did during the war, and they escaped the penalty. Other hazards, however, kept their escape from that penalty from lessening their suspicion of the radicals.[74]

When the British evacuated Philadelphia, the Americans talked loudly of vengeance upon the Loyalists who had joined the retreating British (or upon their abandoned estates) as well as upon the collaborators who did not leave with the British. The Council appointed forty-three commissioners to hunt for traitors. Newspapers speculated on the fate of the guilty. Talk of reprisals circulated in the streets. Friends were specified as a suspect lot, deserving the attention of the forty-three sleuths or inquisitors. The old epistles of 1775 and 1776 were recalled as evidence not of neutrality but of disloyalty and collaboration. Too, the Quakers still refused to affirm allegiance. They allegedly hoarded British goods during the recent occupation to sell at high prices to returning Patriots. A spurious Yearly Meeting paper, containing purportedly treasonable information, was circulated. Events were running true to the form of 1777 and Friends expected a repetition of the consequences. But imprisonment did not come. The cost to Friends amounted to psychological wear and tear.[75]

At least twice again after 1778, Friends feared they might be exiled anew. In the summer and autumn of 1779, paper currency depreciated alarmingly, prices rose, and food was in short supply, all of which made poorer Philadelphians angry and restive. They complained of monopolists, forestallers, and regraters, and demanded that the evils be corrected. Christopher Marshall, a disowned Friend, was the premier organizer of the protests; he had complained loudly about Quaker avarice in 1776. Many of the complainers were militiamen who accused the men who did not serve and complained about the unequal burden of those who did. While their economic grievances went unattended, the militia turned their discontents toward a different object. On 4 October, militiamen met at a city tavern to deliberate on their "plan to drive from the city, all disaffected persons, and those who supported them."[76] The militiamen had to decide specifically who deserved exile.

The first person the militiamen selected was John Drinker, clerk of the Meeting for Sufferings. They apprehended him as he came out of Yearly Meeting, and after permitting him to have his supper, led him about town with three other captives behind a drummer beating the rogue's march. The day's protest escalated into violence and bloodshed between the crowd of militia and some of their conservative antagonists. The city cavalry was summoned and it routed the protestors. No harm came to Drinker and no other Friends were involved. No Friends ended up in exile, but the prospect of exile may be said to have been even greater after the disturbance. The legislature listened to the militiamen and on 10 October passed a law providing for the securing, jailing, or exile of the sort of persons the militiamen had complained of. A person who was suspected of being an enemy of the American cause or had shown "a general disaffection" from it could be reported to the Supreme Executive Council or the Supreme Court, and if inquiry by one of these bodies revealed disaffection, the person could be sentenced to give security, go to jail, or be sent into exile.[77] The Council and the Supreme Court made little use of the law, and the prospect that Friends dreaded did not materialize.

For the last time in the war, in 1780 Friends again sensed the possibility of exile. On 12 August, the *Pennsylvania Packet* republished the Quaker epistles of 1775 and 1776 which had so angered Paine and the military associators and had sparked the exile. Also republished was a crude, spurious "Spanktown Yearly Meeting" epistle from 1777 which an enemy of the Society had then circulated to "prove" the treachery of Friends. The Meeting for Sufferings immediately published a refutation of the potentially damaging materials and succeeded nicely in encouraging sympathy for itself.[78] It did appear, as Friends alleged, that some anonymous, jealous, and malevolent persons were blowing on the ashes of old fires, hoping to rekindle the harassment of Friends. At the time of Yearly Meeting, several weeks after the newspaper stimulus, an effigy of Benedict Arnold was carted around the city accompanied by mounted men with "a great rabble following." The crowd headed for the Yearly Meeting at the Pine Street meeting house, but discovered that the Meeting had already broken up. Later that evening, while John Pemberton and Henry Drinker walked about the streets, they found themselves cursed by collections of angry men.[79] Whatever additional evil design there was in the crowd and in the newspapers, it came to nothing. No one publicly proposed the reincarceration of Friends.

In addition to official sanctions upon Friends, there were a score of occasions during the war when mobs or vandals harassed and rioted against them. Twice yearly Friends might expect trouble—every April and December, when the Supreme Executive Council appointed, respectively, a day of fasting and of thanksgiving.[80] These proclamations usually required that citizens quit their business for the day, and the crowds in the streets might also demand that housekeepers illuminate their windows. When Friends refused to respect these proclamations and demands, people in the streets harassed them, often by breaking their darkened windows, or vandalizing their property in other ways. July fourth often turned into an even greater occasion for vandalizing the homes of Friends. On 4 July 1777, Sarah Logan Fisher lost fifteen windows, Nicholas Waln, fourteen, and William Logan, fifty or more. The following year, Elizabeth Drinker rejoiced at the shortage of candles in the city which prevented the Patriots from lighting up their houses and spared the Quaker Egyptians another Patriot Passover. The violence that marred days appointed for fasting and prayer convinced Friends of the irreligion in the revolutionary regime. "To sport and commit evil . . . cannot reasonably be supposed to be the fast acceptable . . . with God." Knowing that Friends in England were afflicted by fast days proclaimed there to invoke God's favor upon the British armies, John Pemberton reflected upon the irony of it all. How could English and American Friends be expected to implore the same Divine Being for contradictory things? "Lamentable confusion and defection from the Spirit of Christ!"[81]

The greatest American victory and the end of the war gave Friends the greatest trouble. On the twenty-fourth of October, Philadelphia celebrated Cornwallis's surrender. In the evening a mob, or mobs, assembled, fired guns, and raised a great din. The mob searched out houses that were not illuminated and checked especially those belonging to people who were in bad repute with the revolutionaries. Elizabeth Drinker believed that scarcely one Friend's house escaped completely, and some suffered outrageously. Windows, of course, were broken, but the mob, equipped with axes and crowbars, pried off shutters and hinges, smashed sashes and doors, entered some houses and destroyed furnishings. John Drinker, an obvious enemy of the radicals, lost half of the goods in his shop and was beaten. The mob threw flaming materials into one house, shot off guns in another, while Friends and others tried to remain composed through it. The children often became hysterical.[82] The mob returned to Hannah Moore's home twice. Before its third visit a neighbor rushed in with the news that the mob intended to pull the house down this time. He implored the Moores to light candles, but Hannah refused. The neighbor rushed off to get candles and returned to light them in the Moores' windows just as the mob reappeared. Several men who sympathized with Friends joined the mob to discover its intended direction and victims, then outrun it and light candles in the windows of the intended victims. Hannah credited John Dorsey with saving fourteen houses this way. At the end of the day many houses stood ruined, but no one had been killed. As with other riots in America, the lack of resistance to the mob tempered its behavior and forestalled bloodshed.[83]

Friends hardly suspected that the riot was the last violence they would suffer in the Revolution. Quite the opposite, they believed that the victory of the American forces at Yorktown would lead to a great deal more license in the Patriots' treatment of Friends. The riot confirmed their fear; "Philadelphia will no longer be that happy asylum for the Quakers it once was."[84] However quiet the battlefields had become, Friends expected no peace.

The violence of the riot and the prospect of more of the same astonished and embittered Friends. "It must . . . appear strange and extraordinary," they wrote, "in the view of candid inquirers, that so evident a change and contrast have taken place . . . that we . . . descendants of the first settlers, professing the same religious principles . . . who have never forfeited our birth-right, should now be vilified, persecuted, imprisoned." In this address to the Council and House of Representatives, frustrations pent up in Friends since 1776 burst out. You have passed laws calculated to oppress us, Friends accused; you have committed their execution to avaricious, profligate men who preyed on the innocent and industrious. Scurrilous publications have reproached Friends in order to inflame ignorant men against them. Your fasts—filled with animosity, reveling, and oppression—are unacceptable to the Lord, who has given you the "scourge of war" to tell you as much.[85]

Chastising their tormentors appears to have had hardly any effect on the tormentors. In little more than a month, Friends discovered another assault in the making, a novel one. It had originated in 1780, when a number of former Friends, most of whom were disowned for assisting the Revolution, began to meet under the leadership of Timothy Matlack and Samuel Wetherill. The two were brothers-in-law. Matlack was a proven nemesis of the Society, a "loose" individual, disowned before the Revolution for indebtedness, whereas Wetherill, a Quaker minister and genuinely pious man, had been disowned only in 1779 for revolutionary activity. Christopher Marshall also joined the group as did other notable Patriots such as Clement Biddle and Betsy Ross.[86] In December 1781, these persons, styled Free Quakers, petitioned the House to recognize and protect their rights to property in the hands of the Society of Friends. The Free Quakers asked to share in the use of Quaker meeting houses, schools, burial grounds, lots of land, and others estates like records, papers, and books. They complained of Quakers' unpatriotic conduct, or even Loyalism, without ever proving it or explaining its legal connection with the relief they sought. Did they expect that a few innuendos could do the work of a difficult legal brief? Were they trying to rouse the patriotic passions of the legislators against Friends? The legislature did nothing immediately by tabling their petition. In February 1782, the petition was reconsidered together with an address that the Meeting for Sufferings submitted.[87]

James Pemberton felt that the Free Quaker attack "exceeds any we have before experienced, it being made upon the whole body."[88] The Meeting for Sufferings prepared its defense well. Because the Free Quakers had recited the reasons they were disowned, all of them being services on behalf of the Revolution, the Meeting for Sufferings justified its practice of church discipline. It was the best apology for discipline yet written by Friends in Pennsylvania. Quoting John Locke as well as Scripture, Friends protested that no church or private society is bound to toleration. No member has a right to forbearance if he disturbs the constitution of any church. The address showed that Friends perceived the Free Quaker petition as above all a threat to their sectarian mores and use of discipline, and they focused their defense upon their right to order their own church as they wished.[89]

The Free Quakers replied that they did not care about a church's right to disown; they conceded that. However, they proceeded to list still more of their patriotic services which got them disowned, and to rue the Tory-Loyalist behavior of Friends. Their only unambiguous argument concerned their property rights. They believed that having contributed to the church and helped to amass its property while they were members, they retained some vested right in the use of that property now.[90]

In the fall of 1782, the legislature assigned the controversy to a committee for investigation. Here the many accusations were thrashed out, however irrelevant they may have been to the legal questions or the relief petitioned for. Friends' behavior in the Revolution, in other words, was raked over once again—by Timothy Matlack. James Pemberton perceived the Free Quakers' strategy in all of it: "Their proceedings are directed in the same line as former persecutions to misrepresent our conduct and bring in the laws of the land to their assistance amusing the people that we are legally disenfranchised of our liberties and the protection of government and have forfeited our inheritance." We are not traitors, aliens, or pariahs, the Friends insisted; all the history, true or false, that the Free Quakers recited does not add up to that, and we will not abide any public punishment rationalized in the name of such history.[91]

The Society's defense improved immensely because of the address of seventy-five disowned Friends to the House. They, who had joined the Revolution, had no quarrel with the Society which had ousted them. They still respected the Society's use of discipline and they did not want to be confused with the Free Quakers. Their protest struck hard at the standing of the Free Quakers as spokesmen of aggrieved former Friends who were Patriots. It left the legislative committee in confusion.[92]

By late October, the trouble had passed, pretty much as Friends suspected it had. Relief came not especially from the committee hearing—although it offered hope—but from the election early that month. Since 1780, the conservatives in Pennsylvania—the Republican party—had been gaining strength in the legislature. They maintained a slight preponderance over the radicals or Constitutionalist party. In October 1782, the Republicans won even greater control and a signal victory in the Supreme Executive Council. It was their first victory there since the creation of the radical constitution in 1776. The House committee on the Free Quaker question, which already had a majority of moderates, dissembled and the House postponed the business until 1783. Thereafter, it languished. "Blessed be the Lord who hath not given us a prey to their teeth," sighed James Pemberton.[93]

Friends in Pennsylvania had been suffering not only from the Revolution against Great Britain—perhaps not even especially from that Revolution. Their troubles resulted from the domestic upheaval in their state, whereby the most radical Patriots had created a new regime in 1776 and opened a long, bitter struggle with their conservative, local rivals. Conservative Friends identified with the prerevolutionary Galloway party had deeply offended the radicals, and being pacifists, nonjurors, and Loyalists in principle, these Friends had given the radicals a handy means to punish them. Politically innocent Friends too were caught in the nets cast especially for conservatives. But when non-Quaker conservatives like John Dickinson and Robert Morris gained office and power, Friends found they had kindred spirits for their governors.

Seventeen eighty-two ended Friends' trials for the partisan reasons that started most of them. The party of the Free Quakers was eclipsed. Timothy Matlack, midwife to the Free Quakers, was disgraced. The Republican legislature declared him "unworthy of public trust or confidence" because of a defalcation in the tax revenues entrusted to him. He lost the secretaryship of the Council and the respect of even his colleagues.[94] The war would end shortly; the radicals would never regain their earlier eminence. As some Friends suspected, a corner had been turned.

CONSUMMATION

12

Reformation in the Revolution

Suffering and Spiritual Growth

For some twenty years before the Revolution, Quaker reformers urged their brethren to lead more ascetic lives—to moderate or renounce their absorbing interest in property, political office, and power. A more circumscribed life was, in the opinion of the reformers, essential to a truly religious character. Anthony Benezet succinctly described their attitude when he wrote, "It is in nothingness that God is found."[1] But not enough Friends had followed their advice and example to permit the reformers to congratulate themselves or the Society. Instead, they warned that some Friends were susceptible to disappointment because of their misplaced confidence in material things. Trials and testing awaited them; the depths of their religious commitment would be plumbed. The trouble was, the trial did not appear. The years from 1755 to 1775 were not untroubled ones; there were wars with the French and Indians, and confrontations with the Paxton men. But none of these quite fulfilled the reformers' warnings of a wrenching experience. The Friends in need of correction emerged from the prerevolutionary disturbances still needing correction.

The Revolution, on the other hand, disappointed none of the reformers. It was as much a disaster as anything they had predicted. It did not, however, make an end of their labors. There were dull and callous members whom no disaster alone would provoke to reflection and reform. The war's impact had to be supplemented by instruction. God had done his part by granting Friends "a season in which to grow in grace." But Friends were left to choose whether to grow or not.

Plainly, the reformers were not uncomfortable with war. It may do them an injustice to say that they preferred wartime to peace. What they clearly preferred was a thoughtful, pious, ascetic church. The trouble with peace was that it did not lead men and women into that kind of life. Instead, Friends prospered, became proud of their ability to regulate or control their lives, and forgot that there had ever been a time of adversity in their collective past. Their senses were sated with the things of this world and their curiosity rested. It seemed that God did not speak loudly enough in peacetime to awaken them. War was better. The din of it broke through even their impaired faculties and caused them to question their presumptions and situations in the light of God's unfolding will. The war was also as effective a form of discipline as any Friends could have devised. Without an innovation in Quaker codes or administration, the wheat was resifted and the chaff removed.

In 1774, when war was only a prospect, Benezet discovered the reluctance of Friends to confront the inevitable. "People are afraid at being disturbed in their enjoyments, in . . . their confidence in the world & the things of it." As for himself, "I feel but little apprehension at the prospect of things, which to many is so alarming. . . . I fear nothing more than giving way to a spirit whose hope & expectation is from the unchristian . . . measures proposed by many. . . . Its [sic] from God alone . . . deliverance must arise." Once war was a fact, Philadelphia Yearly Meeting in 1776 repeated Benezet's advice for the sake of all Friends: Our principles declare "that we place no Confidence, or dependence in the Arm of the flesh. . . . And as deep Trials, Sufferings, & Revilings may be permitted to come upon us, let us hear the rod, & him who hath appointed it, and not seek for or expect deliverance by the hand of Man, but endeavour to get into that humble, meek, quiet, peaceable Spirit, which beareth all Things: & when it is reviled, revileth not again, but suffereth patiently."[2]

The year 1778 brought the severest losses of the war to Pennsylvania Friends, because the British and American armies occupied the southeastern part of the state. Then the Meeting for Ministers and Elders begged Friends to "join in a deep inquiry into the Causes why the present prevailing Calamities have been suffered to fall so heavy amongst us, in this land. Let a solemn Search pass through every Mind; and we trust as this comes to be the Case, each individual may be entitled to see and know their own standing." "If stripping of Goods, with other Sufferings become yet more our lot," wrote the Meeting for Sufferings, at the same time "let us not be dismayed or murmur, but . . . labour to be established in the same mind, wherein the holy Apostle . . . declared 'I . . . do count them but dung that I may win christ.' " The possibility of self-discovery especially interested Friends. The Meeting for Sufferings enlarged upon this theme in 1780: "May this dispension of his Providence be improved effectually to quicken us . . . to an impartial examination of our standing, and an enquiry how nearly our temporal engagements and pursuits are circumscribed by the standard of pure righteousness."[3]

The Friends who had the most temporal engagements to examine and who were also providentially situated to examine them were the Virginia exiles. Men taken two hundred miles from home and imprisoned might expect to receive condolences from their brethren. They did receive them, but Benezet and George Churchman sent some stern advice appropriate to the merchant and political nabobs of the Society. Benezet asked James Pemberton to consider how much Friends had contributed to the calamity that had overcome them. Pemberton could take the advice either of two ways: His political behavior, along with that of his colleagues in exile, had helped to get him in this fix; or more philosophically, his attachment to property and other earthly things caused the sting of losing them to be a sting indeed. We have lived in conformity to other peoples, Benezet continued. See it in the sumptuousness of our dwellings, equipage, dress, furniture, and tables; these are our gods. Right now we pay homage to them in the resentment we show to the men who take these goods from us. But relief is at hand:

The suffering providence which now is displayed over us seems particularly calculated to bring us to our selves . . . as the tryals & devastation is greater upon those whose possessions are most expensive, & have been at the greatest pains & expenses in adorning their pleasant pictures. . . . If this afflictive providence does induce us to begin anew upon the true foundation of our principles, in that low & humble state . . . which . . . constituted the real followers of Christ, it will have done much for us.[4]

Churchman wrote Thomas Wharton that his situation in prison was better than Churchman's. Wharton was better able to "examine the Foundation" he was upon and "in adversity to be content &

resign'd to [God's] will." Ease and tranquility had drawn some Friends aside from simplicity and purity, and they needed reforming. Now, in the midst of adversity, Wharton and all Friends could "look over the former Part of our Lives, & . . . man by man . . . set our houses in Order." John Fothergill ordered James Pemberton to "mind your own proper business." "The Kingdom we profess to seek is not of this world. . . . Be more attentive to inculcate a regard to that which has been the cause of this deserved awakening than how to gain the favour of this party or that."[5]

To these and other calls to a more ascetic life came some very heartening responses. First, when the revolutionaries threatened Friends' property in order to gain their obedience, some Friends defied them to do what they would. A few Friends did so in particularly inspired language. A Friend who refused to pay his taxes and to execute a public office wrote the Chester County Commissioners that reproving evil usually brought suffering such as they threatened him with. Men of good principle were accustomed to suffering; "Time would fail me to relate the many instances of the Prophets & righteous Men of Old who for reproving Sin . . . & disobeying Men in Earthly Power became the Objects of their Hatred & revenge." The writer's Quaker forefathers had been stoned, stocked, mocked, and banished for the sake of a good conscience; some "joyfully sealed with their Blood" their testimony against evil men and deeds.[6]

The commissioners had repeated a common assertion of the time that the current sufferings of Friends were evidence of God's displeasure with Friends' conduct in the Revolution. God may indeed have a quarrel with Friends, the writer agreed, but he was not angered for the reasons the commissioners were. For Friends' behavior toward the men in power, God had a reward which the commissioners would not understand, and which "the World can neither give nor take away. Blessed be his Name he is turning many of our Hearts to the Rock from whence we were hewn and to the Hole of the Pit from whence we were digged."[7]

Warner Mifflin's defiance and resignation to suffering may have outshone that of any other Friend in the Revolution. This man who imitated John Woolman's testimonies and service on behalf of antislavery, claimed to have discovered the depth of his pacifist commitment while sharing a condition similar to that of the soldier. His leg was badly injured and it pained him immensely each time the dressings of the wound were changed. On these occasions he became convinced that "if every farthing we were possessed of was seized for the purpose of supporting War, and I was informed it should all go, except I gave voluntarily one shilling . . . I was satisfied I should not so redeem it."[8]

The object of Mifflin's defiance was Chief Justice of Pennsylvania Thomas McKean. McKean had roughly handled Friends before his bench because of what Mifflin knew was the clear religious behavior of the Quaker defendants. McKean had harangued them about the enormity of Quaker criminality and Loyalism. Mifflin repeated the alleged crimes in order to shame McKean by their innocent and modest nature. It appears, he said, that you endeavour "to crush and root out of the very earth . . . an innocent harmless people, who are known to you to be such." You show the greatest malice to those who "so far imitate their pattern as to be sheep before their shearers, dumb, and not open their mouths in their own defense."[9]

Because of our pacifism, Mifflin continued, "we [Friends] are looked on as people not worthy to live in the land, notwithstanding it would be at the forfeiture of Our Eternall All to forsake this testimony." But McKean would credit only worldly motives for Friends' pacifism. Do you expect, Mifflin queried, the king has enough posts to reward every pacifist Friend in America? Or do you imagine that Friends are so stupid as to think the king has? The king has not one post or honor "that I would give one bushel of Indian corn for," Mifflin asserted. "I feel no dispostion in me to envy any for what they have of the poor bub[b]le of the riches and honors of this world."[10]

Yet McKean did not believe Mifflin and other Friends, and the confrontation between them had already taken the painful course of numberless, past clashes between secular rulers and religious subjects. "You are permitted to try us," Mifflin conceded, "and on tryal find numbers are what they profess to be." From their witness, "the considerate part of mankind . . . [will] be put upon from thence . . . to experience for themselves that the Lord is good, and worthy to be loved, served, and obeyed above every other consideration. . . . They will experience as many have done that nothing in this world is too much to give up for his name sake, and to be the happy partaker of that peace . . . that the world, nor all the gaols or collectors in it can take away, nor all the kings, and congresses give."[11]

Mifflin's address was bursting with sectarian pugnacity: Friends had a rule, he said, with which to judge their own conduct and the chief justice's Christianity: the Lord said, "if it were of the world, it would be loved by the world, but as it is not, but in opposition thereto, therefore it is hated, and no marvel for it hated me before it hated you."[12]

Ten days after Mifflin wrote that letter, the Meeting for Sufferings recorded that:

the peaceable principle we profess is so opposite to the spirit of the world that it is no marvel if such as endeavor faithfully to maintain it have to partake in measure of that cup of affliction which christ our holy pattern so largely drank of, and is often in mercy handed forth for the refinement of his followers, for it is through tribulation that the righteous in every age enter the Kingdom.[13]

From Virginia came some far less impassioned testimonies to the progress of an ascetic spirit. The condition of the exiles was the proper one to teach men to rely solely upon religious faith—although the testimonies came not from Thomas Wharton or James Pemberton, two exiles who had most misplaced their confidence. The Friend who suffered most in Virginia was the merchant John Hunt—the same John Hunt who had come to Pennsylvania in 1756 as an emissary from London Yearly Meeting to get Pennsylvania Friends to resign from the legislature and stop the tax protest against the war. Hunt became ill and one result was that his leg became infected and paralyzed and had to be amputated in March 1778. The operation was not successful, and Hunt died eight days later. While ill in January, he wrote:

it appears very clear to me, we are called . . . to bear a testimony (by suffering) to the Holy Truth which we as a religious Society have professed nearly 130 years. The doctrines of the Gospel have long been preached in these Provinces, but few have suffered in support of the testimony of Jesus; now the time is come wherein we are called not only to believe, but to suffer. . . . If I am so happy as to be one of those, I shall esteem it a mercy. . . . I have many times thought myself unworthy to suffer for my Lord and Master. For years past I have read with much satisfaction the History of the Primitive Martyrs and our ancient Friends. . . . Those accounts I often admired but till now I never so livingly and experimentally felt such a degree of that power which succored them, and enabled them not only to bear but to rejoyce.[14]

Collective Witness

Most Friends experienced neither exile nor imprisonment, nor did they leave personal accounts of religious growth. Yet the Revolution supplied the means for a host of Friends to witness to their religious convictions in humble and anonymous ways. By persisting in holding their meetings for worship at regularly scheduled places and times, by crossing the belligerents' lines while doing the Society's business, and by refusing to leave their residences, groups of Friends showed their religious mettle. As much as they reasonably could, they were to behave without regard to the war and its indispositions and dangers. In the seventeenth century, English Friends had met in defiance of the Conventicle Acts and had suffered grievously for it.[15] That part of Quaker history lay heavily on the minds of American Friends.

In 1778, the Yearly Meeting reasserted in the discipline that Friends must maintain the worship of God "after the example of our worthy antients in times of close persecution" by meeting as close to the usual times and places as Friends can.[16] Their trials on this account never reached the magnitude of those inflicted by the Conventicle Acts, but some danger and indisposition did arise.

Occupying armies sometimes displaced Friends from their meeting houses. Friends protested and tried to persist in worshipping, sometimes succeeding. Fighting itself sometimes made collecting for worship a fearful prospect, as at the battle of Brandywine. On these occasions many Friends stayed away, but a considerable number nevertheless met together even while, as at Moorestown, New Jersey, cannon fire shook the meeting house. Other Friends met despite the immediate danger of being apprehended while at meeting and pressed into the American army. In 1777, the location of the Yearly Meeting was not changed because of the British occupation of Philadelphia. Friends presumed to cross belligerents' lines to attend, defying prohibitions on any such travel—"as a public testimony . . . of an unshaken Zeal for the Cause of righteousness."[17] Some Friends from Chester County and further west got through; others were stopped. Throughout the war, Quaker ministers traveled on religious journeys, crossing and recrossing lines, raising suspicion that they were spies. Finally, Friends were not to flee the war zones, either out of loyalty to one belligerent or the other, or from concern for personal security. In Pennsylvania, the overwhelming number of Friends remained in residence when the British invaded—as the Patriots invidiously noted—and continued there when the British left. Those who fled to Bucks County when the British invaded, out of fear for their property, found no sanctuary there, for their goods were distressed by the American army. John Pemberton took that as a sign of divine justice.[18]

It is possible to get a still better estimate of the number of Friends

who obeyed their conscience and proved their asceticism. These
Friends volunteered to sacrifice more property than the Society obliged
them to; they voluntarily refused to pay taxes that financed the
Revolution. As it had been in the French and Indian War, the refusal
to pay taxes was a controversial testimony among Friends and was
never added to the discipline. Even so, it appeared to prevail among
a majority of Friends in Chester and Western Quarterly meetings.

Western Quarter reported to Yearly Meeting in 1780 that no one
in that quarter objected to the boycott of the tax collector and that
the "consequence of paying taxes for the support of wars, has made
impressions on the minds of a large number of Friends . . . that they
have rather chose to suffer the spoiling of their goods, than actively
to comply [with the law]."[19] When John Hunt of New Jersey, himself
a very plain, sober person, attended Chester Quarterly Meeting, he
described the assembly as "a very Solid, wise Number of Friends &
Much united in their Testimony against Tax paying & Superfluity. A
very Plain people."[20] Reporting on his visits among Friends, Samuel
Roland Fisher of Philadelphia exulted that Friends in Western Quarter were clearer of complicity with war than any others he knew of,
and that Chester County Friends were faring well except that they
were losing considerable goods because of their refusing to pay taxes.
Remarkably, he did not know of any Friend in Philadelphia County
who was suffering for that reason.[21]

Quantitatively, the records of Chester Quarterly Meeting show
that a large part of the losses by Friends there arose from the tax
scruple. By 1780, 35 percent of the property lost by Friends in Chester Monthly Meeting arose from their refusal to pay taxes. In Concord
Monthly Meeting the proportion was 45 percent and in Darby Monthly
Meeting it was 59 percent. In these three the amounts totaled £1,166.[22]
Extraordinary spite toward the revolutionaries might conceivably
account for Chester County Friends' resistance to the paying of taxes,
instead of a scruple against all warfare. But the remark of Samuel
Roland Fisher discounts that possibility—he wrote that he knew of
no Philadelphian who was suffering from refusing to pay taxes. A
Tory at heart, he was well acquainted with other Philadelphia Friends
who shared that attitude and were likely to be spiteful—former politicians, phobic over Presbyterians and frontiersmen.[23] They were also
the wealthiest Friends in Pennsylvania. Yet, it appears that these
men did not jeopardize their property to satisfy any extraordinary
dislike of the revolutionaries. Some Philadelphia Friends even opposed

the whole idea of not paying one's taxes.[24] It was the rural Friends, poorer and far less political, but consistently more scrupulous, plain, and progressive, who showed the sternest face to the war effort.

Finally, it bears repeating that of the large majority of Friends who did not join the Revolution but practiced the neutrality that their church prescribed for them, probably most were prepared to sacrifice some property in order to witness to their historic pacifist testimonies.

At the end of the war, the Meeting for Sufferings expressed gratification at the number of Friends who had learned spiritual discipline from the trials and sacrifices of the war: "They have measurably seen and felt the sufficiency of his protecting power, and in the day of their humiliation have been permitted to sit under the sensible covering of his paternal care."[25]

The progress of the reformation appeared in other respects or quarters than the growth of an ascetic spirit. The reformers, who were typically long on jeremiads and short with praise, remarked that in general the Society seemed to them to be improving. The Yearly Meeting of 1777 figured very importantly in their good opinion of the times. It was one of those like 1755, 1758, and 1763, which collected, initiated, or renewed the reformist impulses in Friends or directed them into practical work. The reformers in question appeared not yet willing to credit their earlier works with having turned the Society around in its course. At the outset of the 1777 Yearly Meeting it was "clearly discovered that much degeneracy had gotten entrance, & for many years past had been rather increasing."[26] It was a solemn assembly that made that judgment—a smaller than normal meeting whose participants had crossed belligerents' lines to meet in occupied Philadelphia. They felt they had no reason to murmur against the "dispensation of scourging" abroad in the land. "The many deviations from the Simplicity, & Purity of our Profession, which we as a people had slid into . . . justly Provoked the Almighty."[27] With the members laboring under a sense of their own shortcomings, Churchman reported that "the clearness and weight in which that subject [of reformation] opened and spread before the view of friends . . . was such that will not I believe be easily forgotten by many who were favored to attend there."[28] The Meeting proceeded to initiate another round or wave of visitations and inspections of the constituents of Philadelphia Yearly Meeting down to and including families. Committees were to be appointed at every level to examine the spiritual health and ethical practices of Friends and to prescribe changes where needed. Special attention was to be paid to the education of children in families and schools and to the manufacture and abuse of liquor.

The work got underway immediately and, despite the presence of the armies, committee members traveled about the province and the Delaware Valley to an extent that surprised even them. Having got a view of things in his visits to all the quarters in Pennsylvania and some in New Jersey, the ever-critical Churchman finally found himself free to praise:

We have on the whole just reason to acknowledge in humility and reverence, that wisdom and strength above what man of himself is able to obtain has remarkably been manifested in the course of this business; unity of spirit and oneness of sentiment . . . doth prevail and spread amongst friends respecting the important business of searching the camp of our Israel. . . . I believe it is really the case that these difficult and trying times have evidently and remarkably tended to increase love and sympathy amongst friends and a concern to promote the cause of truth and righteousness . . . more than ever was visible to my understanding before; . . . if I am not mistaken a reformation is coming forward.[29]

The following year, after the British and American armies had left the province, Friends were free to journey to Yearly Meeting uninterrupted. A larger number than ever before did so. What is more important, this largest assembly ever was able to continue the solemn spirit of the previous year and resolve ethical questions harmoniously. The reformist 1777 Yearly Meeting, in other words, was no fluke, no select group of reformers who alone succeeded in getting to Philadelphia in that troublesome season.[30]

Pacifism

When there was progress in the discipline of the Society or its enforcement, there was usually tension too. Wars aggravated both and "this [revolutionary war], wrote David Cooper, "has been a proving Dispensation to Friends, wherein Faith, Love, Charity, & Fortitude were closely tryed, the more so by reason of the great diversity of Sentiment in [the] Society."[31] Many of the Friends who were enthusiastic about maintaining discipline, uniformity, and sectarianism were the same Friends who wished to push Quaker testimonies beyond their former reaches. When they innovated or pressed their brethren to do so, they aroused impatience, or worse reactions, among Quaker stand-patters. Both groups revered Quaker history. Its suffering spirit inspired reformers while the letter of its codes transfixed the conservatives. Ultimately, they reconciled differences in a Quaker manner; there was no schism in this era. As often occurs in such reconciliations, neither group could claim to have relinquished its most cherished point, and as uncommonly occurs, one was willing to suffer for the other's sake.

As might be expected, the most divisive ethical issue in the Revolution was paying taxes for war. When a small number of Friends refused to pay in 1756, John Woolman had hoped that their example might unsettle the consciences of others. The response of Friends in the Revolution would not have disappointed him, even though it once again disturbed the peace of Philadelphia Yearly Meeting. The situation had changed since the French and Indian War. After 1776, no Friends served in government. Therefore, no taxpaying Friend could be an accomplice to a Quaker officeholder's use of revenues for war. Woolman's example from 1756 still pertained, however. He and his colleagues had protested as much against paying any taxes to war as they had against paying to Quaker officeholders who used it for war. It was this example that hundreds of Friends imitated in the Revolution and suffered for.

The first and by far the foremost objection of conservative Friends was the old one that Friends must render to Caesar that which is Caesar's—taxes. Friends who believed that the rule had no merit nevertheless respected its antiquity and the determination of conservatives to preserve it. For example, Anthony Benezet always counseled caution to the tax reformers. Moses Brown of Rhode Island, George Dillwyn, and David Cooper, among other eminent Friends, urged the Society toward a moderate course because of the orthodox rule.[32]

In the Revolution the merits of the orthodox rule were more severely tested than at any other time by Samuel Allinson, a New Jersey lawyer and member of Philadelphia Yearly Meeting. Allinson wrote the best brief to this day on behalf of the refusal to pay taxes and added measurably to the progress of pacifist doctrine. His work—"Reasons against War, and paying Taxes for its Support"[33]—is the best Quaker pacifist effort of any to come out of the Revolution.

It seems improbable that Friends would have to have waited until

1780 for someone—Allinson—to point out that Jesus' response to the Pharisees was enigmatic. In his 1780 work, Allinson explained that Jesus' response "was so wisely fram'd that it left [the Pharisees] in doubt, what things belong'd to Caesar and what to God, thus he avoided giving . . . offense which he must inevitably have done by a determination." Even that important criticism appeared minor when Allinson thereupon called into question the inviolability of any or all orthodoxy. "Knowledge is progressive," he began. "Every reform had its beginning." Religious truths can be historically dated; no compendium of them existed at the outset of time. To assert that knowledge is complete in one's own day is to exercise the prerogative of shutting off revelation, which one would not permit his forebears to have done. Some of the truths that contemporary conservatives cherish were novelties to past Friends. Allinson supplied examples from Scripture of progressive revelation and reemphasized the important point among Friends that after Pentecost, Christ taught his disciples by his holy spirit. If examples from Scripture were not sufficient proof, Allinson cited Friends' own progress: Had Friends not embraced antislavery contrary to their ancestors' example? Their English forebears also sold supplies to armies, served as army commissaries, chartered vessels for troop transport, all of which were later forbidden.

Having given Friends a reason for questioning old rules, Allinson introduced them to his reasons for adopting a new practice in place of the old. He reminded them of an argument on taxpaying that was twenty-five years old and very credible in the world's eyes: "That if we are forbidden . . . personally to engage in war . . . we ought not *mediately* to promote it by *actively* giving our money for that use." So cogent had that argument been among men, that when pressed to explain why Friends spurned it, wise men, illiterate, poor Indians, foreigners, and others have replied that Friends have great property and desire that others defend it.[34] They do not reply, Allinson added, that Friends have any respect for a Scriptural precept or that the precept covers the matter in question.

If "Reasons against War" were to change the opinions of conservative Friends, it may not have been wise of Allinson to belittle the fortitude of seventeenth-century Friends, yet he did so. He blamed them for the difficulty Friends now had with paying taxes. The forefathers had drawn a fine distinction between taxes that immediately assisted war (and must not be paid) and taxes that mediately assisted war (and must be paid). When, with Friends' encouragement, the English government smiled ever so patronizingly on that battered band of early Friends, were they "not levened into too great a complaisance for [the] mankind they engaged"? "Without breach of charity, [we] may suppose, that this complaisance to the outward protection . . . of Government, added to the acquisition of much Wealth, which sometimes needs the arm of power to secure, might a little dim the Eyes & stay them from that full and earnest pursuit of their religious duties, which before now would have . . . clear'd up some painful difficulties which the present day produceth. . . ." Thomas Story, the turn-of-the-century apostle to taxpayers, was specifically taken to task and stood on his head. Story had argued that even when Friends in one nation paid taxes to support a war with another nation inhabited by Friends, and the latter did likewise, both Friends had to pay nevertheless. No, said Allinson, that very situation (like the present revolutionary war) is a reason not to pay. That situation illustrated a venerable point among all Friends that whereas civil justice desires to reconcile contradictory things, war promotes them, "for both [belligerents] cannot be right."[35]

In the foregoing arguments Allinson had been addressing conservative critics in the Society. With equal insight and dispatch he discredited some arguments that non-Friends had raised off and on for the past ninety years. Although no part of Quaker tradition, Allinson evidently believed that these arguments troubled some Friends and stopped their inclination to protest. The arguments revolved around the issue of contractualism. Our critics, wrote Allinson to begin, claim that we are as much obliged to pay our taxes as we are to pay our debts and fulfill our contracts (which Friends did very punctually). But the argument is sophistical; there really was no analogy, Allinson went on to demonstrate, using his knowledge of the law to point out the difference. A debtor has no control over a creditor once the debt is paid, nor one party to a contract over the other once the contract is performed. Yet in government the taxpayers have considerable control over the expender of revenue and are partly responsible for the use of the revenue.

Allinson also noted in passing that valid contracts are voluntarily entered into. He probably did not dally over that point because the critics had a response to any Quaker who denied he had ever voluntarily contracted to pay the expense of war in return for its benefits. Since 1740, Governor George Thomas, James Logan, Judge Samuel

Chew, and most recently, the military associators had variously argued that having reaped the benefits of civil society, Friends tacitly had obliged themselves to repay society. The benefit that Friends were accused of enjoying was protection of person and property, and the obligation that critics pressed upon Friends was that they at least ought to pay for war. Friends were allegedly liable under this argument because they did extol and support civil government, law, and magistrates, but they baulked at supporting war. In America, George Keith had first equated civil government and war in order to attack his officeholding Quaker rivals in Pennsylvania. In every war thereafter, someone revived the argument and in the Revolution revived it in order to induce Friends to pay taxes. Allinson's task was to distinguish between civil government and war. This he did more cogently than his Quaker predecessors. Allinson argued that war was a state closer to anarchy than to government or law, and that all the obligations that a citizen may tacitly incur does not oblige him to support the antithesis of civil society. It was not a new argument among Friends, but Allinson stated it exceptionally well.

Allinson concluded on an irenic note; he did not plead that the Society should adopt his position. He asked Friends "to feel each others scruples & concerns as well as patiently to forbear with each other in Love where a sincere desire after the Master's will . . . appear[s] to be uppermost." "Reasons against War" was commended even by Friends who had paid and continued to pay taxes.[36] Allinson's plea for forbearance succeeded.

Another consideration entered the debate over paying taxes. Friends had a testimony against sedition and treason; they were to be loyal to the "powers that be," according to St. Paul's dictum.[37] Civil government was a terror to evildoers and therefore deserved the support of Christians, including their taxes. When revolution broke out in Pennsylvania, the course for Friends was clear: they could not be a party to it without violating testimony. Forbearance from revolution complemented their pacifism and strengthened their refusal to serve in the American armies. But trouble arose in regard to some less hallowed and explicit testimonies of Friends than the refusal to serve personally. Paying taxes is the best example. The injunction to support government (and pay one's taxes) would seem to include in it the qualifier "legitimate" or "established" government—otherwise, it contradicted the Quaker sanction against supporting revolution. But the discipline was brief and ambiguous on this point. Many Friends (perhaps even a majority), with a literalist, uncritical reading of the discipline and Scriptures, heeded two different and contradictory injunctions. They refused to acknowledge the Revolution (i.e., refused to serve in it and swear oaths to it) or its legitimacy and yet they paid taxes to it, which effectively promoted the overthrow of the "established" government.

Some of the Friends who refused to pay taxes took seriously the testimony on behalf of established government and against revolution. They would not pay to support the overthrow of the existing power. Also, it appeared to some Friends that by paying taxes, they symbolically or tacitly acknowledged the legitimacy of a regime. In a manner, one may have pledged his allegiance by paying. Very careful Friends were moved to refuse the tax collector not only by their desire not to *effectively* support revolution, but also a desire not to *symbolically* acknowledge it. To be consistent, Friends who were most troubled by symbolism had to stop paying all taxes—like the poor rates and road taxes—because paying these acknowledged the new regime as much as did paying taxes for war.[38] On the other hand, a small group of Friends attached no symbolic significance whatever to taxpaying and (together with other reasons) urged Friends to pay all taxes.[39]

However clear the reasoning and motives of various individual Friends may appear upon examination, the mixture of motives in groups of Friends who behaved alike is obscure. This much can be said satisfactorily: None of the differences in these ethical positions raised as much controversy within the Society as the allegation that some Friends were using ethics to cover their political bias. While appearing scrupulous, they were really ignoble. They pushed their brethren toward a refusal of taxes, but out of a fondness for the old regime. They were affiliated with it—the Galloway party—and had nailed their flag to its mast while it sank. Their expressions of nostalgia were too common for some Friends to tolerate, and so there was grousing about crypto-Loyalists. Moses Brown, a Friend who refused to pay taxes, worried to Anthony Benezet that the political bias of some boycotters retarded the spread of the scruple. If we who protest all shared the same honorable motive, he speculated, this testimony would overcome all doubters.[40]

Samuel Allinson's father-in-law, David Cooper, raised the biggest fuss over the motives of tax protestors. Cooper, who was also Timothy Matlack's father-in-law, doubted their altruism from the beginning. He believed that the "Spirit of Party" burned concealed within them. In December 1781, he averred that they had unwittingly revealed their base motives by "wheeling about" once British military failure appeared certain.[41] Cooper was a peevish fellow, wise in his own conceits; and his evidence of hypocrisy proved much less than he believed.[42] Granting his assertion that some Friends were "wheeling about" in their allegiance to favor the United States, they were behaving rather in the spirit, if not the letter, of giving their allegiance to the "powers that be." The American victory at Yorktown had done a great deal to prove that Americans wielded sovereign power in America, or were Caesar. It was a reasonable time to switch.

The allegations by Cooper and others of the same sort about the tax protestors were wide of the mark. As good Friends ought, the critics did not specify names of alleged hypocrites in their letters. They broadly asserted that "party" men were pushing the protest. That would mean city Friends of the Galloway party especially. Yet the evidence of tax protest comes overwhelmingly from Chester and Western Quarterly meetings. It may be that the critics of the protestors grasped at straws when they needed something deprecating to say about the protest. They, rather than the protestors, may have had the partisan motives—but for the Americans instead of the British. Whatever the motives of the tax protestors may have been, as a group they remained in good repute. The misfortune is that Friends who served the Galloway party before 1776 gave critics the means to disparage a largely innocent, worthy group of Friends.

A petition to have the Yearly Meeting resolve the tax question reached it in 1778. In Chester Quarter a few Friends were advocating that Friends pay no taxes whatever in these times. The Quarterly Meeting asked the Yearly Meeting for a resolution of that point, but got an inadequate reply. The 1778 Yearly Meeting did not address the question of a complete stop to taxpaying, but asked all Friends not to suppress any scruple they had against paying taxes *for war* and remain open to the scruple. In 1780, Western Quarterly Meeting asked the Yearly Meeting whether it could do more to advance the testimony against taxes for warfare. The Yearly Meeting replied by reaffirming its 1778 statement. The refusal to pay taxes for war remained a voluntary and personal decision, which the Yearly Meeting commended but did not require.[43] The question officially rested where Allinson had urged it remain.

The end of the war and the Treaty of Paris did not remove all the conditions that had troubled Friends' consciences over taxes in the past seven years. The more scrupulous Friends understood that the war had not been financed by taxation entirely—or even mostly—but by the emission of paper currency and government loans. After the war, government indebtedness still had to be paid off and by taxes. Some Friends discovered no significant difference between paying for an ongoing war and a past one; little less reason existed for refusing to pay now than earlier. And so, these Friends did not pay and their goods were distrained. Friends who disagreed with this postwar protest tried to demean it by refusing to record as "sufferings" the property that protestors lost to the authorities. The protestors and their admirers, like Warner Mifflin, would not abide this slight. There was far less doubt over the altruism of these protestors than of earlier ones because one's behavior could not affect the outcome of the war; that was settled—America had won. Only a dislike of warfare remained as an explanation of their protest. The protestors carried their grievance to the Yearly Meeting and in 1786 that friendly assembly decided that the losses of these Friends were as much sufferings as any in the period 1775–83.[44]

Allegiance

The question of political allegiance intruded upon every major ethical question that Friends confronted in the Revolution. Taxpaying was just the most troublesome of them. In the matter of oaths and affirmations, allegiance excluded almost every other consideration. The Quaker prohibition against swearing solemn oaths would seem to be the operative rule in this matter, but it applied only to an attestation invoking God. Affirmations avoided this objectionable feature. In Pennsylvania, most of the performances demanded by the revolutionary regime permitted the choice of an affirmation instead of an oath, which appeared to leave Friends free to decide upon political grounds. The freedom to take an affirmation, however, was eliminated by the Quaker ethic on allegiance. Before a Friend was free to take an affirmation, it had to be tendered by the powers that be. In 1777, when the tests were enacted, it was clear to most Friends that the United States and the Commonwealth of Pennsylvania had not proven themselves to be the powers that be by any reasonable definition of the term. Therefore, without prolonged deliberation the

Yearly Meeting proscribed the taking of oaths and affirmations and paying fines upon the refusal to swear.[45] The ruling remained in force throughout the Revolution and in this respect differed from the taxpaying question, which was never officially resolved one way or the other.

There was murmuring against the prohibition on affirmations. A Friend was obliged to be loyal to the established power and to attest to it by taking an affirmation regardless of his personal preference in regimes. His affirmation was a statement of principle and commitment as well as a reference to the facts of political life. The Friends who murmured believed that no commitment was involved in affirming. Rather, what one did was publicly admit the existence of a temporary de facto power. "To say we own this & deny the other power is the will of the Creature," scoffed David Cooper.[46] Cooper was objecting to the Tory bias he discovered in the Meeting for Sufferings, but he ignored the obligation to Friends to "own" *some* power.

Samuel Allinson took a dim view of swearing or affirming according to the shifting fortunes of nations and revolutions. People who did so swore frequently and, it seemed, casually. Some of these, as well as others who observed their frequent swearing, were troubled about "the rectitude of destroying with their own Breath what they have heretofore uttered and signified they could not destroy or be absolved from." Oaths transcended the facts of the political world and involved principle and personal integrity. Some men felt that even without involving God's name and witness, the person who takes an oath "shall not be excusable in the sight of him who avenges the violations of Truth." Second, without respect to the swearer, "declarations of Abjuration & Allegiance go to the right [of the nation], are *perpetual & final.*"[47] They are not mere statements of political fact about the nations involved. They carry the weight of principle that lesser and more commonplace acts, like paying taxes, do not.

The nature of affirmations was only one of two features in the debate over them. There was also the need to specify in political fact which was the established power or when a change of power occurred. Saint Paul omitted giving the Romans guidelines for determining what power is the established one. At the outset of the Revolution it appeared indisputable that Great Britain was that. The problem was, when did she cease to be? Certainly that would occur whenever she relinquished her claim to sovereignty over Americans. But was that the only conceivable time? Could it not be any time when the United States exercised effective control over the population in question? Or, after a battle won, or some other shift in fortunes? The ambiguity permitted any opinionated Friend to argue on behalf of his rule, and his opponent to suspect that he chose his rule because it accommodated his politics. Moses Brown, who had no party to apologize for, believed that "our former attachment to our old valuable constitutions and the favorable government . . . we have been so long under may in our simplicity and willingness for its continuance . . . induce us to stay too long by it, and by that means the Truth suffer under our being censured and treated as party men.[48] While Brown put the kindest interpretation on Friends' bias for the old regime—fondness for a good constitution—others were less kind. Cooper, who consistently found politics in Friends' resolution of ethical questions, laid the blame squarely on the party loyalties of Friends in the Philadelphia Meeting for Sufferings and their renowned dislike of their rivals. Cooper's unhappiness with the Meeting began in January 1777 with the publication of *The Testimony of People Called Quakers,* "drawn up with a View to please St. James as much, if not more than to be useful in America." "Every line of it," said Cooper, "almost appeared to me Dictated from human Views." Thereafter, "deep rooted Prejudice, Sourness, & even Bitterness . . . [was] frequently to be discovered by expressions from our Friends against the directors of the American measures." Enmity causes the sword to be drawn, he concluded; "I would to GOD we were all as careful to keep the one out of our Hearts as the other out of our hands."[49] By June 1777, Cooper had had all he could bear of the bias and mistaken decisions (and what he felt were personal slights upon him) by the Meeting for Sufferings, and he resigned from it.[50]

There was some of Cooper's bad temper in his accusations, but some truth too. The *Testimony* and other early pronouncements from the Meeting showed unnecessary pique with the revolutionaries. Yet Cooper's protest gained him no following and changed very little. Whatever unhappiness there was with its prohibition on affirmations to the new states, that unhappiness was confined to private letters mostly. In meetings, swearers and affirmers were routinely disowned.

In yet another Quaker protest against the Revolution—the refusal to accept Continental currency—Friends revealed a mixture of motives and scruples. There were fewer protestors than there were against taxpaying or affirming, but they acted because the paper currency, like taxes, supported warfare; because the currency was issued by a revolutionary regime that had also demanded they pledge their allegiance to it; and because they disliked their new rulers. A final reason brought an old testimony to bear on a novel situation: The paper currency depreciated so fast that Friends concluded that it was dishonest to use it.

In June 1775, the Congress voted to print the currency in order to finance the army it had just voted to raise. Paper currency had been familiar to Pennsylvanians for the previous fifty years and Friends had accepted it as readily as anyone else. They accepted it, moreover, after 1739, when it was issued to finance colonial wars. Any Friend who began to boycott the paper in the Revolution and who said that his conscience did not permit him to assist war by using it was initiating a scruple or pushing Quaker pacifism beyond its previous bounds. He was likely to be accused by revolutionaries of disguising his dislike of them with a handy but questionable scruple. Two of the earliest Quaker boycotters, John Drinker and Samuel Roland Fisher, offered just that explanation to the Philadelphia Committee of Inspection. As prominent merchants with suspect political affinities (to the Galloway partly), their explanation did not convince the committee. The two had earlier used Pennsylvania provincial currency which had promoted war, the committee protested, and so it publicly proclaimed them "Enemies to their Country" and shut them off from any trade or intercourse with other Americans.[51] Had Drinker and Fisher explained that there was a difference between using provincial currency and the present stuff—that the present was issued by a revolutionary regime—they would have been treated the same, but would have been more squarely in a Quaker tradition. To plead pacifism was to innovate, whereas to refuse service to a usurping power was to be loyal to the established government. Drinker and Fisher, unlikely reformers, choose to be known as innovators.

In nearby Delaware, the revolutionaries treated another Quaker protestor more severely. John Cowgill was carted through Dover at drum beat and then ostracized. His property was seized; the miller would not grind his grain nor boat owners transport it; and the schoolmaster would not educate his children. But his suffering caused Cowgill's scruple to spread, and one of the people whose attention it captured was Warner Mifflin. Mifflin could not dismiss the recollection of Cowgill's suffering from his mind, but he doubted his own fortitude if he tried to imitate Cowgill. He found the courage to proceed upon reading the thirteenth chapter of Revelation: "He who worships the beast will receive the wrath of God, tormented with fire and brimstone, no rest day or night."[52] Mifflin later spread some of that fire and brimstone among his brethren, for John Hunt (of New Jersey) recollected Mifflin delivering in meeting "a very full plain Clear and Lively Testimony Against friends taking Congress money, which Some Could hardly bear with."[53]

The protest against Continental currency took significant hold in Western Quarterly Meeting. In 1779, this meeting reported that in four of its monthly meetings the prevailing sentiment was disappointment that Friends continued to circulate Continental currency. From Western Quarter came one of the most remarkable testimonies against the money. That father of the reformation John Churchman before his death related to his son and others his disapproval of the money and its "fellowship with the works of Darkness." After Churchman's death, Friends wished to subscribe funds to have his journal published. Yet knowing and respecting his scruple, they understood he would not have wanted the journal published if the cost were paid for in Continental currency. Therefore, the funds were raised without recourse to paper money, so that the propagation of Churchman's message might be consistent with the message.[54]

There was some mild opposition to the paper money protest. Moses Brown believed that the protest was ill conceived. If Friends refused to use Continental currency, they would have to circulate specie, and that the revolutionary governments desired more than paper. Brown, however, was wrong when he deduced therefrom that passing specie promoted the war as effectively as passing paper. Both helped the war, but as Friends correctly understood, paper was "the great sinew of War."[55] When Philadelphia Quarterly Meeting brought the scruple to the attention of Yearly Meeting in 1777, it condemned the circulation of Continental currency as a violation of justice or honesty because it grossly depreciated. The Yearly Meeting recommended that all members use the paper money with caution, be guided by justice, and "keep clear of a polluting Fellowship with the unfruitful works of Darkness." In other words, Friends could use the currency or not and not be disciplined, but the Yearly Meeting looked askance at it use. Two years later, Western Quarterly Meeting wanted something more done, but the Yearly Meeting merely agreed to express concern.[56]

Philanthropy

The American Revolution was not likely to have promoted Quaker philanthropy, with the revolutionaries' distraint of Quaker property, imprisonment of Friends, and accusations of Quaker cowardice and hypocrisy. More likely, the Revolution would have driven Friends in the sectarian direction they had already chosen for themselves—further isolation from American society. In the broadest respect, that is what happened. Friends did not ignore their tormentors or seek revenge upon them, but some Friends took unconcealed satisfaction in the reversals and distress that the revolutionaries suffered. Most commonly (and least reprehensibly), Friends looked upon the whole war as divine punishment for the evils in American society.[57] The Revolution had no estimable benefit as its object, no evil to root out that warranted such violence, that Friends could discover. That left only the unnecessary death and destruction.

Reformer Friends passed no smug judgments upon the belligerents, because reformers included Friends among the judged in this war. For past errors and blackslidden ways, Friends too were suffering. That the revolutionaries and the British should be God's instruments in correcting Friends, however, did not prove that the revolutionaries or the British were God's own. It was the case of Abimilech, one Friend suggested, whom God used to scourge the people of Sechem: when his purpose was served, God disposed of his instrument.[58]

The divine hand could be discovered working justice upon individual revolutionaries too. John Pemberton's journal is sewn with remarkable examples of God's vengeance: Andrew McNeil, who distressed three cows from Friend Everard Roberts and told Roberts he could go to hell for milk, died four days after seizing the cows; a man who helped to strip the Dunkard printer, Christopher Sauer, of his clothes, paint him, and imprison him, wore Sauer's clothes and after several days was seized by a great pain and died miserably.[59] In taking down these supposed evidences of God's justice, Pemberton was not behaving in accord with Anthony Benezet's caution to Friends that "we might pass lightly over the conduct of those who are instruments in God's hand in our sufferings, they . . . know not what they do."[60]

In spite of such feelings, The Society did distribute aid to non-Quaker Americans who suffered from the war—after being reassured that the aid would not appear partisan. But the supply of aid to outsiders was neither a focus of Yearly Meeting attention nor a persistent activity. Much of the aid was directed to New England before 1777, when Friends were better able to help and less alienated from their American critics. Even this early aid caused some recriminations in the Society.[61] In all, the wartime assistance to non-Friends amounted to but little of Quaker philanthropy in terms of expense and effort. As to the motive for giving, it was not, as Sydney James suggests, Friends' desire to justify themselves, compensate for their neutrality, or alleviate their persecution. Reformer Friends did not doubt the correctness of their pacifist course or the providential benefit of their suffering. And the erstwhile politicians and unreformed Friends left in the Society had no love or respect for "Presbyterian" revolutionaries.

The significant philanthropy promoted by the Yearly Meeting and enhanced by the Revolution was consistent with the Quaker withdrawal from American society. Quaker philanthropy was not, in other words, a bond which they inconsistently maintained with the surrounding community while they cut their other connections with it. Quakers showed their benevolence overwhelmingly to Negro slaves and freemen and to American Indians. Both of these, like Friends, were in disrepute with American society. Most Indians were British allies in the Revolution—just as Friends were accused of being. Once the recipients of Quaker philanthropy are examined, they appear, from a Quaker point of view, less like Gentiles and more like kindred.

The promotion of philanthropy began in the jeremiads preached by Quaker ministers during the Revolution and earlier. Jeremiads were not intended to enervate Friends, but to stir them to improvement. There was optimism and promise in some: "Notwithstanding the Declension which hath spread in the time of Ease amongst us," wrote the Meeting of Ministers and Elders to all Friends, "the Bowels of everlasting Love and Compassion are not withdrawn, but still extended for our Recovery; so that as there is a Returning to the Lord . . . he will yet return to us, and bless us as in the days of our Forefathers."[62] War only improved the likelihood that good works would be done, because "the unexpected depredations [of 1778] will loosen [Friends] from that close attachment to temporal possessions . . . which hath . . . prevented their being ready to every good work." God had given Friends the war "for a trial of that Charity which is a principal part of the Christian Character."[63]

At the nadir of their political fortunes, Pennsylvania's Friends found their way to abolition broadening, and the two events—suffering and abolition—were not merely coincidental. More than any other Christian body, Friends were able in their physical crisis to resolve an ancient ambiguity of Christianity in favor of the physically enslaved.[64] Like the Stoic philosophers, and partly from them, Christianity had adopted an ascetic strain which condemned any man's fond attachment to the objects of this world. Such a person was nothing less than a slave to his own passions, fit to be pitied or scorned. By the exertion of his will, man ought instead to master his passions and win his independence from the world. Christianity equated one's bonds to the world with sin; and to break them was to be redeemed and restored to God's grace.

The chattel slave figured into this doctrine in an equivocal way. The slave, having little or nothing at his command, is denied the opportunity to enslave himself to the world's objects. Better that he escape the opportunity to be tempted and bound than chance succumbing to them. His is a superior state to even his master's, said the Stoic Epictetus. And so said a long train of Christian thinkers who extolled humility, obedience, resignation, and similar virtues, all because they evinced one's freedom from sin or spiritual bondage. When asceticism was enhanced, so too it seemed was slavery, measure for measure.

But asceticism did not rest there inertly buttressing chattel slavery. While most Christians easily took up the justification that asceticism afforded for enslaving men, and others more uneasy with the institution salved their consciences with it, some Christians and others understood how the ascetic and religious life indicted the ownership of human beings. Slaves—who were property—were among the objects of the world that tempted men like any other objects. At the same time slaves were a different and more insidious object because they were human beings. Their submission to their masters supported pride, ego, and licentiousness in a way that the ownership of land, or houses, or sheep could not. The ownership of men put an insuperable obstacle in the path of the Christian pilgrim. Friends understood that better than most Christians. As they exalted humility and servanthood more than most, they perceived the enormity of slavery more clearly.

The Revolution helped Friends to end slavery among themselves, but even more it propelled them to abolish slavery beyond the confines of the Society of Friends. While the Revolution brought the word *liberty* into currency all over America, Friends more than ever before expressed their gratitude for their current deliverance from spiritual chains—deliverance at the hands of the revolutionaries. Their task was not so much to free their minds from the pride of owning slaves as to requite their Providential deliverance from sin. That deliverance included, ironically, an attachment to slaves as much as to any objects. Now they had to free the Negro out of gratitude. "We acquaint you that a lively concern continues for the discharge of christian duty towards the oppressed Africans," the Meeting for Sufferings wrote in a long condemnation of the African slave trade. Because God has been "graciously pleased to favour such [Friends] with his paternal regard, owning them as his children, by his judgments instructing them in righteousness . . . it becomes us not to repine. . . . United in this strengthening faith the living members of the Church become qualified to move with propriety in their respective services."[65] Two months after the Yearly Meeting had petitioned the United States Congress to end the slave trade, the Meeting for Sufferings wrote that "In the late stormy season . . . [Friends] have measurably seen and felt the sufficiency of his protecting power, and in the day of their humiliation have been permitted to sit under the sensible covering of his paternal care. . . . To be under this assurance [of God's care] is to be free indeed, to know a happy dwelling place in the liberty of truth, in which wisdom and strength is found to qualify to labour for the liberty of the captive, and to relieve the burden of the oppressed."[66]

The link between the Revolution and Warner Mifflin's antislavery impulse was more specific. Mifflin was the most vigorous antislavery Friend after the death of Anthony Benezet in 1784. In temperament he was certainly Benezet's successor.[67] Mifflin related that when he began boycotting Continental currency, he was "dipped into sympathy with the condition of the blacks," because when the revolutionaries declared him an enemy of his country, he was, like the blacks, "thrown out from the benefit of its Laws." For the slaveholders who disliked his abolitionism, the abolitionism was sufficient reason to prove him a Loyalist. Another time, when crossing lines at the battle of Germantown and discovering his exposure to harm, he "was brought into renewed sympathy with our oppressed African Brethren, who are many of them exposed to the uncontrouled power of Man without any Tribunal on all the Earth whereunto they can appeal for redress of grievances."[68]

Men exposed to war, then, are in a proper condition to better understand the situation of the slave and sympathize with it, because the two are analogous. Mifflin's analogy suggests that he may have been familiar with John Locke's works, for Locke had asserted that war and slavery lie beyond the confines of civil society and the social contract. Both of them lie within the state of nature.[69] Locke's assertion is in keeping with the long-held Quaker assertion that war holds no benefit for human society whereas the state and its laws and courts do.[70]

Having barely experienced the suffering of the Revolution, Friends in 1776 prohibited slaveholding in the Society. The Revolution provided them the opportunity to push further, for abolition in the new states, for an end to the slave trade, and for the care of freed Negroes. Beginning before the war, however, at about 1772, Friends Anthony Benezet, Samuel Allinson, Robert Pleasants, David Cooper, and William Dillwyn had shown an interest in general abolition and opened a correspondence with Granville Sharp, the preeminent British abolitionist.[71] By 1775, Friends had organized in Philadelphia the first abolition society in America.

Although the war did not initiate the Quaker interest in abolition, it could have inhibited it. The abolition society fell an early casualty to wartime disorder. The years of military occupation, 1777–78, saw little activity. But in the fall of 1778, the Yearly Meeting was urging Friends to revive their charities. Friends began to lobby the Pennsylvania government to promote abolition. Allinson warned the governor of New Jersey: "America put up her Petitions for success on her Endeavours to him who is 'Just and Equal in all his Ways,' who 'is no respecter of Persons in Judgments.' . . . America never Can or will prosper in a right manner . . . until she 'proclaims Liberty to the Captives and lets the Oppressed go free.' "[72] Benezet lobbied the Pennsylvania legislature until in 1780 it passed legislation for abolition. Beginning in 1783, Friends directed their abolitionist efforts toward the United States Congress too. From 1778 until 1787, Friends became an engine for abolition that no other body, religious or otherwise, matched.[73]

The experience of Quaker abolitionists adds significantly to the interpretation of the origins of the antislavery impulse in America. Probably no question about abolition has been more extensively debated among historians than the so-called "status-anxiety hypothesis" of David Donald.[74] Rather than ask what might be the most obvious question—How did abolitionists feel so secure that they could challenge an entrenched American institution like slavery?— Donald asked what *in*security in their lives impelled them to challenge it. Briefly, he answered that the abolitionists of the 1830s and beyond were anxious because they had lost power and prestige in their communities and that they engaged in abolition in order to reduce that anxiety or find social fulfillment. Donald provoked a host of critics who attacked both his research and his social psychology. Historians have reexamined the circumstances of nineteenth-century abolitionists to see how well Donald's hypothesis explains their behavior.[75] A great part of the critics' research involved the determination of the social status of the abolitionists and any changes in it. When their research showed (as it almost always did) that abolitionists' status did not decline, it means that Donald misapplied his hypothesis. The hypothesis still remained as potentially useful in explaining the behavior of a people who really did experience a decline.

The unique experience of Quaker abolitionists in the years 1755 to 1776 brings the hypothesis itself into question. The social status of Friends did decline after 1755. Insofar as holding political office and enjoying public power constituted part of their status in Pennsylvania, they lost it when they withdrew from government. In another respect, increased sectarianism, endogamy, "guarded education," and other Quaker peculiarities divorced them from the polite society of their day. The respect in which they did not decline before 1776 was economic—although the Revolution brought economic losses their way too, if not relative decline in status. Decline was theirs by choice, moreover. Those who wanted to escape it could get out of the Society; membership and whatever went with it was voluntary. The reformers who led the Society into such "decline" were explicitly aware of what they were doing. They taught that low and lowered status liberates people from cares that inhibit people from fulfilling their Christian obligations. To put it in modern jargon, maintaining or raising one's status creates tensions of its own and to reduce or free oneself from them, one must give up one's status.[76] In contrast to Donald's hypothesis that becoming an abolitionist was a behavioral reaction to one's declining status, it seems more likely that a Friend who joined the abolitionist movement did so after having made a deliberate alteration in his condition of life. In 1783, the Yearly Meeting recorded that in their recent suffering, Friends experienced the assurance of living under Divine care and that with that assurance, they felt "free indeed," and qualified "to labor for the liberty of the captive." This psychological insight was not original with Friends. On and off for two thousand years, some Christians or others have taught the liberating effect of asceticism. Donald seems to have asked what in this light seems to be the less likely question when he wished to uncover the origins of the antislavery impulse.

Quaker aid to the Indians had to wait until the end of the Revolution. The Indians had removed themselves from the Friends' reach by having taken the British side in the war. Friends could not assist belligerents in the war however much they may have wished to. Friends' desire to do so became apparent at the war's end with a renewal of Quaker interest in the Iroquois as well as older Quaker clients like the Delawares. Then the Meeting for Sufferings directed the renewed effort until Yearly Meeting created a permanent Indian Committee to take up the work. Through the committee, the Society assisted in the treaty-making efforts of the American government, and in a new activity, Friends attempted to physically aid and educate Indians, especially the Seneca.[77]

Although it was never intended or even anticipated, the philanthropic activity of Friends returned a benefit to the Quaker community. Activist Friends who could not agree on such ethical matters as taxpaying and oaths, thrived as a group in their joint promotion of abolition and benevolence. David Cooper, Anthony Benezet, and Moses Brown, conservatives in various respect, worked long and amicably with progressives like Warner Mifflin, Samuel Allinson, and Jacob Lindley. Abolition and family ties seemed to be all that kept testy David Cooper in the Society, yet that was a great deal to him.

The Revolution added no new commandments to the discipline of the Society of Friends. Progress in Quaker ethics was not to be measured by what the church required, but by what the members volunteered to do—with the undisguised encouragement of the church. The number of Friends who refused to pay taxes for war had increased immensely since the French and Indian War, together with the amount of property the protestors lost on account of pacifism. A new scruple had appeared over the use of Continental currency, showing that some Friends were carefully inspecting their lives to weed out conduct inconsistent with their professions. New reasons were discovered to support old protests, like the symbolic significance of taxpaying. The most exacting Friends, like Warner Mifflin and Joshua Evans, found yet other anomalies in their professedly Christian lives—like eating salt, which bore an excise tax for war—and culled these too.

Within the Society, the progress in ethics was not even. Rural members, especially those from Chester County west to York County, deserved the most praise, whereas most members in the city showed little initiative and others positively obstructed progress. In the sternest rebuke administered by one Friend to his fellows during the Revolution, Mifflin wrote to James Pemberton, "you are scarcely sensible what the conduct of a few individuals in your city had done, and the pain it occasioned to many minds and stumbling to many more." "I hope . . . you in the city may . . . give way in your minds for the progression of the precious testimony of truth against all connexions with war, that former practices . . . may be no more remembered in such manner as to limit the spirit of the Holy One, in the advancement thereof."[78] But despite the differences that arose when some men inspected their consciences and behavior, and others' too, the Society preserved community and a great deal of harmony, if not uniformity. Three months after that bugbear of innovators David Cooper resigned from the Meeting for Sufferings in protest, at the Yearly Meeting of 1777 he praised the reformist spirit he found in the Society. At the end of the Revolution, he wrote that "Faith, Love, Charity, & Fortitude were closely tryed,"[79] but that the Society had passed the trial. A century-long retrospective look suggests that not war but peace had held the greater hazards for Quaker community.

Post-revolutionary America was no pacifist Arcadia—states required militia service or its equivalent from Friends and other pacifists; the taxes that Friends paid helped to retire the revolutionary war debt. But despite these problems, the peace with Great Britain had relieved Friends of most of the demands upon them. A minority of Friends were uncomfortable with the relief that the postwar period brought to the Society. Just as these Friends had discovered benefits in their late suffering, they mistrusted their new-found ease. They believed, like John Hunt of New Jersey, "that not all the enemies and persecution that ever rose up against religion, did it [the] hurt that prosperity had."[80] If Friends' own past were any guide, peace would prove to be the greater danger to piety and a spiritual life. The times that try men's souls were just beginning.

Abbreviations

Col. Rec.	*Colonial Records of Pennsylvania; Minutes of the Provincial Council*
FHLS	Friends Historical Library, Swarthmore
HSP	Historical Society of Pennsylvania
Pa. Hist.	*Pennsylvania History*
PLB	Penn Letter Book
PMHB	*Pennsylvania Magazine of History and Biography*
PPOC	Penn Papers, Official Correspondence
QCHC	Quaker Collection, Haverford College
Votes	*Votes and Proceedings of the House of Representatives of the Province of Pennsylvania*
WMQ	*William and Mary Quarterly*

Sources

This essay is not an exhaustive guide to the resources on Quaker or Pennsylvania history, or all the sources used in this volume. I omit secondary sources and refer the reader to the Notes for citations of them and some comment on the more useful ones. Here I wish to indicate the most useful of the primary materials, both manuscripts and printed matter.

The largest single group of manuscripts used in this work were the minutes of nineteen monthly meetings, which contain the more than thirteen thousand violations of discipline tabulated in this study as well as records of marriages and other information. These minutes are on microfilm deposited at both the Quaker Collection at Haverford College Library and at Friends Historical Library, Swarthmore College. Both libraries have a printout of the disciplinary data used in this book. Other essential meeting records are minutes of quarterly meetings, Philadelphia Yearly Meeting, Philadelphia Meeting for Sufferings, and the Meeting for Ministers and Elders of Philadelphia Yearly Meeting. The most nearly complete collection of these as well as all other meeting records is at Friends Historical Library.

For the political history of Pennsylvania, the documents that are in print and are essential are: *Colonial Records of Pennsylvania: Minutes of the Provincial Council* (Harrisburg, 1931–35); *Votes and Proceedings of the House of Representatives of the Province of Pennsylvania,* Pennsylvania Archives, ser. 8 (Harrisburg, 1931–35); Pennsylvania Archives, ser. 2 (Harrisburg, 1874–90); Edward Armstrong, ed., *Correspondence Between William Penn and James Logan and Others, 1700–1750,* 2 vols. (Philadelphia: Historical Society of Pennsylvania, 1872); Leonard W. Labaree and others, eds., *The Papers of Benjamin Franklin,* 21 vols. to date (New Haven: Yale University Press, 1959–). Of considerable usefulness are: John R. Dunbar, ed., *The Paxton Papers* (The Hague: M. Nijhoff, 1957); Theodore Tappert and

John W. Doberstein, eds., *The Journals of Henry Melchoir Muhlenberg*, 3 vols. (Philadelphia: Muhlenberg Press, 1942–45); Paul A. W. Wallace, *Thirty Thousand Miles with John Heckenwelder* (Pittsburgh, 1958); and Louis Mulkearn, ed., *George Mercer Papers Relating to the Ohio Company of Virginia* (Pittsburgh: University of Pittsburgh Press, 1954).

For the issues of the press other than newspapers, I have used the American Antiquarian Society microcard edition of the imprints in Charles Evans, ed., *American Bibliography: A Chronological Dictionary of All Books, Pamphlets and Periodical Publications Printed in the United States . . . 1639 . . . 1820*, 12 vols. (Chicago, 1903–34).

The most important manuscript collections treating the political history of Pennsylvania are at the Historical Society of Pennsylvania. Essential to any study of Quakers and politics are the Pemberton Papers—those by that name alone as well as the Etting Collection, the Parrish Collection, and the Pemberton Family Papers. They are equally central to the study of Quakerism in its religious and social aspects. The Penn Papers, mostly the Thomas Penn Papers, but some of the William Penn Papers too, are second in importance. Penn's secretary, Richard Peters, left a detailed commentary on his times in his letter book and other manuscripts. Of less importance and bulk are, in approximate order of importance, the Letter Books of Isaac Norris II; the John Smith Papers of the Library Company of Philadelphia on deposit at the Historical Society; the James Logan Letter Book; the Robert Proud Papers; and the Gratz Collection. For the mid-eighteenth century and later, the following are useful: the Coates and Reynell Papers; Henry Drinker Letter Book; Christopher Marshall Diaries; Edward Penington Papers; and Thomas Willing Letter Book. The Wharton-Willing Papers and Wharton Letter Book, 1773–74, are useful for Quaker as well as political history. The Historical Society also has transcripts of the Board of Trade papers in the British Public Records Office which treat Pennsylvania affairs.

Finally, the James Logan Copy Book at the American Philosophical Society and the Joseph Shippen Papers in the Library of Congress are of some value.

For the religious aspect of this history there are a number of Quaker diaries, journals, and other manuscripts in print. The largest collection by far is William Evans and Thomas Evans, eds., *Friends Library*, 14 vols. (Philadelphia, 1837–50). Next in size is John Comly and Isaac Comly, eds., *Friends Miscellany*, which appeared as a serial from 1831 to 1859. The most important single journal in print is that of John Woolman. The best edition is Phillips P. Moulton, ed., *The Journal and Major Essays of John Woolman* (New York: Oxford University Press, 1971). For Woolman's formal writings not included in Moulton, I have used Amelia M. Gummere, ed., *The Journal and Essays of John Woolman* (New York: Macmillan, 1922). Almost as valuable is John Churchman's journal, *An Account of that Faithful Minister of Christ John Churchman, Late of Nottingham, in Pennsylvania* (Philadelphia, 1882). Most of the *Life and Travels of John Pemberton* (London, 1844) is useful, although the student should also use Pemberton's manuscript diary at the Historical Society. Samuel Fothergill's journey to America and some of his labors for reform in England are in George Crosfield, ed., *Memoirs of Samuel Fothergill* (New York, 1845). Other significant journals in print are the following, in alphabetical order: Thomas Chalkley, *The Works of Thomas Chalkley* (London, 1791); Joshua Evans, *A Journal of Joshua Evans* (Byberry, Pa., 1837); David Ferris, *Memoirs of the Life of David Ferris, an Approved Minister of the Society of Friends* (Philadelphia, 1825); Samuel Roland Fisher, "Journal of Samuel Roland Fisher, of Philadelphia, 1779–1781," *Pennsylvania Magazine of History and Biography* 41 (1917); John Griffith, *A Journal of the Life, Travels, and Labours in the Work of the Ministry, of John Griffith* (Philadelphia, 1780); John Hunt's Diary in *New Jersey Historical Society Proceedings* 53 (1935); Warner Mifflin, *The Defense of Warner Mifflin* (Philadelphia, 1796); Samuel Neale and Mary Neale, *Some Account of the Lives and Religious Labours of Samuel Neale, and Mary Neale* (London, 1845); William Reckitt, *Some Account of the Life and Labours of William Reckitt* (Philadelphia, 1783); and Daniel Stanton, *A Journal of the Life, Travels, and Gospel Labours of a Faithful Minister of Jesus Christ, Daniel Stanton* (Philadelphia, 1772).

The largest collection of manuscript letters, diaries, and journals on Quaker religious topics (including some of those in print) is at the Quaker Collection at Haverford College Library. George Churchman's journal describes the reformation years more steadfastly than any other and is a resource of inestimable value. The Anthony Benezet Letters show less breadth of reformist interest but are extremely valuable for their evidence on antislavery and asceticism. The Allinson Papers are especially informative on the Revolution, pacifism, and antislavery. David Cooper's diary offers one of the few insights into the resistance to reformation by a Friend in good standing and an antislavery advocate. Elizabeth Wilkinson's Journal of a Religious Visit to Friends in America is valuable for its information on the social aspects of reformation and the Quaker family. The following are less important sources at the Quaker Collection but ones that must be consulted: Richard T. Cadbury Collection, Sarah Logan Fisher Letter Book, Hill Family Papers, Howland Collection, Matlack Family Papers, Pemberton Papers, Edward Wanton Smith Collection, John Smith, part of a diary, Ann Cooper Whitall Diary, and Anna Wharton Wood Collection.

The second most useful collection of narrative materials on Quakerism is at Friends Historical Library. Of these, the three most valuable sources and collections are Joshua Evans Journal, David Ferris Journal, and the Emlen

Papers. Also of use are the James Craft Journal, Samuel Comfort Journal, Benjamin Ferris Journal, Elias Hicks Journal, Jenkins Autograph Collection, and the Proud Manuscripts.

The Historical Society of Pennsylvania also has materials on Quakerism and its reformation. The Cox-Parrish-Wharton Collection is the most fruitful (aside from the Pemberton Papers mentioned earlier). The Emlen Family Papers are especially useful for Ann Emlen's papers. The Elizabeth Drinker Diary provides material on the revolutionary era. The John Smith Papers treat Quakerism as well as provincial politics. The Dreer Manuscripts and the Logan-Fisher-Fox Collection ought to be consulted also.

Records of crime in Pennsylvania were obtained from two printed sources: *Records of the Courts of Chester County, Pennsylvania, 1697– 1710*, transcribed by Dorothy Lapp (Danboro, Pa.: R. T. Williams, 1972) and Colonial Society of Pennsylvania, *Records of the Courts of Quarter Sessions and Common Pleas of Bucks County, Pennsylvania, 1684–1700* (Meadville, Pa.: Tribune Publishing, 1943). More important are the dockets of quarter-sessions courts in the Chester County Clerk of Courts' Office at West Chester. The few remaining dockets of the Mayor's Court of Philadelphia are at the Philadelphia City Hall.

Notes

Preface

1. James, *A People Among Peoples* (Cambridge, Mass: Harvard University Press, 1963).
2. Tolles, *Meeting House and Counting House: The Quaker Merchants of Colonial Philadelphia* (New York: W. W. Norton, The Norton Library, 1963).

Chapter 1: The Context of Reform

1. Falls Monthly Meeting minutes, 2–8 month–1689.
2. For more on the certification of membership and approval of residence and travel see Jack D. Marietta, "Ecclesiastical Discipline in the Society of Friends, 1682–1776" (Ph.D. diss., Stanford University, 1968), pp. 11–21.
3. More information about the organization of the Society in Pennsylvania may be found in Pennsylvania Historical Survey, *Inventory of Church Archives, Society of Friends in Pennsylvania* (Philadelphia: Friends Historical Association, 1941).
4. Falls Monthly Meeting minutes, 3–12 month–1730, 7–2 month–1731, 2–4 month–1731.
5. Newgarden Monthly Meeting minutes, 27–12 month–1755, 3–4 month–1756.
6. Philadelphia Yearly Meeting minutes, 21–7 month–1719.
7. Philadelphia Monthly Meeting minutes, 28–1 month–1757 through 25–1 month–1760. Sadsbury Monthly Meeting minutes, 5–9 month–1759, 7–11 month–1739.

8. Uwchlan Monthly Meeting minutes, 9–12 month–1773, 10–3 month–1774.
9. Bradford Monthly Meeting minutes, 21–12 month–1746, 19–1 month–1747.
10. Uwchlan Monthly Meeting minutes, 9–12 month–1773, 10–3 month–1774. Abington Monthly Meeting minutes, 29–10 month–1753, 25–3 month–1754. Philadelphia Monthly Meeting minutes, 26–1 month–1753 through 22–2 month–1754. Middletown Monthly Meeting minutes, 3–9 month–1761, 3–12 month–1761, 4–3 month–1762, 1–7 month–1762, 5–8 month–1762.
11. Goshen Monthly Meeting minutes, 20–8 month–1753, 11–3 month–1768, 9–11 month–1770.
12. Philadelphia Monthly Meeting minutes, 21–7 month–1719.
13. Wrightstown Monthly Meeting minutes, 4–9 month–1764, 4–4 month–1769. Four years later Z. G. was readmitted to membership.
14. Philadelphia Monthly Meeting minutes, 29–8 month–1697, 29–9 month–1706.
15. Exeter Monthly Meeting minutes, 25–11 month–1756. Newgarden Monthly Meeting minutes, 29–5 month–1727.
16. Philadelphia Monthly Meeting minutes, 25–8 month–1706 through 28–1 month–1707.
17. Philadelphia Monthly Meeting minutes, 25–7 month–1730. Abington Monthly Meeting minutes, 29–9 month–1755. Goshen Monthly Meeting minutes, 20–6 month–1744, 18–3 month–1749. Darby Monthly Meeting minutes, 4–4 month–1749.
18. These conclusions are consistent with the findings of Richard T. Vann regarding the practices of English Friends. Vann, *The Social Development of English Quakerism, 1655–1755* (Cambridge, Mass.: Harvard University Press, 1969), pp. 131–32.
19. Philadelphia Monthly Meeting minutes, 30–5 month–1731.
20. Richland Monthly Meeting minutes, 19–9 month–1765, 17–10 month–1765. Chester Monthly Meeting minutes, 30–5 month–1763, 27–6 month–1763. Radnor Monthly Meeting minutes, 14–12 month–1769. Chester Monthly Meeting minutes, 28–10 month–1776, 30–12 month–1776.
21. Concord Monthly Meeting minutes, 4–7 month–1721, 18–9 month–1752. Middletown Monthly Meeting minutes, 1–11 month–1759, 7–2 month–1760. Newgarden Monthly Meeting minutes, 5–6 month–1762, 1–1 month–1763. Abington Monthly Meeting minutes, 25–3 month–1754.
22. Gwynedd Monthly Meeting minutes, 31–5 month–1768. Middletown Monthly Meeting minutes, 5–7 month–1700.
23. Abington Monthly Meeting minutes, 27–7 month–1722, 21–9 month–

1772, 25–4 month–1774. Philadelphia Monthly Meeting minutes, 29–3 month–1747.

24. Abington Monthly Meeting minutes, 28–11 month–1774.

25. Some regional differences existed in the treatment of fornication. The most significant was the severity of the Friends in Chester Quarterly Meeting. They disowned 80.1 percent of fornicators and 50.6 percent of fornicators with fiance(e)s. Bucks Quarter was the most lenient. They disowned 62.0 percent and 33.9 percent, respectively. Philadelphia Quarter's figures were 69.0 and 30.8 percent. Chester was most consistent in its treatment of the sexes, showing less than 1.5 percent difference between the disownment of men and women for the two sexual offenses. Philadelphia was less consistent. They disowned 13.8 percent more male than female fornicators, and Bucks, 5.1 percent more female than male fornicators with fiance(e)s.

26. David H. Flaherty, "Law and the Enforcement of Morals in Early America," *Perspectives in American History* 5 (1971): 214.

27. Ibid., pp. 230–32. William H. Lloyd, *The Early Courts of Pennsylvania* (Boston: The Boston Book Co., 1910), pp. 90–91. Examination of the dockets of the courts of Chester County and Philadelphia city demonstrates this trend. In Chester, the cases of fornication doubled in the 1740s, but 57 percent of the cases involved bastardy. By the 1770s, 83 percent involved bastardy. In Philadelphia, there were only 6 cases, all of bastardy, out of 217 for 1759–64 (the only period for which dockets exist). The statistics for Chester County are derived from a sampling of the Chester dockets by alternate five-year periods, 1682–1776. Chester County Courthouse, West Chester, Pa. Philadelphia City Hall, Philadelphia.

28. Philadelphia Monthly Meeting minutes, 29–6 month–1759, 29–2 month–1760. Goshen Monthly Meeting minutes, 17–12 month–1734, 16–4 month–1735. Darby Monthly Meeting minutes, 30–8 month–1770, 27–9 month–1770. Abington Monthly Meeting minutes, 26–5 month–1766.

29. Radnor Monthly Meeting minutes, 14–8 month–1752. Abington Monthly Meeting minutes, 28–10 month–1754, 30–1 month–1764, 26–11 month–1770. Darby Monthly Meeting minutes, 1–3 month–1770. Goshen Monthly Meeting minutes, 18–3 month–1747, 7–4 month–1747, 10–9 month–1753. Chester Monthly Meeting minutes, 30–4 month–1746.

30. Bradford Monthly Meeting minutes, 18–10 month–1759, 15–11 month–1759, 14–3 month–1760, 13–6 month–1760.

31. Middletown Monthly Meeting minutes, 1–11 month–1759, 7–2 month–1760.

32. Abington Monthly Meeting minutes, 29–5 month–1758, 28–2 month–

1746, 30–4 month–1746, 25–2 month–1760, 28–4 month–1760, 26–5 month–1760.

33. Emil Oberholzer, Jr., *Delinquent Saints: Disciplinary Action in the Early Congregational Churches of Massachusetts* (New York: Columbia University Press, 1956), pp. 128–29. Twenty of the fornicators were not identified in the meeting records. Women fornicators outnumbered men in the Pennsylvania courts also. An examination of 50 years of the dockets of the Courts of Quarter-Sessions of Chester County shows 50 men and 80 women convicted.

34. Vann, *Social Development of English Quakerism*, pp. 138, 140–41.

35. Abington Monthly Meeting minutes, 28–4 month–1760, 26–5 month–1760. Exeter Monthly Meeting minutes, 30–12 month–1756, 25–8 month–1757, 29–9 month–1757, 27–10 month–1757, 29–12 month–1757, 26–1 month–1758.

36. Darby Monthly Meeting minutes, 1–4 month–1773, 1–8 month–1766, 28–11 month–1765. Middletown Monthly Meeting minutes, 1–5 month–1760, 5–6 month–1760, 7–8 month–1760.

37. Newgarden Monthly Meeting minutes, 21–12 month–1746, 19–1 month–1747.

38. Philadelphia Yearly Meeting minutes, 16–7 month–1749, 15–9 month–1753, 19–9 month–1754. Abington Monthly Meeting minutes, 25–5 month–1748. Middletown Monthly Meeting minutes, 7–6 month–1753, 2–8 month–1753. Falls Monthly Meeting minutes, 5–12 month–1753, 3–7 month–1754.

39. I exclude voluntary withdrawals from the list of priority of severity, since few such offenders ever asked for pardon.

40. Middletown Monthly Meeting minutes, 9–4 month–1690.

41. By 1756–60 in Chester County and 1759–64 in Philadelphia, drunkenness, cursing, and lesser crimes do not appear at all. Contrariwise, in 1691–1705, persons were indicted and convicted of drunkenness, cursing and swearing, scandalizing, geomancy, and violating the sabbath as well as fornication without bastardy.

42. Abington Monthly Meeting minutes, 26–1 month–1756, 25–11 month–1754, 22–2 month–1762. Chester Monthly Meeting minutes, 26–10 month–1720. Philadelphia Monthly Meeting minutes, 30–5 month–1736. For comparison, 27.9 percent of all delinquents (including drunken ones) committed more than one offense.

43. Chester Monthly Meeting minutes, 28–12 month–1737, 7–1 month–1738, 30–4 month–1740, 25–11 month–1741, 22–12 month–1741, 25–12 month–1744. Concord Monthly Meeting minutes, 1–3 month–1756, ?–5 month–1756. J. Smith to John Smith, 9 February 1763, John Smith Papers 6: 40, HSP.

44. Philadelphia Monthly Meeting minutes, 25–1 month–1760 through 27–7 month–1764.

45. Philadelphia Monthly Meeting minutes, 23–12 month–1710. Radnor Monthly Meeting minutes, ?–11 month–1724, 11–2 month–1717. Abington Monthly Meeting minutes, 26–3 month–1712, 25–2 month–1748. Concord Monthly Meeting minutes, 6–10 month–1731, 4–7 month–1732, 9–4 month–1766. Middletown Monthly Meeting minutes, 6–4 month–1706. Chester Monthly Meeting minutes, 28–8 month–1755.

46. Newgarden Monthly Meeting minutes, 26–5 month–1759. Abington Monthly Meeting minutes, 21–9 month–1767. Radnor Monthly Meeting minutes, 10–4 month–1764, 14–6 month–1764, 10–8 month–1764, 13–9 month–1764.

47. Frederick B. Tolles, *Meeting House and Counting House: The Quaker Merchants of Colonial Philadelphia* (New York: W. W. Norton, The Norton Library, 1963), pp. 109–43.

48. Ibid., pp. 58–60. Tolles, *Quakers and the Atlantic Culture* (New York: Macmillan, 1960), pp. 58–64.

49. Philadelphia Monthly Meeting minutes, 30–10 month–1767, 29–3 month–1771. Gwynedd Monthly Meeting minutes, 29–3 month–1739. Uwchlan Monthly Meeting minutes, 7–8 month–1766. Falls Monthly Meeting minutes, 2–2 month–1718.

50. Sadsbury Monthly Meeting minutes, 21–2 month–1770, 21–3 month–1770.

51. These two meetings in present-day Delaware and Montgomery counties were settled predominantly by Welsh Friends who desired to retain some degree of ethnic identity and autonomy.

52. Goshen Monthly Meeting minutes, 11–10 month–1765.

53. A sample from the courts of Lancaster County—all convictions from 1729 to 1739—shows 77 assaults of men upon men, 6 of men upon women, and 3 of women upon men. From reading without tabulating cases from other counties, it is my opinion that the frequency of women as victims is at least as high in York County and lower in Chester and Bucks. Quarter-sessions dockets, Lancaster County Historical Society, Lancaster, Pa. This conclusion is also confirmed by a study of women in the courts of Pennsylvania by Gail S. Rowe, a draft of which I read through the kindness of the author.

54. Albert Cook Myers, *Immigration of the Irish Quakers into Pennsylvania, 1682–1750* (Swarthmore, Pa., 1902). Arthur J. Worrall, "The Impact of Discipline in the Eighteenth Century: Ireland, New England, and New York" (paper presented at the Pacific Coast Branch meeting of the American Historical Association, 21 August 1975), p. 9 and Appendix. Jack D. Marietta, "Chester County Friends and the Reformation of Pennsylvania Quakerism" (paper presented to the Friends Historical Association, 6 May 1973).

55. In a crosstabulation of sex by resolution of case, the value of Phi was

0.11. Phi for crosstabulation of each of the five offenses was: theft
(0.32), gambling (0.28), slander (0.20), "loose" conduct (0.17), and fornication (0.16).

56. Mary Maples Dunn, "Saints and Sisters: Congregational and Quaker
Women in the Early Colonial Period," *American Quarterly* 30 (1978):
582–601. Henry J. Cadbury, "George Fox and Women's Liberation,"
The Friends Quarterly 18 (October 1974): 370–76.

57. J. William Frost, *The Quaker Family in Colonial America* (New York:
St. Martin's Press, 1973), p. 183.

58. Mary Maples Dunn, "Women of Light," in Carol R. Berkin and Mary
Beth Norton, eds., *Women of America: A History* (Boston: Houghton
Mifflin, 1979), p. 132.

59. Mary Maples Dunn, "Saints and Sisters: Congregational and Quaker
Women in the Early Colonial Period," *American Quarterly* 30 (1978):
591–94. Also useful are Nancy F. Cott, *The Bonds of Womanhood:
"Women's Sphere" in New England, 1780–1835* (New Haven: Yale
University Press, 1977), pp. 126–59; Ann Douglas, *The Feminization of
American Culture* (New York: Alfred Knopf, 1977); and Michelle
Zimbalist Rosaldo, "Women, Culture, and Society: A Theoretical
Overview," in M. Z. Rosaldo and Louise Lamphere, eds., *Women,
Culture, and Society* (Stanford: Stanford University Press, 1974), pp.
17–41.

Chapter 2: The Beginnings of Reform, 1748–1755

1. *An Account of the Gospel Labours and Christian Experiences of that
Faithful Minister of Christ John Churchman, Late of Nottingham, in
Pennsylvania* (Philadelphia, 1882), pp. 83–86. William Evans and
Thomas Evans, eds., *Friends Library* 11 vols. (Philadelphia, 1837–45),
6: 191.

2. Evans and Evans, *Friends Library* 6: 191. *Account of Churchman*, pp.
17–18, 26, 34–35.

3. Evans and Evans, *Friends Library* 6: 203.

4. *Account of Churchman*, pp. 102, 107. John Pemberton to Israel and
Rachel Pemberton, 10–4 month–1752, Pemberton Papers 8: 21, HSP.

5. *Account of Churchman*, p. 103. Churchman was not the only Quaker
minister who made a point silently and English Friends were not alone
in need of it. Churchman did the same in America, as did other ministers like John Griffith, David Ferris, and Mary Peisley. *A Journal of the
Life, Travels, and Labours in the Work in the Ministry, of John Griffith*
(Philadelphia, 1780), p. 390. Benjamin Ferris's Journal, 3: 31, FHLS.

6. *Account of Churchman*, pp. 93–94, 113–15, 195.

7. Evans and Evans, *Friends Library* 6: 230–31.

8. *Account of Churchman*, pp. 195, 197.

9. Evans and Evans, *Friends Library* 6: 209, 212, 232. *Account of Church-man*, pp. 108, 145. *Life and Travels of John Pemberton* (London, 1844), p. 20. John Griffith to John Pemberton, 17–12 month–1753, Pemberton Papers 8: 134. John Pemberton to Israel Pemberton, Jr., 7–10 month–1751., ibid. 7: 134. John Pemberton to Israel and Rachel Pemberton, 20–6 month–1752, ibid. 8: 47. Payment of tithes was so widespread that the Society tried to arrange a face-saving accommodation of this delinquency. Norman C. Hunt, *Two Early Political Associations* (Oxford: Clarendon Press, 1961), pp. 64–72.

10. Evans and Evans, *Friends Library* 6: 209, 231. *Life of John Pemberton*, p. 13.

11. *Life of John Pemberton*, p. 13. John Pemberton to Israel and Rachel Pemberton, 12–7 month–1752, Pemberton Papers 8: 55.

12. *Account of Churchman*, pp. 34–35, 95.

13. Evans and Evans, *Friends Library* 6: 222, 232. John Pemberton to Israel and Rachel Pemberton, 26–6 month–1753, Pemberton Papers 9: 21. Mary Weston to John Churchman, 17–8 month–1755, Henry H. Albertson Collection, QCHC. Robert Valentine to John Pemberton, 13–6 month–1784, Pemberton Papers 41: 69.

14. *Account of Churchman*, pp. 145, 159–60. *Life of John Pemberton*, p. 13. John Pemberton to Israel Pemberton, Jr., 30–6 month–1753, Pemberton Papers 9: 26. Mary Weston to John Churchman, 17–8 month–1755, Henry H. Albertson Collection.

15. Mary Weston to John Churchman, 17–8 month–1755, Henry H. Albertson Collection. John Griffith to John Pemberton, 4–6 month–1757, Pemberton Papers 12: 25.

16. *Account of Churchman*, p. 199.

17. Israel Pemberton to wife, 14–10 month–1754, Pemberton Papers 10: 43. Joseph E. Illick, *Colonial Pennsylvania: A History* (New York: Charles Scribners' Sons, 1976), p. 218. See also Anonymous, "The Christian Orator on Hearing Samuel Fothergill Preach in Philadelphia," Pemberton Papers 34: 30. *Journal of the Life of Benjamin Ferris* (1740–71), FHLS. George Churchman's Journal 2: 4, QCHC. John Reynell to Elias Bland, 3 October 1754 and to John Fothergill, 2–6 month–1756, John Reynell Letter Book, 1754–56, Coates and Reynell Papers, HSP. Thomas Brown, "Memorandum of his last expressions," 9 August 1756, Parrish Collection: Pemberton Papers, HSP. John Williams to John Pemberton, 12–7 month–1755, Pemberton Papers 10: 145.

18. George Crosfield, ed., *Memoirs of the Life and Gospel Labours of Samuel Fothergill* (Liverpool, 1858), pp. 167, 187.

19. Ibid., pp. 281–82. In 1750, before Fothergill and Churchman met and had the opportunity to exchange ideas about the Society, Fothergill characterized British Friends in a similar way. Evans and Evans, *Friends Library* 9: 126–27.

20. Evans and Evans, *Friends Library* 9:163. Crosfield, *Memoirs of Fothergill*, pp. 218, 240, 167, 187. John Smith, "part of a diary," Howland Collection, QCHC.

21. *Some Account of the Lives and Religious Labours of Samuel Neale, and Mary Neale* (London, 1845), pp. 339-40, 353-54. Mary Peisley married Samuel Neale, a minister who visited America.

22. The only biography of Pemberton is Theodore Thayer, *Israel Pemberton, King of the Quakers* (Philadelphia: The Historical Society of Pennsylvania, 1943). Thayer concentrates on Pemberton's political activities.

23. *Col. Rec.* 4: 389-94. *Votes* 3: 2555-57. Charles P. Keith, *Chronicles of Pennsylvania from the English Revolution to the Peace of Aix-la-Chapelle, 1688-1748* (Philadelphia: Patterson & White Co., 1917), pp. 799-801.

24. Richard Peters to Thomas Penn, 21 November 1742, 4 June 1743, 5 June 1743, Richard Peters Letter Book, HSP.

25. James Hamilton to Thomas Penn, 14 September 1751, PPOC 5: 173. Thomas Penn to Richard Peters, 18 March 1752 and 15 November 1760, PLB 3: 118-29 and 6: 328-36. Richard Peters to Thomas Penn, 13 July 1750 and 20 June 1752, PPOC 5: 37, 249-57.

26. Errol T. Elliot, *Quakers on the American Frontier* (Richmond, Ind.: Friends United Press, 1969), p. 398.

27. Richard Peters to Proprietor, 13 July 1750, PPOC 5: 37. In 1753, Pemberton remarked that he disliked Norris as a "senseless muddy headed, perplexed Creature . . . of no good moral Disposition." Peters to Proprietors, 11 September 1753, PPOC 6: 101.

28. Mary Weston to Israel Pemberton, Jr., 25-11 month-1750, Pemberton Papers 6: 159. William Brown to Israel Pemberton, Jr., 29-4 month-1752, ibid. 8: 22. Israel Pemberton, Jr., to John Pemberton, 7-7 month-1751, ibid. 7: 106. Evans and Evans, *Friends Library* 9: 141-50.

29. William Logan to John Smith, undated but following a letter of 1 July 1769, John Smith Papers, Library Company of Philadelphia, on deposit at HSP. Paul A. W. Wallace, *Conrad Weiser, 1696-1760: Friend of Colonist and Mohawk* (Philadelphia: University of Pennsylvania Press, 1945), p. 428. John Churchman to Israel Pemberton, Jr., 19-4 month-1749, Pemberton Papers 5: 115. Israel Pemberton, Jr., to P. Kearney, 27-4 month-1750, ibid. 6: 44.

Chapter 3: Social Reforms

1. The average for 1683-85 was 10.0 offenses per year. In only five of the succeeding thirty years did the number per year exceed 10.

2. On immigration see W. F. Dunaway, "The English Settlers of Colonial Pennsylvania," *PMHB* 52 (1928): 324; and James T. Lemon, "Urbaniza-

tion and the Development of Eighteenth-Century Southeastern Pennsylvania and Adjacent Delaware," *WMQ*, 3d ser., 24 (1967): 502.

3. There were only three major crimes (felonies) in the period—two of witchcraft and one of counterfeiting. Lawrence H. Gipson, *Crime and Its Punishment in Provincial Pennsylvania* (Bethlehem, Pa.: Lehigh University, 1935), pp. 10–11. In the Chester County Quarter-Sessions, there were 11 convictions for 1681–85, 52 for 1691–95, and 25 for 1701–5. The records for 1711–15 are mostly missing. To determine the overlap between Quaker and public court records for the whole colonial period as well as for the first thirty-two years, I examined a sample of 166 criminals from five five-year periods in the Chester records. The names of 166 criminals were checked against Quaker birth and death records for duplications (more positive identification being impossible in most cases). Eleven percent of the names were duplicates; these Quakers accounted for 8 percent of the crimes. For the period 1681–85, Friends were 3 of 7 criminals; for 1691–95, 6 of 42; for 1701–5, 2 of 17; for 1721–25, 4 of 31; for 1751–55, 4 of 69. In the records of the Philadelphia Mayor's Court, 1759–64, Friends were 4 or 5 of the 189 criminals, and they accounted for about 2 percent of the crime.

4. Chester Quarterly Meeting minutes, 7–2 month–1688. A copy of the 1760 Philadelphia census is at Friends Historical Library. Also, it was described in *The Friend* 71 (1897): 10.

5. Barry John Levy, "The Light in the Valley: The Chester and Welsh Tract Quaker Communities and the Delaware Valley, 1681–1750" (Ph.D. diss., University of Pennsylvania, 1976), pp. 89, 92. Levy's study showed 70 Quaker families in Chester Monthly Meeting and 5.69 children per family. See also Levy, "Tender Plants: Quaker Farmers and Children in the Delaware Valley, 1681–1735," *Journal of Family History* 3 (1978): 116–35.

6. If doubling the Chester figure to arrive at the Philadelphia Quaker population and halving the Philadelphia total population to estimate Friends is exorbitant, the error is discounted because Nash and Smith's estimate of Philadelphia population in 1693 is the lowest encountered. John K. Alexander, for example, estimated 4,389 persons in Philadelphia in 1700, whereas for 1709 Nash and Smith estimated 2,464. Other estimates are higher than Alexander's. Gary B. Nash and Billy G. Smith, "The Population of Eighteenth-Century Philadelphia," *PMHB* 100 (1976): 362–68. Alexander, "The Numbers Game: An Analysis of Philadelphia's Eighteenth-Century Population," *PMHB* 98 (1974): 314–24.

7. Isaac Sharpless, Rufus Jones, and Amelia Gummere, *The Quakers in the American Colonies* (London: Macmillian, 1923), pp. 522, 524.

8. Robert V. Wells, "Quaker Marriage Patterns in a Colonial Perspective," *WMQ*, 3d ser., 29 (1972): 416.

9. I have tried an alternative method which used the rates of monthly meetings' annual contributions to the Philadelphia Yearly Meeting stock or treasury. It produced a population of 8,345 Friends in Pennsylvania. *Quaker History* 59 (1970): 40–43.

10. Of the daughters born before 1786, 57.3 percent married; born after 1786, 45.5 percent. Celebacy among women was 9.8 percent before 1786 and 23.5 percent after 1786. Age at marriage of women born before 1730 was 22.0; born after 1755, 23.4. Wells, "Quaker Marriage Patterns," pp. 420–21, 426–27. Levy, "Light in the Valley," pp. 154, 156, 201.

11. These are estimates for all Pennsylvania based upon statistics from Philadelphia and Concord Monthly meetings.

12. Philadelphia Yearly Meeting minutes, 20–9 month–1755.

13. Ibid. Meeting for Ministers and Elders of Philadelphia Yearly Meeting minutes, 20–9 month–1755. Ten of the draftsmen of the new discipline were appointed to the committee to inspect meetings. This was the committee which met jointly with the nascent Meeting for Sufferings in December 1755, and some of whose members drafted "An Epistle of Tender Love and Caution." See chap. 7.

14. Standard deviation for 1682–1755 was 25.4 months and for 1756–76, 7.0 months.

15. The percentage of cases ending in disownment slightly increased between 1751–55 and 1756–60, from 40.1 percent to 45.3 percent.

16. Philadelphia Monthly Meeting certainly disowned 17.4 percent of its 1760 population—though not necessarily the very same persons belonging to it in 1760.

17. Arthur J. Worrall, "The Impact of Discipline in the Eighteenth Century: Ireland, New England and New York" (an unpublished paper), and the appendix especially of his *Quakers in the Colonial Northeast* (Hanover, N.H.: University Press of New England, 1980).

18. Sectarian errors subsided somewhat in 1766–70, by 22.3 percent from those in 1756–60; but the decrease was more than offset by the growth of violations of sectarian marriage regulations.

19. The importance of inattendance in disownment was determined by employing a discriminant analysis of multiple-offenders who were disowned with ones who were pardoned. The program correctly classified 69.3 percent of the cases. Following inattendance in weighing toward disownment were contempt for disciplinary proceedings, and incest.

20. Middletown Monthly Meeting minutes, 7–6 month–1690.

21. Philadelphia Monthly Meeting minutes, 30–1 month–1705.

22. John Griffith, *Some Brief Remarks upon Sundry Important Subjects, Necessary to be Understood and Attended to By all Professing the Christian Religion* (London, 1764). George Crosfield, ed., *Memoirs of*

the Life and Gospel Labours of Samuel Fothergill (London, 1858), pp. 167, 187, 189, 281.

23. Samuel Fothergill, *The Heads of a Sermon Preached by Samuel Fothergill at Horsley Down Meeting . . . The 19th of the 11th mo 1767,* Miscellaneous Manuscripts, FHLS.

24. John Griffith, *Some Brief Remarks,* pp. 10–11. Diary of Ann Cooper Whitall, 22–11 month–1760, QCHC.

25. Elizabeth Wilkinson, Journal of a Religious Visit to Friends in America, p. 71, QCHC. John Pemberton to M. Sparks, 25–8 month–1750 and to children of Israel Pemberton, Jr., 11–8 month–1752, Pemberton Papers 6:122, 8:63, HSP. Samuel Comfort, Journal of Samuel Comfort, pp. 1–2, FHLS.

26. See the journals and diaries of John Churchman, Samuel Comfort, David Cooper, Joshua Evans, Benjamin Kite, John Pemberton, Catherine Payton Phillips, William Savery, Thomas Scattergood, Daniel Stanton, and John Woolman. Some of these are in print and those which are not are to be found in manuscript at either the Quaker Collection at Haverford or Friends Historical Library, Swarthmore. The only exception is Pemberton's diary at the Historical Society of Pennsylvania. The best work on Quaker education, marriages, and families, is J. William Frost, *The Quaker Family in Colonial America: A Portrait of the Society of Friends* (New York: St. Martin's Press, 1973). As the subtitle indicates, Frost does not take a chronological approach to these subjects as I have done.

27. Woodbury Monthly Meeting Manuscript Discipline, p. 26. Middletown Monthly Meeting minutes, 6–11 month–1775, 4–12 month–1755.

28. Michael Walzer, *The Revolution of the Saints: A Study in the Origins of Radical Politics* (New York: Atheneum, 1969), p. 49.

29. For details see Jack D. Marietta, "Ecclesiastical Discipline in the Society of Friends, 1682–1776" (Ph.D. diss., Stanford University, 1968), pp. 37–42. Falls Monthly Meeting minutes, 2–10 month–1771, 6–11 month–1771, 4–12 month–1771, 6–5 month–1772.

30. Philadelphia Yearly Meeting minutes, 1778.

31. Elizabeth Wilkinson's Journal, p. 12. Sarah Logan Fisher to Charles Logan, n.d., Sarah Logan Fisher Letter Book, 1783–ca. 1789, QCHC.

32. Mary Peisley to Francis Parvin, Jr., n.d., Cox-Parish-Wharton Collection 11:17, HSP. Ann Emlen, "Notes on Religion," 18–3 month–1781, 13–4 month–1781, Emlen Family Papers, HSP. Emlen noted that she was influenced by Mary Peisley and Catherine Payton when they were traveling in America in the 1750s.

33. The derogation of parental authority and the estrangement of children from parents was at least as old as Calvinism, as Walzer points out, and was a characteristic of Quakerism in the Interregnum according to Vann. Walzer, *Revolution of the Saints,* pp. 47–49. Richard T. Vann,

The Social Development of English Quakerism, 1655–1755
(Cambridge, Mass.: Harvard University Press, 1969), pp. 174–76, and
"Nurture and Conversion in the Early Quaker Family," *Journal of
Marriage and the Family* 31 (1969): 641–42. See also Edwin G. Burrows
and Michael Wallace, "The American Revolution: The Ideology and
Psychology of National Liberation," *Perspectives in American History*
6 (1972): 169–89.

34. Samuel Comfort's Journal, p. 5.

35. Ibid.

36. Moses West, *A Treatise Concerning Marriage* . . ., 4th ed. (London,
1780), pp. 31, 44.

37. Note that admission of children could occur only after the Quaker
parent who had married exogamously had repented and been pardoned.
The automatic admission of children has been referred to as "birthright" membership. It began long before it got a name or was officially
acknowledged as Quaker practice in 1737, in America as well as
England. Vann, *Social Development of English Quakerism*, pp. 155–56
and, generally, pp. 143–57.

38. Many monthly meeting clerks did not describe precisely the nature of
the marriage offenses, often using only "married out" to identify the
offense. In these cases one cannot separate exogamy from its necessary
complement, marriage solemnized outside the Society. The records of
eight monthly meetings appear more precise and reliable and from
them calculations were made. The meetings are Concord, Darby,
Exeter, Goshen, Gwynedd, Philadelphia, Radnor, and Uwchlan, whose
membership is estimated to have been 48 percent of the Society in
1760. They represent urban and rural areas, large meetings and small.
In these meetings exogamy in 1751–55 rose 94.7 percent over the
previous five years, and then 100 percent between the periods 1751–55
and 1756–60. Pardons for exogamy in these three consecutive periods
remained a fairly steady 42 percent to 47 percent. The increase in abso-
lute number of offenses meant, therefore, that more children would
become members by reason of only one Quaker parent, and more non-
Quaker spouses might informally participate in the religious community. By 1775, the pardon rate had been cut in half (24.8 percent),
whereas because of increased apprehensions the number of pardons
decreased slightly (11 percent). In 1751–55, exogamy comprised
17.7 percent of all marriage offenses in the eight meetings and by
1771–75 had risen to 33.7 percent. For reasons explained below, the
amount and percentage of exogamy recorded before 1762 may
be low.

39. Sadsbury Monthly Meeting was permitting the meetings therein to do
so. Such blatantly irregular marriages were not recorded in the
Monthly Meeting business, which is proof that exogamy was more

common than the records indicate. Sadsbury Monthly Meeting minutes, 22–4 month–1761.

40. *Account of Samuel Neale and Mary Neale,* pp. 353–54. John Pemberton to James Pemberton, 25–5 month–1785, Pemberton Family Papers 3: 337–40, HSP.

41. Emil Oberholzer, Jr., *Delinquent Saints* (New York: Columbia University Press, 1956), pp. 239–41. Sidney E. Mead, "Denominationalism: The Shape of Protestantism in America," *Church History* 23 (1954): 309–10, 313.

42. West, *Treatise Concerning Marriage,* p. 31. William Evans and Thomas Evans, *Friends Library* (Philadelphia, 1837–50), 6: 220–21.

43. Elizabeth Wilkinson's Journal, pp. 78–79.

44. See, for example, Chester Monthly Meeting minutes, 26–4 month–1732.

45. In his study of nineteenth-century Friends, Philip S. Benjamin supplies evidence that those Friends behaved in much the way the eighteenth-century reformers complained of regarding their contemporaries. Specifically, Benjamin found that "Active involvement in the Society of Friends was rarely found among those who looked beyond their own religious community for a marriage and proceeded to 'marry out of Meeting.' " Ninety-one percent of the "weighty" Friends investigated had married regularly, whereas "fully 88 percent of those who married non-Friends fell into the Nominal category." "Philadelphia Quakers in the Industrial Age, 1865–1920" (Ph.D. diss., Columbia University, 1967), pp. 121–22. The information in Benjamin's dissertation appears also in his book *The Philadelphia Quakers in the Industrial Age, 1865–1920* (Philadelphia: Temple University Press, 1976).

46. Ann Cooper Whitall's Diary, 1–7 month–1760, QCHC.

47. West, *Treatise on Marriage,* pp. 45–46. It may be added that when a Friend was forgiven for exogamy, the Society required one to criticize one's spouse, which promoted marital disharmony and no model home. Therefore, by reason of its own discipline, the Society had another reason to disown exogamously married Friends.

48. Philadelphia Monthly Meeting minutes, 27–6 month–1760. Philadelphia Quarterly Meeting minutes, 4–8 month–1760. George Churchman's Journal 1: 17, QCHC. Philadelphia Yearly Meeting minutes, 30–9 month–1761.

49. Elizabeth Wilkinson's Journal, pp. 72–75. Philadelphia Yearly Meeting minutes, 1–10 month–1762.

50. Philadelphia Yearly Meeting minutes, 1–10 month–1762.

51. See fig. 5. The count for offenses and offenders is the same. Whereas irregular marriage increased its share of total delinquency by 4.9 percent, 1761–65 over 1756–60, it increased its share of all disownments by 9.7 percent.

52. Wells, "Quaker Marriage Patterns in a Colonial Perspective," pp. 417, 423, 438, 439. Of all marriages by Quaker men, 88.8 percent were first marriages, and of all by women, 97.5 percent were.
53. A similar case might be made for the effect of disownments for fornication. The age of fornicators is not known, but one may reasonably presume they were of child-bearing age. Another prospect for Friends was that the Society would contain more older people than it had earlier.
54. Vann, *Social Development of English Quakerism*, pp. 45–46, 174–78.
55. Ibid., pp. 89–92. Hugh Barbour, *The Quakers in Puritan England* (New Haven: Yale University Press, 1964), pp. 94–110, 224–33. Gerald R. Cragg, *Puritanism in the Age of the Great Persecution, 1660–1688* (Cambridge: Cambridge University Press, 1957), pp. 39, 47, 50–51, 64, 88–91, 95, 112–13.
56. Vann, *Social Development of English Quakerism*, pp. 139–40, 164, 167. "In the early eighteenth century, for the first time, the majority of Friends were the children of Friends."
57. Ibid., pp. 143–57.
58. Abington Monthly Meeting minutes, 29–4 month–1702.
59. An excellent study of the Quaker family in perspective is Barry J. Levy's essay "The Birth of the 'Modern Family' in Early America: Quaker and Anglican Families in the Delaware Valley, Pennsylvania, 1681–1750," in Michael Zuckerman, ed., *Friends and Neighbors: Group Life in America's First Plural Society* (Philadelphia: Temple University Press, 1982), pp. 26–64.
60. For a comparison of the detection and knowledge of grace in the seventeenth century with that in the Great Awakening, see J. M. Bumsted and John E. Van de Wetering, *What Must I Do To Be Saved: The Great Awakening in Colonial America* (Hinsdale, Illinois: The Dryden Press, 1976), pp. 78–79, 110–15. David D. Hall, *The Faithful Shepherd: A History of the New England Ministry in the Seventeenth Century* (New York: W. W. Norton, The Norton Library, 1974), pp. 163–65, 205. Robert Middlekauff, *The Mathers: Three Generations of Puritan Intellectuals, 1596–1728* (New York: Oxford University Press, 1971), pp. 98, 100–101. Robert G. Pope, "New England Versus the New England Mind: A History of the New England Ministry in the Seventeenth Century," *Journal of Social History* 3 (1969): 107.
61. Sidney E. Mead, *The Lively Experiment: The Shaping of Christianity in America* (New York: Harper & Row, 1963), pp. 32, 33. Edwin Scott Gaustad, *The Great Awakening in New England* (Chicago: Quadrangle Books, 1968), p. 139.
62. Mead, *Lively Experiment*, pp. 122, 125.
63. Gaustad, *Great Awakening*, pp. 113–14.
64. Oberholzer, *Delinquent Saints*, p. 239.

65. Hall, *Faithful Shepherd*, pp. 55, 62, 158–59, 162, 170, 248–50, 257, 260.
66. Ibid., pp. 227–48. Middlekauff, *Mathers*, pp. 262–78. Perry Miller, *The New England Mind from Colony to Province* (Boston: Beacon Press, 1961), pp. 262–63, 283–84, 307–8, 375–78, 384, 408–9, 415. T. H. Breen, *The Character of the Good Ruler: Puritan Political Ideas in New England, 1630–1730* (New York: W. W. Norton, The Norton Library, 1974), pp. 97–109. Oberholzer, *Delinquent Saints*, p. 245.
67. Edmund S. Morgan, *The Puritan Family: Religion and Domestic Relations in Seventeenth-Century New England* (New York: Harper & Row, 1966), pp. 133–47, 173. Morgan believes that in the seventeenth century, Puritan parents exalted their children because of their mere genealogical tie to them, and the Congregational churches consequently moved toward ascribed membership. Morgan calls this a shift to sectarianism because of or concomitant with increased emphasis on the family. I cannot accept the characterization, however, because Morgan's definition of sectarianism is very limited—exclusive, ascribed membership. It is plain that Puritan families in the seventeenth century were adopting more of secular culture, and that certainly makes them more Church-like, even though they made a genealogical aristocracy of Congregationalism. When I say below that Congregationalism hypothetically could have turned the sectarian direction, I mean toward the rejection of secular culture.
68. Hall, *Faithful Shepherd*, p. 169. John Demos, *A Little Commonwealth: Family Life in Plymouth Colony* (New York: Oxford University Press, 1971), p. 183. Lawrence A. Cremin, *American Education: The Colonial Experience, 1607–1783* (New York: Harper & Row, 1970), pp. 485, 519.

Chapter 4: The Labors and Faith of the Reformers

1. George Churchman to James Pemberton, 4–12 month–1761, Pemberton Family Papers 2: 180–82, HSP. Anthony Benezet to Moses Brown, 1–7 month–1780, Anthony Benezet Letters, QCHC. *Some Account of the Life and Gospel Labours of William Reckitt* (Philadelphia, 1783), p. 111. In some places the subject's name is spelled Rickett.
2. John Pemberton to James Pemberton, 17–6 month–1752, Pemberton Papers 8: 45, HSP.
3. George S. Crosfield, ed., *Memoirs of the Life and Gospel Labours of Samuel Fothergill*, (London, 1858), p. 256. It is difficult to find any considerable evidence of the labors of the opponents of reform beyond their resistance to pacifism and abolition. Even in these areas, the information comes principally from the reformers and meeting records. For example, Isaac Norris II recorded very little about the Society, and after 1750 he rarely appears in the Society's business records.

4. "Friends in the ministry from Europe who have visited America on Truth's Service," Sheppard Family Papers, box 3, vol. 13, and an equivalent list for Americans visiting Europe, QCHC. Benjamin Ferris's Journal, 11–3 month–1756, 3: 32, FHLS.

5. Churchman testified that a sympathetic spouse was necessary in order that he leave their farm so often (almost weekly in 1763) on journeys in the service of the Society. He had one, who "was willing to encourage, & help to open the Way for me to take little journeys on such an Embassy." George Churchman's Journal 1: 41–42, 86, and throughout, QCHC.

6. Journal of Daniel Stanton in William Evans and Thomas Evans, eds., *Friends Library* (Philadelphia, 1837–45), 12: 167. George Churchman's Journal, 27–6 month–1761, 4: 59–60. John Hunt Diary in *New Jersey Historical Society Proceedings* 53 (1935): 32. John Hough and Mahlon Janney to Henry Drinker, 14–2 month–1780, Allinson Papers, Samuel Allinson Letterbook, 1764–91, pp. 174–75, QCHC. George S. Brooks, *Friend Anthony Benezet* (Philadelphia: University of Pennsylvania Press, 1937), p. 75.

7. *An Account of . . . John Churchman* (Philadelphia, 1882), pp. 205–6, 240. George Churchman's Journal 1: 52–53, and 3: 15. George Churchman to Israel Pemberton, 8–12 month–1777, Pemberton Papers 31: 61. Philadelphia Quarterly Meeting minutes, 1760s.

8. John Pemberton to James Pemberton, 25–5 month–1785, Pemberton Family Papers 3: 337–40. Also, George Churchman's Journal 1: 15.

9. John Williams to John Pemberton, 12–7 month–1755, Pemberton Papers 10: 145.

10. David Cooper's Diary, p. 31, QCHC.

11. Leonard Hugh Doncaster, *Quaker Organization and Business Meetings* (London: Friends Home Service Committee, 1958), chap. 1. Richard T. Vann, *The Social Development of English Quakerism, 1655–1755* (Cambridge, Mass.: Harvard University Press, 1969), pp. 197–99.

12. Note that, as stated in chap. 7, differences existed in Philadelphia Yearly Meeting but that they revolved about the question of advancing the pacifist testimony of the Society beyond the point that English Friends practiced. The English reformers defeated the attempt to censure American Friends who fulfilled the orthodox pacifist discipline. The Americans continued to differ over whether boycotting all wartime taxes ought to become part of Quaker discipline.

13. Philadelphia Yearly Meeting minutes, 26–9 month–1776.

14. George Churchman's Journal 1: 52–56. Bradford Monthly Meeting Miscellaneous Papers, 1760–69, FHLS. Western Quarterly Meeting minutes, 21–2 month–1763.

15. George Churchman's Journal 1: 52–56. Western Quarterly Meeting minutes, 20–2 month–1764 and generally through 1768.

16. Western Quarterly Meeting minutes, 19–5 month–1760, 18–8 month–1760, 17–11 month–1760. Sadsbury Monthly Meeting minutes, 18–5 month–1763, 23–6 month–1763, and 17–4 month–1776. Alan Tully, *William Penn's Legacy: Politics and Social Structure in Provincial Pennsylvania, 1726–1755* (Baltimore: Johns Hopkins University Press, 1977), pp. 84, 86, 90–91, 96–97. More information on the Wrights appears in Tully's manuscript version of his book which he kindly permitted me to read.

17. Buckingham Monthly Meeting minutes, 1–2 month–1760. Chester Quarterly Meeting minutes, 8–5 month–1758. Philadelphia Yearly Meeting minutes, 30–9 month–1780. George Churchman's Journal 2: 12–14; 4: 4.

18. Phillips P. Moulton, *The Journal and Major Essays of John Woolman* (New York: Oxford University Press, 1971), p. 140. David Ferris's Journal (1740–71), 3: 12–13, 35–36. Joseph White to John Pemberton, 14–10 month–1772, Letters of American Friends, QCHC. Thomas E. Drake, *Quakers and Slavery in America* (New Haven: Yale University Press, 1950), pp. 60–62. Considering numbers alone, *disownments* under the pre-1758 disciplinary articles, rather than *disablings* under the 1758 amendments to the discipline, more likely promoted reform; because between 1758 and 1774, only thirty-six slaveholding Friends were placed under the 1758 sanctions and no officeholders. The thirty-six slaveholders were 34 percent of the total apprehended.

19. Sophia Hume to ?, 15–4 month–1757, Miscellaneous Manuscripts, FHLS. John Pemberton to Israel and Rachel Pemberton, 29–9 month–1752, Pemberton Papers 8: 80. George Churchman's Journal 1: 49. John Reynell to Elias Bland, 14–3 month–1769, Coates and Reynell Papers, John Reynell Letter Book, 1769–70, HSP. Some Account of Samuel Fothergills Service at several places in the Course of a Religious Visit . . ., Anna Wharton Wood Collection, QCHC. Anne Emlen, Notes on Religion, Emlen Family Papers, HSP. John and Isaac Comly, eds., *Friends Miscellany* (Philadelphia, 1831–59), 12: 322–23.

20. George Churchman's Journal 1: 53–55. Philadelphia Meeting for Sufferings minutes, 20–11 month–1783, Epistle to New England Meeting for Sufferings. Woodbury Monthly Meeting Manuscript Discipline, pp. 51–55.

21. Western Quarterly Meeting minutes, 16–11 month–1761.

22. *Life and Travels of John Pemberton* (London, 1844), p. 22. Evans and Evans, *Friends Library* 9:168–69. *Some Account of the Lives and Religious Labours of Samuel Neale and Mary Neale* (London, 1845), p. 354. John Reynell to Elias Bland, 28–12 month–1746/47, Coates and Reynell Papers, John Reynell Letter Book, 1745–47. Anne Emlen Mifflin, Anne Mifflin's Book on Religious Subjects, Emlen Family Papers.

23. Elizabeth Wilkinson, Journal of a Religious Visit to Friends in America, entry for 14–12 month–1762, QCHC. John Reynell to sister, 15–4 month–1766, Coates and Reynell Papers, John Reynell Letter Book, 1754–56, HSP. Journal of Joshua Evans, pp. 9, 18, FHLS. Anne Emlen (Mifflin), Account of her religious progress, Emlen Family Papers.

24. John Griffith, *Some Brief Remarks upon Sundry Important Subjects* . . . (London, 1764), p. 100. George Churchman's Journal 2: 50. In their jeremiads, New England Puritans had earlier used wall and hedge images and had alluded to Nehemiah. T. H. Breen, *The Character of the Good Ruler: Puritan Political Ideas in New England, 1630–1730* (New York: W. W. Norton, The Norton Library, 1974), p. 100.

25. *Account of Samuel and Mary Neale*, pp. 347–48.

26. Account of Fothergill's Service.

27. George Churchman's Journal, 2: 79. John Pemberton to James Pemberton, 17–6 month–1752, Pemberton Papers 8: 45. Philadelphia Yearly Meeting minutes, 9 month–1776. Comly and Comly, *Friends Miscellany* 12: 319; 1: 97.

28. Anthony Benezet to Morris Birbeck, 16–10 month–1781, Miscellaneous Manuscripts, FHLS.

29. James Craft, Journal of Occurrences, 8–8 month–1773, Miscellaneous Manuscripts, FHLS. George Churchman's Journal 2: 81. John Griffith, *Some Brief Remarks*, pp. 15–16. Philadelphia Quarterly Meeting minutes, 4–8 month–1777.

30. Anthony Benezet to Morris Birbeck, 16–10 month–1781, Miscellaneous Manuscripts.

31. John Griffith, *Some Brief Remarks*, p. 87. Comly and Comly, *Friends Miscellany* 1: 100. George Churchman's Journal 2: 56–57.

32. Benjamin Ferris's Journal 3: 12, FHLS. Comly and Comly, *Friends Miscellany* 1: 97–98. Evans and Evans, *Friends Library* 6: 275.

33. Evans and Evans, *Friends Library* 9: 167–68. James Pemberton to Joseph Phipps, 15–11 month–1763, Pemberton Family Papers 1: 223–26. *New Jersey Historical Society Proceedings* 53: 35–36.

34. Evans and Evans, *Friends Library* 6: 275. Samuel Fothergill to William Logan, 1–2 month–1759, Jenkins Autograph Collection, FHLS. John Churchman to Israel Pemberton, 1–12 month–1755, Pemberton Papers 11: 24.

35. Comly and Comly, *Friends Miscellany* 1: 97–99. George Churchman's Journal 1: 21, 61. John Churchman to James Pemberton, 6 month–1764, Pemberton Papers 17: 68. *New Jersey Historical Society Proceedings* 53: 237–39.

36. Moulton, *Journal of Woolman*, pp. 102–3, 104. See Woolman's chapter "On Divine Admonitions" in *Considerations on the True Harmony of Mankind* in Amelia M. Gummere, ed., *The Journal and Essays of John Woolman* (New York: Macmillan, 1922), pp. 456–58.

37. George Churchman's Journal 2: 66–68.

38. Moulton, *Journal of Woolman*, p. 155.

39. Hugh Barbour, *The Quakers in Puritan England* (New Haven: Yale University Press, 1964), pp. 209–10. Gerald R. Cragg, *Puritanism in the Period of the Great Persecution, 1660–1688* (Cambridge: Cambridge University Press, 1957), pp. 67–68. Brooks, *Benezet*, p. 315. *Account of Churchman*, p. 308. John Pemberton to Benjamin Evans, 15–9 month–1753, Pemberton Papers 9: 69.

40. Epistle to New England Meeting for Sufferings, Philadelphia Meeting for Sufferings minutes, 15–11 month–1781. Moulton, *Journal of Woolman*, pp. 202–5. George Churchman's Journal 2: 67.

41. Yet among the reformers there was a sense of special mission for Pennsylvania. See Philadelphia Monthly Meeting minutes, 15–1 month–1762.

42. *Account of Churchman*, pp. 109–11.

43. Crosfield, *Memoirs of Fothergill*, p. 257. Evans and Evans, *Friends Library* 9: 168–69.

44. Samuel Fothergill to William Logan, 1–2 month–1759, Jenkins Autograph Collection. Moulton, *Journal of Woolman*, p. 98.

45. Garry Wills, *Bare Ruined Choirs: Doubt, Prophecy, and Radical Religion* (Garden City, New Jersey: Doubleday, 1972), p. 250.

46. The quotation is from *An Epistle to the Quarterly and Monthly Meeting of Friends*, Woolman's farewell before he sailed to England in 1772, the journey on which he died. Philadelphia Meeting for Sufferings distributed two thousand copies of it. Gummere, *Journal and Essays*, pp. 475, 482–83. Also, Moulton, *Journal of Woolman*, pp. 147, 188.

47. Moulton, *Journal of Woolman*, p. 24. George Churchman's Journal 1: 74. Samuel Fothergill to William Logan, 1–2 month–1759, Jenkins Autograph Collection.

48. Henry Drinker to James Thornton, 31–8 month–1788, Richard T. Cadbury Collection, QCHC.

49. Elizabeth Wilkinson's Journal, p. 71. Anne Emlen (Mifflin) to Dear Brother, November 1781, Parrish Collection, Pemberton Papers, HSP.

50. Moulton, *Journal of Woolman*, p. 99. Woolman's authorship of the epistle appears virtually certain.

51. Ibid., p. 207.

52. Elizabeth Wilkinson's Journal, pp. 91–93. George Churchman's Journal 1: 27–28.

53. "Some Account of Samuel Fothergill's Service."

54. Moulton, *Journal of Woolman*, pp. 46–47.

55. Ibid., p. 304. Evans and Evans, *Friends Library* 6: 220–21.

56. Moulton, *Journal of Woolman*, p. 72.

Chapter 5: The Fruits of Reformation

1. Richard T. Vann, *The Social Development of English Quakerism,
   1655–1755* (Cambridge, Mass.: Harvard University Press, 1969), p. 208.
   Hugh Barbour, *The Quakers in Puritan England* (New Haven: Yale
   University Press, 1964), p. 242.
2. Hugh Barbour, *Quakers in England*, pp. 167–68. Edward C. O. Beatty,
   William Penn as Social Philosopher (New York: Columbia University
   Press, 1939), p. 193. Robert Barclay, *Apology for the True Christian
   Divinity* (Philadelphia: Friends Bookstore, 1908), p. 484.
3. Frederick B. Tolles and E. Gordon Alderfer, eds., *The Witness of
   William Penn* (New York: Macmillan, 1957), pp. 44–49. Frederick B.
   Tolles, *Quakers and the Atlantic Culture* (New York: Macmillan,
   1960), pp. 55–65. Arthur Raistrick, *Quakers in Science and Industry*
   (New York: Philosophical Library, 1950).
4. Barclay, *Apology*, p. 488. William Penn, *England's Present Interest
   Discover'd* (London, 1675), p. 32. William I. Hull, *William Penn: A
   Topical Biography* (New York: Oxford University Press, 1937), pp. 314–
   15. William Hepworth Dixon, *A History of William Penn* (New York:
   New Amsterdam Book Co., 1902), pp. 274–78.
5. Tolles, *Meeting House and Counting House: The Quaker Merchants of
   Colonial Philadelphia, 1682–1783* (New York: W. W. Norton, The
   Norton Library, 1963), pp. 109–43. George Churchman's Journal 4: 50–
   51, QCHC. The data for this conclusion comes from Philadelphia
   Quarterly Meeting, where Quaker wealth in Pennsylvania was concentrated. By 1786, no Quaker elite (the top 2.5 percent of all persons on
   the tax lists) were among the ministers and elders who represented
   Philadelphia Quarterly Meeting at Yearly Meeting. For this data I am
   indebted to Robert Gough who permitted me to read his manuscript
   "The World of the Rich: Wealth and Social Cohesion in Late
   Eighteenth-Century Philadelphia," p. 436.
6. Phillips P. Moulton, ed., *The Journal and Major Essays of John Wool-
   man* (New York: Oxford University Press, 1971), pp. 139–40. Anthony
   Benezet to Moses Brown, 1–7 month–1780 and to George Dillwyn, 4
   month–1780, Anthony Benezet Letters, QCHC. John Pemberton to
   James Pemberton, 16–12 month–1752, Pemberton Papers 8: 108, HSP.
   Elizabeth Wilkinson's Journal, pp. 84–85, QCHC.
7. Anthony Benezet to Moses Brown, 1–7 month–1780, Anthony Benezet
   Letters. Anthony Benezet to Samuel Allinson, 30–3 month–1774,
   Allinson Papers, box 6, folio 41, QCHC. Anthony Benezet to George
   Dillwyn, 4 month–1780, Anthony Benezet Letters.
8. This letter is an extensive and candid criticism of urban Friends and
   discloses some urban-rural mistrust in the Society. It helps to explain

the invidious comment of William Logan made in 1767, when Churchman became clerk of Yearly Meeting, that "the Nottinghamites are all
in their Glory." Churchman was from Nottingham, Chester County.
George Churchman to James Pemberton, 4–12 month–1761, Pemberton Family Papers 2: 180–82; William Logan to James Pemberton, 30
September 1767, John Smith Papers, HSP.

9. George Churchman's Journal 4: 50–51, 56–57.
10. Some of Woolman's drafts of the essay bore only the final subtitle.
Moulton, *Journal of Woolman*, p. 284.
11. Ibid., pp. 118–19, 238–72, 252–53. Amelia M. Gummere, ed., *The
Journal and Essays of John Woolman* (New York: Macmillan, 1922), p.
495.
12. John Griffith, *Some Brief Remarks upon Sundry Important Subjects*
(London, 1769), pp. 9–10. Elizabeth Wilkinson's Journal, pp. 78–79.
Anthony Benezet to Moses Brown, 1–7 month–1780, 9–5 month–
1774, Anthony Benezet Letters.
13. John Griffith, *Some Brief Remarks* (London, 1769), 107–8. Some
account of Samuel Fothergill's service at Several places in the Course
of a Religious Visit . . . , Anna Wharton Wood Collection, QCHC. Philadelphia Meeting for Sufferings minutes, 20–11 month–1783. Epistle
to New England Meeting for Sufferings, Meeting of Ministers and
Elders (Philadelphia Yearly Meeting) minutes, 27–9 month–1766.
Anthony Benezet to Moses Brown, 1–7 month–1780, Anthony Benezet
Letters.
14. George S. Brookes, *Friend Anthony Benezet* (Philadelphia: University
of Pennsylvania Press, 1937), pp. 337, 392–93. Samuel Neale to Israel
Pemberton, 7–10 month–1773, Pemberton Papers 25: 126. Anthony
Benezet to George Dillwyn, 4 month–1780, Anthony Benezet Letters.
15. James Logan, "To Robert Jordan, and others the Friends of the Yearly
Meeting for Business, now conven'd in Philadelphia," in *PMHB* 6
(1882): 402–11. Samuel Chew, *The Speech of Samuel Chew, Esq.; Chief
Justice of the Government of New-Castle, Kent and Sussex upon Delaware; Delivered from the Bench to the Grand Jury of the County of
New-Castle, Nov. 21, 1741; and now published at their Request* (Philadelphia, 1741); and *The Speech of Samuel Chew Esq.; Chief Justice . . .
Aug. 20, 1742* (Philadelphia, 1742). Chew was disowned for publishing
the pamphlet.
16. Moulton, *Journal of Woolman*, pp. 94–95, 98–101.
17. Ibid., pp. 19, 255.
18. James A. Henretta, *The Evolution of American Society, 1700–1815: An
Interdisciplinary Analysis* (New York: D. C. Heath, 1973), pp. 138–42.
19. Isaac Comly and John Comly, eds., *Friends' Miscellany* (Philadelphia,
1831–59), 1: 99–100.

20. Brookes, *Benezet*, p. 326. Anthony Benezet to Moses Brown, 1–7 month–1780, Anthony Benezet Letters.
21. Jones, *The Quakers in the American Colonies*, pp. 531, 269. Beatty, *William Penn as Social Philosopher*, pp. 296, 298, 299. Chester Monthly Meeting minutes, 28–12 month–1737, 7–1 month–1738, 30–4 month–1740, 25–11 month–1741, 22–12 month–1741, 25–12 month–1744. Concord Monthly Meeting minutes, 1–3 month–1756, ?–5 month–1756. J. Smith [nephew] to John Smith [uncle], 9 February 1763, John Smith Papers 6: 40.
22. Abington Monthly Meeting minutes, 26–1 month–1756. Jack D. Marietta, "Ecclesiastical Discipline in the Society of Friends, 1682–1776" (Ph.D. diss., Stanford University, 1968), pp. 62–68.
23. Marietta, "Ecclesiastical Discipline," pp. 62–68.
24. *An Account of the Gospel Labours and Christian Experiences of that Faithful Minister of Christ, John Churchman* . . . (Philadelphia, 1882), pp. 264–65. Moulton, *Journal of Woolman*, pp. 19, 156, 244–48. For a longer reference on Friends' belief in their forefathers' abstinence, see David Cooper's Diary, p. 116, QCHC.
25. Joshua Evans's Journal, pp. 20–21, FHLS.
26. Philadelphia Monthly Meeting minutes, 16–1 month–1762, 31–12 month–1762, 27–4 month–1764, 25–5 month–1764, 29–6 month–1764, 28–4 month–1769, 24–4 month–1774. Abington Monthly Meeting minutes, 28–5 month–1764, 30–1 month–1769, 27–11 month–1769.
27. Benezet, *The Mighty Destroyer Displayed, In Some Account of the Dreadful Havoc Made by the Mistaken Use as Well as Abuse of Distilled Spirituous Liquors* (Philadelphia, 1774).
28. Philadelphia Yearly Meeting minutes, bk. 1747–79, pp. 375–76, 442.
29. Thomas E. Drake, *Quakers and Slavery in America* (New Haven: Yale University Press, 1950), p. 45.
30. Moulton, *Journal of Woolman*, pp. 119–21, 143, 156, 162n, 186–87, 190.
31. Ibid., p. 145. Joshua Evans's Journal, pp. 13–15.
32. Moulton, *Journal of Woolman*, pp. 167–68, 180, 183.
33. Joshua Evans's Journal, pp. 13–14, 16–17, 22–23. David Cooper's Diary, p. 111.
34. David Cooper's Diary, pp. 48–52. To "Beloved Friend" from unsigned, no date, Matlack Family Papers, QCHC. Joshua Evans's Journal, pp. 24–25.
35. Anne Emlen [Mifflin], "Notes on Religion," HSP. "Anne [Emlen] Mifflin's Account of Warner Mifflin," Emlen Family Papers, HSP. Milcah Martha Moore to Hannah Moore, no date, Edward Wanton Smith Collection, box 5, QCHC. See also David Cooper's Diary, pp.

48–52, 117; and Samuel Comfort's Journal, p. 2, FHLS.

36. For a review of the literature on Quaker antislavery, see J. William Frost, "The Origins of the Quaker Crusade against Slavery," *Quaker History* 67 (1978): 42–58. Thomas E. Drake, in his important work *Quakers and Slavery* does not discuss coeval developments in the Society and in the larger, secular political and intellectual spheres. Earlier and much briefer accounts by Isaac Sharpless and Amelia Gummere are similarly restricted. Since Drake's work, Sydney James's account in *A People Among Peoples* has become the standard explanation of the rise of Quaker antislavery, reappearing in such important works as David B. Davis's *The Problem of Slavery in Western Culture* (Ithaca: Cornell University Press, 1966), and *The Problem of Slavery in the Age of Revolution, 1770–1823* (Ithaca: Cornell University Press, 1975), and Winthrop D. Jordan, *White Over Black: American Attitudes Toward the Negro, 1550–1812* (Baltimore: Penguin Books, 1969), p. 271. Abolition is one of the philanthropies that James discovers arising or thriving in the Society after 1755, and which he correctly treats as interrelated with Quaker sectarianism and dependent upon other changes in Quakerism. But James characterizes abolition and other charities as qualifications upon Quaker exclusiveness or a diminution of it. What is missing from his account is the record of severe discipline and disownments—that is, the full dimensions of Quaker exclusiveness. To say that in the midst of so severe a purge of the church as this, Friends desired to qualify their exclusiveness with new philanthropies is more or less to say that they contradicted their exclusiveness or reversed themselves. It is more than just a qualification. Historiographically, it would be far more economical of explanation to discover that philanthropy were consistent with Friends' other behavior than a contradiction or qualification of it.

A second problem with James is the great emphasis that he places upon the 1755 political crisis as the originator of Quaker abolition and other philanthropies, to the depreciation of their reformist motives. Had Friends not desired to be more pure and exclusive, there need not have been a political crisis in 1755. "Impure" consciences had permitted Friends to trim before; they could do it again. *First* comes the will to be pure and exclusive. To attribute abolition to a desire to qualify exclusiveness and yet posit the 1755 crisis of conscience is to contradict oneself by respectively, qualifying exclusiveness and depending on it. Antislavery impulses, like other reform impulses, existed before 1755. They were among the causes of the crises and changes of 1755 and later, as much as or more than they were the effects.

37. Drake, *Quakers and Slavery*, pp. 5–9. Richard S. Dunn, *Sugar and Slaves: The Rise of the English Planter Class in the English West*

Indies, 1624–1713 (New York: W. W. Norton, The Norton Library, 1972), pp. 103–6.

38. Drake, *Quakers and Slavery,* pp. 11–23, 39–47. John F. Watson, *Annals of Philadelphia and Pennsylvania* 2 vols. (Philadelphia: Elijah Thomas, 1857), 2: 263.

39. Darold D. Wax, "Quaker Merchants and the Slave Trade in Colonial Pennsylvania," *PMHB* 86 (1962): 148–49. Tolles, *Meeting House and Counting House,* p. 43. Samuel Carpenter, Samuel Richardson, and Jonathan Dickinson were conspicuous examples of such immigrants.

40. Philadelphia Monthly Meeting minutes, 27–12 month–1716, 30–1 month–1717, 27–10 month–1717, 28–8 month–1720. Drake, *Quakers and Slavery,* pp. 43, 45. Philadelphia Yearly Meeting minutes, 16–7 month–1738. Benjamin Lay, *All Slave Keepers That Keep the Innocent in Bondage, Apostates . . .* (Philadelphia, 1737). Ralph Sandiford, *A Brief Examination of the Practice of the Times* (n.p., 1729).

41. Jean Soderlund, "Pennsylvania Quakers and Slavery" (paper delivered at the Conference of Quaker Historians and Archivists, 27 June 1980). Soderlund's excellent work also appears in "Conscience, Interest, and Power: The Development of Quaker Opposition to Slavery in the Delaware Valley" (Ph.D. diss., Temple University, 1982).

42. Davis, *The Problem of Slavery in Western Culture,* p. 330.

43. Watson, *Annals* 2: 265. Drake, *Quakers and Slavery,* pp. 53–56. Moulton, *Journal of Woolman,* pp. 36–38, 44–45, 47. Philadelphia Quarterly Meeting minutes, 5–8 month–1754. See J. William Frost, *The Quaker Family* (New York: St. Martin's Press, 1973), p. 222, for an explanation of Quaker censorship.

44. Philadelphia Yearly Meeting minutes, 20–9 month–1755.

45. Goshen Monthly Meeting minutes, 18–7 month–1757, 15–8 month–1757, 17–10 month–1757, 21–11 month–1757. Philadelphia Monthly Meeting minutes, 30–9 month–1757, 28–10 month–1757, 24–2 month–1758. Slaveholding was definitely an urban practice among Pennsylvania Friends. Fifty-five of the 116 offenses against the discipline on slaveholding and purchasing occurred in Philadelphia. Considering that Philadelphia Monthly Meeting sponsored Woolman's pamphlet in 1754, and continued to show antislavery vigor, one may deduce that the city slaveholders exercised little influence in Monthly Meeting councils. Leadership had changed since the 1740s.

46. Moulton, *Journal of Woolman,* pp. 91–93.

47. The proliferation of slaves and slaveholders did not occur in Chester and Lancaster counties or even in Philadelphia County outside the city. Gary B. Nash, "Slaves and Slaveholders in Colonial Philadelphia," *WMQ,* 3rd ser., 33 (1973): 244–45. Forbearance from buying slaves was not necessarily accompanied by antislavery attitudes. In Chester, the

two went together, but the Welsh Tract monthly meetings, Gwynedd and Radnor, showed no antislavery sentiment, yet had few slaves compared with Philadelphia.

48. Darold Duane Wax, "The Negro Slave Trade in Colonial Pennsylvania" (Ph.D. diss., University of Washington, 1962), pp. 47–48.

49. These figures differ from those arrived at by Nash, "Slaves and Slave-holders," p. 253. From the 1760 Philadelphia Monthly Meeting census of 1760 and the records of subsequent disownments, I count 2,153 Friends in the city and suburbs in 1767. Nash and Billy G. Smith in "The Population of Eighteenth-Century Philadelphia," *PMHB* 99 (1975): 366, list 22,814 residents in the city and suburbs in 1767. Of the whole, Quakers amounted to 9.9 percent, whereas Nash found 12.8 percent. I find 54 Quaker slaveholders in the 1767 city tax assessors' lists (in the Van Pelt Library of the University of Pennsylvania) whereas Nash found 88. Six equivocal identifications might raise my total to 60. Using 54, the Quaker percentage of all slaveholders (517) is 10.4; using 60, it is 11.6. Nash found 16.9 percent Quaker slaveholders in a whole population of 521 slaveholders.

50. Philadelphia Yearly Meeting minutes, 28–9 month–1758. From 1758 to 1774, 31 Friends were placed under the 1758 disabilities.

51. Gwynedd Monthly Meeting, 30–10 month–1770. Radnor Monthly Meeting minutes, 8–2 month–1771.

52. Philadelphia Monthly Meeting minutes, 29–2 month–1760, 29–7 month–1763. Falls Monthly Meeting minutes, 4–2 month–1767.

53. Philadelphia Monthly Meeting minutes, 1–3 month–1764, 30–3 month–1770. Abington Monthly Meeting minutes, 28–4 month–1760, 20–9 month–1762. Falls Monthly Meeting minutes, 6–4 month–1763, 7–11 month–1764, 6–3 month–1765.

54. Abington Monthly Meeting minutes, 21–9 month–1760. Wrightstown Monthly Meeting minutes, 5–3 month–1776. James Pemberton to Joseph Phipps, 15–11 month–1763, Pemberton Family Papers 1: 223, HSP.

55. The offenders who were completely disowned had committed an offense or offenses in addition to buying or selling slaves. Those offenders unaccounted for after disowned, disabled, and pardoned are counted, were unresolved cases.

56. Goshen Monthly Meeting minutes, 11–2 month–1763. Buckingham Monthly Meeting minutes, 6–8 month–1759. Philadelphia Monthly Meeting minutes, 31–8 month–1764, 30–11 month–1764, 31–5 month–1765, 26–9 month–1765. Chester Monthly Meeting minutes, 27–12 month–1773, 26–2 month–1776.

57. Demands for repurchase began in 1775.

58. David Ferris's Journal 3: 12–13, FHLS. George Churchman's Journal 1: 38, 93.

59. Moulton, *Journal of Woolman*, p. 201. *Account of Churchman*, pp. 209–10.

60. Falls Monthly Meeting minutes, 4–8 month–1773. Philadelphia Monthly Meeting minutes, 25–2 month–1774, 29–4 month–1774. Philadelphia Yearly Meeting minutes, 1–10 month–1774. Gwynedd Monthly Meeting minutes, 25–7 month–1775.

61. Drake, *Quakers and Slavery*, p. 72.

62. The figure for all delinquents was obtained from a sample of the same.

63. Drake, *Quakers and Slavery*, pp. 74–76. Western Quarterly Meeting minutes, 19–2 month–1781.

64. For the Pennsylvania abolition see Edward Raymond Turner, *The Negro in Pennsylvania: Slavery, Servitude, Freedom, 1639–1861* (New York: Arno Press, 1969); Arthur Zilversmit, *The First Emancipation: The Abolition of Slavery in the North* (Chicago: University of Chicago Press, 1967); Wayne J. Eberly, "The Pennsylvania Abolition Society, 1775–1830" (Ph.D. diss., Pennsylvania State University, 1973).

   For the Quaker role in resistance to the Atlantic slave trade see Roger Anstey, *The Atlantic Slave Trade and British Abolition, 1760–1810* (London: Macmillan, 1975); Judith Gaile Jennings, "The Campaign for the Abolition of the British Slave Trade: The Quaker Contribution, 1757–1807" (Ph.D. diss., University of Kentucky, 1975).

65. See chaps. 6 through 10 for political events referred to here and in the next paragraph.

66. Donald L. Robinson, *Slavery in the Structure of American Politics, 1765–1820* (New York: W. W. Norton, The Norton Library, 1971), pp. 54–55. Davis, *The Problem of Slavery in the Age of Revolution*, pp. 317, 321–26.

67. Davis, *The Problem of Slavery in the Age of Revolution*, pp. 35–36. Zilversmit, *The First Emancipation*, pp. 208–10, 216–17. Claudia Dale Golden, "The Economics of Emancipation," *Journal of Economic History* 33 (1973): 70.

68. Fredrika Teute Schmidt and Barbara Ripel Wilhelm, "Early Proslavery Petitions in Virginia," *WMQ*, 3rd ser., 33 (1973): 133–46.

69. Davis, *The Problem of Slavery in the Age of Revolution*, pp. 216–17, 238–39. John Michael Shay, "The Antislavery Movement in North Carolina" (Ph.D. diss., Princeton University, 1971), pp. 410–14, 422–24, 213–14.

70. Shay, "Antislavery Movement in North Carolina," p. 61. James D. Essig, "Break Every Yoke: American Evangelicals Against Slavery" (Ph.D. diss., Yale University, 1978), pp. 45–152. Donald G. Mathews, *Slavery and Methodism: A Chapter in American Morality, 1780–1845* (Princeton: Princeton University Press, 1965), pp. 18–29.

71. Aileen S. Kraditor, *Means and Ends in American Abolitionism* (New York: Pantheon Books, 1967), pp. 20–22, 274–76. George Santayana,

Character & Opinion in the United States (New York: Charles Scribner's Sons, 1921), pp. 205–6.

72. *Annals: The Debates and Proceedings in the Congress of the United States* (Washington, 1834–   ), 1st Cong., 2d Sess., 1458.
73. Santayana, *Character and Opinion*, pp. 216–17.
74. James, *A People Among Peoples*, p. 238. Richard Bauman repeats this interpretation in *For the Reputation of Truth: Politics, Religion, and Conflict Among the Pennsylvania Quakers, 1750–1800* (Baltimore: Johns Hopkins University Press, 1971), pp. 196–97, 210.
75. Essig, "Break Every Yoke," pp. 120–44.
76. Reinhold Niebuhr, *Beyond Tragedy: Essays on the Christian Interpretation of History* (New York: Charles Scribner's Sons, 1937), p. 62.
77. Essig, "Break Every Yoke," viii–xi, 28–40, 51–62, 65–68. Mathews, *Slavery and Methodism*, pp. 3–17.
78. Essig, "Break Every Yoke," pp. 72–77, 82–88, 145–60, 164–73, 178–79. Mathews, *Slavery and Methodism*, pp. 17–29.
79. Mathews, *Slavery and Methodism*, pp. 11–12, 20–21. Shay, "Antislavery in North Carolina," p. 119.
80. Mary Maples Dunn, "Women of Light," in Carol R. Berkin and Mary Beth Norton, eds., *Women of America: A History* (Boston: Houghton-Mifflin, 1979), p. 125.

Chapter 6: Prologue to Reform, 1739–1755

1. Verner W. Crane, *Benjamin Franklin and a Rising People* (Boston: Little, Brown, 1954), p. 174.
2. The political fighting is detailed in Edwin B. Bronner, *William Penn's Holy Experiment* (New York: Temple University Press, 1962); and Gary B. Nash, *Quakers and Politics: Pennsylvania, 1681–1726* (Princeton: Princeton University Press, 1968).
3. Thomas Wendel, "The Keith-Lloyd Alliance: Factional and Coalition Politics in Colonial Pennsylvania," *PMHB* 92 (1968): 289–305.
4. For the best coverage of the period 1730–50 see Alan Tully, *William Penn's Legacy* (Baltimore: Johns Hopkins University Press, 1977).
5. Nash, *Quakers and Politics*, pp. 187–198, 205–6, 218–24, 242–51.
6. Board of Trade Papers, Proprietaries, 1697–1776, Bundle T, no. 42, Public Records Office.
7. The record of requests and refusals, recriminations between the executive and the House is contained in *Votes* 3: 2512– 4: 3190.
8. William Allen to Thomas Penn, 24 October 1741, PPOC 3: 201, HSP. Board of Trade Papers, Proprietaries, Bundle T, no. 57. John Fothergill to Israel Pemberton, Jr., 8–2 month–1742, Pemberton Papers 2: 2, HSP.
9. Richard Partridge to John Kinsey, 16–3 month–1743, Pemberton Papers 3: 65. John Fothergill to Israel Pemberton, Jr., 14–3 month–1743,

Pemberton Papers 34: 4. William Allen to Thomas Penn, 3 October 1743, PPOC 3: 275. Richard Peters to Thomas Penn, 3 October 1743, Richard Peters Papers, HSP. Thomas Penn to William Allen, 8 February 1743/44, PLB 2: 76–77, and to James Logan, 18 June 1747, PLB 2: 204–5, HSP.

10. Israel Pemberton, Jr., to Edmond Peckover, 13–2 month–1745, Pemberton Family Papers 1: 148, HSP. Richard Peters to Thomas Penn, 2 November 1744, Peters Letter Book, HSP. A copy of the Petition is in the Pemberton Papers 3: 152. Israel Pemberton, Jr., to John Haslam, 10–10 month–1744, Pemberton Papers 3: 142. Richard Partridge to John Kinsey, 11–11 month–1744, 2–12 month–1744, 30–2 month–1745, 19–5 month–1745, 19–6 month–1745, 25–10 month–1745, 8–11 month–1745, 3–12 month–1745, 12–12 month–1745/46, Pemberton Papers 3: 147, 150, 160, 170, 174; and 4: 18, 21, 23.

11. Isaac Norris to Dr. Charles, 26 October 1741, Isaac Norris Letter Book, 1719–56, HSP. Richard Peters to Thomas Penn, 24 October 1741, Peters Letter Book.

12. William Allen to Thomas Penn, 8 July 1742, PPOC 3: 227. For accounts of the election riot see Norman S. Cohen, "The Philadelphia Election Riot of 1742," *PMHB* 92 (1968): 306–19; and William T. Parsons, "The Bloody Election Riot of 1742," *Pa. Hist.* 36 (1969): 290–306. Contemporary accounts are in *Votes* 4: 2843–50.

13. Hermann Wellenreuther, *Glaube und Politik in Pennsylvania, 1681–1776* (Cologne: Bohlau, 1972), pp. 430–41.

14. Herbert L. Osgood, *The American Colonies in the Eighteenth Century* (New York, Columbia University Press, 1924), 4: 56–57.

15. For an excellent discussion of the question see Frederick B. Tolles's essay "Quakerism and Politics," in his *Quakers and the Atlantic Culture* (New York: Macmillan, 1960), pp. 36–54.

16. Among the critics were George Keith, James Logan, Samuel Chew, and Governor George Thomas. Quaker willingness to fill public offices and exercise force in peacetime fundamentally distinguished their nonviolent ethic from that of the anabaptists, who refused to serve in public office.

17. The best recent account of Quaker pacifism in early America is Peter Brock, *Pacifism in the United States from the Colonial Era to the First World War* (Princeton: Princeton University Press, 1968), pp. 1–258. The portion of the foregoing on Quakers has been published separately as *Pioneers of the Peaceable Kingdom* (Princeton: Princeton University Press, 1968).

18. The Quaker pacifist ethic and its implications for Pennsylvania legislators was made plain in the first two colonial wars, partly by Pennsylvanians ignoring it and the consequent reprimands addressed to them.

Their behavior may be followed in: *Col. Rec.* 1: 361–460; 2: 138–49, 467–86, 521–22; *Votes* 1: 279–80, 414–37, 860–78, 903–32, 985–1001. William Penn to Arthur Cook, Jr., J. Simcock, et al., 5 November 1695, Gratz Collection, Governors, HSP. *Epistles From the Yearly Meeting Of the People called Quakers, Held in London To The Quarterly and Monthly Meetings in Great Britain, Ireland, and Elsewhere From the Year 1675, to 1759, inclulsive* (London, 1760), p. 67. No book in English contains an accurate understanding of the Quaker pacifist ethic in this era. Two journal articles do accurately represent it and were the first to do so: Hermann Wellenreuther, "The Political Dilemma of the Quakers in Pennsylvania, 1681–1748," *PMHB* 94 (1970): 156–72; and my own "Conscience, the Quaker Community, and the French and Indian War," *PMHB* 95 (1971): 3–27. In other histories, the spurious issue of "mixed taxes" (a term never defined) is often specified as the Quakers' grievance. "Mixed taxes" do no figure in their ethic, however, and never occasioned a controversy in colonial Pennsylvania. Taxes for war, whether mixed with anything else or not, had to be paid if levied by "Caesar." Most recently, Richard Bauman used the "mixed taxes" explanation repeatedly in his *For the Reputation of Truth* (Baltimore: Johns Hopkins University Press, 1971) to explain Friends' conduct in this period (see pages 44, 55, 69, 145, 163). Because he finds that such taxes constituted the provocation to reformers in 1755, he claims that the rift in the Society appeared only then, whereas the Assembly's conduct as far back as 1745 caused it. Other works on the Quakers' pacifist ethic and its application in Pennsylvania are: Jack D. Marietta, "The Course of Quaker Pacifism: The Pennsylvania Legislatures in the Colonial Wars, 1693–1748" (paper delivered at the Conference of Quaker Historians and Archivists, 28 June 1980). Marietta, "William Rakestraw: Pacifist Pamphleteer and Party Servant," *PMHB* 98 (1974): 53–58.

19. The Whig assemblymen's drive for local power has been described well in the following: Charles M. Andrews, *The Colonial Background of the American Revolution, Four Essays in American Colonial History*, rev. ed. (New Haven: Yale University Press, 1931), pp. 3–66; Bernard Bailyn, *The Origins of American Politics* (New York: Vintage Books, 1970); and a work on Southern assemblies, but important for the study of comparative progress among all assemblies, Jack P. Greene, *The Quest for Power, The Lower Houses of Assembly in the Southern Royal Colonies, 1689–1776* (New York: W. W. Norton, The Norton Library, 1972).

20. The contest between the Assembly and Thomas Penn is described in detail in James H. Hutson, "Benjamin Franklin and Pennsylvania Politics, 1751–1755: A Reappraisal," *PMHB* 93 (1969): 303–71.

21. Jack D. Marietta, "Transatlantic Friends: Cooperation and Conflict" (paper delivered at the Organization of American Historians, Pacific Coast Branch, 21 August 1975).

22. *Votes* 5: 3637.

23. Ibid., 3653–55, 3686–87, 3689, 3698, 3703–13, 3731.

24. Ibid., 3719–23, 3728, 3731, 3742, 3751–52, 3755–57, 3766–68, 3771– 3842.

25. *Col. Rec.* 4: 448–50.

26. *Votes* 5: 3841.

27. The committee included Norris and Joseph Fox, who were Quaker assemblymen, and John Mifflin and Samuel Smith, who were Quakers but not assemblymen. Reese Meredith was also on the committee. *Votes* 5: 3877–78.

28. Isaac Norris and William Callender to Meeting for Sufferings in London, 12 January 1755, Isaac Norris Letter Book, 1719–56. James Pemberton to Henton Brown, 15–1 month–1755, Pemberton Papers 10: 73–75.

29. Marietta, "Transatlantic Friends," pp. 8–10.

30. Isaac Norris to Robert Charles, 18 May 1755, Isaac Norris Letter Book, 1719–56, p. 73.

31. Arthur Herbert Basye, *The Lords Commissioners of Trade and Plantations Commonly Known as the Board of Trade 1748–1782* (New Haven: Yale University Press, 1925), pp. 35–37, 56, 103–4.

32. Thomas Penn to Governor Hamilton, 5 June 1752, 13 July 1752, 17 July 1752, PLB 3: 138–62. Thomas Penn to Governor Morris, 17 October 1754, to Richard Peters, 17 November 1754 and 21 February 1755, to Morris, 26 February 1755 and 10 May 1755, PLB 4: 12, 22, 29, 32– 35, 46, 58–63, 82–83.

33. Thomas Penn to Governor Morris, 21 March 1755, PLB 4: 71–72.

34. Lois Mulkearn, ed., *George Mercer Papers Relating to the Ohio Company of Virginia* (Pittsburgh: University of Pittsburgh Press, 1954), viii, xi, xiii, 2–5, 394, 409–10. Alfred P. James, *The Ohio Company: Its Inner History* (Pittsburgh: University of Pittsburgh Press, 1959), pp. 9– 27. A. T. Gary, "The Political and Economic Relations of English and American Quakers, 1750–1785" (D. Phil. thesis, Oxford University, 1935), pp. 30, 34, 35, 50, 62–69, 73, 79. Thomas Penn to Governor Hamilton, 1 May 1750 and 9 March 1752, PLB 2: 302, 3: 113–18; Penn to Hamilton, 26 September 1751, Penn-Hamilton Correspondence, p. 14, HSP.

35. Thomas Penn to Governor Hamilton, 26 September 1751, Penn-Hamilton Correspondence, p. 14, HSP.

36. Norman C. Hunt, *Two Early Political Associations* (Oxford: Clarendon Press, 1961), pp. 1–112.

37. Governor Hamilton to Thomas Penn, 30 April 1751, PPOC 5: 135 and

27 June 1751, Penn Papers, Additional Miscellaneous Letters 1: 70, HSP.

38. Albert F. Gegenheimer, *William Smith: Educator and Churchman* (Philadelphia: University of Pennsylvania Press, 1943).

39. Ibid. Charles Gordon Bolam, et al., *The English Presbyterians* (Boston: Beacon Press, 1968), pp. 181, 204, 204n.

40. William Smith, *A Brief State of the Province of Pennsylvania* (London, 1755).

41. Gegenheimer, *Smith*, pp. 36–37, 39. William Smith to Thomas Penn, 1 May 1755, PPOC 7: 29, 31. Thomas Penn to Governor Morris, 26 February 1755, and to Richard Peters, 26 March 1755, PLB 4: 58, 79–81. Earlier Penn had privately predicted that a deepening defense crisis would lead to Quakers' being disabled. Thomas Penn to Governor Hamilton, 10 June 1754, and to Richard Peters, 31 July 1754, PLB 3: 341–342, 369.

42. Dr. John Fothergill to Israel Pemberton, 8–7 month–1755, Pemberton Papers, Etting Collection 2: 3, HSP.

43. Hutson, "Benjamin Franklin," p. 350. *Votes* 5: 3901–2, 4027. Israel Pemberton to John Fothergill, 19 May 1755, in Leonard W. Labaree et al., eds., *The Papers of Benjamin Franklin*, 21 vols. (New Haven: Yale University Press, 1959–   ), 5: 53.

44. William Smith to Thomas Penn, 1 May 1755, PPOC 7: 29, 31. Philadelphia Quarterly Meeting to London Meeting for Sufferings, Philadelphia Quarterly Meeting minutes, 5–5 month–1755. The signers of the letter included Israel Pemberton.

45. Philadelphia Quarterly Meeting to London Meeting for Sufferings, Philadelphia Quarterly Meeting minutes, 5–5 month–1755.

46. Israel Pemberton to Dr. John Fothergill, 27–11 month–1755, Pemberton Papers 11: 20.

47. Thomas Penn to Governor Morris, 2 July 1755 and to Richard Peters, 3 July 1755, PLB 4: 101, 108–20. London Meeting for Sufferings to Philadelphia Quarterly Meeting, 3–10 month–1755, Philadelphia Meeting for Sufferings minutes.

48. William Evans and Thomas Evans, *Friends Library* (Philadelphia, 1837–50), 11: 229–30.

49. Phillips P. Moulton, *The Journal and Major Essays of John Woolman* (New York, 1971), pp. 48–50.

50. Ibid.

51. Ibid.

Chapter 7: Withdrawal from Government, 1756

1. "Extracts from the Diary of Daniel Fisher, 1755," *PMHB* 17 (1893): 274. *Col. Rec.* 6: 645, 703–5, 710–11, 736, and generally 645–784. The story of Logan and others' greed and fraud in the land and fur trade is to be found in the work of Francis Jennings as follows: "The Indian Trade of the Susquehanna Valley," *Proceedings of the American Philosophical Society* 110 (1966): 410, 413–14, 416–17; "Incident at Tulephocken," *Pa. Hist.* 35 (1968): 237–54, 336, 344–45; "The Scandalous Indian Policy of William Penn's Sons: Deeds and Documents of the Walking Purchase," *Pa. Hist.* 37 (1970): 21, 24, 27–38; "The Delaware Interregnum," *PMHB* 89 (1965): 181, 185–89, 191–92.
2. Jennings, "The Delaware Interregnum," *PMHB* 89 (1965): 181, 185–89, 191–92. Thomas Willing to John Perks, 19 November 1755, and to Thomas Willing, 17 December 1755, Thomas Willing Letter Book, HSP. William Evans and Thomas Evans, eds., *Friends Library* (Philadelphia, 1837–45), 9: 165.
3. Conrad Weiser to Thomas Penn, 25–2 month–1756, PPOC 8: 61, HSP. *Col. Rec.* 6: 705. Thomas Willing to Thomas Willing, 17 December 1755, Thomas Willing Letter Book.
4. *Votes* 5: 3937, 3939, 3941–47, 3958–60. Thomas Penn to Governor Morris, 4 October 1755, 14 November 1755, PLB 4: 159–163, 180–86, HSP.
5. *Votes* 5: 4004, 4041, 4077. Morris's consent too was needed in order to expend. The expenditure provision irked Morris because the Assembly had phrased it so that the Assembly presumed the right solely to expend the money, but waived its right on this occasion. Ibid., p. 3962.
6. *Votes* 5: 4100–4103.
7. Ibid., 4105–64. Rev. William Smith to Thomas Penn, 27 November 1755, PPOC 7: 173.
8. William Foster to John Smith, 4–10 month–1755, John Smith Papers 34: 238, HSP. Phillips P. Moulton, ed., *The Journal and Major Essays of Woolman* (New York: Oxford University Press, 1971), pp. 75, 77. Israel Pemberton to Dr. John Fothergill, 27–11 month–1775, Pemberton Papers 11: 20.
9. James Pemberton to Richard Partridge, 7–10 month–1755, Pemberton Papers 11: 9/, HSP.
10. Israel Pemberton to Dr. John Fothergill, 17–12 month–1755, Pemberton Papers, Etting Collection 2: 8, HSP. Samuel Fothergill to John Churchman, 12–10 month–1755, Emlen Papers, Correspondence, FHLS.
11. *Votes* 5: 4100–4103. Evans and Evans, *Friends Library* 9: 165. Moulton, *Journal of Woolman*, p. 81.
12. *Pennsylvania Archives, First Series* (Philadelphia, 1852), 2: 487–88. *An*

Account of the Gospel Labours and Christian Experiences of John Churchman (Philadelphia, 1882), pp. 205–6. Friends like Fothergill, John Woolman, and John Evans, who were present at the Assembly, probably did not sign the address because they were not citizens of Pennsylvania. Norris specifically defended the procedure the twenty now condemned. Norris to Dr. Charles, 7 October 1754, Isaac Norris Letter Book, 1719–56, pp. 55–58, HSP.

13. *Votes* 5: 4173, 4103–4. These five Friends later resigned from the Assembly for reasons of conscience.

14. Israel Pemberton to John Fothergill, 17–12 month–1755, Pemberton Papers, Etting Collection 2: 8.
     For a different account of this clash, the events of 1755–56, and the pacifist principles involved, see Hermann Wellenreuther, "The Quest for Harmony in a Turbulent World: The Principle of 'Love and Unity' in Colonial Pennsylvania Politics," *PMHB* 107 (1983): 537–76. Wellenreuther's account is of a complex and ambiguous ethical situation where an "old" and a "new" pacifist ethic were in contention. I find that the ethical points in question were simple and clear and had been so at least since 1711. A clear explanation of them can be found in John Fothergill's letter to Israel Pemberton, 2–8 month–1756, Pemberton Papers, Etting Collection 2:16, which means the point of the pacifist protest was understood among eminent Friends on both sides of the Atlantic.

15. One of the committees, representative of every quarter in the Yearly Meeting, was charged to correspond with London Meeting for Sufferings. It later became the Philadelphia Meeting for Sufferings. The second committee was appointed to visit the quarterly and monthly meetings in order to promote reformation in the church. Moulton, *Journal of Woolman*, p. 77. Philadelphia Yearly Meeting minutes, 23–9 month–1755, Also, members of the committees are neatly listed by Hermann Wellenreuther, *Glaube und Politik in Pennsylvania, 1681–1776* (Cologne: Bohlau, 1972), pp. 448–49.

16. Moulton, *Journal of Woolman*, pp. 84–86. Evans and Evans, *Friends Library* 9: 170.

17. Evans and Evans, *Friends Library* 9: 170.

18. Israel Pemberton to Dr. John Fothergill, 17–12 month–1755, Pemberton Papers, Etting Collection 2: 8. Henton Brown to James Pemberton, 18–2 month–1756, Pemberton Papers 2: 50.

19. *Col. Rec.* 7: 78–90. *Votes* 5: 4217. Richard Peters to Thomas Penn, 17 February 1756, PPOC 8: 29–33. Thomas Penn to Richard Peters, 8 May 1756, PLB 4: 277–91, and to Governor Morris, 12 June 1756, PLB 4: 311–12. Philadelphia Monthly Meeting minutes, 30–4 month–1756. Only William Logan among the councilors disapproved of the declaration and bounties. Joseph Fox was profiting from the war. He was

awarded £8,000 to build an army barracks in Philadelphia and £3,700 to purchase and outfit a ship of war. *Votes* 6: 4875, 4879.

20. *Votes* 5: 4216–18. *Col. Rec.* 7: 78–90. The six Friends who addressed the Council were Samuel Powell, Anthony Morris, John Reynell, Samuel Preston Moore, Israel Pemberton, and John Smith.

21. *Col. Rec.* 7: 85–86.

22. Israel Pemberton to John Fothergill, 26–4 month–1756, Pemberton Papers, Etting Collection 2: 12.

23. Ibid.

24. Ibid. *Votes* 5: 4099.

25. *Col. Rec.* 7: 103–4. Richard Peters to Thomas Penn, 25 April 1756, PPOC 8: 71–75.

26. *Votes* 5: 4245–46. Committee to correspond with London Meeting for Sufferings minutes, 21–5 month–1756. Israel Pemberton to John Fothergill, 26–6 month–1756, Pemberton Papers, Etting Collection 2: 14. James Pemberton, Joshua Morris, William Callender, William Peters, Peter Worral, and Francis Parvin resigned.

    Hermann Wellenreuther claims that the six Quaker assemblymen did not resign for the reason I state. From circumstances he infers that they were responding to pressure from English Friends. But one need not infer. The reader should see Israel Pemberton's clear explanation of the reason the six had for resigning, in Pemberton's letter to John Fothergill on 26–6 month–1756. Wellenreuther, "Quest for Harmony," *PMHB* 107 (1983): 570n.

27. George S. Brookes, *Friend Anthony Benezet* (Philadelphia: University of Pennsylvania Press, 1937), p. 220.

28. Ibid.

29. Thomas Penn to William Allen, 9 January 1756, PLB 4: 196–98. John Fothergill to Israel Pemberton, 2–8 month–1756, John Smith papers 5: 5.

30. Henton Brown to James Pemberton, 18–2 month–1756, Pemberton Papers 11: 50.

31. Ibid.

32. Leonard W. Labaree, et al., eds., *The Papers of Benjamin Franklin* (New Haven: Yale University Press 1959–   ), 6: 231–32. Thomas Penn to William Allen, 14–2 month–1756, PLB 4: 238–39. See Mabel P. Wolff, *The Colonial Agency of Pennsylvania, 1712–1757* (Ph.D. diss., Bryn Mawr College, 1933), for a fuller account of the Board of Trade transactions.

33. Wolff, *Colonial Agency*, pp. 181–82. Charles J. Stille, "The Attitude of the Quakers in the Provincial Wars," *PMHB* 10 (1886): 294–307. Stille has reprinted the petition and the arguments of petitioners' counsel.

34. Wolff, *Colonial Agency*, p. 180.

35. Thomas Penn to Richard Peters, 27 January 1756, PLB 4: 216–18. Ferdinand John Paris to William Allen, 14 February 1756, PPOC 8: 35.
36. John Fothergill to Israel Pemberton, 16 to 19–3 month–1756 and 3–4 month–1756, Pemberton Papers, Etting Collection 2: 10, 11.
37. Wolff, *Colonial Agency*, pp. 180–81, 183. Isaac Sharpless, *A Quaker Experiment in Government* (Philadelphia: A. J. Ferris, 1898), p. 253. Ferdinand John Paris to William Allen, 14 February 1756, PPOC 8: 35.
38. John Fothergill to Israel Pemberton, 16 to 19–3 month–1756, Pemberton Papers, Etting Collection 2: 10. Sharpless, *Quaker Experiment*, pp. 253–56. Henton Brown to James Pemberton, 11–3 month–1756, Pemberton Papers 11: 55.
39. John Fothergill to Israel Pemberton, 16 to 19–3 month–1756 and 3–4 month–1756, Pemberton Papers, Etting Collection 2: 10, 11.
40. London Meeting for Sufferings minutes, 9–7 month–1756.
41. Thomas Penn to Richard Peters, 13 August 1755, PLB 4: 134–35. Thomas Penn to James Hamilton, 14 February 1756, PLB 4: 240–41. Thomas Penn to James Hamilton, 13 March 1756, Penn-Hamilton Correspondence, p. 34, HSP. Norman S. Cohen, "William Allen: Chief Justice of Pennsylvania, 1704–1780" (Ph.D. diss., University of California, 1966), p. 206.
42. Joseph White to Israel Pemberton, 9–10 month–1759, Pemberton Papers 13: 117.
43. John Fothergill to Israel Pemberton, 2–8 month–1756, Pemberton Papers, Etting Collection 2: 16.
44. Ibid. Robert Foster to John Pemberton, 9–9 month–1756, Pemberton Papers 11: 119.
45. John Fothergill to Israel Pemberton, 2–8 month–1756, Pemberton Papers, Etting Collection 2: 16.
46. Samuel Fothergill to John Pemberton, 26–10 month–1756, Emlen Papers, Correspondence, HSP.
47. London Meeting for Sufferings minutes, 9–7 month–1756.
48. Israel Pemberton to John Fothergill, 26–6 month–1756, Pemberton Papers, Etting Collection 2: 14. Richard Peters to Thomas Penn, 13 August 1756, Peters Letter Book, HSP, and 4 September 1756, PPOC 8: 151.
49. William Logan to John Smith, 1–10 month–1756, John Smith Papers 5: 20–21. James Pemberton to Samuel Fothergill, ?–11 month–1756, Pemberton Papers 34: 43. Christopher Wilson and John Hunt to "Dear Friends," 4–11 month–1756, 33029 Newcastle Collection, p. 355, British Museum. Copy in FHLS.
50. Philadelphia Meeting for Sufferings minutes, 17–12 month–1756. James Pemberton to Samuel Fothergill, ?–11 month– 1756, Pemberton Papers 34: 43. Richard Peters to Thomas Penn, 30 October and 4

November 1756, PPOC 8: 181–89.

51. Isaac Norris to Dr. Charles, 27 November 1755, Isaac Norris Letter Book, 1719–56, pp. 90–91.

52. The four were Mahlon Kirkbride and William Hoge of Bucks County, and Peter Dicks and Nathaniel Pennock of Chester County. *Votes* 6: 4385.

53. Richard Peters to Thomas Penn, 30 October 1756 and 11 December 1756, PPOC 8: 181–89, 208. Thomas Penn to Governor Morris, 10 September 1756, to William Smith, 6–10 month–1756, and to Richard Peters, 11 December 1756, PLB 4: 359–62; 5: 4–7, 51.

54. Israel Pemberton to John Fothergill, 26–7 month–1756, Pemberton Papers, Etting Collection 2: 15.

55. Israel Pemberton to Samuel Fothergill, 14–9 month–1757, Pemberton Papers 34: 61. Moulton, *Journal of Woolman*, p. 84.

56. Isaac Norris to Richard Partridge, 15 June 1758, Isaac Norris Letter Book beginning 16 June 1756, HSP. John Churchman to John Pemberton, 22–5 month–1758, Pemberton Papers 12: 119.

57. Samuel Fothergill to Israel Pemberton, 7–9 month–1758, Pemberton Papers 34: 82. Israel Pemberton to Samuel Fothergill, 8–12 month–1757, Pemberton Papers 34: 66. John Smith to Jonah Thompson, 3–12 month–1757, Thompson MSS, FHLS. ? to Samuel Fothergill, 21–10 month–1757, Cox-Parrish-Wharton Collection 12: 15, HSP.

58. London Yearly Meeting minutes, 17–2 month–1758, FHLS.

59. Samuel Fothergill to John Smith, 19–9 month–1757, John Smith Papers 5: 48. John Griffith to John Pemberton, 9–2 month–1758, Pemberton Family Papers 2: 122, HSP.

60. Samuel Fothergill to James Pemberton, 10–3 month–1758, Pemberton Papers, Etting Collection 2: 31. Samuel Fothergill to John and to Israel Pemberton, 22–4 month–1758, and 1–3 month–1758, Pemberton Papers 34: 77, 69.

61. John Griffith to John Pemberton, 4–6 month–1757, and 21–5 month–1758, Pemberton Papers 12: 25, 118. Samuel Fothergill to Israel Pemberton, 7–9 month–1758, ibid. 34: 82. Magistrates seized property of Friends who refused to pay tithes, sold the property, and kept the amount of the tithes. Any surplus amount from the sale they offered to return to the Friend in question. If the Friend took it, he or she in effect paid tithes, which aside from the inconvenience involved, might just as well be compliance with the law as a protest against it. All this in the context of widespread Quaker compliance with the tithe law.

62. Samuel Fothergill to Israel Pemberton, 7–9 month–1758, Pemberton Papers 34: 82. John Griffith to John Pemberton, 21–5 month–1758, ibid. 12: 118, and 23–6 month–1764, ibid. 17: 63.

63. John Griffith to John Pemberton, 18–6 month–1760, Pemberton Papers

14: 41. John Griffith to ?, 1–6 month–1761, Cox-Parrish-Wharton Collection 11: 28.

64. W. Morris to John Smith, 14–12 month–1756, John Smith Papers.

Chapter 8: Perfecting Pacifism, 1756–1758

1. Margaret E. Hirst, *The Quakers in Peace and War: An Account of Their Peace Principles and Practice* (New York: George H. Doran, 1923), pp. 44, 115, 152, 159, 166. Peter Brock, *Pacifism in Europe to 1914* (Princeton: Princeton University Press, 1972), pp. 260–61, 269, 271–76, 304.

2. Brock, *Pacifism in Europe*, 260–61, 269, 271–76, 304.

3. J. T. Mitchell and Henry Flanders, eds., *Statutes at Large of Pennsylvania from 1682 to 1801* (Harrisburg, 1896–1908), 4: 17–19; 5: 203. If tax collectors refused to enforce the law, they were fined £10; tax assessors and county commissioners were fined £20 for the like offense.

4. John Churchman to Israel Pemberton, 14–12 month–1756, Pemberton Papers 11: 156, HSP. George Churchman's Journal 2: 60, QCHC.

5. Israel Pemberton to Samuel Fothergill, 11–1 month–1757, and James Pemberton to Samuel Fothergill, ?–11 month–1756, Pemberton Papers 34: 49, 43, HSP.

6. Samuel Foulke, "A Collection of some Scriptural texts . . . ," 10–2 month–1756, Miscellaneous Manuscripts, FHLS.

7. Israel Pemberton to Samuel Fothergill, 11–1 month–1757, and James Pemberton to Samuel Fothergill, ?–11 month–1756, Pemberton Papers 34: 49, 43.

8. *Votes* 6: 4553.

9. Israel Pemberton to Samuel Fothergill, 14–9 month–1757, Pemberton Papers 34: 61.

10. Woodbury Monthly Meeting Manuscript Discipline, p. 331. See also George Fox, Epistle no. 176 (1659), *Epistles* 1, in *Works of George Fox*, 8 vols. (Philadelphia: M. T. C. Gould, 1831), 7: 168.

11. Phillips P. Moulton, ed., *The Journal and Major Essays of John Woolman* (New York: Oxford University Press, 1971), pp. 75–84.

12. John Pemberton to Abraham Farrington, 13–10 month–1757, Anna Wharton Wood Collection, QCHC. ? to Samuel Fothergill, 21–10 month–1757, Cox-Parish-Wharton Collection 12: 15, HSP. Israel Pemberton to Samuel Fothergill, 14–9 month–1757, Pemberton Papers 34: 61.

13. Philadelphia Yearly Meeting minutes, 23 and 24–9 month–1757.

14. *Col. Rec.* 7: 110, 591–92.

15. James Pemberton to Samuel Fothergill, ?–11 month–1756, Pemberton Papers 34: 43. Philadelphia Meeting for Sufferings minutes, 28–6

month–1757, 14–7 month–1757. *An Apology for the People called Quakers*, 29–6 month–1757 (Philadelphia, 1757).

16. Thomas Penn to William Denny, 9 October 1756, PLB 5: 26–28, HSP. *Votes* 6: 4390–93.
17. *Votes* 6: 4597.
18. Philadelphia Meeting for Sufferings minutes, 30–3 month–1757.
19. James Pemberton to John Hunt, 18–1 month–1759, Pemberton Papers, box 3.
20. Philadelphia Meeting for Sufferings minutes, 30 and 31–3 month–1757, 14–4 month–1757.
21. Ibid.
22. John Fothergill to Israel Pemberton, 12–6 month–1758, Pemberton Papers, Etting Collection 2: 32, HSP. Philadelphia Meeting for Sufferings to London Meeting for Sufferings, 1–2 month–1759, Philadelphia Meeting for Sufferings minutes, 1–2 month–1759.
23. See chaps. 2 and 3.
24. George Crosfield, ed., *Memoirs of the Life and Gospel Labours of Samuel Fothergill* (Liverpool, 1858), p. 240.
25. Mitchell and Flanders, *Statutes of Pennsylvania* 5: 291–94, 330–34.
26. Philadelphia Yearly Meeting minutes, 28–9 month–1758.
27. Chester Quarterly Meeting minutes, 14–8 month–1758. John Churchman to John Pemberton, 17–8 month–1758, Pemberton Papers 12: 142. James Pemberton to John Hunt, 18–1 month–1759, ibid., box 3.
28. James Pemberton to John Hunt, ?–11 month–1758, Pemberton Papers, box 3. Philadelphia Yearly Meeting minutes, 28–9 month–1758. Reformers and ministers were ably represented on that committee by John and George Churchman, William Brown, John Woolman, Joseph White, Anthony Benezet, and Israel Pemberton.
    The words "any act" permitted disciplinarians to proceed against magistrates who required services other than wagons; tax collectors could be apprehended too. James Pemberton indicated that at least one official was disowned for distraining Friends' property in lieu of their paying taxes. Monthly meeting records, however, do not identify him or his offense. James Pemberton to John Hunt, 8–10 month–1763, Pemberton Papers, box 3.
29. James Pemberton to John Hunt, ?–11 month–1758, Pemberton Papers, box 3.
30. Chester Quarterly Meeting minutes, 14–4 month–1759, 13–8 month–1759.
31. James Pemberton to John Hunt, 18–1 month–1759, Pemberton Papers, box 3.
32. John Fothergill to Israel Pemberton, 9–4 month–1759, Pemberton Papers, Etting Collection 2: 40, HSP.

33. Anthony Benezet to John Smith, probably 20–2 month–1759, Anthony Benezet Letters, QCHC. In a letter to John Smith, Benezet was much less temperate. John Smith Papers 5 (n.d.): 268, HSP. Benezet's commitment to reform was uneven. He was deeply committed to abolition and asceticism, but his commitment to pacifism was conditioned by several temporal considerations in the French and Indian War and the American Revolution.

34. Philadelphia Yearly Meeting minutes, 28–9 month–1758.

35. John Griffith, *Some Brief Remarks upon sundry important subjects* (London, 1764), p. 109.

36. Chester Quarterly Meeting minutes, 13–8 month–1759.

37. Committees multiplied after 1755. They were created to visit and counsel not only nonpacifists and magistrates, but slaveholders, all monthly meetings, and families or households. One committee often had several charges. Their progress at monthly meeting level was to be reported in answers to quarterly and yearly meeting queries. The answers appear laconic, but the contemporary querists found them informative and insisted they be punctually submitted. Philadelphia Quarterly Meeting minutes, 7–2 month–1763, 2–5 month–1763. Western Quarterly Meeting minutes, 16–2 month–1761.

38. George Churchman's Journal 1: 31.

39. Ibid., pp. 39–40.

40. Ibid., p. 47.

41. Bucks Quarterly Meeting minutes, 25–8 month–1763 and 24–11 month–1764. James Pemberton to Thomas Goodwin and William Horne, 16–11 month–1763, Dreer Manuscripts, boxes, HSP. James Pemberton to Joseph Phipps, 15–11 month–1763, Pemberton Family Papers 1: 223–26, HSP.

42. Mitchell and Flanders, *Statutes of Pennsylvania* 5: 202–6, 291–302, 330–34, 337–52, 377–96; 6: 7–22. James Pemberton said that half, or eighteen members, of the Assembly qualified by affirmation rather than oath, which might lead people to believe that they were Friends. James Pemberton to William Logan, 5–2 month–1761, Pemberton Family Papers 1: 199–200.

43. Edward Shippen, Jr. to ?, 5 April 1760, Joseph Shippen Papers, 1727–83, Library of Congress.

44. Philadelphia Meeting for Sufferings minutes, 25–3 month–1760.

45. Ibid., 25–3 month–1760, 17–4 month–1760, 24–9 month–1760, 29–9 month–1760, and Philadelphia Meeting for Sufferings Papers, box 11, 1760.

46. Philadelphia Meeting for Sufferings Papers, box 11, 1760.

47. Philadelphia Meeting for Sufferings minutes, 29–9 month–1760 and Papers, box 11, 1760.

48. Philadelphia Meeting for Sufferings minutes, 1–2 month–1759.
49. George S. Brookes, *Friend Anthony Benezet* (Philadelphia, 1937), pp. 224–25.
50. Richard Peters to Thomas Penn, 13 August 1756, Richard Peters Letter Book, HSP.
51. Israel Pemberton to John Fothergill, 22–11 month–1758, Pemberton Papers, Etting Collection 2: 34.

Chapter 9: Reformation Stalled, 1763–1765

1. Sydney V. James, *A People Among Peoples: Quaker Benevolence in Eighteenth-Century America* (Cambridge, Mass.: Harvard University Press, 1963), pp. 178–79, 186–90. Richard Peters's Diary, Peters Manuscripts, 21 October 1758, HSP. Richard Peters to Thomas Penn, 30 October 1756, PPOC 8: 181–89, HSP.
2. Accounts of Pemberton's role may be found in Theodore Thayer, *Israel Pemberton, King of the Quakers* (Philadelphia: Historical Society of Pennsylvania, 1943), and in Anthony F. C. Wallace, *King of the Delawares: Teedyuscung, 1700–1763* (Philadelphia: University of Pennsylvania Press, 1949).
3. James, *People Among Peoples*, pp. 186–90. Wallace, *Teedyuscung*, pp. 254–61, 264.
4. Howard H. Peckham, *Pontiac and the Indian Uprising* (Princeton: Princeton University Press, 1947), pp. 92–170.
5. Ibid., pp. 214–20. Wallace, *Teedyuscung*, pp. 258–61, 264.
6. Paul A. W. Wallace, *Thirty Thousand Miles with John Heckenwelder* (Pittsburgh: University of Pittsburgh Press, 1958), pp. 71–76.
7. *Col. Rec.*, 9: 89–90, 100–103. Brooke Hindle, "The March of the Paxton Boys," *WMQ*, 3d ser., 3 (1946): 467. William Logan to John Smith, 30–12 month–1763, John Smith Papers 6: 102, HSP.
8. *Col. Rec.* 9: 110–12. David Cooper's Diary, 26–28, QCHC.
9. *Col. Rec.* 9: 121–23, 126–27, 131. Wallace, *Thirty Thousand Miles*, pp. 78–80. James Pemberton to Dr. Fothergill, 7–3 month–1764, Pemberton Papers 34: 125–28, HSP. James Logan, Jr., to John Smith, 25 March 1764, John Smith Papers.
10. George Fisher to Israel Pemberton, 16–3 month–1764, Pemberton Papers, QCHC. William Cox to Israel Pemberton, 22–3 month–1764, Cox-Parris-Wharton Collection 11: 33, HSP.
11. Wallace, *Thirty Thousand Miles*, p. 80. John R. Dunbar, ed., *The Paxton Papers* (The Hague: M. Nijhoff, 1957), p. 39. Hindle, "March," pp. 475–76. James Pemberton to Dr. Fothergill, 7–3 month–1764, Pemberton Papers 34: 125–28, HSP.
12. Dunbar, *Paxton Papers*, pp. 50–51.

13. Ibid., pp. 85–86.
14. Ibid., pp. 104, 109, 189–90, 212, 272–73, 320.
15. Ibid., pp. 108, 193, 213.
16. Ibid. pp. 190, 108. Color counted most, because the Christianity of the Indians did not gain them a whit more consideration from the Presbyterian frontiersmen nor protect them from the assumption that Christian Indians would always prefer other Indians to other Christians.
17. Ibid., pp. 85, 211, 344. Burton A. Konkle, *George Bryan and the Constitution of Pennsylvania, 1731–1791* (Philadelphia: W. J. Campbell, 1922), p. 49.
18. Dunbar, *Paxton Papers*, pp. 188, 211, 271, 341–42, 375–77. For an excellent account of the Assembly-executive struggle see James H. Hutson, *Pennsylvania Politics, 1746–1770: The Campaign for Royal Government* (Princeton: Princeton University Press, 1972) pp. 41–121.
19. Theodore Tappert and John W. Doberstein, eds., *The Journals of Henry Melchior Muhlenberg*, 2 vols. (Philadelphia: Muhlenberg Press, 1942–45), 2: 20, 22. Dunbar, *Paxton Papers*, pp. 151, 175, 177, 212. James Pemberton to Dr. John Fothergill, 7–3 month–1764, Pemberton Papers 34: 125–28. On February 7, the city again became alarmed that Paxton men were approaching, and although no Quakers turned out, an innocent gesture by Friends compounded their trouble with their public image. The volunteers on the seventh drilled at the marketplace square. When it began to rain, they asked to wait out the rain in the Quaker meetinghouse on the square and were admitted. In the hostile press the meetinghouse had been converted into an armory for drilling and Quaker ministers passed out powder and shot, wine and liquor.
20. Israel Pemberton printed a letter of his cousin Charles Read and another Friend printed a mild reply to *The Quaker Unmasked*. Otherwise, Friends remained silent. James Hutson makes a great deal of the numerous pamphlets opposing the Paxtonites by attributing them to Friends. Hutson appears unaware that the Society censored the publications of members, and at that time, 1764, was dealing with a member for unsanctioned publication (not, however, regarding the Paxtonites). Also, the apologists for the Paxtonites had exerted themselves to discover the opposition authors and were disappointed to find that they had no Quakers to debate and that no opponents even professed to be Quakers. Dunbar, *Paxton Papers*, pp. 79–82, 133–38. Hutson, *Pennsylvania Politics*, pp. 96–111. James Pemberton to John Hunt, 11–4 month–1764, Pemberton Papers, box 3, and to Samuel Fothergill, 13–6 month–1764, Pemberton Papers 34: 130–32. Philadelphia Meeting for Sufferings minutes, 17–5 month–1764. John Hunt to John Pemberton 1–3 month–1764, Pemberton Papers, box 3.
21. John Hunt to Israel Pemberton, 10–12 month–1763, Pemberton Papers,

box 3. James Pemberton to Dr. John Fothergill, 7–3 month–1764, Pemberton Papers 34: 125–28, and to John Hunt, 11–4 month–1764, Pemberton Papers, box 3.

22. Dunbar, *Paxton Papers*, pp. 339–51, 365–86. Hutson, *Pennsylvania Politics*, pp. 109–12. James Pemberton to Dr. John Fothergill, 7–3 month–1764, Pemberton Papers 34: 125–28.

23. Thomas Wharton, "An Account of what I recollect of the Vile Affidavit taken by Wm Plumsted on the 10th of Febry 1764, sworn to by Thomas Swiney with the Circumstances relative thereto," Wharton-Willing Papers, box D, HSP. Hutson, *Pennsylvania Politics*, pp. 109–12. James Pemberton to Dr. John Fothergill, 5–9 month–1764, Pemberton Family Papers 1: 279–80, HSP.

24. James Pemberton to Dr. John Fothergill, 5–9 month–1764, Pemberton Family Papers 1: 279–80. Hutson, *Pennsylvania Politics*, pp. 113–26, 180. Governor John Penn had demanded that the Penns' land be assessed for taxes at a rate no higher than the worst of the people's lands.

25. If there were 200 Friends who turned out, they comprised a conspicuously large number of the Philadelphia Quakers. The census of Philadelphia Monthly Meeting of 1760 discloses 1001 male members, of which 464 appear to be minors. Probably 1 in 4 Friends who might be regarded as potential volunteers because of their age did in fact take up arms.

26. Philadelphia Monthly Meeting minutes, 30–3 month–1764 through 29–5 month–1767.

27. Edward Penington Papers, HSP. Quoted by David Sloan, " 'A Time of Sifting and Winnowing': The Paxton Riots and Quaker Non-Violence in Pennsylvania," *Quaker History* (Spring, 1977), pp. 19–20.

28. Philadelphia Yearly Meeting minutes, 30–3 month–1767. William Logan to John Smith, 2–8 month–1767, John Smith Papers.

29. James Pemberton to John Hunt, 11–4 month–1764, Pemberton Papers, box 3. James Pemberton reported there were fourteen Friends in the House in 1764; the Meeting for Sufferings said sixteen. Historians have counted from ten to fifteen. James Pemberton to Dr. John Fothergill, 7–3 month–1764, Pemberton Papers 34: 125–28. Philadelphia Meeting for Sufferings minutes, 3–9 month–1764. Arthur J. Mekeel, *The Relation of the Quakers to the American Revolution* (Washington: University Press of America, 1979), pp. 19, 30n. Mekeel's account of the Quakers and the American Revolution is the most complete and accurate yet published. Hermann Wellenreuther, *Glaube and Politik in Pennsylvania* (Cologne: Bohlau, 1972), pp. 432–37. Wayne Bockelman and Owen Ireland, "The Internal Revolution in Pennsylvania: An Ethnic-Religious Interpretation," *Pa. Hist.* 41 (1974): 159.

30. Philadelphia Yearly Meeting minutes, 28–10 month–1764.
31. James Pemberton to John Hunt, 11–4 month–1764, Pemberton Papers, box 3. J. T. Mitchell and Henry Flanders, eds., *Statutes at Large of Pennsylvania from 1682 to 1802* (Harrisburg, 1896–1908), 6: 311–19, 344–67. See also the statute of 1763 for hiring wagons, which revived the problem of 1758. Ibid., pp. 293–97. *Col. Rec.* 9: 189.
32. James Pemberton to John Hunt, 8–10 month–1763, Pemberton Papers, box 3. James Pemberton to Thomas Goodwin and William Horne, 16–11 month–1763, Dreer Manuscripts, boxes, HSP. Bucks Quarterly Meeting minutes, 15–8 month–1763, 24–11 month–1763. James Pemberton to Dr. John Fothergill, 18–12 month–1756, Pemberton Papers 34: 138.
33. Hutson, *Pennsylvania Politics*, p. 227.
34. James Pemberton to Dr. John Fothergill, 7–3 month–1764, 3–9 month–1764, Pemberton Papers 34: 125–28, 133. William Logan to John Smith, [October 1764], John Smith Papers. Israel Pemberton to David Barclay, Sr., 6–11 month–1764, Pemberton Papers 17: 103.
35. James Pemberton to Dr. John Fothergill, 11–10 month–1764, and to Henton Brown and Dr. John Fothergill, 17–12 month–1765, Pemberton Papers 34: 134, 137. The pamphlets of the 1764 election campaign, which focused upon Franklin, could easily have raised Pemberton's partisan spirit. See J. Philip Gleason, "A Scurrilous Colonial Election and Franklin's Reputation," *WMQ*, 3d ser., 18 (1961): 68–84.
36. Israel Pemberton to David Barclay, Sr., 6–11 month–1764, Pemberton Papers 17: 103. Richard Peters to Thomas Penn, 5 June 1756, PPOC 8: 7.
37. *An Address to the Rev. Dr. Alison, the Rev. Mr. Ewing, and others, Trustees of the Corporation for the Relief of Presbyterian Ministers, their Widows and Children: Being a Vindication of the Quakers From the Aspersions of the said Trustees in their Letter published in the London Chronicle, No. 1223 . . . By a lover of Truth* (Philadelphia, 1765). Leonard W. Labaree et al., eds., *The Papers of Benjamin Franklin* (New Haven: Yale University Press, 1959–   ), 12: 136–38.
38. Tappert and Doberstein, *Journals of Muhlenberg* 2: 22. William Logan to John Smith, 4 October 1764, John Smith Papers. James Logan to John Smith, 27 July 1764, John Smith Papers. Henry Drinker to Frederick Pigou, 30–4 month–1764, Henry Drinker Letter Book, 1762–86, HSP.
39. Ashbridge was the Franklin party candidate for speaker of the House in October 1764, but lost to Joseph Fox. John Dickinson to Isaac Norris, 24 October 1764, Isaac Norris Letter Book Beginning 16 June 1756, HSP.
40. Philadelphia Meeting for Sufferings minutes, 21–6 month–1764, 19–7 month–1764, 3–9 month–1764.

41. John Churchman to James Pemberton, 6 month–1764, and Israel Pemberton to David Barclay, Sr., 6–11 month–1764, Pemberton Papers 17: 68, 103.

42. Philadelphia Yearly Meeting minutes, 22 to 29–9 month–1764 (Epistle to London Yearly Meeting) and 28–10 month–1764.

43. Hutson exaggerates the number of Quaker signers of petitions for royal government. He states that half of the 3500 signers were Friends, that very few country Friends signed, and that city Friends generally did. However, in 1760 there were only some 537 adult, male Friends in the city. Hutson, therefore, has exaggerated the Quaker signers from the city by a factor of two or more, or else has exaggerated the total number of Quaker signers in the province. Hutson, *Pennsylvania Politics*, pp. 127–29.

44. Ibid., pp. 170, 175, 178–80. Israel Pemberton to David Barclay, Sr., 6–11 month–1764, Pemberton Papers 17: 103.

45. Hutson, *Pennsylvania Politics*, pp. 176, 180–90, 204, 219, 227. James Pemberton to Henton Brown and to Dr. John Fothergill, 17–12 month–1765, 18–12 month–1765, Pemberton Papers 34: 137, 138. Labaree et al., *Papers of Benjamin Franklin* 12: 142, 145, 313. Philadelphia Meeting for Sufferings minutes, 20–11 month–1766 (Epistle from London Yearly Meeting for Sufferings dated 28–8 month–1766).

46. Tappert and Doberstein, *Journals of Muhlenberg* 2: 123.

47. Konkle, *Bryan*, pp. 48–49.

48. James Pemberton to Dr. John Fothergill, 3–9 month–1764, Pemberton Papers 34: 133.

49. David Barclay to Israel Pemberton, 5 July 1764, Cox-Parrish-Wharton Papers 11:34. James Logan to John Smith, 27 July 1764, John Smith Papers. James Pemberton to Dr. John Fothergill, 3–9 month–1764, and Israel Pemberton to David Barclay, Sr., 6–11 month–1764, Pemberton Papers 34: 133; 17: 103. Meanwhile, James Pemberton treated Allen as one of his greatest adversaries and confronted the man personally. Labaree, *Franklin Papers* 13:295.

50. Franklin B. Dexter, ed., *Extracts from the Itineraries and Other Miscellanies of Ezra Stiles, D.D., L.L.D. 1755–1794 with a Selection from His Correspondence* (New Haven: Yale University Press, 1916), pp. 425–26.

51. John Dickinson to Isaac Norris, 22 and 24 October 1764, Isaac Norris Letter Book beginning 16 June 1756.

52. George Churchman's Journal 1: 79–80, QCHC.

Chapter 10: The Exhaustion of Quaker Politics, 1765–1775

1. This story may be followed in James H. Hutson, *Pennsylvania Politics, 1746–1770* (Princeton: Princeton University Press, 1972), pp. 178–227, and in Benjamin H. Newcomb, *Franklin and Galloway: A Political Partnership* (New Haven: Yale University Press, 1972), pp. 105–60.

2. Samuel Fothergill suspected that Franklin penned acerbic messages from the House to Governor Morris and the proprietors in order to make the Society more obnoxious to Englishmen. According to gossip in Philadelphia, Franklin expected to exclude Friends from office with oaths once he came to the head of a royal regime in Pennsylvania. Israel Pemberton, at a meeting between Fothergill and Franklin, promised to raise Morris's salary by subscription if Franklin and the House did not pay it. William Evans and Thomas Evans, eds., *Friends Library* (Philadelphia, 1837–45), 9: 176. William Peters to Thomas Penn, 4 January 1756, PPOC 8: 3, HSP. Richard Peters to Thomas Penn, 5 June 1756, PPOC 8: 7.

3. An important exception to the urban residence of the group was George Ashbridge, Chester County assemblyman, unflagging political activist, and candidate of the Franklin party for House speaker against Joseph Fox in 1764. E.g., Leonard W. Labaree et al., eds., *The Papers of Benjamin Franklin* (New Haven: Yale University Press, 1959–), 13: 273.

4. Ibid. 13: 257–58; 16: 200n. Newcomb, *Franklin and Galloway*, pp. 106, 148–49, 212. Theodore Thayer, *Pennsylvania Politics and the Growth of Democracy, 1740–1776* (Harrisburg: Pennsylvania Historical and Museum Commission, 1953), p. 135. Oliver C. Kuntzleman, *Joseph Galloway, Loyalist* (Ed.D. diss., Temple University, 1941), pp. 14–15. Bruce R. Lively, "Toward 1756: The Political Genesis of Joseph Galloway," *Pa Hist.* 45 (1978): 125n. Galloway's biographers do not specify his Quaker membership, but the evidence of it is found in the Philadelphia Monthly Meeting census of 1760, FHLS. Also, Richard Peters called him "a young nosey Quaker Lawyer." Joseph E. Illick, *Colonial Pennsylvania: A History* (New York: Charles Scribner's Sons, 1976), p. 215. Samuel Wharton, often counted an Anglican, was a nominal Friend disowned in 1774 for slaveholding. Philadelphia Monthly Meeting minutes, 2–4 month–1772, and occasionally through 7 month–1774. Manuscript dated 14 and 20 August 1764, Wharton-Willing Papers, box 1, HSP.

5. Labaree, *Franklin Papers* 8: 81–82. Carl Bridenbaugh, *Mitre and Sceptre: Transatlantic Faiths, Ideas, Personalities, and Politics, 1689–1775* (New York: Oxford University Press, 1962), pp. 171–339. James

Pemberton to Dr. John Fothergill, 14–11 month–1766, Pemberton Papers 34: 148, HSP.

6. Labaree, *Franklin Papers* 12: 250–51. William S. Perry, ed., *Papers Relating to the History of the Church in Pennsylvania, A.D., 1680–1778* (Hartford, 1871), p. 368.

7. Through 1785, Pemberton continued to regard the political division in Pennsylvania as one between Presbyterians and others, largely Episcopalians. "Our politicians continue active in their separate views, distinguished by two parties termed Constitutionalists which consists chiefly of Presbyterians and the Republicans who are mostly Episcopalians." James Pemberton to William Dillwyn, Pemberton Family Papers 3: 368–69, HSP.

8. James Pemberton to Samuel Fothergill, 13–6 month–1764, and to Dr. John Fothergill, 1–3 month–1766, 34: 130–32, 140. Galloway and John Hughes, a Stamp distributor, shared almost the same attitude toward the Presbyterians. Labaree, *Franklin Papers* 13: 37. Edmund S. Morgan and Helen M. Morgan, *The Stamp Act Crisis: Prologue to Revolution* (New York: University of North Carolina Press, 1962), p. 323, and elsewhere.

9. James Pemberton to Henton Brown and Dr. John Fothergill, 17–12 month–1765, Pemberton Papers 34: 137.

10. Labaree, *Franklin Papers* 12: 145, 145n, 146; 13: 324. Hutson, "The Campaign to Make Pennsylvania a Royal Province, 1764–1770, Part II," *PMHB* 95 (1971): 28–29. Newcomb, *Franklin and Galloway*, pp. 108–13.

11. James Pemberton to Henton Brown and Dr. John Fothergill, 17–12 month–1765, Pemberton Papers 34: 137.

12. Labaree, *Franklin Papers* 12: 265–66, 269–70, 271–74, 315–17, 372–75; 13: 294. Morgan and Morgan, *Stamp Act Crisis*, pp. 314–16.

13. James Pemberton to Dr. John Fothergill, 18–12 month–1765, Pemberton Papers 34: 138. Philadelphia Meeting for Sufferings minutes, 20–2 month–1766.

14. Labaree, *Franklin Papers* 12: 357–58, 372–73. Arthur L. Jensen, *The Maritime Commerce of Colonial Philadelphia* (Madison, Wisc.: State Historical Society of Wisconsin, 1963), pp. 160–61. Arthur J. Mekeel, *The Relation of the Quakers to the American Revolution* (Washington: University Press of America, 1979), p. 20.

15. Labaree, *Franklin Papers* 12: 357–58. *Pennsylvania Gazette*, 14 and 28 November 1765. "To the Merchants, & Manufacturers of Great Britain, the Memorial of the Merchants, and Traders of the City of Philadelphia," Franklin Papers, American Philosophical Society. The list includes 269 individuals and 28 business firms. Of the 269, 85 were Friends. Of the 28, 9 possibly included Friends among the partners in the firms.

16. Labaree, *Franklin Papers* 12: 372–73, 377. James Pemberton to Dr. John Fothergill, 18–12 month–1765, Pemberton Papers 34: 138.

17. James Pemberton to Dr. John Fothergill, 18–12 month–1765, Pemberton Papers 34: 138.

18. Lyman H. Butterfield, ed., *The Letters of Benjamin Rush* (Princeton: Princeton University Press, 1951), 1: 18.

19. John Pemberton to James Pemberton, 2–10 month–1769, Pemberton Papers 21: 75. And yet from his egocentric outlook, James believed he was a nonpartisan assemblyman who behaved that way by not joining party quarrels in the House. His obsession with the Presbyterian menace—his motive for holding office—was not politically partisan because he believed he was, in the public interest, merely countering Presbyterian activism. His was a definition of the public interest that many Pennsylvanians, including possibly most Quakers, did not accept. James Pemberton to Dr. John Fothergill, 14–11 month–1766, Pemberton Papers 34: 147–48.

20. Labaree, *Franklin Papers* 13: 272, 282–85. *Pennsylvania Gazette*, 22 May 1766. James Pemberton to Dr. John Fothergill, 7–6 month–1766, Pemberton Papers 34: 143–45.

21. Friends had not been entirely consistent in their behavior and the face they showed the public, and it was primarily city Quakers who marred the record. When, in March 1765, the news reached Philadelphia that Franklin had arrived safely in England, bent upon a change of government for Pennsylvania, his followers celebrated in the streets. Bells rang almost all night, Governor John Penn complained; the whole city seemed in motion, "especially the Quaker part of it." Penn doubted that these Quakers would have shown half as much joy at the most signal British victory in wartime. Governor John Penn to Thomas Penn, 16 March 1765, PPOC 10: 5, 7.

22. The supporters of Franklin had as much reason to celebrate as most other Pennsylvanians for they were relieved of the need to act duplicitously and their opponents lost a very useful canard against Franklin. Henry Drinker to Samuel Emlen, Jr., 20–9 month–1766, Henry Drinker Letter Book, 1762–86, HSP.

23. Labaree, *Franklin Papers* 15: 71; see also pp. 39–41, 88–90.

24. Newcomb, *Franklin and Galloway*, p. 182.

25. *Votes* 7: 6181–92, 6243–44, 6271–80. Labaree, *Franklin Papers* 15: 91–92, 189. Hutson, *Pennsylvania Politics*, p. 227.

26. James Pemberton to Dr. John Fothergill, 20–10 month–1768, 30–1 month–1769, Pemberton Papers 34: 154, 157. Of the committee created by the merchants to memorialize British merchants, five of eight members were Friends. Labaree, *Franklin Papers* 15: 266–67.

27. Newcomb, *Franklin and Galloway*, pp. 199–200, 203.

28. Mekeel, *Relation of Quakers to the Revolution*, p. 44. Of a committee

of seventeen members who informed Franklin of the nonimportation agreement, seven were Friends. Labaree, *Franklin Papers* 16: 115–16. In August 1769, in a letter to London Friends, the Philadelphia Meeting for Sufferings claimed that some of the Friends named to the nonimportation committee accepted in order to moderate the actions of the body; others were named to it without their consent or knowledge. The Meeting's picture is one of general Quaker suspicion of the committee. Yet the picture may be doubted. Friends had generally joined the agreement of 1765 and had consistently expressed Whiggish views about parliamentary taxation. Perhaps the Meeting for Sufferings wished to characterize more Friends as sharing its attitude. Philadelphia Meeting for Sufferings minutes, 5–8 month–1769.

29. Philadelphia Meeting for Sufferings minutes, 5–8 month–1769. *Pennsylvania Gazette*, 20 July 1769.

30. Philadelphia Meeting for Sufferings minutes, 5–8 month–1769, 1–9 month–1769. The meeting circulated two-thousand copies of an "Epistle of Caution" among Friends.

31. Ibid., 5–8 month–1769.

32. Dr. John Fothergill to James Pemberton, 16–9 month–1768, 16–5 month–1769, Pemberton Papers, Etting Collection 2: 58, 60, HSP.

33. Philadelphia Meeting for Sufferings minutes, 5–8 month–1769.

34. James Pemberton to Dr. John Fothergill, 3–5 month–1771, Pemberton Papers 34: 159–60.

35. After the summer of 1769, two or three of the twelve committeemen were Friends, which was down from eight. *Pennsylvania Journal*, 20 and 27 September 1770. Jensen, *Maritime Commerce*, p. 184. Franklin, *Letters, to the Merchants' Committee of Philadelphia* . . . (Philadelphia, 1769).

36. For a recapitulation of these debates see Jensen, *Maritime Commerce*, pp. 190–93.

37. *Pennsylvania Journal*, 20 and 27 September 1770, 4 October 1770.

38. Labaree, *Franklin Papers* 17: 287–88.

39. *Pennsylvania Gazette*, 27 September 1770. William Goddard, *The Partnership* (Philadelphia, 1770). Newcomb, *Franklin and Galloway*, pp. 212–16.

40. Newcomb, *Franklin and Galloway*, pp. 218–19. Labaree, *Franklin Papers* 17: 228–29. *Pennsylvania Gazette*, 20 September 1770, 19 August 1772, 22 September 1773. *Pennsylvania Chronicle*, 27 September 1773. *Fellow Citizens and Countrymen* (Philadelphia, 1772).

41. James Pemberton to Dr. John Fothergill, Jacob Hagan, Danl Mildred, and David Barclay, 30–10 month–1773, Pemberton Papers 34: 169, and to Dr. John Fothergill, 1–7 month–1774, Pemberton Papers, Etting Collection 2: 68. Philadelphia Meeting for Sufferings minutes, 20–1 month–1774, 16 and 28–6 month–1774, 21–7 month–1774, 15 and

23–12 month–1774. Philadelphia Yearly Meeting minutes, 24–9 month to 1–10 month–1774.

42. The other three commissioners were Isaac Wharton, a Friend until disowned early in 1773, Jonathan Browne, and Gilbert Barkly. The latter two did not figure much in the controversy between tea commissioners and resistors. Jensen, *Maritime Commerce*, p. 201.

43. *Pennsylvania Gazette*, 22 September 1773. *Pennsylvania Chronicle*, 27 September 1773.

44. Jensen, *Maritime Commerce*, pp. 200–202. Pennsylvania Gazette, 20 September 1773.

45. James Pemberton to Dr. John Fothergill and others, 30–10 month–1773, Pemberton Papers 34: 169, and to Daniel Mildred, 22 July 1774, quoted by Jensen, *Maritime Commerce*, p. 214. Henry Drinker to Lancelot Cowper and Company, 27–3 month–1775, Henry Drinker Letters, Foreign Letters, 1772–85, HSP.

46. James Pemberton to Dr. John Fothergill and others, 30–10 month–1773, Pemberton Papers 34: 169. Pemberton said that one "unsteady young" Friend agreed to be a member of the committee appointed on October 16.

47. Arthur M. Schlesinger, *The Colonial Merchants and the American Revolution, 1763–1776* (New York: Atheneum, 1968), pp. 290, 343, 345. *Pennsylvania Gazette*, 8 June 1774, 18 June 1774. And see the sources cited at n. 40.

48. Newcomb, *Franklin and Galloway*, pp. 243–44.

49. *Pennsylvania Gazette*, 8 June 1774. The committee also included Quaker radicals like Thomas Mifflin and Benjamin Marshall. Five of 19 members were Friends.

50. Schlesinger, *Colonial Merchants*, pp. 345–46. *PMHB* 33 (1909): 436, 439. *Pennsylvania Gazette*, 22 June 1774. Of the eight Friends, five were moderates and three were radicals.

51. James Pemberton to Dr. John Fothergill, 1–7 month–1774, Pemberton Papers, Etting Collection 2: 68.

52. Philadelphia Meeting for Sufferings minutes, 16–6 month–1774, 28–6 month–1774, 21–7 month–1774.

53. Schlesinger, *Colonial Merchants*, pp. 456–58. Robert F. Oaks, "Philadelphia Merchants and the Origins of American Independence," *Proceedings of the American Philosophical Society* 121 (1977): 428–29, and "Philadelphia Merchants and the First Continental Congress," *PMHB* 40 (1973): 158, 159, 164–65. Richard A. Ryerson, "Political Mobilization and the American Revolution: The Resistance Movement in Philadelphia, 1765–1776," *WMQ*, 3d ser., 31 (1974): 571, 585. *Pennsylvania Gazette*, 16 November 1774. Historians have commonly overestimated the number of Friends in the revolutionary era committees, as well as the number of Friends in the Assembly. The exaggerations

usually occur because historians have counted disowned Friends. Whereas I differ with Mekeel's figures by only one, others differ by a greater number, especially Ryerson. Ryerson counted reputed Friends, producing greater totals, which supported his thesis of approximate balance in the makeup of the committees. Ryerson, *The Revolution Is Now Begun: The Radical Committees of Philadelphia* (Philadelphia: University of Pennsylvania Press, 1978), pp. 10n, 188, 188n. While the thesis of Wayne L. Brockleman and Owen S. Ireland is sound, their figures too on Friends are inaccurate. Brockleman and Ireland, "The Internal Revolution in Pennsylvania: An Ethnic-Religious Interpretation," *Pa. Hist.* 41 (1974): 124–59.

54. Newcomb, *Franklin and Galloway*, pp. 244–47.
55. Ibid., pp. 250–58, 271–72. Edward Penington and Thomas Willing lost the 1774 election in the city to Thomas Mifflin and Charles Thomson (a collaborator with Friends in the French and Indian War negotiations with the Indians). Thomas Wharton attributed the setback to Presbyterians and their lower-class followers. Thomas Wharton to Samuel Wharton, 4 October 1774, Wharton Letter Book, 1773–74, HSP.
56. *Votes* 8: 7162. Philadelphia Meeting for Sufferings minutes, 15–12 month–1774.
57. James Pemberton to Dr. John Fothergill, 15–2 month–1775, Pemberton Papers 27: 75. Newcomb, *Franklin and Galloway*, pp. 276–79.
58. Philadelphia Meeting for Sufferings minutes, 20–1 month–1774, 21–7 month–1774. James and Drinker to Pigou and Booth, 11 June 1774, Henry Drinker Letters, Foreign Letters, 1772–85. In the *Pennsylvania Gazette*, 1 June 1774, James Pemberton, John Reynell, and Samuel Noble published a notice that, contrary to the news in the *Pennsylvania Packet* of 30 May 1774, Friends had not joined the other denominations which had planned the fast, and that any Friend who countenanced the fast was violating discipline.
59. Philadelphia Yearly Meeting minutes, 24–9 month–1774.
60. "To our Friends & Brethren in these & the adjacent Provinces," Philadelphia Meeting for Sufferings minutes, 5–1 month–1775. "The Testimony of the People called Quakers given forth by a Meeting of the Representatives of the said People, in Pennsylvania and New Jersey held at Philada the twenty fourth day of the first Month 1775," ibid., 24–1 month–1775. James Pemberton to Joseph Oxley, 6–11 month–1774, Dreer Collection, Boxes, HSP. James Pemberton to "Esteemed Friend," 31–1 month–1774, Cox-Parrish-Wharton Collection 11: 69. Philadelphia Meeting for Sufferings minutes, 21–7 month–1774. Philadelphia Monthly Meeting minutes, 26–8 month–1774. Philadelphia Yearly Meeting minutes, 24–9 month to 1–10 month–1774.
61. Philadelphia Yearly Meeting minutes, 24–9 month to 1–10 month–1774. Philadelphia Meeting for Sufferings minutes, 5–11 month–1774.

62. Newcomb, *Franklin and Galloway*, pp. 261–62. Dr. John Fothergill to James Pemberton, 3–1 month–1775, 26–1 month–1775, 17–3 month–1775, Pemberton Papers 34: 170–73. David Barclay to James Pemberton, 18–3 month–1775, Pemberton Family Papers 2: 356–61. James Pemberton to Dr. John Fothergill, 6–5 month–1775, Pemberton Papers 27: 138.

Chapter 11: Beleaguered Quakers, 1775–1782

1. Christopher Marshall Diaries, 30 December 1774, 2 January 1775, HSP. "To our Friends & Brethren in these & the adjacent Provinces." "To the Monthly & Quarterly Meetings of Friends in Pennsylvania & New Jersey." "The Testimony of the People called Quakers given forth by a Meeting of the Representatives of said people, in Pennsylvania and New Jersey held at Philada the twenty fourth day of the first Month 1775." These three epistles and notices are found in Philadelphia Meeting for Sufferings minutes, 5, 19, and 24–1 month–1775. The second message was printed in two thousand copies and the third, three thousand.
2. Christopher Marshall Diaries, 24 January 1775, 14 February 1775. Martha Allinson to Samuel Allinson, 29–4 month–1775, Allinson Papers, box 2, QCHC.
3. Thomas Wharton to Samuel Wharton, 31 January 1775, Thomas Wharton Letter Book, HSP.
4. James Pemberton to Dr. John Fothergill, 15–2 month–1775, Pemberton Papers 27: 75, HSP. David Barclay to James Pemberton, 18–3 month–1775, Pemberton Family Papers 2: 356–61, HSP.
5. David Barclay to James Pemberton, 18–3 month–1775, Pemberton Family Papers 2: 356–61. James Pemberton to Dr. John Fothergill, 15–2 month–1775 and 6–5 month–1775, Pemberton Papers 27: 75, 138.
6. *An Earnest Address to such of The People Called Quakers As are Sincerely Desirous of Supporting and Maintaining the Christian Testimony of their Ancestors* (Philadelphia, 1775).
7. "B. L.," *Pennsylvania Journal*, 1 February 1775. *Argumentum ad Hominem: Being an Extract from a Piece Entitled, England's Present Interest considered by Wm. Penn* (Philadelphia, 1775).
8. Edward Stabler to Israel Pemberton, 16–5 month–1775 and 19–6 month–1775, Pemberton Papers 27: 144, 172.
9. *Votes* 8: 7230, 7236–38, 7245–49.
10. Edward Burd to Jasper Yeates, 7 June 1775, Yeates Papers, Correspondence, 1762–1770, HSP. Jasper Yeates to James Burd, 11 July 1775, Shippen Family Papers, vol. 7, HSP. The laws of the province did not yet prescribe militia duty.
11. Worthington C. Ford, ed., *Journals of the Continental Congress, 1774–*

1789, 34 vols. (Washington: U.S. Government Printing Office, 1903–37), 2: 187–90. *Votes* 8: 7258–63, 7310–13, 7324–29, 7334–43.

12. *Votes* 8: 7262. Friends had heard the argument—one based upon the contractural nature of society and government—first in the 1740s from James Logan and Judge Samuel Chew. And through the 1750s Quaker legislators were accused of ignoring their societal obligations to protect the property and lives of Pennsylvanians. In 1748, John Churchman had replied that Pennsylvania was a different society, explicitly pacifist, and that the complainers could leave if they did not like it.

13. Samuel Allinson to Elias Boudinot, 20–12 month–1790, Samuel Allinson Letter Book, 1764–91, Allinson Papers, box 11B.

14. *Votes* 8: 7311–13, 7326–30. Philadelphia Meeting for Sufferings minutes, 20–10 month–1775, 24–10 month–1775.

15. *Votes* 8: 7335–36, 7338, 7342–43. The addresses to the Assembly were also published in the newspapers. See *Pennsylvania Packet* and *Pennsylvania Gazette* for October and November.

16. *Votes* 8: 7334, 7339. See also Charles Wetherill, *History of the Religious Society of Friends called by Some the Free Quakers in the City of Philadelphia* (Philadelphia, 1894), p. 14.

17. *Votes* 8: 7259, 7334, 7338–39.

18. Ibid., pp. 7351–52.

19. Ibid., pp. 7399, 7402–7, 7422, 7426, 7440, 7443, 7487.

20. John Reynell to Joshua Williams, 28–11 month–1775, John Reynell Letter Book, 1774–84, HSP.

21. Eric Foner, *Tom Paine and Revolutionary America* (New York: Oxford University Press, 1976), pp. 79, 85.

22. "The antient Testimony & Principles of the People call'd Quakers renew'd with respect to the King and Government, and touching the Commotions now prevailing in these and other parts of America, addressed to the People in General," Philadelphia Meeting for Sufferings minutes, 20–1 month–1776. The Meeting printed three thousand copies.

23. Ibid.

24. Philip S. Foner, ed., *Complete Writings of Thomas Paine*, 2 vols. (New York: The Citadel Press, 1945), 2: 56–59. The appended letter appeared in the third edition of *Common Sense* and thereafter.

25. Ibid.

26. Theodore Tappert and John W. Doberstein, eds., *The Journals of Henry Melchior Muhlenberg* (Philadelphia: Muhlenberg Press, 1942–45), 2: 753, 756. Christopher Marshall Diaries, 30 June 1776.

27. Foner, *Writings of Paine* 2: 97–98.

28. For the history of the proprietary government of Pennsylvania in its last year and of its overthrow see David Hawke, *In the Midst of A Revolution* (Philadelphia: University of Pennsylvania Press, 1961).

29. For a description of these men see ibid., pp. 102–6 and Foner, *Paine and Revolutionary America*, pp. 108–16.
30. Tappert and Doberstein, *Journals of Muhlenberg* 2: 720–21. Philadelphia Meeting for Sufferings minutes, 18 and 27–4 month–1776. The Meeting published 2000 copies of its order against the fast. Hawke, *Midst of Revolution*, pp. 133–34.
31. Hawke, *Midst of Revolution*, p. 155.
32. Ibid., pp. 186–95.
33. Philadelphia Yearly Meeting minutes, 28–9 month–1776.
34. Hawke, *Midst of Revolution*, pp. 189–90.
35. Peter Brock, *Pacifism in the United States* (Princeton: Princeton University Press, 1968), pp. 285–329.
36. Philadelphia Yearly Meeting minutes, 21 to 28–9 month–1776.
37. Arthur J. Mekeel, *The Relation of the Quakers to the American Revolution* (Washington: University Press of America, 1979), pp. 334–35. The information on the volunteers from Bucks, Chester, and Philadelphia counties is found in Kenneth Alan Radbill, "The Socioeconomic Background of Nonpacifist Quakers During the American Revolution" (Ph.D. diss., University of Arizona, 1971).
38. Radbill, "Socioeconomic Background," pp. 96, 97. Charles Royster, *A Revolutionary People at War: The Continental Army and American Character* (Chapel Hill: University of North Carolina Press, 1979), chap. 1.
39. Radbill, "Socioeconomic Background," pp. 1, 95.
40. Ibid., p. 26. Yet by 1781, the economic status of the volunteers who appeared in both the 1774 and 1781 tax lists was approximately equal to that of the regular Friends who appeared in both lists.
41. Ibid., pp. 15, 19.
42. Ibid., p. 76.
43. Wells, "Quaker Marriage Patterns in a Colonial Perspective," *WMQ*, 3d ser., 39: 417. Barry J. Levy, "The Birth of the 'Modern Family' in Early America," in Michael Zuckerman, ed., *Friends and Neighbors* (Philadelphia: Temple University Press, 1982), pp. 44–45.
44. Radbill, "Socioeconomic Background," pp. 32–34. In Philadelphia, Chester, and Bucks counties, 74.2 percent, 95.3 percent, and 44.6 percent, respectively, of the volunteers occupations (while or after they were disowned) were ascertained.
45. Ibid., pp. 81–83.
46. Ibid., pp. 90, 93.
47. Ibid., pp. 58, 60, 63–65.
48. *Pennsylvania Gazette*, 18 September 1776.
49. *An Act to Regulate the Militia of the Common-Wealth of Pennsylvania* (Philadelphia, 1777).
50. *Laws Enacted in the Second General Assembly of the Representatives*

of the Freemen of the Common-Wealth of Pennsylvania (Lancaster, 1778), chaps. 38, 46.

51. *Laws Enacted in the Third Sitting of the Third General Assembly of the Representatives of the Freemen of the Common-Wealth of Pennsylvania* (Philadelphia, 1779), chap. 130. E. James Ferguson, *The Power of the Purse: A History of American Public Finance, 1776–1790* (Chapel Hill: University of North Carolina Press, 1961), p. 32. Continental currency depreciated 30 to 1 relative to specie by October 1779.

52. John Paul Selsam, *The Pennsylvania Consitution of 1776* (Philadelphia: University of Pennsylvania Press, 1936), pp. 164, 193–94.

53. "An Act obliging the male white inhabitants of this state to give assurances of allegiance to the same, and for other purposes therein mentioned," *Laws Enacted in a General Assembly of the Representatives of the Freemen of the Common-Wealth of Pennsylvania Begun and held at Philadelphia the Twelfth day of May, A.D. One Thousand Seven Hundred and Seventy-seven, and continued by adjournments to the Nineteenth day of June, A.D. One Thousand Seven Hundred and Seventy-seven* (Philadelphia, 1777).

54. "A Supplement to the Act, intitled 'An Act obliging the male white inhabitants of this State to give assurances of allegiance to the same, and for other purposes therein mentioned,' " *Laws Enacted in a General Assembly of the Representatives of the Freeman of the Common-Wealth of Pennsylvania* [12 May 1777 to 14 October 1777] . . . *Laws Enacted in the Second Sitting of the General Assembly of Common-Wealth of Pennsylvania* (Lancaster, 1778), chap. 61.

55. *Laws Enacted in the Third Sitting of the Third General Assembly of the Common-Wealth of Pennsylvania* (Philadelphia, 1779), chap. 117. Philadelphia Meeting for Sufferings minutes, 3–11 month–1779.

56. On the other hand, the full punishment prescribed by the laws was not consistently applied.

57. Philadelphia Meeting for Sufferings minutes, 20–12 month–1776. Norman C. Hunt, *Two Early Political Associations* (Oxford: Clarendon Press, 1961), pp. 64–72.

58. Elizabeth Drinker Diary, 15 June and 14 September 1779, 1 May, 27 June, and 7 July 1780, HSP.

59. John Smith Futhy and Gilbert Cope, *History of Chester County, Pennsylvania* (Philadelphia: L. H. Everts, 1881), pp. 244–45.

60. Mekeel, *Relation of the Quakers to Revolution*, p. 202.

61. Arthur J. Mekeel, "The Quakers in the American Revolution" (Ph.D. diss., Harvard University, 1940), pp. 155–56.

62. Nicholas B. Wainwright, " 'A Diary of Trifling Occurrences,' Philadelphia, 1776–1778," *PMHB* 82 (1958): 411–65. Elizabeth Drinker Diary, 25 January 1781, HSP.

63. For their neutrality Friends got no more favor from the British than the

British showed to other Americans. For John Adams's testimony to the neutrality of Friends see Charles Francis Adams, ed., *Works of John Adams*, 10 vols. (Boston: Little, Brown, 1850–56), 9: 459, and Charles Francis Adams, ed., *Letters of John Adams Addressed to His Wife*, 2 vols. (Boston: C. C. Little and J. Brown, 1841), 1: 194.

64. Moses Roberts, "A Narrative of my Going to and Living in the New Purchase . . .," 5–5 month–1780, Philadelphia Meeting for Sufferings Papers, box 1779–80. Philadelphia Meeting for Sufferings paper dated 6–9 month–1780 signed by Isaac Zane, James and John Pemberton, and Nicholas Waln, ibid.

65. John Pemberton Diary, 1777–81, 28–3 month–1780, Pemberton Papers, box 3. For other Friends jailed at Lancaster, see Meeting for Sufferings minutes, 29 and 30–6 month–1778.

66. The most complete account of the exiles in print is the documents collected in Thomas Gilpin, *Exiles in Virginia* (Philadelphia, 1848). A recent account is Robert F. Oaks, "Philadelphians in Exile: The Problem of Loyalty During the American Revolution," *PMHB* 96 (1972): 298–325. And see Mekeel, *Relation of the Quakers to Revolution*, pp. 173–88.

67. Robert L. Brunhouse, *The Counter-Revolution in Pennsylvania, 1776–1790* (Ph.D. diss,. University of Pennsylvania, 1942), pp. 23–24.

68. Ford, *Journals of the Continental Congress* 8: 689, 694–95. James Pemberton Diary, 1777–78, 5–2 month–1778, HSP. William Evans and Thomas Evans, eds., *Friends Library* (Philadelphia, 1837–50) 6: 294.

69. *Col. Rec.* 11: 283–84, 288–90, 293, 295–96. Brunhouse, *Counter-Revolution*, p. 43.

70. The president and secretary of the Council were, respectively, disowned Friends Thomas Wharton, Jr., and Timothy Matlack. Matlack proved to be the most persistent antagonist of the Society in the Revolution. George Churchman's Journal, vol. 3, 9–month–1777, QCHC.

71. James Pemberton Diary, 12–10 month–1777.

72. James Pemberton had a Negro servant with him. Samuel Wharton went well supplied with money. See Pemberton's diary and Wharton's letters in the Wharton-Willing Papers, box 1, HSP.

73. Evans and Evans, *Friends Library* 6: 292–93, 298. James Pemberton Diary, 1 and 2–10 month–1777.

74. James Pemberton Diary, 15–4 month–1778.

75. Ibid., 2–10 month–1777. Brunhouse, *Counter-Revolution*, p. 50.

76. John K. Alexander, "The Fort Wilson Incident of 1779: A Case Study of the Revolutionary Crowd," *WMQ*, 3d ser., 31 (1974): 593–602. Elizabeth Drinker Diary, 4 October 1779.

77. *Laws Enacted in the Third Sitting of the Third General Assembly of the Common-Wealth of Pennsylvania* (Philadelphia, 1779), chap. 130.

78. *A Short Vindication of the Religious Society called Quakers Against*

the *Aspersions of a nameless Writer in the Pennsylvania Packet of the 12th Instant* (Philadelphia, 1780).

79. Evans and Evans, *Friends Library* 6: 300.
80. *Pennsylvania Archives*, 4th ser. 3: 652–53, 661–62, 665–66, 699–700, 744–46.
81. Wainwright, "Diary of Occurrences," pp. 437–38. Elizabeth Drinker Diary, 4 July 1778. Evans and Evans, *Friends Library* 6: 290.
82. Elizabeth Drinker Diary, 19 October 1781 [*sic*]. William Brooke Rawle, "Laurel Hill," *PMHB* 35 (1911): 403.
83. Hannah Moore to Milcah Martha Moore, n.d. Hill Family Letters, QCHC. Leonard L. Richards, *"Gentlemen of Property and Standing"; Anti-Abolitionist Mobs in Jacksonian America* (New York: Oxford University Press, 1971), p. 111. Gordon Wood, "Note on Mobs in the American Revolution," *WMQ*, 3d ser., 23 (1966): 635–42.
84. Rawle, "Laurel Hill," pp. 401–3.
85. "To the President and Executive Council, the General Assembly of Pennsylvania, and others whom it may concern," Philadelphia Meeting for Sufferings minutes, 16 and 22–11 month–1781. Five thousand copies were printed.
86. David Cooper Diary, pp. 69–71, QCHC. For a history of the Free Quakers by a descendant of its leading member, see Wetherill, *History of the Religious Society of Friends.*
87. *Journals of the House of Representatives of the Commonwealth of Pennsylvania* (Philadelphia, 1781) 2: 547–48, 568.
88. James Pemberton to John Pemberton, 14–9 month–1782, Pemberton Papers 37: 30.
89. "To the General Assembly of Pennsylvania: An Address and Memorial on Behalf of the People Called Quakers," Meeting for Sufferings minutes, 21–3 month–1782; also in *House Journals* 2: 574–77.
90. *House Journals* 2: 667–71.
91. Ibid., pp. 682–83. James Pemberton to John Pemberton, 20–9 month–1782, Pemberton Papers 37: 36–37.
92. James Pemberton to John Pemberton, 1–9 month–1782, Pemberton Papers 3: 172–75.
93. Brunhouse, *Counter-Revolution*, pp. 88–124. *House Journals* 2: 707. James Pemberton to John Pemberton, 20–9 month–1782, 10–11 month–1782, Pemberton Papers 37: 36–37, 93.
94. James Pemberton to John Pemberton, 20–9 month–1782, 10–11 month–1782, Pemberton Papers 37: 36–37, 93. Brunhouse, *Counter-Revolution*, pp. 126–27.

Chapter 12: Reformation in the Revolution

1. Anthony Benezet to George Dillwyn, ?–4 month–1780, Anthony Benezet Letters, QCHC.
2. Anthony Benezet to Samuel Allinson, 23–10 month–1774, Allinson Papers, box 6, QCHC. Philadelphia Yearly Meeting minutes, 21 to 28–9 month–1776.
3. Meeting of Ministers and Elders minutes, 24–3 month–1778. Four thousand copies were distributed. Philadelphia Meeting for Sufferings minutes, 19–2 month–1778, 21–1 month–1780.
4. George S. Brookes, *Friend Anthony Benezet* (Philadelphia: University of Pennsylvania Press, 1937), pp. 326–27.
5. George Churchman to Thomas Wharton, 8–12 month–1777, Wharton-Willing Papers, box 1, HSP. Dr. John Fothergill to James Pemberton, 24–4 month–1778, Pemberton Papers, Etting Collection 4: 178, HSP.
6. Anonymous, "To the Commissioners of Chester County," 1–4 month–1779, Parrish Collection, Pemberton Papers, HSP.
7. Ibid.
8. Warner Mifflin, *The Defense of Warner Mifflin* (Philadelphia, 1796), p. 19.
9. Warner Mifflin to Thomas McKean, 5–11 month–1781, Cox-Parrish-Wharton Collection 9: 79, HSP.
10. Ibid.
11. Ibid.
12. Ibid.
13. Philadelphia Meeting for Sufferings minutes, 15–11 month–1781.
14. John Hunt to Elizabeth Morris, 13–1 month–1778, Cox-Parrish-Wharton Collection 14: 28.
15. Gerald R. Cragg, *Puritanism in the Age of the Great Persecution* (Cambridge: Cambridge University Press, 1957), pp. 18, 57, 67.
16. "Rules of Discipline of Philadelphia Yearly Meeting. 1781," QCHC.
17. William Evans and Thomas Evans, eds., *Friends Library* (Philadelphia, 1837–45), 6: 288. John Comly and Isaac Comly, eds., *Friends' Miscellany* (Philadelphia, 1831–59), 1: 103–4, 108–9. George Churchman's Journal 3: 5–6, 8–9, QCHC.
18. Elias Hicks's Journal, 1748–1822, p. 15, FHLS. Comly and Comly, *Friends' Miscellany* 1: 103–4.
19. Philadelphia Yearly Meeting minutes, 30–9 month–1780.
20. *New Jersey Historical Society Proceedings* 50: 235.
21. Samuel Roland Fisher to Tabez Fisher, 19–2 month–1799, Logan-Fisher-Fox Collection, box 3, HSP. This and other evidence critically disables Richard Bauman's thesis that the policy of the Society and Friends' abhorrence of the Revolution was imposed upon Quakerism by the city "politiques" (political activists). Narrative and quantitative

evidence shows that resistance to the Revolution, if not abhorrence of it, flourished among rural Friends and in Chester County especially, not in Philadelphia where politiques allegedly used Philadelphia Monthly Meeting and the Meeting for Sufferings to impose their attitudes. Richard Bauman, *For the Reputation of Truth* (Baltimore: Johns Hopkins University Press, 1971), p. 152.

22. Chester Quarterly Meeting minutes, 14–8 month–1780. Monthly meetings were irregular about recording this category of loss.

23. "Journal of Samuel Roland Fisher, of Philadelphia, 1779–1781," *PMHB* 41 (1917): 145–97, 274–333.

24. At Philadelphia Quarterly Meeting "it was manifestly felt there was a spirit prevalent that was for Saving Self, & opposing . . . the Peaceable Testimony against the . . . paying taxes for the promoting of it." John Pemberton Diary, 1777–81, 7–2 month–1780, Pemberton Papers, box 3, p. 157, HSP.

25. Philadelphia Meeting for Sufferings minutes, 20–11 month–1783.

26. George Churchman's Journal 3: 8–9.

27. Ibid. David Cooper Diary, pp. 47–48, QCHC.

28. George Churchman's Journal 3: 8–9.

29. George Churchman to John Pemberton, 5–2 month–1778, Pemberton Papers 31: 108. George Churchman's Journal 3: 10, 24, 46.

30. George Churchman's Journal 3: 41. Philadelphia Yearly Meeting minutes, 26–9 month- to 5–10 month–1778. The 1779 Yearly Meeting was a quiet and satisfactory one too. James Pemberton to Dr. John Fothergill, 14–10 month–1779, Pemberton Papers 34: 180.

31. David Cooper Diary, p. 72.

32. Brookes, *Benezet*, pp. 347, 353, 427–28. Moses Brown to John Pemberton, 30–4 month–1776, Pemberton Papers 29: 32.

33. 13–6 month–1780, Allinson Papers, box 11B.

34. Ibid.

35. Ibid.

36. Brookes, *Benezet*, p. 435. Benezet circulated Allinson's work. His arguments began to appear among other Friends. See Anne Emlen Mifflin, "Some Notes on the Payment of Taxes for military Purposes," Emlen Family Papers.

37. Romans 13:1–2.

38. Chester Quarterly Meeting minutes, 11–5 month–1778.

39. For this argument see Timothy Davis, *A Letter from a Friend to Some of His Intimate Friends, on the Subject of paying Taxes &c* (Watertown, Mass., 1776). Davis's arguments became popular among discontented and former Friends in Pennsylvania. See Isaac Gray, *A Serious Address to Such of the People called Quakers on the Continent of North-America, as profess Scruples relative to the Present Government* . . . (Philadelphia, 1778). For a nice discernment of these various posi-

tions see Moses Brown to John Pemberton, 21–10 month–1778, Pemberton Papers 32: 115.

40. Brookes, *Benezet*, p. 432.
41. David Cooper Diary, pp. 91, 92.
42. David Cooper to Catherine Haines, 28–7 month–1788, 5–11 month–1788, Allinson Papers, box 7B.
43. Chester Quarterly Meeting minutes, 11–5 month–1778, 10–8 month–1778. Philadelphia Yearly Meeting minutes, 3–10 month–1778, 25 to 30–9 month–1780.
44. *New Jersey Historical Society Proceedings* 53: 39, 42–43. David Cooper Diary, pp. 106–7, 114–15. Philadelphia Yearly Meeting minutes, 25 to 30–9 month–1786.
45. Philadelphia Meeting for Sufferings minutes, 30–6 month–1778. Philadelphia Yearly Meeting minutes, 1–10 month–1778.
46. David Cooper to "Loving Son," 25–6 month–1778, Allinson Papers, box 7B.
47. Samuel Allinson to Governor William Livingston, 13–7 month–1778, Samuel Allinson Letter Book, 1764–91, Allinson Papers, box 11B.
48. Moses Brown to John Pemberton, 21–10 month–1778, Pemberton Papers 32: 115. Richard Bauman alleges that Quaker ethics were so equivocal regarding revolution that when Friends renounced it in 1775 and 1776, they were guided by a partisan political spirit—that of the Philadelphia "politiques." While crediting the "politiques" with an influence they did not have, Bauman also misconstrues the ethic. If one chooses to disavow his allegiance to "the powers that be" whenever local persons conspire to revolt or declare revolution, what does one's allegiance ever count for? If Friends were to have switched as early as 1775 or 1776, they would have effectively proclaimed themselves Patriots and guided by a partisan spirit. Like David Cooper, Bauman ignores the significance of eight years of war in resolving who are "the powers that be"; it is perfectly in order to wait and see who wins. Bauman, *For the Reputation of Truth*, pp. 157, 176.
49. David Cooper Diary, pp. 72–79.
50. Meeting for Sufferings minutes, 19–6 month–1777.
51. *In Committee of Inspection and Observation, Feb. 5, 1776* (Philadelphia, 1776).
52. Warner Mifflin, "Statement concerning his refusal to use and circulate Continental currency," 8 month–1779, FHLS.
53. *New Jersey Historical Society Proceedings* 52: 235. See also Martha Harris's ministry in Anne Emlen, "Account of her religious progress," Emlen Family Papers.
54. Philadelphia Yearly Meeting minutes, bk. 1747–79, p. 431. George Churchman to John Pemberton, 3–1 month–1779, Pemberton Papers 32: 152.

55. Moses Brown to John Pemberton, 30–4 month–1776, Pemberton Papers 29: 32. Anne Emlen, "Account of her religious progress."
E. James Ferguson, *The Power of the Purse* (Chapel Hill: University of North Carolina Press, 1961), p. 44.

56. Philadelphia Yearly Meeting minutes, 20–9 month– to 4–10 month–1777 and bk. 1747–79, p. 431.

57. Samuel Allinson to William Livingston, 13–7 month–1778, Samuel Allinson Letter Book, 1764–91, pp. 145–46, Allinson Papers, box 11B.

58. "To the Commissioners of Chester County," 1–4 month–1779, Parrish Collection, Pemberton Papers.

59. Evans and Evans, *Friends Library* 6: 297, 299. John Pemberton Diary, 1777–81, pp. 156–57, 186–87, Pemberton Papers, box 3. Quakers' antecedents in Restoration England recorded similar cases of retribution upon their persecutors. Cragg, *Great Persecution*, pp. 77–78.

60. Brookes, *Benezet*, p. 326.

61. For Quaker dislike of New Englanders see "Some Strictures on certain Parts of the Epistle from the Y. Meeting . . . in the Year, 1774 Signed by James Pemberton," Proud Manuscripts, FHLS. Four thousand pounds were spent in New England. After 1777, much of the aid dispensed in America came from British Friends. Sydney V. James, *A People Among Peoples* (Cambridge, Mass.: Harvard University Press, 1963), pp. 260–63. Arthur J. Mekeel, *The Relation of the Quakers to the American Revolution* (Washington: University Press of America, 1979), pp. 294–310.

62. Meeting of Ministers and Elders minutes, 24–3 month–1778.

63. Philadelphia Yearly Meeting minutes, 26–9 month– to 5–10 month–1778. Samuel Allinson to William Livingston, 12–8 month–1778, Samuel Allinson Letter Book, 162. Gerald Cragg writes of sufferers in Restoration England: "If prison was the school where men learned the lessons of faith, the wider world was the sphere where they must apply them; the mercies received in gaol must inspire greater service abroad." Cragg, *Great Persecution*, pp. 121–22.

64. My synopsis of this problem here and through the next two paragraphs comes from David B. Davis, *The Problem of Slavery in Western Culture* (Ithaca: Cornell University Press, 1966), pp. 76–78, 84–85, 89, 94, 109, 293, 319, 341–42.

65. Meeting for Sufferings minutes, 21–1 month–1780.

66. Ibid., 20–11 month–1783.

67. J. P. Brissot de Warville remarked of Mifflin: "It seems that to love mankind, and to search to do them good constituted his only pleasure, his only existence." J. P. Brissot de Warville, *New Travels in the United States of America* (London, 1797), 1: 157, quoted by Thomas Drake, *Quakers and Slavery in America* (New Haven: Yale University Press, 1950), p. 108.

68. Mifflin, *Defense of Mifflin*, pp. 12, 17.
69. Davis, *Problem of Slavery in Western Culture*, p. 119.
70. Friends had to assert the distinction in order to defend their participation in the punishment of criminals while they forbore serving in wars. See Samuel Smith, *Necessary Truth: Or Seasonable Considerations for the Inhabitants of the City of Philadelphia and Province of Pennsylvania In Relation to the Pamphlet call'd Plain Truth: And Two Other Writers in the News-Paper* (Philadelphia, 1748).
71. Their activity may be traced in the Allinson Papers, box 8.
72. Samuel Allinson to William Livingston, 13–7 month–1778, Samuel Allinson Letter Book, pp. 145–46. John Churchman and Anthony Benezet had used the jeremiad in reference to slaveholding as early as the French and Indian War. *An Account of the Gospel Labours . . . of . . . John Churchman* (Philadelphia, 1882), pp. 209–10. Benezet, *Observations on the Inslaving, Importing and Purchasing of Negroes* (Germantown, Pa., 1759).
73. Drake, *Quakers and Slavery*, pp. 90–113.
74. In the writings on American history, the hypothesis is original with Richard Hofstadter, who applied it to reformers in the late nineteenth- and twentieth-century United States. Hofstadter, *Age of Reform: From Bryan to F. D. R.* (New York: Alfred A. Knopf, 1955).
75. An excellent bibliography and comment on the historical studies emanating from Donald's hypothesis and on others' work similar to Donald's is Gerald Sorin, *The New York Abolitionists: A Study in Political Radicalism* (Westport, Conn.: Greenwood Publishing Corp., 1971), pp. ix–24, 139–52. The most famous critique of Donald is Martin B. Duberman, ed., *Antislavery Vanguard* (Princeton: Princeton University Press, 1965). Also, useful for its analytic insights is Robert F. Berkhofer, Jr., *A Behavioral Approach to Historical Analysis* (New York: Free Press, 1969), especially pp. 64–74.
76. The experience of the Southern evangelicals with abolition, discussed in chap. 5, illustrates the case. Their concern for affluence and the society it permitted them to enter ended their freedom to be abolitionists.
77. James, *People Among Peoples*, pp. 289–311. Rayner W. Kelsey, *Friends and the Indians* (Philadelphia, 1917), pp. 89–98.
78. Warner Mifflin to James Pemberton, ?–8 month–1781, Pemberton Papers 35: 180. Some New Jersey Friends likewise impeded the progress of new testimonies and even resisted ones that were part of the discipline. John Hunt Diary, *New Jersey Historical Society Proceedings* 52: 235; 53: 28, 31.
79. David Cooper Diary, p. 72.
80. John Hunt Diary, *New Jersey Historical Society Proceedings* 52: 232; 53: 209. James Thornton to Samuel Neal, 23–5 month–1784, James

Thornton Manuscripts, FHLS. Moses Brown to Samuel Allinson,
11–11 month–1785, Samuel Allinson Letter Book, p. 202, and Brown
to "Dear Friend," 21–6 month–1787, Cox-Parrish-Wharton Collection
11: 88.

Index

abolition, 94, 111–27, 272–78; and asceticism, 125–27, 274–75; and consensus in U.S., 123–25; and David Donald thesis, 276–78; disownment of slaveholders, 120, 303, 312; emancipations, 121; enforcement of, 116–18; and evangelicals, 126–27; and Friends before 1740, 111–13; in nineteenth century, 123–24; origins and circumstances of, 113–14; 1755 reform, 114; 1758 reform, 115, 116; 1774 reform, 119–20; 1776 reform, 120; and American Revolution, 122–23; and sectarianism, 121–27, 309–10; and sale of slaves, 118; and Quaker sufferings, 274; and Whig politics, 121–22
Adams, John, 241
adultery, 18–19
affirmations. *See* oaths
Allen, William, 43, 159, 162, 202
Allinson, Samuel, 77, 261–64, 265, 266, 268, 276, 278; and abolition, 276; on oaths, 268; "Reasons against War and paying taxes for its Support," 261–64
Arnold, Benedict, 244
Asbury, Francis, 126
Ashbridge, George, 199, 202
Assembly, Pennsylvania: appropriations power, 138–40; challenge to Quaker presence in, 132–35, 159–61; contest with Thomas Penn, 138–42; endorses

Continental Congress, 219; Friends in resist pacifism, 183–84; Friends' resignation from, 158, 164–65, 320; Friends refuse to resign from, 165, 195–96; and pacifists, 152–54; and pacifists' sufferings, 155–56; war appropriations of, 140–41, 147, 151–53

Baker, Jeremiah, 238
Barclay, David, 162, 169, 198, 220, 224
Barclay, Robert, 98
Bauman, Richard, 315, 344, 346
Bellers, John, 169
Benezet, Anthony, 45, 73, 75, 82, 85, 89, 90, 99, 100–105, 108, 114, 121, 158, 174, 180, 185, 251–53, 261, 265, 272, 275, 276, 278, 325; and abolition in Pennsylvania, 276; criticizes James Pemberton, 253; criticism of wealth, 100; *The Mighty Destroyer Displayed*, 108; on public power, 185; on suffering, 252, 253
Biddle, Clement, 246
Biddle, Owen, 223
Boorstin, Daniel, 125
Braddock, General Edward, 146, 149, 150, 158–60, 162, 190
Bradford Monthly Meeting, obstructs reform, 78–79
Brown, Henton, 141, 159, 161
Brown, Moses, 261, 265, 269, 271, 278